Studies in Temporal Urbanism

Fabian Neuhaus
Editor

Studies in Temporal Urbanism

The urbanTick Experiment

 Springer

Editor
Fabian Neuhaus
Centre for Advanced Spatial Analysis
University College London
London
United Kingdom
fabian.neuhaus@ucl.ac.uk
www.urbantick.blogspot.com

Every effort has been made to contact the copyright holders of the figures and tables which have been reproduced from other sources. Anyone who has not been properly credited is requested to contact the publishers, so that due acknowledgment may be made in subsequent editions.

ISBN 978-94-007-0936-2   e-ISBN 978-94-007-0937-9
DOI 10.1007/978-94-007-0937-9
Springer Dordrecht Heidelberg London New York

Library of Congress Control Number: 2011932790

Printed on acid-free paper

Springer is part of Springer Science+Business Media (www.springer.com)

Acknowledgments

There were a lot of people involved in the past year in the creation of the content of urbanTick. Foremost I would like to thank Andy Hudson-Smith who actually persuaded me to write this blog, but also supported me throughout the year and still does. Thanks go to the supporting CASA team, especially Mike Batty as one of my supervisors, also to Andrew Crooks and Duncan Smith for continuous input and encouragement, Richard Milton for great technical advice and information. Thanks for graphic and layout advice go to Urs Stampfli of P'inc. I am also grateful to my fellow PhD researchers Ateen Patel, Sung-Hyun Jang, Taneha Bacchin, Joel Dearden, James Cheshire and Daniel Lewis. Also a big thanks goes to all the participants of the UrbanDiary project who have been or still are carrying the GPS tracking device to collect data. I also want to thank Sandra and Malik for support and their tolerance of late nights and sleepy mornings.

Contents

About the Authors

Sandra Abegglen is a PhD researcher at Goldsmiths, University of London. Her research is concerned with the use of photographs as a research tool, especially in combination with semi-structured interviews. Before her postdoctoral study, she did a master degree in social research at the University of Plymouth (UK). Her masters thesis was entitled 'The woman in my wallet – An investigation of photography in everyday life'. Her bachelor degree was in social work at the University of Applied Science Basel HPSABB (Switzerland). Sandra has worked as a research assistant at the University of Basel (Switzerland) and the University of Freiburg (Germany) where she was involved in different projects concerned with migration and the care of elderly people. She is also doing fieldwork for the Connected Communities Project of the Royal Society of Art (RSA) and the University of the Arts. www.everydayclick.blogspot.com.

Zahra Azizi has recently finished an MArch degree in Urban design at the Bartlett School of Architecture with a distinction award on the topic of 'Memory & Movement', following a BSc Architecture degree (RIBA Part one) at the Bartlett. Her main interests, both on the architectural and urban scale, stem from curiosity about human behaviour and perception in the built environment and the psychology of space. She is currently working in Iran on architecture and urban design projects.

Matthew Dance is completing a Masters of Arts at the University of Alberta, in Edmonton, Alberta, Canada. His thesis is focused on how people understand location and express that understanding with new web-based Geographic Information Systems tools. As part of his research, he is building an application (www.WiserIsThePath.org) that combines mapping, social network and collaboration elements that will enable the citizens of Edmonton to collaboration on the how they use Ed-monton's River Valley Network. Prior to starting graduate school he worked as an independent consultant primarily for Alberta Environment helping with the development of environmental policy. He filled project management, facilitation, research and strategic advice roles on several policy projects. In addition, he worked as a Senior Project Manager for the Clean Air Strategic Alliance on Air Quality policy projects such as the development of a regulatory framework for the thermal electricity sector and an Ambient Air Monitoring Strategy for Alberta. Twitter @mattdance, www.wiserpath.blogspot.com.

Jeff Kon-Chung Ho is an urban planner and urban designer chartered in the UK and Hong Kong with international working experience in the UK, Italy, Hong Kong, Mainland China and Vietnam. He is currently leading a masterplanning team in Hong Kong responsible for a few Hong Kong new town projects, Mainland China and Southeast Asia masterplanning projects. He has been involved in a wide range of planning studies, urban design, masterplanning, railway planning and GIS analysis. Jeff's interests range from adaptive urbanism and urban regeneration to spatial politics. In his spare time, Jeff has been involved in writing commentaries on Hong Kong urban design issues and organizing events of urban issues. He was invited to be one of the event organizers in London Festival of Architecture 2008 to organize an event called "Feeling High", which explored the sustainability and humanity of high rise development in London. Jeff received a Masters in urban planning from the University of Hong Kong and a Masters in urban design from the Bartlett School of Architecture, UCL. After a few years working in Mainland China and the UK, he returned to Hong Kong.

Ana McMillin She has worked on several masterplanning projects in China, Poland and the UK, and regeneration studies in Manchester and Dover. Her experience in urban design started in Lisbon where she worked for RBD.APP with the head of the Architecture Faculty, Professor Rui Barreiros Duarte, on the urban regeneration and conservation of the Alfama Historic Centre of Lisbon. Her interest in revitalization of urban areas continued in London with the work on the urban design and integration of the Gazprom Tower in the historic fabric of St Petersburg, a UNESCO listed site. Ana received a Licentiate Degree in Architecture from the Technical University of Lisbon. She also holds a Masters of Science in Urban Design from the Bartlett School of Architecture where she received an award for her Design Thesis in Cinematic Urbanism. Recently, she has returned to the Bartlett as a guest critic for mid and final-year reviews. Ana McMillin lives and works in London.

Fabian Neuhaus (editor) is currently a PhD researcher at CASA, the Centre for Advanced Spatial Analysis at UCL. His main research interests are temporal aspects of the urban environment in general and cyclical, repetitive temporal patterns specifically. He has been teaching at the University of Plymouth as well as the Bartlett School of Architecture. For his Masters of Science in urban design at the Bartlett School of Architecture, he developed a concept for a floating city in the Thames estuary (available at www.jafud.com) and for his Master thesis on cycles in urban environments (available on www.cyclesinurbanenvironments.blogspot.com) he was awarded a distinction. Fabian also received a Masters of Architecture from FHNW Basel for the design project 'Ambassador' and his thesis 'am Ring' investigating elements of urban patterns in Basel, Switzerland. He has worked with architecture and urban design practices in the UK and Switzer-land on projects ranging from policy planning, consultancy and construction to master planning. He also worked on research projects at universities in Switzerland, Germany and the UK. www.urbantick.blogspot.com.

Luis Suarez was born, in Bogotá, Colombia and graduated from The University of Florida in design, construction and planning in 2005. He received a master in science of urban design from The Bartlett School of Architecture, University College London. He is currently pursuing a Masters in Bioclimatic Architecture from the Isthmus School of Architecture for Latin America and the Caribbean. He is designing and building multiple projects in South and Central America with his established firm, Estudio ArQ.

Contributors

Sandra Abegglen   Goldsmiths, University of London, London, UK
e-mail: s.abegglen@gold.ac.uk

Zahra Azizi   Bartlett School of Architecture, University College London, London, UK
e-mail: zahra.azizi@gmail.com

Matthew Dance   WEB Mapping Consultant, Edmonton, CA
e-mail: matt@matthewdance.ca

Jeff Kon-Chung Ho   JLF Urban Research, Hong-Kong, China
e-mail: kchojeff@hotmail.com

Ana McMillin   ACGRM, London, UK
e-mail: ana.mcmillin@gmail.com

Fabian Neuhaus   Centre for Advanced Spatial Analysis, University College London, London, UK
e-mail: fabian.neuhaus@ucl.ac.uk

Luis Suárez   Estudio ARQ, Bogotá, CO
e-mail: luis@estudio-arq.com

Introduction

This book is very much about what the name urbanTick literally says, about the ticking of the urban, the urban as we experience it every day on the bus, in the park or between buildings. It is about the big orchestrated mass migration of commuters, the seasonal blossoms of the trees along the walkway and the frequency of the stamping rubbish-eater-trucks. It is also, not to forget, about climate, infrastructure, opening hours, term times, parking meters, timetables, growing shadows and moon light. But most of all it is about how all this is experienced by citizens on a daily basis and how they navigate within this complex structure of patterns.

The content of this book is based on the content of the urbanTick blog between 2008–2010. One year of blogging about this topic brought together a large collection of different aspects and thoughts. It is not at all a conclusive view: to the contrary, it is a work in progress, trying to capture as many facets of the topic as possible.

For this publication the written content has been structured under seven topics that appear here as chapters and the text has been reproduced as continuous content. Therefore individual blog posts are only indicated and additional information has to be found in the footnotes. However, information is given to find the cross links between the chapters, as there are a series of other topics, besides the chosen seven, buried in the content.

Each chapter is led in by an essay, each written by an academic or professional with a specific interest and expertise in the particular topic. It will set the scene for the topic and beyond.

urbanMachine investigates the impact of modernist ideas on city planning and the perception of function as a defining activity. Examples are drawn from a range of sources to create a picture of how today's city came to be understood as a machine. The machine here largely stands for an abstract model of repetition in the sense of clockwork. The machine is examined as part of planning, under the aspect of its function or usage, but also in terms of experience and models of power.

timeSpace will investigate the conceptions of time and space as a result of the social configuration of the city as well as critically reviewing the founding concepts in time-geography. The first part discusses the different units of the calendar type time organisation as modelled on natural repetitive phenomena. This will establish the rhythms in a larger context, but ultimately in relation to the city as the place. Together with time the concept of 'place' and 'space' also have to be integrated in a holistic view. The second part discusses approaches in time geography to deal with the time phenomena. A special focus will lie on the discussion of the Hagerstrand model and the attached visualisation.

The bodySpace chapter defines the rhythmic structure as a function of the human body as well as investigating the body city relationship. The body functions are discussed as the ultimate point of reference to actually 'measure' any repetitive pattern. Very much in the sense of Lefebvre's 'Rhythmanalysis', this establishes the human capacity to perceive cycles and relate to them. The second part of the chapter discusses the connection and cycles external to the body and focuses especially on the relationship between the body and the city. It examines the relationship overall as a model, but also specifically related to individual or sets of cycles.

urbanNarrative outlines concepts of structure as a sequence of events constituting a overall story. The narrative is here discussed as an element of structure to describe and capture the nature of ongoing processes. It is used to provide a framework that can actually integrate the numerous different aspects examined as part of the everyday experience.

The chapter locationInforamation draws together a number of applications based on location information as well as discussing aspects of city sensing in regard to everyday life in an urban context. These examples range from software-based mobile gadget apps to physical interventions to raise location awareness. It closely ties in with the other topics and expands on planning, social and identity topics. To do so it draws from personal, technical and machine based sources.

UrbanDiary is the chapter that summarises the writings around the research project of the same name. It can be read as a live coverage of the project development, as update reports, but at the same time as the place to develop guiding thought. In this sense it is the central element of the project. Together with the facebook group, this is where the magic happens.

The last part of the book brings together the reviews. A great variety of media, topics and concepts have been reviewed and this now forms a dense tapestry of critical thoughts on contemporary activity as well as examples from the past. It covers a selection of books, software applications, events and more.

Comments, discussion and feedback are welcome and can be posted directly to the blog on www.urbantick.blogspot.com.

Don't worry about typing all the links listed in the footnotes into your browser to get to the content. Simply go to urbantick.blogspot as above and click on the book link. There you find all the links listed by chapter and with the corresponding number.

Part I
urbanMachine

Cycle Study as the Basis of Adaptive Urbanism

Jeff Kon-Chung Ho

Current Situation/Status

Our cities grow very fast and hence societies become increasingly arbitrary, interchangeble and contingent. The changes on even the cycles in our societies, e.g. economic, product and development cycles, etc. become quicker and shorter. It is getting more difficult to predict the trends and therefore to foresee our future. Planning our cities is about control—to frame our cities to some extent and direct the development directions or themes. However, perfect control has never been achieved in human history, and hence urban planning becomes a dilemma between the belief of stability and instability.

On the other hand, if we look into our neighbourhood, we will realize that our cities are shaped more by the forces of everyday life than by formal design and official plans as people can always not only adapt to the environmental changes, but also respond to the social and economic needs from time to time. Everyday emphasizes a social and communal condition which changes the way things are manifested physically in space. Even though the environment is relatively stable, people have the intuition to adapt to an increasing unpredictable future. It has little pretence about the perfectibility of the built environment, nor is it about utopian form. Meanwhile, urbanists are still required to provide a plan as a blueprint for the future of cities. Some people raised a concept of "non-plan" or "open-plan" as they do not believe in an absolute masterplan, but a strategy of conceptual pragmatism. They think cities are evolving—cities are like self-generative organisms growing organically and responding to the changes of the environment naturally. However, cities have been being designed in human history, whether via masterplan or organic development—it is just a matter of planning mechanism. How we learn from the past and create better cities is the key subject for urbanists.

J. K.-C. Ho (✉)
JLF Urban Research, Hong-Kong, China
e-mail: kchojeff@hotmail.com

F. Neuhaus (ed.), *Studies in Temporal Urbanism,*
DOI 10.1007/978-94-007-0937-9_1, © Springer Science+Business Media B.V. 2011

Subjects that Urbanists Should Study

In order to understand about the changes and how those changes may affect our cities, urbanists should investigate the "forces". Forces dominating the changes of cities could be categorized into two simple types—global and local forces. Global forces are those trends and changes initiated by technological improvement and thought movements as they holistically change the relationship between cities and social structure. Though their influential powers vary from cities to cities, they have influence over the whole world. The speed of change of this kind of force is getting faster and faster. On the other hand, local forces are initiated by the local communities' needs. It could be the change in life pattern or family structure. More people would like to spend more time on restaurants, bars and entertainment, reducing the significance of the private home. Such life patterns causes different demands on land use patterns, which affects the planning criteria as well as the urban form.

It may not be difficult to understand the definitions of global and local forces, but to understand how they react with each other could be a life-long project. When the global and local forces meet, the dominant forces could change rapidly and unpredictably and boundaries of different forces are created. The porous nature of the boundaries between cultivated and developed land is a symptom of the flows which are identified as the prevailing metaphor for urbanism. Flows of goods in the global economy, flows of information in advanced communication technology, flows of population from countryside to city and from country to country, flows between cultural theory and architectural practices are all appropriated as means to represent and understand the urban conditions. The forces mentioned before could also be interpreted as virtual dynamic flows mixing in cities. As the weight and number of these flows vary with time, geographical location, culture and the combinations of flows would be complicated like chaos in different scales. The crucial issue is that with changes of global and local forces due to remarkable evolution, such as revolutionary technological improvement and social structure, flows of new categorcauses would be imposed in the city, in which no trend can be predicted. Functions of spaces created have multiplied, so that people are allowed to work, shop, watch movies, and hold lecture at homes, café or even in an open space. The boundaries between functional areas are no longer distinguishable, thus when and why people commute in the city cannot be accurately estimated. The organisational structure of the city becomes more dynamic and the land use demands on housing, offices or industries, etc. are hard to predict.

How could a person be in a less defining space or how to redefine the function, purpose or target users of spaces and buildings becomes a major question to the urbanists. Urbanists must be able to narrate and construct a habitat/living style/pattern and design opportunities for people from an urban design point of view, drawing in the above mentioned changing environment.

Rise of Adaptive Urbanism

Adaptive urbanism is a study to investigate the underlying principles or rules of those long lasting successful cities over changes and apply them into our future planning practices.

The masterplan should focus more on organization, production and technique as potential generators of form, instead of form, functions, uses or intensity only. It should encourage an undetermined process, rather than a fixed form. Since there is a discernable link between spatial parameters and forms of social organization, such planning concepts will allow permanent and temporary structures for the flexibility of social organization. In other words, hierarchy of organization and space are emphasized as comprehensive hierarchy can divert or channel the flows in the city, indirectly enhancing the adaptability of a city system. In the building scale, flexibility of building form, its adaptability and durability are specifically identified as aids to the creation of a sustainable urban environment.

The masterplan should maintain its openness, allowing for creativity instead of limiting. Apart from the top-down approach, which emphasizes political, economic, social and environmental issues, the underlying concern and psychological experiences, which based on living patterns, are also major underlying forces that should be considered and directly translated into design elements in the masterplan. More open typologies are designed in order to encourage creation and changes with needs. However, unstable typologies require more and more structure in terms of technical equipment and manpower, and unlimited resources may be drawn.

Relationship Between Adaptive Urbanism and Cycle

It is impossible for the urbanists to investigate or understand all forces and predict how those forces mix completely. Our society is evolving, and sometimes revolution happens. However it does not mean that we have no clue about our society and nothing we can do. Something is repeating in our cities—which are cycles.

The adaptive urbanism allows mobile organization structure to deal with scenarios for multiple futures of urban evolution to some extent. Since urban change is subject to transient forces that are never completely predictable and controllable, temporal elements in city cannot be quantitatively masterable in spatial practice. Temporal elements may temporarily change the organization fixing the problem raised by the instability of city and indirectly inform a mode of generative operation and a resulting organisational temporality. With the study on cycles in our cities, we could understand how the internal and external logistics flows change in terms of volume and direction. A city with high level of adaptive structure may adjust its internal links over time by allowing re-distributing flows in its flexible infrastructure system.

In terms of the period of repetition, cycles could be categorized into daily, weekly, monthly, seasonally, annually or eventually in our life. Daily resting time, Saturday and Sunday work off, monthly telephone bill, seasonal sale, yearly Christmas holiday or 4-yearly Olympic Games are patterns repeating in our lives unstoppably. There are lots of other cycles in our society such as the economic cycle, the political cycle (change of dominating party in the government), the financial cycle (up and down in stock market) and weather season, etc. highly affecting our quality of life. All these cycles are crucial elements in our everyday life generation by generation. Without a certain understanding of these cycles and their implications on our life patterns, urbanists can hardly formulate the criteria for the masterplan.

Limitation of Adaptive Urbanism as well as Cycle

Nevertheless, as mentioned, our society is also evolving and sometimes revolution happens. Since the speed of development become faster and faster, breakthroughs/evolutions from technology discoveries such as electronic, computer, nanotechnology, bio technology and internet, imply changes in life pattern to an unpredictable way is foreseeable. Some new forces will be raised inevitably and highly interrupt the existing cycles. Such reality is the ultimate limitation of cycle study as well as an adaptive urbanism as some nowadays dominating cycles and rules of adaptive urbanism may be outdated tomorrow without notice. The speed of reaction of human being, which initializes changes, is much faster than that of the development of cycle study and adaptive urbanism, and so as that of built environment. Lifespan of everything becomes very short while we need long-lasting masterplan as it is also very important to the sustainability of our Earth.

Instead of fully predicting the forces, maybe urbanists should aim at designing opportunities for making organization, which is initialized by the living pattern. Strategies to create coherence within the idea of temporality and fragmentation allowing changes of cycles should be studied. Meanwhile, human beings should understand more about their own desires, preferences for life patterns, their cycles, and relationship with nature—it maybe the ultimate solution.

urbanMachine

Fabian Neuhaus

1   *IDENTITY*[1] A specific interest in the field of cycles are the three areas to deal with the interaction between the people in the city and the city itself. The hypothesis here is that cycles as repetitive actions are involved in the construction of orientation, memory and identity in the urban context (Fig. 1).

The following examples are taken from my Masters thesis "Cycles in urban environments". The thesis developed from the project AKA www.jafud.com[2] and is based on researching the topic in London.

Identity of the place or the genius loci can be mainly driven by the rhythm of events filling and emptying the space. As a very simple example can be named a local street market. Every week the Saturday is the market day. The road is traffic free for the duration of the market while the stands occupy the street and the people gather round to do their weekly shopping and have a chat (Fig. 2).

The example documents the street market at Queens Crescent in Kentish Town, London. How the identity of the place changes between the two identities of market day and local street day are best documented with photographs. The changes range from function e.g. the road, the walkways, to the role of the defining elements, such as local shops to distances, density and usage. Also certain secondary elements change dramatically. For example colours, materials and smells transform the space dramatically. These are the changes that follow directly from transformation. But from the repetition of the cycle, the space, in this case the road, generates its special identity consisting of the two aspects of street day and market day.

2   *TOWARDS A MORE HUMAN ARCHITECTURE*[3] The title of a book I have come across today in the library. I only just flipped through, but what I picked up

---

[1] *IDENTITY*, 9 October 2008 21:46, urbanMachine, rhythm, cycle, identity

[2] http://www.jafud.com.

[3] *TOWARDS A MORE HUMAN ARCHITECTURE,* 10 October 2008 14:26, inspiration, cycles, urbanMachine.

F. Neuhaus (✉)
Centre for Advanced Spatial Analysis, University College London, London, UK
e-mail: fabian.neuhaus@ucl.ac.uk

F. Neuhaus (ed.), *Studies in Temporal Urbanism,*
DOI 10.1007/978-94-007-0937-9_2, © Springer Science+Business Media B.V. 2011

Fig. 1 Image taken from 'Cycles in Urban Environments' (Neuhaus 2010) / Market Day

Fig. 2 Image taken from 'Cycles in Urban Environments' (Neuhaus 2010) / Street Day

was that the author is saying that today's (whatever publication date the book has) architecture and urbanism are disconnecting the people living in those structures from their natural habits and the way humans are meant to live. Although I do not entirely agree with this claim, I could relate the topic of cycles and rhythms to this argument. It is a fact that we are no longer living like people did in ancient times, when everyone was a farmer and completely relying on what they were able to produce on their own fields with their own hands. But I would assume that the natural cycles still apply to modern life, even in the city. The book is: Allsopp, B., 1974. Towards a Humane Architecture, London: Muller.

3   *TRANSPORT RHYTHM*[4] A completely different approach to capture the rhythm of the city can be through image or video capturing. I have been playing around with timeLapse techniques. There are a number of tutorials out there, really good ones on DigitalUrban[5] (Fig. 3).

---

[4] *TRANSPORT RHYTHM,* 27 January 2009 16:50, tube, stop motion, bus, transport, London, timeLapse, wave, urbanMachine, rhythm.

[5] http://digitalurban.blogspot.com/search/label/TimeLapse.

Fig. 3 Clip by urbanTick on Vimeo. (http://vimeo.com/2986171)

Transport networks are quite simple and steady producers of rhythms. It all relates to a timetable and the frequency of the stops. Here is a clip from a Tube stop in London. Passengers are swiped in and out of the carriages onto the platform in waves. The journey on the bus gives a similar impression. Here especially the frequency of the bus stops indicates a rhythm. It is stop motion in the most literal sense of the word (Fig. 4).

4 *VISUALISING GPS DATA—CABSPOTTING*[6] The web based project Cabspotting[7] traces San Francisco's taxi cabs as they travel throughout the Bay Area. See clip on Youtube[8]. The patterns traced by each cab create a living and always-changing map of city life. This map hints at economic, social, and cultural trends that are otherwise invisible. The Exploratorium has invited artists and researchers to use this information to reveal these "Invisible Dynamics." See clip on Youtube[9]. They must have a great collection of GPS tracks as the project was launched in 2006. So it could be two and something years worth of tracking data. There are also some nice animations on their website. Some artists were invited to use the data for their work: some of these examples are here[10]. Two example movies from their visualisations.

5 *LONDON BEATS DIFFERENTLY—CYCLES DISRUPTED*[11] There is a lot of snow today in London. It has been snowing since yesterday evening and it still is. The city is not really used to it or prepared for it, so it means the daily routine is disrupted or hasn't even started. The BBC writes, "Heavy snowfall has left roads

---

[6] *VISUALISING GPS DATA—CABSPOTTING,* 29 January 2009 11:31, animation, San Francisco, GPS tracks, cabspotting, tracking, visualisation, urbanMachine.

[7] http://www.cabspotting.org/.

[8] http://www.youtube.com/v/NDoL7w8hcOM&hl=en&fs=1&.

[9] http://www.youtube.com/v/PECHheSP1Lc&hl=en&fs=1&.

[10] http://www.cabspotting.org/projects/.

[11] *LONDON BEATS DIFFERENTLY—CYCLES DISRUPTED,* 2 February 2009 14:40, snow, London, cycles, urbanMachine, rhythms, weather.

Fig. 4 Clip by urbanTick
on Vimeo. (http://vimeo.
com/2985856)

closed, and public transport running a skeletal service or nothing at all." This means
not many options to travel around. Probably a lot of people cannot even get to work
if they tried and schools are closed all day. London has seen the heaviest snowfall
in 18 years, weather experts said, according to BBC. It is around 10 cm of snow
until now, but could be more towards the evening. Last time something like this
happened, in January 2003, there was what was called the heaviest snowfall in 10
years with about 1 inch (2 cm) of snow. The normal everyday rhythm has been completely changed by the weather. There is no 09 h00–17 h00 working hours today,
no scheduled transport, even the airports have closed their busy runways. The city
beats differently under the snow (Fig. 5).

Businesses have already calculated loss of £ 1 bn because of the disrupted routines. The market reacts quickly to changing conditions. According to the BBC,
shares in British Airways, which has cancelled all flights from Heathrow, were
down 4.25% at 115 pence, while Go-Ahead, which runs Southeastern rail services,

Fig. 5 Image by urbanTick /
A lot of snow in London! See
clip on Vimeo. (http://vimeo.
com/3059482)

was down 2% at 963.5p. These only because it is a day not going according to plan, but when does it go according to plan? Finally, at around 15 h00 UCL has decided to send out an email to all staff and students with instructions on how to deal with these exceptional circumstances. Trying to introduce some sort of rhythm they wrote the following line "All attempts are being made to keep UCL running but it is necessary for reasons of safety and security and on account of unavoidable short staffing to switch to the Friday shut-down routine for all buildings. Procedures in place for week-end working therefore apply…" If it is not the Monday rhythm there will be an other one to apply. A not quite accurate but idealistic impression of today in London.

6   *HOW DISRUPTION REMINDS US OF THE ROUTINE WE FOLLOW*[12] Suddenly after our everyday activities are interrupted, one naturally is reminded of how smoothly it "normally" works out. Yesterday's weather condition has brought London to a standstill and even today there is plenty of reasons to stay home. In the news the routines are the big topic. The articles cover the whole range from complaints to positive remarks about the capitals happiness, but mainly revolve around the normal routine. I put together a collection of how the terms cycles, rhythms and routines suddenly are used a lot as something disruptive happens. 10 cm of snow does change the way the city beats. Following up from yesterday's disruption of the city's everyday activities there is much talk today about the daily cycles. One of the phrase used in the news yesterday and today is: "… this snowfall is a once in a lifetime experience…" "London struggled back to work through snow and ice today." (Dick Murray, Transport Editor, Evening Standard, 03.02.09)[13]. An article in the online Evening Standard, titled "This transport collapse is inexcusable", questioning the transport collapse, also uses the terms. "THIS has been the worst weather-related transport chaos in living memory." and "…no point spending tens of millions on snow ploughs and other equipment that will be used once in a generation…" (Christian Wolmar, Evening Standard 03.02.09)[14]. Boris Johnson, the Mayor of London was of course also talking about the events and is quoted with this: "This is the kind of snow we haven't seen in London in decades…" on www.streathamguardian.co.uk[15]. The former Mayor of London immediately used this opportunity to attack his procedure and told the BBC "There has never been a day where the bus service has been cancelled for bad weather. Not in 100 years," (on the guardian) In an other article by the same newspaper the evening venues are described. "London's streets empty as snow shuts theatres and bars." The street life was described as "…frozen trade: the normally bustling streets of Soho, including

---

[12] *HOW DISRUPTION REMINDS US OF THE ROUTINE WE FOLLOW*, 3 February 2009 10:38, urbanMachine, twitter, rhythm, timeLapse, London, routine, language, cycles.

[13] http://www.thisisLondon.co.uk/standard/article-23632831-details/More+commuter+pain+on+the+trains%2C+Tubes+and+buses/article.do

[14] http://www.thisisLondon.co.uk/standard/article-23632831-details/More+commuter+pain+on+the+trains%2C+Tubes+and+buses/article.do.

[15] http://www.streathamguardian.co.uk/news/4096044.Snow_brings_more_disruption/.

Old Compton Street, were virtually deserted as the icy weather forced restaurants and bars to close…" (Rashid Razaq, Evening Standard 03.02.09)[16].

Regarding the conditions the weather was compared to the past as "…The biggest snowfall to hit London in 18 years idled the city's trademark red buses and Underground trains…" by The Associated Press on msnbc.[17] "A brief history of snow" is a collection of important snow related events in the UK in the past, going as far back as 1600. Collected by Charlie English, Tuesday 3 February 2009[18].

For a real time crowed sources UK snow mapsee benmarsh[19] a Twitter based snow map.

Again the weather compared to the past by the Guardian titles "Certainly not a blizzard, but it was the heaviest snowfall since 1991" and it concludes "This is the heaviest fall since 1991, and so there's a whole generation of children who haven't seen snow like this. If I were a teenager I would love to be out tobogganing." (Michael Fish, The Guardian, Tuesday 3 February 2009)[20] (Fig. 6).

Twitter was employed to spread information of course. Everything from closed school updates in Camden[21], numbers of snowmen[22] and of course amount of snow[23] was integrated. Anyway updates on conditions, weather, travelling and more can be found on the Guardian News Blog[24]. An other timeLapse to show the snow conditions in London, by, MosReel[25] (see fig. 6), February 02, 2009.

7   *THE PULSE OF THE PLANET*[26] An animation to visualise the pulse of the world was created by using phone call data. Centred on New York, the pulse is generated visualizing the amount of phone calls going to or from different parts of the world to or from NY. The different time zones influence this rhythm, also does the day and night cycle (Fig. 7).

The size of the area shrinks or grows according to the phone call data and international cities with the highest amount of calls are highlighted. Produced by MIT SENSEable City Lab[27].

8   *THE PULSE OF THE TRANSPORT NETWORK*[28] The pulse of the transport network does play a big role in the constitution of the city's pulse. The pace of the

---

[16] http://www.thisisLondon.co.uk/standard/article-23633505-details/London%27s+streets+empty+as+snow+shuts+theatres+and+bars/article.do.

[17] http://www.msnbc.msn.com/id/28972533/.

[18] http://www.guardian.co.uk/uk/2009/feb/03/snow-history-britain-weather.

[19] http://uksnowmap.com/.

[20] http://www.guardian.co.uk/uk/2009/feb/03/weather-michael-fish.

[21] http://twitter.com/camdentalking.

[22] http://twitter.com/anonymoustom/status/1172593264.

[23] http://www.benmarsh.co.uk/snow/.

[24] http://www.guardian.co.uk/news/blog/2009/feb/03/snow-transport-weather.

[25] http://uk.youtube.com/user/MosReel.

[26] *THE PULSE OF THE PLANET,* 24 February 2009 15:08, urbanMachine, pulse, rhythm, MIT.

[27] http://senseable.mit.edu/.

[28] *THE PULSE OF THE TRANSPORT NETWORK,* 24 February 2009 15:35, movement, transport, rhythm, pulse, urbanMachine, timeLapse.

Fig. 6 Clip by Mos-Reel on Youtube. (http://www.youtube.com/v/buvK66X1iBE&hl=en&fs=1)

Fig. 7 Clip by the MIT SensableCity lab on Vimeo. (http://vimeo.com/1997184)

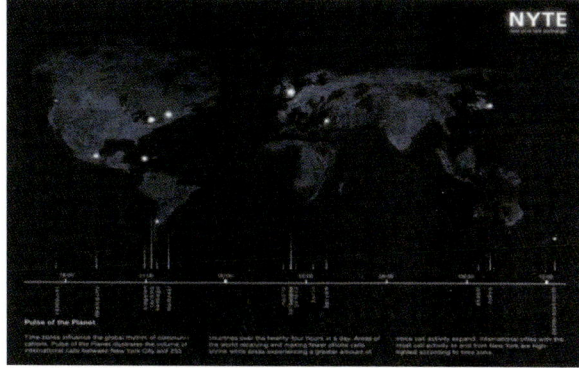

Fig. 8 Clip by urbanTick on Vimeo. (http://vimeo.com/2986171)

departure of the public transport, the frequency of the stops, but also the location of the stations spatially drive this rhythm. Any live tracking transport site gives a good idea of the pulse of the transport network (Fig. 8).

The timeLapse captured at a tube station visualises the pulse from a different angle and shows how the arrival and departure of trains pump the commuters through the network.

9   *DISRUPTION SECOND TAKE*[29] A major strike on the Tube in London is announced for today. From Today Tuesday 19 h00–Thursday 19 h00 there will be no Tube services in London if the strike goes ahead as announced. This will mean that thousands of commuters and travellers will be forced to search for alternatives. We already had this once this year. The heavy (12 cm:) snowfall from February 2nd brought a major disruption to London's transport network and an extra day of for thousands of Londoners. This event was covered in posts here[30] and here[31]. And again this disruption will change the rush hour for two days. Maybe everyone will be using the riverboat service, as the Mayor Boris Johnson has arranged for all of us to travel for free. We'll see how London and Londoners will manage the situation. In terms of routines it will definitely be different (Fig. 9).

Transport for London[32] promotes cycling and walking; this is the cheapest option for them. Walking maps are available from the tfl.gov.uk site. The maps are not very good and hardly any better as a normal tourist guide. Maybe another project would actually be a bit more successful here. The shortwalk[33] project is aiming at promoting the information about distances between inner London tube stations. While doing some research the people behind the project discovered that sometimes it is actually quicker to walk than squeezing into the tube. A nice map visualises this. Other option is to plan your journey as a walk on walkit.com[34] or even Google Maps[35] could help you find the shortest route…A micro blogger community has formed and collects a variety of suggestions and options to beat the strike. A good collection of them is available on TimesOnline[36].

Unlike with the snowfall in February, people seem to be determined to get in to work tomorrow. We'll see how it goes and whether or not Londoners can make it again a positive disruption of their weekly rhythms. First Images start to emerge on the web, Image from Canary Wharf[37]. A new central London transport map on Flickr, click for details:

---

[29] *DISRUPTION SECOND TAKE,* 9 June 2009 15:00, routine, urbanMachine, London, rhythm, cycle.

[30] http://urbantick.blogspot.com/2009/02/London-beats-differently-cycles.html.

[31] http://urbantick.blogspot.com/2009/02/how-disruption-reminds-us-of-routine-we.html.

[32] http://www.tfl.gov.uk/.

[33] http://shortwalk.blog.co.uk.

[34] http://www.walkit.com.

[35] http://maps.google.com.

[36] http://www.timesonline.co.uk/tol/travel/news/article6464101.ece.

[37] http://img265.yfrog.com/img265/5972/tek.jpg.

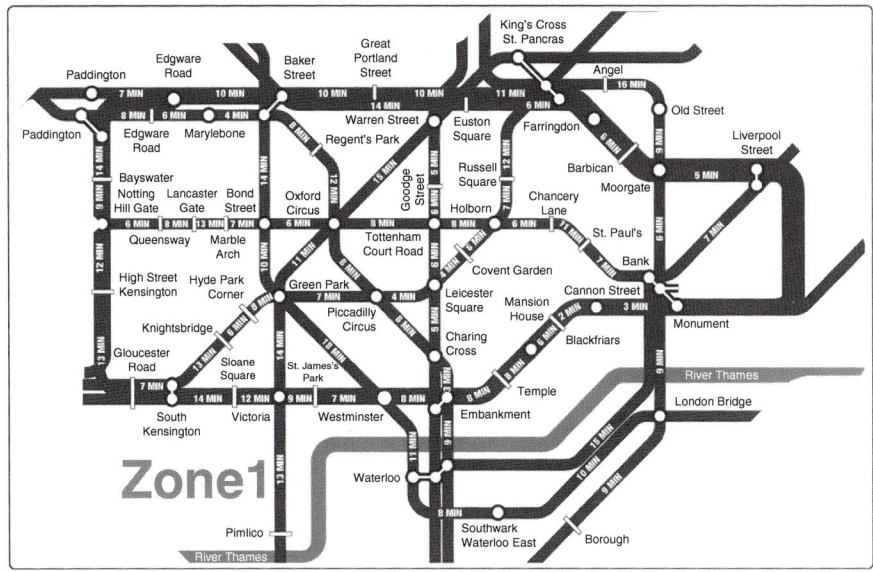

Fig. 9 Image by shortwalk / Central London map with walking times

Fig. 10 Image by urbanTick / TFL temporary transport map at Euston station

FOLLOWING THE DISRUPTION[38] The tube strike in London did go ahead and is in action since yesterday 19 h00. Operation on all tube lines is disrupted. But actually some lines have a service (Fig. 10).

---

[38] *FOLLOWING THE DISRUPTION,* 10 June 2009 12:44, urbanMachine, London, rhythm, traffic, commuting.

Fig. 11 Clip by urbanTick
on Vimeo. (http://vimeo.
com/5100930)

What a surprise the Northern Line has a good service since morning. It was the first line to be open, but during the morning other lines opened. Staff at Euston kept a map to inform passengers what service is available. At around 10 h15 already a number of lines operate a very delayed and interrupted service. The clip starts in Tufnell Park where there is little to see from the strike impact, as the Northern Line is in good service. Only buses coming down towards Kentish Town are jammed. There are obviously a lot of commuters on the bus who usually take the tube. At each stop a number of people ask the driver for advice and information on where the bus goes and how to get to certain places. On a normal day on the bus, hardly anyone speaks to the driver. Same at Mornington Crescent, tube station is open and not busy. Towards Euston it gets busier and a lot of people are walking down the street, as the road is jammed with buses (Fig. 11).

Euston runs a taxi service with a special taxi marshal, and the queue reaches through the big entrance hall. Other tube stations are deserted and ticket offices closed. Music from mp3 unsigned by Andrew Bowsher & The Sceptics (Experimental) A man at one with his bedroom[39].

11   *BRITISH GAS—A SUBJECTIVE WORLD VIEW*[40] Following up from the topic of space creation and individual world views in yesterdays post on Mental Maps[41], an example of an ad campaign that takes these aspects to an extreme trying to make it look funny but probably render it ridiculous. See clip on Youtube[42]. British Gas[43] runs this campaign visualizing British households as individual planets floating around independently in space only connected by the British Gas service van shuttling between them. What exactly the story is, I am not sure. It must be something that persuades you to switch to the British Gas service. I am really not sure about the abstraction, especially the isolation. Advertisement is usually largely about ste-

---

[39] http://www.mp3unsigned.com/showmp3.asp?mp3ID=53501&aid=761.

[40] *BRITISH GAS—A SUBJECTIVE WORLD VIEW,* 7 August 2009 12:07, urbanMachine, mental-Map, personal, spaceCreation, advertisement.

[41] http://urbantick.blogspot.com/2009/07/space-perception-and-mental-maps.html.

[42] http://www.youtube.com/v/Ptpbuuza7K4&hl=en&fs=1&.

[43] http://www.britishgas.co.uk/.

Fig. 12 Image by MArch Urban Design 2009 / Invitation Flyer

reotypes, but this stereotype of space here is a rather sad example. A major aspect of personal space perception is indeed that the corporate's centre is placed on the individual's location, as it is a subjective perspective. The crucial point is where these different world views overlap and interact. To create the personal story of the day the interaction with external realities is an essential part of the narrative. Boiling it down to the British Gas service man is a bit cheap, but obviously the ad designer (this is probably CHI & Partners[44]) thought it to be enough for this project.

MARCH ANNUAL SHOW 2009—CURIOSITIES[45] The Bartlett School of Architecture[46] calls for the MArch Annual Show 2009 (Fig. 12).

The Master of Arts course students present their work at the Wates House, 22 Gordon Street[47]. The bash starts from 17 h30 on the ground floor of the Wates House. Work presented will be of students from both masters courses, MArch Architecture as well as MArch Urban Design[48]. The Urban Design students present their work under the title CurioCities. They have been working on the topic of Urban Mutations and produced an impressive wealth of project (Fig. 13).

As usual each student's background played a key role and helped shaping the diversity again archived in this year's fifty something projects. Some project impressions can be found on UD-unit-06[49] (Fig. 14).

THE WAY THINGS GO—URBAN INTERLOCK[50] One thing leads to another—it could be called a sentence of very old wisdom. But somehow it is also part of our daily experience. A lot of the actions we take will have some form of impact on how we do something afterwards. As for my day there are some elements that are interlocked. I need the key as I leave the house to lock the door, I can take the tube that

---

[44] http://www.chiandpartners.com/.

[45] *MARCH ANNUAL SHOW 2009—CURIOSITIES,* 18 September 2009 09:45, exhibition, city, architecture, London, urban form, urban, urbanMachine.

[46] http://www.bartlett.ucl.ac.uk/architecture/index.php.

[47] http://maps.google.com/maps?f=q&source=s_q&hl=en&geocode=&q=London,+UK+gordon+street+22&sll=51.501103,-0.123339&;sspn=0.033554,0.071325&ie=UTF8&ll=51.526101,-0.132415&spn=0.008384,0.017831&z=16.

[48] http://www.bartlett.ucl.ac.uk/architecture/programmes/march_ud/march_ud.htm.

[49] http://ud0809g06.blogspot.com/2009/09/final-crits-2009-march-urban-design.html.

[50] *THE WAY THINGS GO—URBAN INTERLOCK,* 21 September 2009 09:22, art, time, cycle, urbanMachine, repetition.

Fig. 13 Image by Zahra Azizi / Urban curiosity and memory, installation

Fig. 14 Image by urbanTick / SpeeD, Daria Shipukhina and Stavroula Papafotiou, Adaptive toolkit for urban growth. Tactile urbanism

would be faster, but on the bus I can read something and it is not as crowded, both ways I need my travel card to get on. The packed lunch depends on the leftover of the evening before and the daily hits on the blog depend on what time I upload the new post. Early is good for European readers, whereas later it will be picked up by readers overseas. On the way back the transport issue applies again and if I am late because I wanted to write this additional email, I have to take the tube to get home on time where I will need the key to let myself in. Our decisions are not only driven by what is, but by the consequences it might have. I suppose this is called planning. Still, there are a lot of moments when things are not going according to plan and even this will influence everything thereafter. Here in Britain, superstition has quite a tradition. Things like not walking under ladders, black cats, numbers and so on are part of people's decision making process moment by moment. On an individual daily level it might look as described above. These aspects apply to the whole range of scales too though. On the level of city infrastructure an incident can have the same consequences. An accident on a road in central London will disrupt the commute of thousands of commuters. Greater events, such as 10 cm of snow[51] can bring the city to a standstill. However, it somehow works most days and this is all we care for. The city can be imagined as gigantic machinery with hundreds of thousands of little elements' switches and circuits that work in sync. The most quoted visualisa-

---

[51] http://urbantick.blogspot.com/search/label/snow.

tion in this context is probably Metropolis, the city machine. What actually happened behind the scene of the real city and how it all works together hardly anyone cares, maybe no one even knows. For a large city it is hard to imagine, that there is one person that REALLY knows why and how everything interlocks. Imagine if this person were superstitious, would the city still work? This would probably cause the whole city to fear about a certain aspect. This might even be the case with London. Everyone is very excited about 2012 with the Olympics to be held here in London. But on the other hand it does put on a lot of pressure and certainly sparks some fear.

See clip on Youtube[52]/"Der Lauf der Dinge" (the way things go).

However, the aspect of interlocking events have been subject to great works in the world of art. The artists Peter Fischli und David Weiss created the famous movie "Der Lauf der Dinge" (The Way Things Go[53]) in 1987. Similar to a chain reaction, a motion is unleashed that travels through a setting, constantly changing its form, shape and character. On youtube the full movie is available in three parts.

See also the clip on Youtube[54], a Honda add based on the 1987 Fischil—Weiss film.

Surprisingly the movie manages to build up a tension carried by curiosity over the just 30 min. As a metaphor for an urban machine it works rather well. The same topic has been used for a car advert by Honda. It is obviously modelled on the above original. There are even some direct quotes. A very recent interpretation of the theme was hyped on the internet the last week. This time a fundamental shift has taken place (Fig. 15).

From the very physical and body/object centred original the latest interpretation has replaced the physical aspect with … technology I suppose. The different elements do not touch to pass the motion on any longer. It is all magic here. Nevertheless it is a great demonstration of RFID technology. There are fundamental aspects of the original "Der Lauf der Dinge" are missing, however, it does very much resemble the daily life of interlocked actions. It is not so much the curiosity, but the familiarity that builds up the tension in this new example. It is realized by Nearness, a collaboration of Berg[55] and Timo[56].

14   *UNDERGROUND IS OVERGROUND*[57] In terms of the environment we live in there is a lot of hidden function that we are not aware of at times. Normally we do not want to know about everything that is going on in the city and a lot of them cannot be seen from the everyday perspective. Still the city machine is rumbling and rotating: in the air, behind the block, around the corner and underneath our feet.

---

[52] http://www.youtube.com/v/QfEkPgfA7wo&hl=en&fs=1&.

[53] http://en.wikipedia.org/wiki/The_Way_Things_Go.

[54] http://www.youtube.com/v/rYabfifhEPE&hl=en&fs=1&.

[55] http://bergLondon.com/blog/2009/09/15/nearness/.

[56] http://www.nearfield.org/2009/09/nearness.

[57] *UNDERGROUND IS OVERGROUND,* 15 October 2009 08:34, advertisement, urbanMachine.

Fig. 15 Clip by Timo and
BERG on Vimeo /
Nearness, by Timo and
BERG, clip based on the
1987 Fischli—Weiss film.
(http://vimeo.com/6588461)

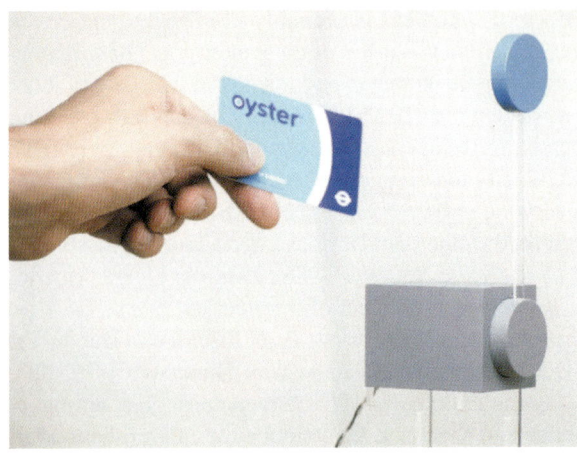

Fig. 16 Clip by Max Brill
on Vimeo. (http://vimeo.
com/4084789)

See clip on Vimeo[58]. A intriguing visualisation developed as an ad for the metro
Madrid by lahuellafx[59].

Same approach used for an ad for foxsportsdesign[60] this time for an HD sports
channel.

15   *LUNCH TIME TIMELAPSE*[61] Once more a nice timeLapse. I think the title of
the clip actually is a bit misleading, or at least it unveils much of the detail about
making it (Fig. 16).

However the colours and the blending in is really nice and makes you want to go
to Liverpool Street for a lunch break.

---

[58] http://vimeo.com/614175.

[59] http://www.lahuellafx.com/.

[60] http://foxsportsdesign.com/2009/01/nascar-underground/.

[61] *LUNCH TIME TIMELAPSE,* 20 November 2009 timeLapse, transport, urbanMachine, traffic

Part II
timeSpace

Memory: Collective vs. Individual Narratives

Zahra Azizi

Introduction

"Memory is one of the key ingredients in the creation of place. It is subject to political as well as physical operations" (Borden et al. 2001).

The main interest throughout the course of my studies at the Bartlett, has been to observe the relationship between memory and our experience of the city bearing in mind the importance of everyday routines. This was studied at an individual scale using narratives to explore further how the passage of time contributes to this experience and how events of the past have an impact on the future of a place. The context of this study is set in Clerkenwell/London which bears a strong element of time and stands as a symbol of the passage of time. With the city growing and daily routines becoming modernized, people inhabiting the city are growing to become less and less in contact with each other, especially face to face; and their daily activities leave them more and more isolated from one and another. Hence the focus was to create a subconscious basis for encouraging more social interaction based on very specific narratives. The inevitable argument, which automatically gets involved, is about the creation of space and its role in place making: in other words, the way we perceive space and our definition of it. The 'box space' created by walls holding a volume of space versus the experience of space. The important factor to be argued here is that it is precisely the experience and the function of a particular space which forms its identity. It is the movement within it and with movement comes interaction; going from A to B, adjustments have to be made on the way. Consequently daily stories and memories are formed through these transitions and interactions.

Z. Azizi (✉)
Bartlett School of Architecture, University College London, London, UK
e-mail: zahra.azizi@gmail.com

F. Neuhaus (ed.), *Studies in Temporal Urbanism,*
DOI 10.1007/978-94-007-0937-9_3, © Springer Science+Business Media B.V. 2011

Memory: Collective vs. Individual Narratives

Within the report, I have taken this at a larger scale to explore the effects of collective memory on the urban fabric and how this subjective element, hand in hand with the actual physique of the city, implements itself in the way the inhabitants move around it. The formation of curiosity and of curious spaces. The project will strive to encompass political, cultural and social entities in our experience of urban life, as they are important variable factors which determine the quality of our experience. A change in these factors over time will ensure a change in the nature of these experiences. The notion of collective memory implies memory which is shared, passed on, constructed by groups or modern society. Jan Assmann in his book of 'Cultural Memory' distinguishes between the Cultural memory and the Communicative memory. Whereas the former fulfils a storage function, and the latter fulfils the function of an everyday memory that is situated in the present (http://en.Wikipedia.org/wiki/Collective_memory). The notion of collective memory brings together the role of space and places of shared memory.

Talking on a larger scale, the collective memory on the scale of a nation spatially manifests itself by the memorials it chooses to erect. Whatever a nation chooses to memorialize in physical monument, or perhaps more significantly, what not to memorialize, is an indicator of the collective memory. As objects they gradually conquer the space they sit upon and become a place; a place of reminiscence and a place of congregation. At the same time, they also become tools of orientation; devices which certain routes are measured around. The idea though that memorials are somehow a means of triggering events of the past has been put to debate and many argue that it is vastly illusory to assume so. Ian Sinclair argues that "memorials are a way of forgetting, reducing generational guilt to a grid of albino chess pieces, bloodless stalagmites. Shapes that are easy to ignore stand in for the trauma of remembrance" (Borden et al. 2001). In a bizarre way after a while it seems that these memorials change their roles from being tools of remembrance to places for gathering. Therefore one can think of this as a two-way concept; that 'place' can itself become a tool of remembrance, a device which triggers different images of different memories for different people. Yet "it is seeing which establishes our place in the surrounding world" (Berger 1990) and consequently our perception of the viewed space.

Memory: Space and Time

Memory distinguishes place from space. "Place is the product of a relationship—part subjective projection, part internalization of an external reality…correspondingly amnesia is an operation which reverses that process and dissolves place back into the indifference of space." (Curtis 2001)

Memory brings to attention the relationship of the past with the present and sparks elements of the future and therefore highlights the continuum of 'time'.

"Social relations in the city are dynamic ones, and although we argue for the importance of space, time is increasingly entering into discussions of the social production of spaces—not solely the time of historical materialism, but also personal and irregular times: bodily rhythms, unconscious and conscious memories, the flux of complexity and chaos" (Borden et al. 2001). The importance of time in the formation of memory cannot be denied. Layers of memory build up and overlap on one another through the passage of time; some parts of these layers are see-through (accessible/retrievable) and some parts conceal one another. Experiences in each layer are separate but may also at times be interconnected. Each could act as a trigger or cue to another one. In the city, space and time are both experienced in forms of representation and are etched between the layers of memory. The built form in relation to memory is highly significant in the way that it holds on to the past and is necessary in to the personal negotiation of change. It also translates itself into the public elaboration of narratives of time. The built form of the city is indeed what makes our experience of urban space more dynamic and curious. Time allows these experiences to be diversified, to be repeated, to progress and to regress, to fulfil the unexpected and to surprise the inhabitant. Time is not independent of place but dominates the place in which the stories occur and emerge; it is "represented consciously, experienced passively, reimagined actively and embedded into all the myriad of social practices that constitute social being" (Borden et al. 2001). Time must be considered as an entity which varies from the ephemeral to a very brief moment to the longer time of future generations and cycles of life. Time flows together with space. The city is part of this flow and a macro home to the micro events happening in little pockets within it.

mi·cro·cosm (m?'kr?-k?z'?m) 'A small, representative system regarded as encapsulating in miniature the characteristics of something much larger' (http://www.bartlett.ucl.ac.uk/architecture/programmes/units/unit05_08.htm, June 2009).

Micro movements, micro spaces, slight cases of disequilibrium (vs. equilibrium) assert themselves upon the complex urban landscape we inhabit. According to Neil Denari, 'the complexity of human-physical systems is generated from the buildup of micro events and actions'; of the niches of worlds within worlds.

Movement: The Concept of the Mask

A day in the life of each person experiencing their spatial surroundings is different to one another. The nature, quality and level of every individual's comprehension of the city is diverse, even if they take the same routes, go to the same locations (gardens in this case) and carry out the same activities. Every inhabitant has a different perception of the space they live in and experiences it based on their own expectations and previous memories. What's important is the 'past', 'present' and the 'future' which all keep layering on top of each other. A lot of the everyday activities we do or routes we take may seem mundane but actually they are part of the bigger picture of the everyday narrative. The Urban fabric (interior or exterior) is a host to the formation of these narratives, memories and various experiences. "The streets stand for shared existence, a common understanding. A place that is owned by no one but is used by everyone" (Williamson 1986); people as recipients of the streets and the spaces held within, behind, or amongst them are the primary narrators of the biography of the city. Realistically, there is a direct relationship between the layers of people's memories and the physical layers of the city fabric (together with layers of its history). There also exists a mutual dialogue between movement and mobility within this fabric and the formation of memories (especially memory of a place).

"The possibilities for engaging with the city and its architecture are spatial and temporal, determined by internal desires, boundaries, thresholds|that define possibilities for the self, as well as through the politics of external spaces, events and moments. Although the self is in part constituted through an occupation of space and an understanding of the city, and the city is too created by the actions of its inhabitants, neither can be completely collapsed into the other" (Borden et al. 2001). Therefore the body becomes the site; the site of retention and propagation of memory and the site of the experience of urban life. The lack of social interaction in the rapidly modernizing world is an issue that I mentioned in the previous section. For people, as inhabitants of the city, there seems to be the gathering of psychological together with physical masks which causes this sense of isolation. Both cases prevent city dwellers from getting closer and crossing their boundaries.

It is only via movement that everyday stories and memories are born. The relation of a place to the self is made by moving points of view within the city by way of narrative and parallax. The movement of the body as the site of memory and the mental and physical movement from one place to another. Mental movement here implies the quality of seeing/hearing/feeling something which acts as a cue and triggers a memory of another experience: in other words, causes us to reminisce. Therefore space becomes a dynamic entity taken over by a range of all these movements. The contained space of a city is very much similar to memory in the way that it is "a play of perspectives and constellations created by points of view adapted in time and space" (Borden et al. 2001). Speaking from a personal perspective, while exploring the nature of individual memory my own body became the site of this exploration and it was through personal judgments and comprehension that these interests took themselves a step further into the discussion of the collective. Movement within the site took itself beyond going from 'a' to 'b' and became about discovering the encapsulated space within these existing forms and layers, physical layers and layers of time. A lot of the conclusions drawn from the experience and the 'feel' of Clerkenwell are therefore highly personal and may of course differ to that of another individual.

References

Barry Curtis (2001) That place where: some thoughts on memory and the city. In: Ian Borden, Joe Kerr, Jane Rendell with Alicia Pivaro(eds) The unknown city. The MIT Press
Ian Borden, Joe Kerr, Jane Rendell with Alicia Pivaro (2001) The unknown city. The MIT Press
John Berger (1990) Ways of seeing. BBC and Penguin Books
Judith Williamson (1986) Consuming passions: the dynamics of popular culture. M. Boyars, London

timeSpace

Fabian Neuhaus

16 *TIME MAP—SOME MORE EXAMPLES*[1] Here are two software examples that are specifically designed to tackle the time-space-visualisation-problem. One of them is GeoTime[2] developed by Oculus[3] a leading and award winning provider of visualisation solutions, as they call themselves on the website. It is aiming at professional analysts and is priced similar to other ESRI extensions. The other one is a Google Code project called timeMap[4] developed at the MIT[5] in connection with the SIMILE project and freely available. With GeoTime is it possible to visualise time-based tracking data in an aquarium sort of way, as developed by the Lund School in the 1970s. It also uses the third dimension to show the passage of time. So spatial locations are shown as X and Y and the time is shown as Z-coordinate. Recently Oculus efforts have focused on analytical tools and performance enhancements within GeoTime. The Web 2.0 support could also be interesting. The GeoTime application does integrate with ESRI and Microsoft Products, as well as GeoRSS feeds (Fig. 1).

The really nice thing about the program, compared to the aquarium visualisations[6] in Google Earth, is that the ground plane is interactive and can be moved in the Z-dimension. Effectively the plane with the spatial configuration of the surrounding represents the present and divides virtually the past from the future. What is useful is that the connection between activity on the vertically extruded path is always relatively close to the surface that displays the context information. For in-

---

[1] *TIME MAP—SOME MORE EXAMPLES*, 22 January 2009 16:23, visualisation, time, map, Geo-Time, timemap, timeSpace.

[2] http://www.oculusinfo.com/SoftwareProducts/GeoTime.html.

[3] http://www.oculusinfo.com/index.html.

[4] http://code.google.com/p/timemap/.

[5] http://simile.mit.edu/.

[6] http://urbantick.blogspot.com/2008/11/plymouth-aquarium.html.

F. Neuhaus (✉)
Centre for Advanced Spatial Analysis, University College London, London, UK
e-mail: fabian.neuhaus@ucl.ac.uk

F. Neuhaus (ed.), *Studies in Temporal Urbanism,*
DOI 10.1007/978-94-007-0937-9_4, © Springer Science+Business Media B.V. 2011

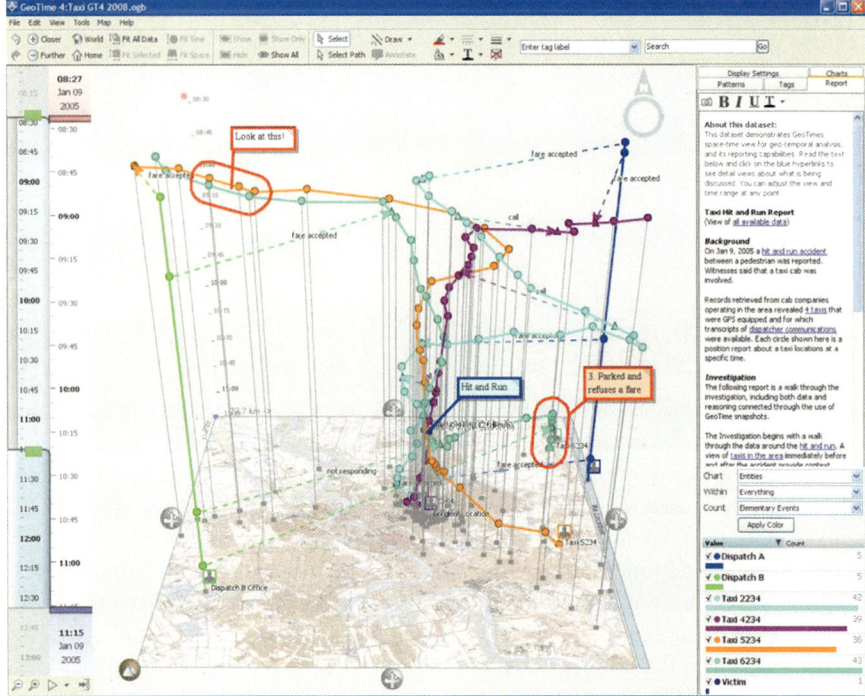

Fig. 1 Image taken from GeoTime website / Movement path represented in time and space. (http://www.oculusinfo.com/SoftwareProducts/GeoTime.html)

formation purposes Oculus has published a nice flash presentation[7] to introduce the GeoTime software (Fig. 2).

The open source software on the other hand is a set of code that can be used and reused. It is basically a Java Script library and it uses the SIMILE time line and displays on Google Maps. Different data sets can be loaded including Json and KML. It reads the location information and the time information. The time line is in the top part and is visualised as one or more bands that can be moved horizontally in order to move back and forward in time. The map sits below and displays by default events that are visible in the time line frame. By scrolling through the time bands the map adjusts. With some simple code elements it is possible to visualise data interactive. I had a go with the data from the Christmas aquarium[8] that I used to play with the Google Earth gadget earlier this month.

So with a bit of clipping and pasting from different examples I was able to load the KML file and have it displayed in the browser.

There are a lot of possibilities to play around with this code. I am really looking forward to spending some time on this. It is not only the layout and the settings in

[7] http://www.oculusinfo.com/flash/Taxi_Nov28.html.

[8] http://urbantick.blogspot.com/2009/01/gadget.html.

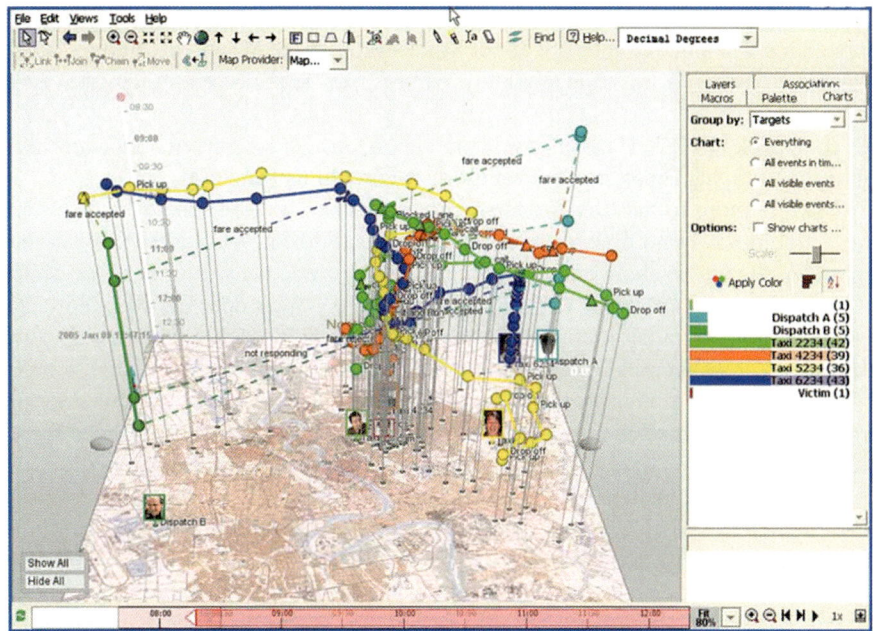

Fig. 2 Image taken from GeoTime website / Space Time path example. (http://www.oculusinfo. com/SoftwareProducts/GeoTime.html)

the code that are exciting, but also the possibilities of integrating different data sets. The recorded tracks could for example be accomplished with some live information feed from online sources, e.g. Flickr, Twitter or News. The KML setting also need to be sorted out. The current production line for GPS track files is not very convenient. I will try to put the version above live soon on my web space to see how it runs on-line. In the mean time have a look at these examples. Timemap examples with Json data—Artists and Authors of the Renaissance[9], Time line SIMILE example—The JFK Assassination Time line[10].

TIME PASSES IN PHOTOGRAPHY[11] The book Ortszeit-Local time[12] featured on the blog earlier as a method to investigate the passing of time. Time over a long period is really difficult to document and photography is just one of the ways of doing this, but probably the most widely used.

Danny Wills[13] achieves a similar effect with his photographs. In this case it is not a direct comparison between two photographs taken at the same place at different

---

[9] http://timemap.googlecode.com/svn/trunk/examples/artists.html.

[10] http://simile.mit.edu/timeline/examples/jfk/jfk.html.

[11] *TIME PASSES IN PHOTOGRAPHY,* 29 August 2009 08:00, body, time, photography, memory, timeSpace.

[12] http://urbantick.blogspot.com/2009/08/book-ortszeit.html.

[13] http://dannywills.com/miketyson.

times as in Ortszeit. Rather it is relying on the individual memory people have of something. The photographs are about Mike Tyson, more exactly about one of his abandoned house. A lot of people know Mike Tyson as the boxer shown above. A public celebrity with ups and downs in his career. He has finally retired in 2005 after his comeback in 1995. He spent some time in prison and once bit an opponent's ear off during a fight. Those are the events you might remember.

There is more to his life of course and there is a lot more time to it than just these highlights. From time to time Tyson is again in the news. Earlier this year he promoted the movie about his life, at one point there was the sad news of the death of one of his young children in the newspaper. Danny Wills does not show any images of Tyson but rather pictures of one of his houses. It appears do be empty and abandoned now, but still has some of its glory. It speaks of a different time, a time Tyson was on top of his career maybe. It also speaks of the time Tyson was not in front of cameras, the time we don't really know what he was doing. Maybe there was some "real life" time in between the events? Head over to Danny's really nice page[14] to see more photographs of Mike Tyson's villa.

18   *MAPPING DISTANCE AND TIME*[15] Time as an element of space (simplification) is a tricky thing. Mapping the time is even worse.

It pops up here and there and some nice examples have been developed recently, mainly in connection with digital application. A series of posts on this blog have been dedicated to this problem. There was an early one on aquarium and one on different approaches[16] that I have tried with my data and an other one with examples of software[17] to deal with this. What is really interesting on those time space maps is how a distorted image emerges. Space, or rather the shape we know, looks different as distances become longer or shorter due to the aspect of time it takes to travel it. On the above map the South East of England almost vanishes as it is quite accessible from London where as western and northern areas are quite stretched out. Since 1981 the Eurostar Tunnel has been opened and travel times to mainland Europe have changed. Paris is only just over two hours away from London these days. For the construction of Euralille the leading planning office OMA has produced a set of nice graphics visualizing how Europe moves closer together with the Eurostar and TGV network expansion. Time can also be very interesting on a smaller scale. Again, OMA used it during the planning of a project in Yokohama. It was part of the programming process. Mapping the different uses over twenty-four hours gave a good insight into how the development will be used. Density and location are adjusted as needed.

The use of technology such as GIS, database and mapping services such as Google Maps, Yahoo Maps or Open Street Map have give rise to a new breed of interactive time maps on the internet. One such example on London commuting

---

[14] http://dannywills.com/miketyson.

[15] *MAPPING DISTANCE AND TIME,* 9 September 2009 16:47, timeSpace, time, timemap, mapping, commuting.

[16] http://urbantick.blogspot.com/2009/01/time-map-different-approaches.html.

[17] http://urbantick.blogspot.com/2009/01/time-map-some-more-examples.html.

Fig. 3 Image by mysociety.
org. / Showing areas reach-
able in a certain time period.
(http://www.mysociety.
org/2007/more-travel-maps/
SW1P4DR_20km_
contours_800.png)

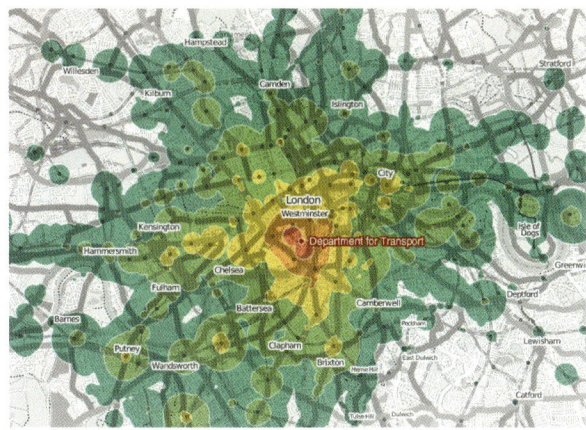

times can be seen here[18]. You can use the two sliders above the map to adjust desired travel time and property prices. The visualisation is based on excluding informa- tion. The map does not distort as seen above, the sliders basically simply direct a black overlay that turns areas of the map invisible. In this sense it is a rather simple visualisation (Fig. 3).

But it gives a good sense of the geographical area that a certain time frame ap- plies to mainly for map reading trained people though. For others this might just add to the confusion. The simple travel times provided by Transport for London might be, in most cases, more helpful. In terms of accuracy, one can argue here, that there will be a delay or any sort of other complication anyway and it hugely depends on what time of the day you are actually travelling. So basically the time frame for the time frame would be important. In short the perception of travel time is a very important factor. This is probably more important than the actual travel time. TfL somehow has the problem, that people expect it to be slow and unreliable and this probably affects the perception of travel time dramatically.

BBCone[19] has produced an animation of crime over time in Oxford. They are looking at a week and document how the amount of crime builds up. Again it is based on a normal map and colour dots fade in and out to indicate locations and a time slider on the top gives information about the time of the day and the day of the week.

ON CYCLES—THE BEGINNING OF URBAN SETTLEMENTS[20] A book by Jo- sef H. Reichholf titled "Warum die Menschen sesshaft wurden[21]", translated why men started settling, and explores a new theory to explain why the first settlements started forming. As generally known, the early humans were not settled at one place

---

[18] http://www.mysociety.org/2007/more-travel-maps/morehousing.

[19] http://www.bbc.co.uk/truthaboutcrime/crimemap/.

[20] *ON CYCLES—THE BEGINNING OF URBAN SETTLEMENTS,* 16 April 2009 10:07, cycles, history, rhythm, routine, religion, timeSpace, urban, theory.

[21] http://www.amazon.de/Warum-die-Menschen-sesshaft-wurden/dp/3100629434.

but rather nomadic, moving around to ensure the supply of food. The current theory to explain why they started settling down assumes, that around 15,000 to 11,000 years ago there was a shortage of animals to hunt and people started farming plants and simultaneously started domesticating animals. Josef Reichholf argues this view is wrong and develops in his book a different explanation for the big change from nomads to citizens. His two main arguments are that at this time, in the area where farming first started, the ground must have been very good and therefore it must have had plenty of food. The second argument is, that starting to farm grain from early forms of these plants would have been much too labour intensive as these early plants must have had such tiny grains. Only much later crossings of these plants produce the grain we know today. So he sets out to set up his own theory on how all this happened. His main idea is that it all started from having too much rather than not enough. He suggests that it started with the production of beer, or rather an early form of it, which is quite simple to brew from grains and water. This drink was sweet and nutritive. It was mainly consumed as part of events related to cult and religion. The buildings for rites and cult are the oldest ones known, for example Goebekli Tepe (Turkish for "Hill with a Navel") in south Turkey. These grew into permanent settlements. It wasn't therefore hunger that lead to permanent settlements but excessive consumption and surplus of supply. This theory of how settlements started is very interesting in the context of the research work on cycles in urban environments, not so much because of the beer and how the early settlers had started farming, but more in context with the rites and events that were based on a cyclical repetition but also based at one specific location in space. In connection to this cult site a permanent settlement could have started growing, but it would still be based, through the cycle of the cult event, on a repetition. This would then suggest that the rhythm of the rite was the main driving force behind the settlement, and it must have influenced all areas of everyday activity in these early hamlets from the start. As an example a quote[22] about the calendar system developed for Goebekli Tepe: "The Mesopotamian year of Goebekli Tepe in southeast Anatolia, Urfa-region, north of the Syrian Harran plain, 11 600–9 500 BP, and the calendar of Upper Mesopotamia in later times, for example in the Halaf period, 6th millennium BC, had (I believe) a month of 30 days, a year of 12 months plus 5 additional days, while 63 continual periods of 30 days yield 1890 days and equal 64 lunations" This would link in with the earlier post[23] on week and calendar concepts, that also derive largely from religious rites and cults and at the same time have their spatial manifestation. To have the event or rite as the starting point for the settlement give a very interesting dimension for the research on cycles in the current urban environment.

20   *TIME—AN ADDITIONAL DIMENSION*[24] While thinking of cycles, time plays a very important role. A cycles always has a time duration associated with it. Actually time is the defining element of the rhythm. This opens the possibility to read a cycle

---

[22] http://www.seshat.ch/home/calendar.htm

[23] http://urbantick.blogspot.com/2009/03/time-concept-of-week.html.

[24] *TIME—AN ADDITIONAL DIMENSION,* 18 August 2009 09:25, visualisation, clock, time, timeSpace.

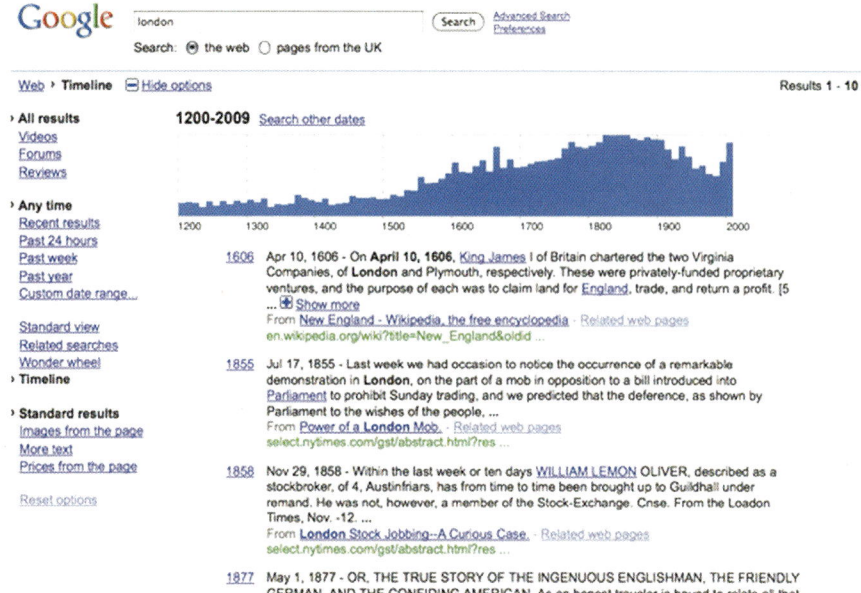

Fig. 4 Screen shot taken from the Google Search page / Showing search results for London on a time line

disconnect from its spatial dimension. It is possible to have two or more cycles in sync in time but not in space. But the problem to visualise time is a fascinating one. The simplest thing is often very complicated. Looking at some ways time is integrated as an option in services. I only recently came across the time option on the Google page. It is possible to search for key words or a combination of words and seeing the result ordered by the data. It is mainly meant to improve search results related to historic event or person. The only thing I found about the definition is that it shows the referred date. It is not really clear how things get lined up whether the data has to be in the text body or as a reference for a blog entry for example. The Google help[25] is not very detailed (Fig. 4).

I tried it with urbanTick, but the result is not very exciting. Nothing shows up bejond the last two years in the time line view, how surprising. Only if tested in the experimental section it does come up with some decent results. Although here it becomes clear that the time line responds to the dates integrated in the body of the text. Unfortunately Google has not yet integrated the function for the general blog search. So we play with something else then. It works well for terms like London: On the other hand in the Google News section[26] the time line option is brilliant. Here it works really well as it is pretty clear what the time and date mean and how it is used. In this context it is rather surprising that it did not exist from the beginning

[25] http://www.google.com/support/websearch/bin/answer.py?hl=en&answer=156089.

[26] http://newstimeline.googlelabs.com/.

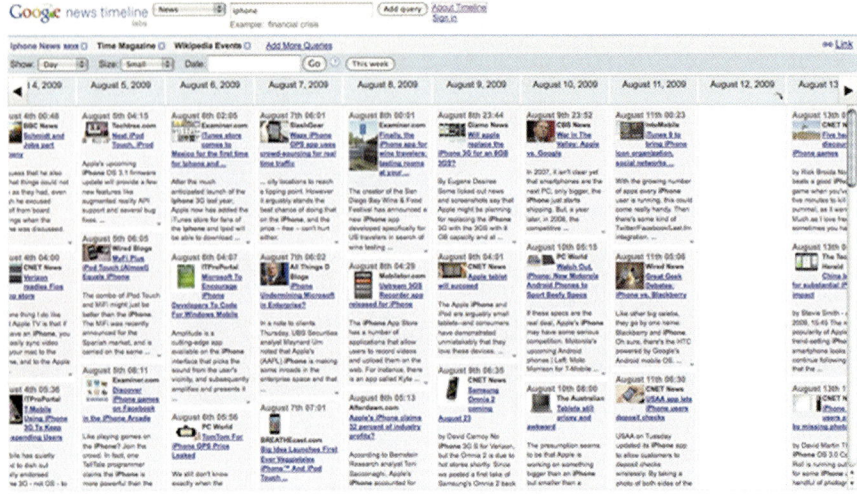

Fig. 5 Screenshot taken from Google Search page / Google News section on a time line

as news live on time. There are a number of setting that can be made, including user queries. Then the time span and time frame can be adjusted. Even with messages the aspect of time has become much more important. Looking at e-mails, they used to be a simple letter. The date sent was a general ordering indicator. Only much later did a sequence of correspondence with the same topic or same person become highlighted in some email programs (Fig. 5).

Google Mail has then introduced the conversation as an organizing criterion. Moving towards a proper chat communication with email messages shows the effort Google takes with the development of WAVE[27], the next generation of messaging application. The same goes for the iPhone message board. It is no longer arranged by date and time, but by conversation, what a leap!

21 ONE YEAR IN TEN MINUTES—THE BARTLETT SCHOOL OF ARCHITEC-TURE[28] The Bartlett summer show[29] has only just closed. It was as usual a great show and very inspirational. It is a long tradition that the Bartlett School of Architecture[30] shows off the work that has been done during the year, of course it is a selection! Each unit from undergraduate to diploma are involved and in the last few weeks this is the main focus of the school. As the show is now over and the work has retreated back in to the Wates House maze what remains is the catalogue and some clips that have been posted online. He he, there we go, there is one particular

---

[27] http://wave.google.com/.

[28] ONE YEAR IN TEN MINUTES—THE BARTLETT SCHOOL OF ARCHITECTURE, 7 July 2009 15:46, timeLapse, timeSpace, cycle, architecture.

[29] http://www.bartlett.ucl.ac.uk/architecture/events/summer/summer.htm.

[30] http://www.bartlett.ucl.ac.uk/index.php.

clip I am talking about, as you might have guessed. The Bartlett Year in ten minutes, another type of timeLapse one year summary—enjoy. See clip on youtube[31].

22   *CHARACTER MAPS*[32] Mental maps[33] have recently featured quite a lot on the blog here. It is an interesting field, even though currently they are not very popular in planning and urban design. It seems almost as if they are seen as late sixties stuff and have some sort of hippie touch to them, which puts a lot of people off. However, I believe they are very interesting in connection with the late seventies Hagerstrand time-space aquarium[34]. Both techniques have been critiqued on some points. The space-time aquarium is very top down, from a distant observer's point of view, disconnecting the subject completely from its surrounding through the rising of the path and denying any sort of procedural creation of the individual. The mental map on the other hand is not objective enough, too subjective and "inaccurate", very difficult to summarize. The aspect of time is in both approaches very static. Even the time-space diagram, from my view, is very much thought of in a linear way, time as an undefined never-ending arrow. This leaves the focus on the space. As a conclusion it would be interesting to have a time focused visualisation and with it we might get a different view on the spatial aspect.

A funny representation is the summary of movie characters by XKCD[35]. It solely focuses on the time aspect in relation to the narrative. In this respect it completely lacks the spatial aspect and the loops and hoops are to me not directly plausible, but nevertheless this is interesting. Regarding the UrbanDiary[36] project, it would be interesting to come up with a similar approach and visualise the relationship of spatial encounters in a similar linear fashion. Thanks to Matt from wiseristhepath[37] for he link. An update to the post—Thanks to Chris[38] for pointing it out. Daniel McLaren[39] has already implemented a dynamic version[40] of the above visualisation. He worked in flash. Head over to his page[41] to see it in action.

23   *LONDON DIARY VISUALISATION IN GEOTIME*[42] After a lot of complicated file manipulations, the data is in a format or better in a location or just is set up to be usable. Well, it is not exactly complicated to handle the data, I was just not quite sure how best to store it. The main problem is the date format, a misinterpretation seems to happen during one of the steps, still have to figure out where exactly. So

[31] http://www.youtube.com/v/KsYUjd2q27U&hl=en&fs=1&.

[32] *CHARACTER MAPS,* 9 November 2009 10:10, visualisation, mentalMap, timeSpace, mapping.

[33] http://urbanTick.blogspot.com/search/label/mentalMap.

[34] http://urbantick.blogspot.com/search/label/aquarium.

[35] http://xkcd.com/.

[36] http://urbantick.blogspot.com/search/label/UrbanDiary.

[37] http://wiserpath.blogspot.com/.

[38] http://www.oddnumber.co.uk/.

[39] http://danielmclaren.net/.

[40] http://danielmclaren.net/2009/11/03/experimenting-with-graph-visualisations-on-a-timeline.

[41] http://danielmclaren.net/2009/11/03/experimenting-with-graph-visualisations-on-a-timeline.

[42] *LONDON DIARY VISUALISATION IN GEOTIME,* 18 February 2009 15:39, cycles, GPS tracks, London, data handling, visualisation, GeoTime, timeSpace, rhythm.

Fig. 6 Image by urbanTick /
Showing a meeting point in
GeoTime

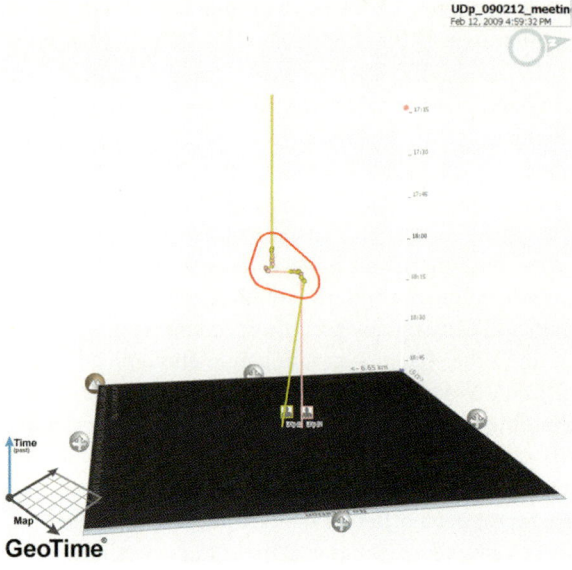

it took a few trial and error investigations to figure out what might be usable. The
solution for the moment is GPX to CSV to database and then to put into Google
Earth or GeoTime it has to go back into a CSV to Excel. So from Excel it can simply be linked to GeoTime. While installing GeoTime it will automatically install
the GeoTime Excel Plug-In that can then be used to link the open spreadsheet to
GeoTime (Fig. 6).

There is a setup to be made but this is rather straightforward, basically telling
GeoTime which column of the spreadsheet contains what kind of information. Several different settings can be saved for later use, which is great, as it is likely that
the same source will be used a number of times. Then the data is in GeoTime after
some processing. Funny enough, this time the meeting query tool works. After fail-
ing to use it in my first go with the Plymouth365 data, I was tempted to get this to
work with the new UD data set. And there you go it worked right away. I guess I
was just not patient enough with the larger PLY365 set, it probably just takes long,
longer than I was willing to wait…. Anyway, interesting who has met during this
first week of data collection. Surprisingly, some people who do not know one another have actually met within a few minutes time difference in the same location.
According to the data they just crossed path briefly, but still. Telling from those
screen shots, GeoTime's ability to output information apart from the screen is pretty
bad. As a designer and visual person I want much more control over this than this
program offers. It is essentially a screen shot in PNG format. It should at least offer
an option to output some vector format to allow further use and especially endless
sizing options.

24   *TIME-SPACE SEMINAR IN NEWCASTLE*[43] This will be a short summary of
yesterdays ESRC seminar with the title Time-Space and Life-Course. It is the fifth
and last seminar in a series over two years. It is chaired by Helen Jarvis[44] from the
University of Newcastle. Unfortunately it is the first seminar I have been to so I
won't be able to comment on the progress and the rest of the work that has been re-
sented and discussed over this time period. As it was the last seminar the topic of the
series as a whole and retrospective views have come up quite frequent. It has provided some insight on what has happened and how things could be related in a wider
context. For a full brief of the seminar series have a look at the synopsis page.[45]

This is a type up during the presentations and discussions so bare with me regarding formulation and construction of sentences. It might often be more sort of
fragments and notes than actual sentences but hopefully it brings the content across
anyway. We are starting the day with live connection to Australia. The researcher
Lyndall Strazdins[46] introduce her presentation "Time Scarcity—Another health in-
equity" After the introduction though the presentation is run on a DVD locally. This
already is a really interesting setting under the time aspect. What time is it right
now in Australia? I don't know just from the top of my head. It is roughly on the
other side of the world. After looking it up on the internet, they are actually nine
hours ahead down under, this means at the time of presentation eleven UK time it is
around eight o'clock at Australian National University in Canberra. In her research
she is looking at the length of time, in particular the perception of the length of time
in different contexts. This is investigated by symptoms such as stress, busyness, and
boredom? As her focus is on health the side of medical symptoms and impact on the
body are important and outweigh other aspects of manifestation of such experinces.
When moving on to the policy side of her talk she shows the example of the march
for the 8 h day (Australia- 8 h rest, 8 h, sleep, 8 h education) in Australia that took
place in Melbourne in 1866[47] (Fig. 7).

She is pointing out that nowadays in connection with the shifting time budget-
spending pattern, there are 8 h missing for childcare. She points out that there is a
great desire to look after children increasingly also from men. In a series of graphs
though, she also points out that the amount of work time in relation to time spent on
child care is still only reduced by women, while men keep on working long hours.
This implies that they want to add this part of the time budget on to the leisure or
educational time but not cutting back on work presumably. She then goes on to ask
whether this time inequality impacts on women's health? In an example from the
States, the quality of food was used to improve women's health. This health food
involved some extended preparation time, as it was prepared from raw ingredients.
The impact on the change of food preparation was an additional 2 h that somehow

---

[43] *TIME-SPACE SEMINAR IN NEWCASTLE,* 15 September 2009 08:01, tracking, rhythm,
spaceCreation, repetition, pattern, time, timeSpace, conference, cycles.

[44] http://www.ncl.ac.uk/gps/staff/profile/helen.jarvis.

[45] http://time-space-life-course.ncl.ac.uk/theme.html.

[46] http://www.linkedin.com/pub/lyndall-strazdins/14/26b/435.

[47] http://en.wikipedia.org/wiki/Eight-hour_day.

Fig. 7 Image taken from Wikipedia / Eight Hour Day Banner, Melbourne, 1856. (http://en.Wikipedia.org/wiki/File:8hoursday_banner_1856.jpg)

had the reverse effect, as the stress level rose. Regarding public health and efforts to improve it, she has found that respondents often quote not enough time as the main argument for not exercising, resting or using public transport. Lyndall concludes from that, to improve public health, policies are needed to integrate time aspects as a health resource. For the discussion and question session Skype is switched back on to allow real time responses. Time poverty as a term is quite interesting. It seems to be related to developed and undeveloped economies. A large study in Germany has looked at time poverty and developed a new multidimensional description of poverty. There was also the question of how far already existing underlying health conditions affect people's use of time, such as inability to manage time and end up being even more stressed. Lyndall argues that, beyond underlying conditions, she found that income is directly related to personal time management resulting in a health impact. A further question comes back to the policy aspect of activities in time. Can activities be stacked and multiplied, resulting in multitasking. If addressed in policy, does it really capture the problem if time is integrated in policy? There might be some other aspects related to this. Here, Lyndall replies that it might be related to the redefinition of activities into a combined time, such as a walk with your kids, or jogging while on the mobile phone. Research has shown that women actually already do multitask in their leisure time. Doing childcare, socializing, …. From my perspective, I am missing here the space dimension. How do the distance, location and travel time affect the time budget? Location of cheaper homes for poorer families and distance to work or health care access are the main points. Nancy Worth—Conceptualizing time space and space over the life course—PhD at Newcastle School of Geography, Faculty of Environment. She gave a very compact overview of the past four seminars in the first part of her presentation. This give a very good impression of what the series was and draws out the context of the work presented on the day. It was too compact and brief to actually follow and summarize on the spot, so I apologize for the lack of information here. But you can probably find some information on past seminars on the web by starting here[48]. Some inter-

---

[48] http://time-space-life-course.ncl.ac.uk/.

esting terms she dropped while talking about previously presented papers though I managed to write down: The concept of different times, illustrated by the difference between child and adult time-space. Adults are oriented to result and intersection of traces (meetings, goals), whereas children's "young" time-space are more self oriented and less production orientated. Time is produced by everyday practice. The term GeoNarrative, introduced by Kahn, understanding the daily routines of everyday life. You can see here the direct link to the UD project[49] and other topics related to urbanNarrative[50]. Nancy also mentioned a very interesting project of long-term life course research, capturing the life course in a documentary "the up series" reconnecting with people every seven years and documenting the progress. Nancy also asks the question, towards the end, whether theory on space and time can be more than just clock time or distance space. Throwing up terms such as embodied time, lived time,..From the audience some more reflections on the past seminar series are provided. For example religion as a fractal of everyday life time-space, how did the seminar series relate to this question? Eric Laurier[51]—Mobile Technologies and the Coordination of Daily Life—University of Edinburgh School of Geoscience (he's got this fancy slide swap breaking down the slides into the RGB colours) He starts with Hagerstrand's space-time diagram, focusing on bends and twists in the daily course, while criticizing the sort of logistics or particle feel of it. Moving on to examples of time-space research tools, he starts with the family calendar pointing out time restrictions similar to those as discussed by Carlstein and Hagerstrand. Also pointing at the moral order of the timetable. He also mentions that his own child started school this month throwing over the family calendar. Showing work using mobile phones and pointing out the summons morality of the phone as a device similar to a baby crying. Someone will have to get up and answer it. The interesting aspect here would be the new mobility and location aspect of phone and calls while on the move, either one party or all. I suppose the more recent opening question is not any longer how are you, but where are you? He comes back to this point at a later stage. Eric then shows parts of his own work, starting with Habitable Cars an ESRC project. He plays a brilliant clip staring a family going to work/school in the morning—the routines of five family members have to be coordinated during this time in the car and all are issued their tasks. The mother is leading the timetable while driving the car, briefing all members including the husband in the front seat. What a beautiful scene! An other project called Location Family Values: A Field of Trial of the Whereabouts Clock is logging family members by mobile phones transmitted into the kitchen and assigning all family members to activities. He provides insight by playing an audio file of an anxious mother talking about how this has helped her to visualise where the children are and that they have arrived at the destination. The device would also allow sending messages directly into the kitchen to exchanging information—but what for? The interesting aspect is probably the location of the device itself in the kitchen to mark the home location and the space to

---

[49] http://urbantick.blogspot.com/search/label/UrbanDiary.

[50] http://urbantick.blogspot.com/search/label/urbanNarrative.

[51] http://homepage.mac.com/eric.laurier/ordinary_life/index.html.

relate to. He also points out that tracking raises the question about observation. Just like questions around the UD project[52]. The device originally features only three locations for a status display. Additional locations can be added and very often also the preset titles of locations did change meaning. For individual families, the meaning of school changed over the weekend into a different activity such as playing football. There is a lot of flexibility while pointing in the direction of routine. Going back to the old days with family phones as a very defined location in the family home. Related to the installation with notepaper, blackboard and telephone directory. Pointing out that the place here is very well defined and it is more of a place to place call, whereas the mobile phone turns it more into a person to person phone call. (Is this true? Why should this be more personal?) He is then finally jumping to the iPhone and the Facebook application as something between the terms of timetable, diary, notes, messages and so forth. Modelling social network using these kind of applications makes Hagerstrandian geographers quite exciting to map information. His interest seems to be more in the area of how people use it and how responses and activity are generated. The questions and comments session comes back to restrictions and proposes to look at travel patterns in terms of dependencies of movement and restrictions probably. A second comment picks up the more nostalgic view through what might be the differences between the patterns of pre mobile phones activities to now mobile phones directed actions. Fifty years ago children could leave the house in the morning, returning six or eight hours later. Whereas now, who ever is leaving the house needs checking back. In relation to this the question, has the technology produced more anxiousness? This is probably directly a response to the whereabouts clock project. At this point I might run out of battery power soon... POWER!

Later, back up with some juice... The afternoon session starts with a panel discussion being introduced also to collect a pool of ideas to take the series into a next stage and also looking at a publication. So there can be something expected in terms of a product, probably next year. It is then again a review of previous papers with the panel member all reflecting on three previous papers in relation to their own work on the topic. Again this is going to be a brief summary of the panel session. Eric Laurier[53] throws up the thought that the research on everydaylife is very much about not to overlook the simple hidden information that we are so much used to see that is easily overlooked. Steve Cummins picks up on this and relates it to routine activities that had more impact in the older days, 70s. The meaning of market days and church going and so on. The setting nowadays is very different and the routines have changed and opened. He quotes Elisabeth (earlier paper) with the idea of sequencing and going on to analyse the individual and the collective in term of sequencing related to being selfish. Recent time data analysis seems to show that the time spent together by men and women seem to suggest that women catch up. Rhythms over the different scales might not be comparable. Steve also throws up the thought about a nested concept of time in terms of scale. Especially in connec-

[52] http://urbantick.blogspot.com/search/label/UrbanDiary.

[53] http://urbantick.blogspot.com/search/label/UrbanDiary.

tion to life course as a concept of time how far can we go in terms of time perception from childhood to late age?—What does that mean in terms of tracking and travel distance?

Miles Tight[54] is then talking about his research on walking and cycling and reasons why people choose to do so. He is doing walkalongs while they speak to participants on what they actually experience and how they take decision. (Could be an interesting part of the UD project). He also has done some GPS tracking looking at tracks relating them to sociospatial aspects of the environment participants travel through. He raises the question of the sampling, how can it cover representative group, a problem I am currently facing in my research work. He also has got a great example/story on routines and repetition and how he times his walking speed to meet the sequence created by the series of traffic light on the way from the train station to his office every morning. Rachel Pain[55] picks up on the issue of sample and represented groups. The panel agrees that previous papers presented, have mainly looked at middle class settings. It seems that, since academics are part of this group, they are more interested in it than other groups of society, since academics like to reflect upon themselves. She then also raises critique on the recent WOW techniques and visual methods, such as GIS and GPS, technology and so on. There is a WOW effect in the first place but afterwards remains the question, but what now? There seems to be a lack of theory, contextual work and methods to approach or take the questions further. During the discussion/question session some additional points are raised about interdisciplinarity, founding, down to the definition of terms used during the discussion such as space-time, time-space. Also the uncertainty of the result or application of this field of research, if there is something such as time research and the question is whether we are on the way to nothing with this discussion, even though or because everyone is currently talking about this from artists to scientists. During the afternoon tea breake the host of the event, the Culture Lab University of Newcastle[56], gives tours on their recent research projects in technology. We are moving on to get a motion capturing[57] demonstration. The culture lab here at Newcastle University has very expensive equipment to track and trace markers in space. It is similar to the technology used in large-scale Hollywood animation films for the imitation of body movement, facial expression and gestures. Downstairs in the interactive technology room, some newly developed touch screen tables are demonstrated and the ambient kitchen[58] project. In the lab they have installed a kitchen that is equipped with sensors to respond to chefs' actions (Fig. 8).

For example by using RFID technology the information projected onto the kitchen wall can suggest recipes corresponding to the ingredients placed on the work top. The project team aims at using the kitchen in an environment with elderly people and mental health patients to help them keeping up their routines and activities.

---

[54] http://www.its.leeds.ac.uk/staff/staffProfile.php?personId=758.

[55] http://www.dur.ac.uk/geography/staff/geogstaffhidden/?mode=staff&id=352.

[56] http://www.ncl.ac.uk/culturelab/.

[57] http://culturelab.ncl.ac.uk/mocap/.

[58] http://culturelab.ncl.ac.uk/ambientkitchen/.

Fig. 8 Image by urbanTick /
Motion capturing at Culture
Lab University of Newcastle

Fig. 9 Image by
urbanTick / Interactive
work tops at Culture Lab
University of Newcastle

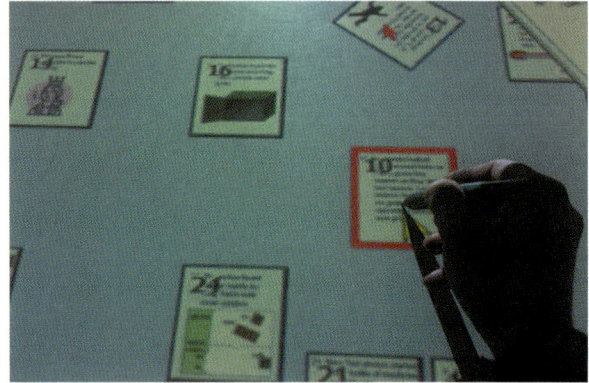

Some thoughts on the day from my experience. There has been a lot of retrospective talking across the series. It is creating a sort of framework and context for the work presented as I pointed out in the introduction. However it is demanding for first time attendees (Fig. 9).

On the other hand it probably also highlights the fact that an overarching concept of time related research is actually missing and the community of researchers in this field lacks this overarching understanding of each other's approach. In this sense, papers presented were all bits and pieces of the greater picture. To aim for a publication of the series to this reflection and contextualisation of the aspects make sense. There has been surprisingly a lot of indepth critique to understand technology as part of this investigation. I do agree that a lot if not most of the currently "exciting" project and works in the area of technology are born out of the technology itself aiming back at the technology without creating some sort of context. Nevertheless the technologies are so quickly entering into everyday life (at least for the middle class) that neglecting this area of research by the technology by social researcher, geographers and health experts will definitely put them in a bad position to continue. Even in this, the time aspect is a topic and related to technology time has definitely speed up. Picking up on the idea of slow and fast time I was surprised to hear so much about the old days. The old days and the current days as a concept of time organisation shines through in a number of contributions. This definitely raises the question if there is a real concept missing? Maybe even beyond this there is a lack of language and terms to talk about time and to exchange ideas and concepts. In this respect the seminar and especially the series, as far as I can judge from the reviews, has and can in the future contribute quite a bit to the discussion around time.

25 *STOPPING TIME—THE MOST PRECISE MEASUREMENTS*[59] Time measuring is nowadays very precise and this we take for granted. To some extend in some sense time has become natural. This is probably a safe assumption to say. Most people would regard time as a natural occurring "substance" and the watch around their wrist as a piece of technology "measuring" this phenomenon. In reality it might be the other way round. The little and in some cases beautifully crafted piece of engineering is actually inventing the time as it ticks. Certainly time is not a natural phenomenon even though we have grown to think of it as fundamental it is little more than a social convention or a cultural agreement that has developed over the last century and managed to extend its importance. The first wave came with the industrial revolution, the synchronisation of working hours. Time entered individual households and then accompanied each individual. Even more so, time plays "behind the scenes" a crucial role. Not much would work in today's highly timed society arrangements. From computer networks to complex shipping and transport schedules, everything ticks. GPS as a technology for example is based on time sync. Each satellite has three atom clocks to keep track of the time and provide accurate time, for the receiver to synchronise. Behind the visual field of images, time is probably the second most important field of technology in our era. There are two big groups of time applications, one side is the technology and the other is the consumer side of time keeping. An application that somehow sits in between, is the discipline of time keeping for major sports events such as the Olympics. The determination of the accurate measurement of the new 100 m sprint world record has both aspects. It is completely technical and a question of applied engineering, but on the other hand it is highly emotional and the reason why millions of people are drawn into the world of sport. The company Swiss Timing[60] is delivering this crucial bit of the games since the 1932, Olympic games in Los Angeles[61]. It is all very accurate, on time and in sync. In this job one cannot make mistakes: there is only one chance to take the time of a potentially new world record and the time ticks. So backup systems are in use. If mesuring time fails, what do you do? What can you rely up on that compares? The other problem is the accurate stopping of the time in relation to the finish. Who crossed the line first? When exactly was the line crossed? Surprisingly, but probably obvious, the backup is a visual method. It is all recorded on camera, the finishing as well as the backup start signal. The power of the "true image" is striking.

Decisions in the dimension of a thousandth of a second not only decide over who the winner is, but decides a number of attached and most likely very valuable exten-

---

[59] *STOPPING TIME—THE MOST PRECISE MEASUREMENTS*, 27 October 2009 10:12, timeSpace, time, beat, advertisement.

[60] http://www.swisstiming.com/.

[61] http://en.Wikipedia.org/wiki/1932_Summer_Olympics.

Fig. 10 Image by urbanTick / Plymouth 365, one year worth of GPS tracks

sions. From sponsors to advertisement and supporters, sport is about money. The truth and evidence are important and it seems that once more the visual is dominant. It seems that most of these types of measuring the time are all very much exterior and so far athlete centred technologies are not yet accepted by the IOC. Positioning systems and RFID technology are in trials, probably the future of time measuring.

26   *TIME MAP—Different APPROACHES*[62] The problem of how to visualise time has been and is still challenging. There is a number of approaches out there, but the one general applicable approach has not been found yet. So far a number of different approaches have been used and tested in this research work. The first one was plain tracking paths. The time is actually inherent in these images as the path is a sequence of points and these points where recorded in time one after the other. Also different lines are distinct in time as one tracked individual can only produce one path at the time. Theoretically this explanation works very well, but in practice when it comes to analysing these drawings all one can see is dense areas, hotspots and trends. The aspect of time gets completely lost, specifically when one tries to look at one path relative to one another. They all seem to have the same time. The second approach was playing the track record as a movie. With this technique it became possible to replay the recorded sequence and, with the help of the movie, simulate the passage of time. The recorded sequence of points is replayed according to the time stamps saved with each point (Fig. 10).

---

[62] *TIME MAP—Different APPROACHES,* 20 January 2009 08:26, timeSpace, time, time-space Diagram, GPS tracks, tracking.

For analysing purposes the tracks are replayed simultaneously at the same time. In this way the tracks can be followed relative to all the others. With this technique it is possible to distinguish between moving and static records. In the first example the path only shows the location and time for activity on the move, e.g. going from A to B, but A and B are not included as a time period. This lies in the nature of the maps which is solely spatial, whereas in the movie the duration of A or B is displayed with a static dot that stays at this specific location of A or B for the relative time. The difficulty with the replay movies is the speed of replay. If it is too slow it is boring. Also there is a limit to how much of a time period one can manage to oversee. If it gets too long it is not possible to directly link the activities at the beginning of the sequence and the end of the sequence. Nevertheless this approach has been very popular with a wider community. The clips replaying the Plymouth365 track records have been watched over 5500 times in past two month. The third approach in visualizing time was the introduction of the third dimension. This dimension was not used to display the height, but time. There is originally already height information in the GPS record, but this has been replaced by the time information. This created 3D matrix with Lat and Long as X and Y, but then time as Z (height). This visualisation has been developed by Torsten Hagerstrand[63] and the Lund School in the 1970s. It was called the Space-Time Aquarium. This is probably at the same time the first time researchers in geography developed ideas for this topic of movement analysis. This technique produces very nice 3D shapes and are visually very pretty. For analysis purposes they tend to become very quickly much too complicated. For a limited number of tracks it can be useful and meaning full, but for a large number, such as the Plymouth365 full record, it is in the current way of the 3D model not very useful. Although the main features do show up. The "home" location as the major spine, "work" locations as a secondary spine and the "wall" for busy connection lines do pop out. Also there are nice smaller elements such as the "steps" for activities with stop and motion or the "spiral" for activities that took place over a longer period of time in more or less the same location, e.g. playground, lunch breake. A major problem is the connection between the model and the surface that provides the sense of location.

The more time passes the more this connection gets lost and later in the afternoon or in the evenings it often is completely lost. Another problem at the moment is the presentation of these models. They just don't look good on images as one naturally wants to rotate them. The fourth and latest approach is the visualisation of time on a map using colours to give time information. Each path segment here is coloured according to time. It starts in the morning with bright red changes to yellow and green over noon, the afternoon is blue and the evening changes again to purple. This actually give a pretty good sense of time while reading the map and also enables the reading of the tracks relative to one another. The main problem is probably that it is static. Once generated it is a drawing and bears not much of a time representation as a dynamic element. Very much like the first approach it captures and frames a point in time.

---

[63] http://en.Wikipedia.org/wiki/Torsten_H%C3%A4gerstrand.

27   *TRACK LOGS—VISUALISATION CLIPS*[64] I have been working on the improvement of the visualisation.

See clip on Vimeo[65] / Showing track location over the period of one year.

The main concern was the representation of the data in terms of time. So far the data was displayed only when there was a track point. Each track point would fade out after a representation time of approximately 30 min. What gets lost in this representation is the times I stay in one place for a longer period, say being at work for a half a day or a day. This new clip takes this into account and the represents exactly those times I haven't moved for a while. See clip on Vimeo[66]/Showing track location over the period of one year.

Interesting how those clusters build up and dissolve. Compared to the point version, the movie below shows the movement with longer duration times. It displays a time frame of 30 min. See clip on Vimeo[67]/To give a stronger sense of time the effect of day and night have been introduced.

After this time the tracks and points fade out. Similarly to the version above, records that represent a longer attendance in one place stay even though the set time frame has past. To set the duration of 24 h in a more realistic context, the clip below integrates the amount of daylight. So at night it's dark and during the day the sun is shining! Even though it is Plymouth …! Anyway the darker periods of this day are quite long. This is due to the fact that the model uses January the first to calculate daylight conditions. So it's winter then.

28   *THE CYCLES OF THE MOON—ALUNA*[68] Peoples fascination with the moon had for a long time now had a bit of a low. It is just there on the sky changing somehow a bit everyday and might get recognized in good weather conditions at full moon. Historically the lunar calendar had a big influence, today the only real lunar calendar is the Islamic calendar or Hijri calendar (wiki[69]). Most calendar in the past where in fact lunisolar. "All these calendars have a variable number of months in a year. The reason for this is that a year is not evenly divisible by an exact number of lunation, so without the addition of intercalary months the seasons would drift each year. This results in a thirteen-month year every two or three years." (wiki[70]) The lunar cycles are not in sync with our currently used time units. The lunar day is not 24 h, but 24 h and 50 min. The most visual impact of this shift is the tide cycle and the fact that the tide is not everyday at the same time, but is roughly 25 min later every day. Aluna now, is a large-scale permanent installation to visualise and communicate the lunar cycles. It is proposed to be built in London in the East India

---

[64] *TRACK LOGS—VISUALISATION CLIPS,* 4 December 2008 22:43, plymouth365, movement, duration, time, timeSpace.

[65] http://vimeo.com/2431381.

[66] http://vimeo.com/2436289.

[67] http://vimeo.com/2436280.

[68] *THE CYCLES OF THE MOON—ALUNA,* 9 July 2009 10:54, timeSpace, rhythm, cycle, moon, tide.

[69] http://en.Wikipedia.org/wiki/Lunar_calendar.

[70] http://en.Wikipedia.org/wiki/Lunar_calendar.

Fig. 11 Image by Laura Williams taken from aluna. org / Visualisation of the proposal. (http://www.alunatime. org/London/index.htm)

Fig. 12 Images by Martin Callanan / Screenshot, showing search terms "Summer" and "Winter". (http://text-trends.greyisgood.eu/)

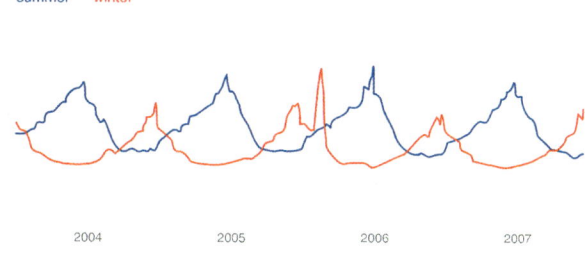

Dock Basin by 2012. "Aluna is a unique proposal for the world's first tidal powered Moon Clock. It will change the way we consider time and understand our planet. Larger than Stonehenge, Aluna's 40 m wide, five storey high structure is made up of three concentric translucent recycled glass rings. By looking at how each ring is illuminated, you can follow the Moon's movements, its current phase and the ebb and flow of the tides. This animation of light is called Alunatime." (alunatime.org[71]). Three rings of glass will display the wax and the wane of the moon in 29.5 calendar days (largest ring), the rise and sink of the moon in 24 h and 50 min (middle ring) and the ebb and flow of the tide in 6 h 25 min (smallest ring) (Fig. 11).

A brilliant animation of the sculpture is on the website[72]. It is a 3D rendering, but in sync with the three rings are also displayed the tide of the river Thames and the moon on the sky, absolutely amazing.

For lunar geeks, there is also a Google Gadget[73] for your iGoogle displaying the lunar calendar.

THE SEARCH FOR TIME—SEARCH TERMS OVER THE PAST FEW YEARS[74]
Another project by artist Martin J Callanan is looking at internet search terms and visualises the amount of hits per term over the period of three years (Fig. 12).

---

[71] http://www.alunatime.org/html/what.htm

[72] http://www.alunatime.org/video_page/video_page.html.

[73] http://www.google.com/ig/adde?moduleurl=hosting.gmodules.com/ig/gadgets/file/105027660719045078773/lunarcalendar.xml.

[74] *THE SEARCH FOR TIME—SEARCH TERMS OVER THE PAST FEW YEARS,* 10 April 2009 16:47, art, time, timeSpace, cycles, search term.

The project is called text trends[75], its speciality is the lineup of terms. How do terms like sex and love compare in a graph? Check it out for your self, but surprising enough the up and down is at times surprising. Especially the terms related to time show an unexpected rhythm, e.g. see summer and winter.

30   *YEARLY CREATION OF SPACE—THE SERPENTINE PAVILION*[76] Every year during the late summer months, the Serpentine Gallery[77] in London erects a pavilion outside in the park. It is usually a famous architect or an architecture team. There is already a long list of buildings, of whom some have become very famous. This year it is SANAA[78], Kazuyo Sejima and Ryue Nishizawa[79] from Japan. The pair has developed a very distinct stile and are building icons of buildings all over the world. One of the most recent completed works is the new Museum of Contemporary Art in New York, opened in 2007. This year's Serpentine Summer Pavilion is a free flowing open shape and mainly consists of a floor plate and a roof plate.

The project of having a Summer Pavilion[80] started in 2000. Together with some very thin columns it defines the space. It seems that this kind of spatial experience is rather difficult for most of the visitors and they don't really know what to do with, in or around it. Most people end up standing around the "object" and looking at it. 2009—SANAA, 2008—Frank Gehry, 2007—Olafur Eliasson and Kjetil Thorsen, 2007—Zaha Hadid (temporary), 2006—Rem Koolhaas and Cecil Balmond, 2005— Alvaro Siza and Eduardo Souto de Moura, 2004—MVRDV (not realized), 2003— Oscar Niemeyer,2002—Toyo Ito, 2001—Daniel Libeskind, 2000—Zaha Hadid

31   *INAUGURAL CEREMONY 2009—OBAMA ONE PEOPLE*[81] "For President Obama's 100th day in office, the MIT SENSEable City Lab has created visualisations of mobile phone call activity that characterize the inaugural crowd and answer the questions: Who was in Washington, D.C. for President Obama's Inauguration Day?" The team around Carlo Ratti has not only recently visualised and analysed mobile phone data. They have been experimenting with this data source for a while and produced number of interesting projects. There are the great visualisations for Rome that show mobile phone activities during the Madonna concert, done mainly by Jon Reades. Reades is again involved with this project set up around Obama's inauguration day back in January. This time the mobile phone call data from around the ceremony's location is analysed. It is analysed regarding amount of activity and destination of the call, either worldwide or per American state. The time period they are looking at is the full week in which the inauguration took place. The Vimeo clip can be found HERE[82]. Isn't it amazing what can be done with a mobile phone call

---

[75] http://texttrends.greyisgood.eu/.

[76] *YEARLY CREATION OF SPACE—THE SERPENTINE PAVILION,* 28 July 2009 09:30, timeLapse, timeSpace, cycle, architecture.

[77] http://www.serpentinegallery.org/.

[78] http://www.dezeen.com/2009/07/13/serpentine-galley-pavilion-by-sanaa-3/.

[79] http://www.sanaa.co.jp/.

[80] http://www.serpentinegallery.org/architecture./

[81] *INAUGURAL CEREMONY 2009—OBAMA ONE PEOPLE,* 5 June 2009 08:25, visualisation, timeSpace, mobile phone, mapping, MIT.

[82] http://www.youtube.com/v/H0-EiXerCkc&hl=en&fs=1.

Fig. 13 Image taken from Sensable City Lab / Mapping the call volume during Obama's inauguration speech in 2009. Showing the number of calls vertically

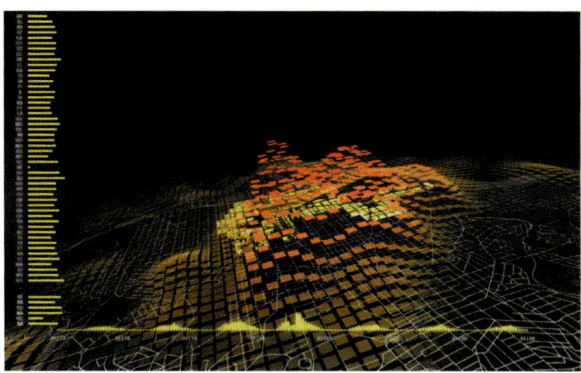

data set? Yes and No. Yes, because there is a great deal of information hidden in the data and results of who is watching and presumably reporting this back home is interesting compared to the results of the election. Questions like did states who voted for Obama attend the ceremony or did mainly states that voted for McCain follow the ceremony live, are of interest. But it has to be said that the visualisations from the clip are very difficult to understand. There is probably too much being communicated at the same time. The two lines of information along the left hand side and the bottom together with the animation in the centre are confusing. Earlier visualise coming out of the lab where using a different graphic and I found where simpler to understand, such as the New York Talk exchange[83] or the Pulse of the Planet[84]. The No for the second part of the answer probably goes for "if we can do it, we might not want to do it" or not everything we can do, we actually want to do. The MIT shows here that it is possible to map and animate this kind of information. Potentially even in real time, although they are taking 100 days to do it (this is most likely a problem with the mobile phone companies, but nevertheless it might be possible to generate instant visuals of this kind of data). The problem lies with the interpretation of it. This is not as instant as the visual (Fig. 13).

It takes time to understand the content and to define a reasonable part to compare it to as shown in this example (the pro Obama votes). So it is not quite what they say it is, but it is still a great visualisation of space-time data—the Obama aquarium[85] if you want.

NATURAL CYCLE—THE TIDE TIMELAPSE[86] In terms of cycles the tide is one of the most direct and powerful examples. While being away for a few days I enjoyed roughly fourteen tide cycles. The constancy and continuity is very impressive together with the force. Assuming all of us have once tried to defend a sandcastle from the incoming waves or keeping the little channel connected to the water as the

---

[83] http://www.youtube.com/watch?v=YXVM6ivpmyE.

[84] http://urbantick.blogspot.com/2009/02/pulse-of-planet.html.

[85] http://urbantick.blogspot.com/search/label/aquarium.

[86] *NATURAL CYCLE—THE TIDE TIMELAPSE,* 2 July 2009 10:23, tide, stop motion, nature, timeLapse, cycle, timeSpace, rhythm.

Fig. 14 Clip by urbanTick
on Vimeo / A line in the sand
marks the tide going out.
(http://vimeo.com/5430860)

tide goes out. The task is doomed, but only for the moment. There will be a next timeframe where it is possible again, this is the fascinating aspect of the rhythm. The problem with this is that our ability to deal with these time spans is limited (Fig. 14).

Music "fire whistle" by Jorya at mp3unsigned[87]. We very much live in the here and now and the speed and repetition of the tide is somehow just about outside our time perception. On one hand it move too slow in order to be properly perceived on a short term basis and it suddenly reaches your towel. On the other hand the cycle of two high tides is too long to be directly related in our experience. Therefore the timeLapse is a good tool to get to grips with the rhythm, enjoy.

33   *TIME—THE CONCEPT OF THE WEEK*[88] There are a number of concepts to structure our lives in time. The primary structure is the day and night rhythm with the period of darkness followed by a period of light. This is only a rough guide, as the duration of these periods changes over the course of one year according to seasons. Within this structure the average day of 24 h is constructed. This fixed time span is mainly set for calculation purposes and interferes with natural rhythms quite often, e.g. daylight, tide, … from this day unit the week is extrapolated as a seven day cycle. The structure of the week is built on work/activity days and days of rest. There has been a strong religious influence on this concept (Fig. 15).

The day of rest was loaded with religious commitments, but has since, specially in western culture, faded in importance. The basic weekly structure although remained. Basically the week is divided in two units, the five days of work from Monday to Friday and the weekend on Saturday and Sunday (Fig. 16).

In the Christian culture the Sunday, the Lord's day, is the main day of worship without having to do commercial work. It is the day of rest and socializing with the community. Interestingly, other religions have a different structure (Fig. 17).

In the Jewish week the day to rest is not the Sunday, it is the Saturday. On Saturdays, the Sabbath, Jews are asked not to do any work, but only save this day for

---

[87] http://www.mp3unsigned.com/showmp3.asp?mp3id=5583.
[88] *TIME—THE CONCEPT OF THE WEEK,* 26 March 2009 15:41, rhythm, week, London, time, religion, timeSpace, cycles.

Fig. 15 Image by Chris Tate, taken from timeout.com / There are over 149,000 Jews in London, over half the Jewish population of Britain. (http://www.timeout.com/london/big-smoke/features/3974/London-s_religions_map.html)

Fig. 16 Image by Chris Tate, taken from timeout.com / There are over 603,000 Muslims in London, two-fifths of the UK Muslim population. (http://www.timeout.com/london/big-smoke/features/3974/London-s_religions_map.html)

Fig. 17 Image by Chris Tate, taken from timeout.com / Over 58% of Londoners say they are Christians (far fewer are practicing). (http://www.timeout.com/london/big-smoke/features/3974/London-s_religions_map.html)

Fig. 18 Image by Chris Tate, taken from timeout.com / Over 29,000 Hindus live in London, more than half the Hindu population of Britain. (http://www.timeout.com/london/big-smoke/features/3974/London-s_religions_map.html)

family and community. The Muslim week has the Friday, the day of assembly, as the main day of rest from work (Fig. 18). (source[89] Wikipedia/sabbath)

Looking at this simple weekly structure from the UrbanDiary perspective, there must be a an impact on movement dependent on religions. Looking at the three religions Islam, Christianity and Judaism in the London area the different patterns between Friday, Saturday and Sunday could be very interesting to observe closer.

34   *REAL TIME VISUALISATION—APP STORE HYPERWALL*[90] Sales in the iPhone App store have amazed a lot of people. Together with the popularity of the iPhone, or the other way round, the iTunes app store's sales have rocketed sky high. Around 3000 apps per minute are sold online. A great success for Apple, and even though we are apple fans here, why should this feature on the blog? Well, interesting is the visualisation that has been produced to impress visitors at this years WWDC 2009.

A massive Hyperwall with 16 screens shows the live sales directly from the app store (some 5 min delay). This visualisation is fascinating because it shows the rather virtual activity of the iTunes store. People are downloading applications for their iPhones/iPod touch's in thousands per minute. The wall visualised live which of the 20,000 most popular app is sold with a blink of this app's icon. The screen is ordered according to colour that makes it look nice, but which is otherwise probably not helpful. It shows the variety of apps and starting to categorize them would probably only end in a very confusing table with sub tables. As it is live one could probably stand there and buy an app and watch the icon go blink. I can imagine that this could become addictive. The time in visualisation has always been important, but has recently become much more so. It still is a very difficult element to usefully integrate, but in this case it serves the purpose brilliantly.

It needs a lot of processing power, as you have read above in Apple's statement. 20 Mac Pro towers are running for this visual, very impressive. Some more, almost realtime projects I came across:

---

[89] http://en.Wikipedia.org/wiki/Sabbath.

[90] *REAL TIME VISUALISATION—APP STORE HYPERWALL,* 16 July 2009 09:30, visualisation, timeSpace, realtime.

Fig. 19 Image taken from
Sensable City Lab / Amount
of phone calls and texts during a concert. (http://sense-
able.mit.edu/realtimerome/
sketches/index.html)

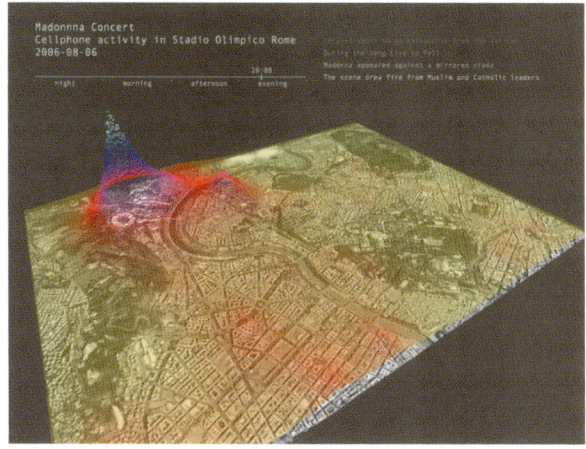

Facebook activity around the globe by Facebook[91] "This video showcases a
Hackathon project that visualises all the data Facebook receives." See clip on Face-
book[92]. Or real time data visualisation of data traffic in the network of Deutsche
Telecom in Germany. Clip can be seen here[93] (Fig. 19).

Experiments have also been undertaken by the MIT sensableCity lab[94]. Their
best known example is probably the Rome Real Time work for the Biennale. They
were using six different types of real time visuals to draw a comprehensive picture
of the city (Fig. 20).

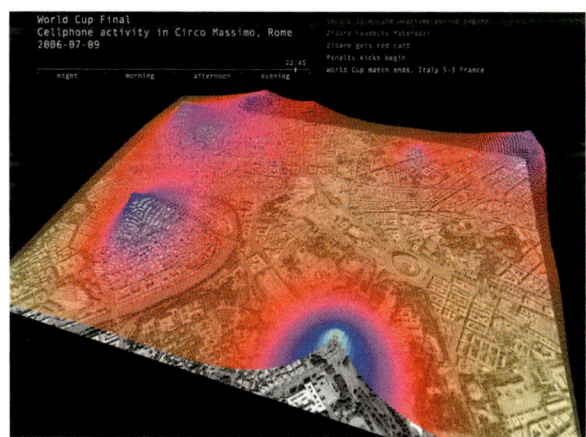

Fig. 20 Clip by MIT
Sensable City Lab on Vimeo.
(http://vimeo.com/1875286)

---

[91] http://www.Facebook.com/video/video.php?v=37403547074&ref=nf#/video/video.
php?v=37403547074.

[92] http://www.Facebook.com/v/37403547074.

[93] http://projects.zumkuckuck.com/realtime/.

[94] http://senseable.mit.edu/.

Fig. 21 Clip by MIT
Sensable City Lab on Vimeo.
(http://vimeo.com/1875387)

The data came live from the Italian Telephone company where sent to the US to the MIT lab to be processed and be made available as a download for the mobile stations in Rome. Not strictly real time but with some 10 min delay still fairly quick. A similar project was run on Obama's inauguration day in Washington earlier this year. See earlier post on this blog, but in this case it was not processed immediately (Fig. 21).

The visualisation of the cell phone activity during the Madonna concert in August 2006 in Rome. And a second visualisation of pedestrian real time activity based on cell phone data.

35   *THE LINK T*[95] A more detailed image of the coloured time map (Fig. 22).

36   *HOW DIFFERENT GROUPS SPEND THEIR DAY—TIME USE SURVEY*[96] The New York Times[97] has published a graphic on how Americans spend their time during the day. The data was collected in a large survey by the American Bureau of Labour Statistics[98]. Participants were asked to recall every minute, as the Times puts it, of their day. The interactive graphic allows detailed access to time and activity and some control over the group. Different groups obviously spend their day differently. There are differences between different races and ages, but the major difference is between the working population and the none-working population, i.e. unemployed. This is the main interest for the US in this statistic because of the high number of unemployed people. It is at 1 in 10, a level not seen in 27 years.

The graph is not as sharp as maybe expected. There seems to be quite a large time frame for change of activity. Nevertheless the structure is quite clear, with a large number having a very similar daily rhythm. The American Bureau of Labour Statistics[99] has a really detailed archive of time-use data. It is all accessible through

---

[95] *THE LINK T,* 21 January 2009 11:38, timeSpace, Solothurn, timeColour, GPS tracks, timemap.

[96] *HOW DIFFERENT GROUPS SPEND THEIR DAY—TIME USE SURVEY,* 3 August 2009 15:33, time, timeSpace, cycle.

[97] http://www.nytimes.com//interactive/2009/07/31/business/20080801-metrics-graphic.html?hp.

[98] http://www.bls.gov/tus/#data.

[99] http://www.bls.gov/tus/#data.

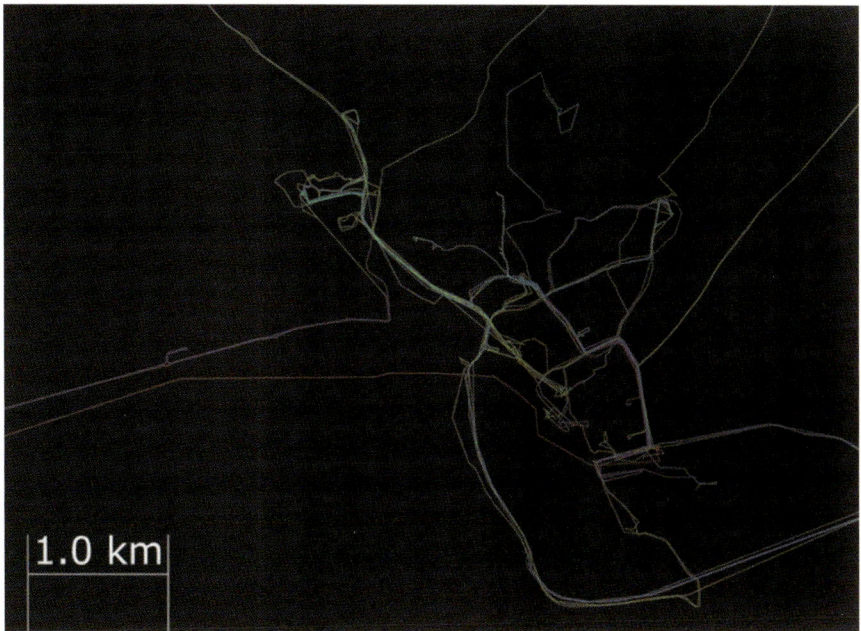

1.0 km

Fig. 22 Image by urbanTick / GPS track map coloured according to time

their webpage. The data is ready to download in different formats. They cover the time periods from 2003 on a yearly cycle. Beside the raw data also some processed data is available, including graphs. You can compare the UrbanDiary graphs[100] from earlier this year here. It does show similar patterns, but is based on GPS records and therefore accounts only for movements.

BIRTH AND DEATH OF THE SUN—THE DAILY CYCLE IN ANCIENT EGYPT[101] The role of cycles and routines in culture have been explored in various ways earlier on this blog. From early settlements[102] to the concept of time[103] in terms of units such as days, weeks and month. One of the cultures that had throughout a very strong concept of repetition in the more literal sense is ancient Egypt, the culture of the Pharaohs. There is so much research on this culture out there and for Europe and especially Britain this has been a deep fascination for centuries. The British Museum is stuffed to the roof with artifacts and knowledge collected in Egypt. What I want to look at is the "simple" concept of the birth and death of the sun during the course of one day. Two elements in Egypt have had a fundamental impact on how the Egyptian culture has formed. This is on one hand the Nile as the life spending river that runs through the deathly desert from south to north and the sun that spends

---

[100] http://urbantick.blogspot.com/2009/03/diary-in-graphs.html.

[101] *BIRTH AND DEATH OF THE SUN—THE DAILY CYCLE IN ANCIENT EGYPT,* 22 July 2009 10:21, animals, history, repetition, time, cycle, timeSpace, religion, culture

[102] http://urbantick.blogspot.com/2009/04/on-cycles-beginning-of-urban.html.

[103] http://urbantick.blogspot.com/2009/03/time-concept-of-week.html.

Fig. 23 Clip by Perseids
on Vimeo. (http://vimeo.
com/1478408)

the warmth and makes the plants grow that travels from east to west. These two
elements might also had a fundamental influence in how orientation and navigation
was developed. (Yi-Fu Tuan (1974), Topophilia. Columbia University Press, New
York) It is believed, that the Egyptian culture hated the darkness that arose together
with the cold as soon as the sun has touched the horizon in the west. The dark and
the cold were associated with death, just like the daily death of the sun. As an opposition to this there was the daily birth of the sun as it rose over the horizon in the
east. For this miracle the Scarab beetle was responsible.

The beetle was an important character that took care of the death and was associated with the Egyptian god, Khepri. He did take care of the sun and made sure
that after she died in the evening she was reborn in the morning in the east. To do so
he rolled the sun just like a ball backwards along the sky, just like a Scarab beetle
would roll a ball of dung. So the beetle rolled the sun during the night from west
to east. The Egyptian name for this important insect was "Kheper". The scarab
beetle was also a symbol of rebirth after death. To believe in being reborn led to the
mummification of the dead body, to preserve it for its next life. When the Egyptians
mummified a body they would remove the heart and put a stone carved like the
beetle in its place (Fig. 23).

Just as the sun would be reborn every day, also humans would be sent back from
the death to be reborn. The idea of cycles and repetition as observed in nature was
deeply embedded in the culture of ancient Egypt. Some sort of visualisation with a
time lapse of the night sky.

Part III
bodySpace

Body, Space and Maps

Sandra Abegglen

Introduction

The term space has a long history and is subject to discussions in various fields, for example in physics where Isaac Newton via his spokesman Samuel Clarke and Gottfried Leibniz had a great debate about the notions of space and time (Absolutism versus Realism). The aim of this article is to critically reflect on the term space in a sociological context and to relate it to the body as means through which we experience, but also create, space. As such, the article will argue that we are not only situated in space, but also form space with and through our body. Obviously, there are other ways in which space can be thought about (for example, historical, mathematical or physical) that the article does not want to argue against. Rather, the article proposes an alternative viewing of space, namely as a physical event but also as a social phenomenon. The attempt is to relate space not only to abstract (mathematical) formulas, but also to man. It is hoped that this perspective allows a new approach to space, especially in social research settings.

Body, Space and Place

Space is an abstract concept and its definition often merges with place. Tuan (1977) sees space as something which allows movement. We go from A to B, and back. We move. If space is movement then place is, according to Tuan (1977), pause. We stop short. We look, hear, smell, taste and touch. We transform an anonymous space in place, a location we know better and endow with value. We feel at home. However, we can also become passionately attached to places of enormous size, such as a city, a region or nation-state, of which we have limited direct experience (Tuan 1977). We define ourselves, for example, as Londoners, Southwesterners and Eng-

S. Abegglen (✉)
Goldsmiths, University of London, London, UK
e-mail: s.abegglen@gold.ac.uk

F. Neuhaus (ed.), *Studies in Temporal Urbanism,*
DOI 10.1007/978-94-007-0937-9_5, © Springer Science+Business Media B.V. 2011

lish. However, we also know the role of the outsider, the stranger and the tourist: the person who is not familiar with the environment and feels disorientated and lost.

We need time, therefore, to experience and understand the world[1]. According to Tuan (1977) 'the child has no world'. This means that the baby feels, but his or her sensations are not localized in space. He or she is simply there. However, during the first weeks the senses develop and the child gets a feeling of different positions and daytimes. Despite this, the infant's space lacks structure and permanence (Tuan 1977). Things appear and disappear, and the dummy is not recognized if is presented the wrong way round. However, when the child starts crawling his or her world expands significantly. Space opens up. He or she is now able to explore the world on his or her own. According to Tuan (1977, p. 25), 'spatial opposites are clearly distinguished by a child two to two and a half years old'. This means that a child of this age knows spatial directions such as up and down, here and there, and inside and outside. Despite this, the development of abstract geometrical concepts follows much later. Children may recognise certain shapes but are not able to draw or describe them. As Tuan (1977, p. 26) states, 'a child's spatial frame of reference is restricted'. This means that human ability to recognise and understand spatial relations has to develop. However, this development is not only dependent on biological growth but is also subject to cultural influences.

Inuit have, for example, a very different understanding of space from Chinese people and they again have another understanding of space than the Americans. 'Nonetheless certain cross-cultural similarities exist, and they rest ultimately on the fact that man is the measure of all things' (Tuan 1977, p. 34). Tuan (1977) refers thereby to the posture and structure of the human body, and the relations between human beings. This means, for example, that we not only define a front and back region of our body, but also speak about front and back gardens. We move up and down the job ladder and we feel in a high or low mood. But space is also related to power and wealth. Who possesses what, where and how much? Apart from that, tools and machines influence the experience of space. Cars, for example, help us to reach other cities; aeroplanes let us see far away countries; and spaceships allow us to explore the cosmos. But we also look through microscopes and telescopes to see things close up and far away. As Tuan (1977, p. 53) states, 'when the Paleolithic hunter drops his hand ax and picks up a bow and arrow, he takes a step forward in overcoming space and yet space expands before him: things once beyond his physical reach and mental horizon now form a part of his world'. This means that space can expand beyond what we can perceive with our senses.

As a consequence, we do not only experience space with and through our body, but we also create space in our mind. We dream, for example, of faraway places and imagine a better world—utopias. Pfrunder (2002) describes in her book Neotopia: Atlas zur gerechten Verteilung der Welt (Neotopia: Atlas of Equitable Distribution of the World) such a place. In her world, all people have the same rights and are therefore entitled to the same proportion of everything. This means that each person

---

[1] For a detailed description of a child's cognitive development see Piaget (1952), especially the first of the four stages of cognitive development (Sensorimotor Stage).

gets the same plot of land measuring 291.5 m by 291.5 m, containing an island, with an arctic and an antarctic region, with desert, farmland and urbanized land. People in this world smoke on average two cigarettes a day, three on weekends. They get a new pair of jeans every seventy years and send an email every day, but only five letters a year. As Pfrunder (2002, p. 24) states:

'Every human being has a personal piece of property which is absolutely identical to all other pieces of property. And all the people can be absolutely certain that there is nothing left anywhere that they do not already own. Because everything that was distributable has been equitably distributed'.

Obviously, this world challenges our understanding of justice. But it also challenges our perception of space. Does a world where everything is distributed equitably give us more room to live and act?

We could therefore say that space is not static. It is constantly created and recreated (physically, socially and mentally). According to Löw (2001), space is a social phenomenon and an ongoing process—in contrast to the notion of space as a container. This means that space is never given but always created and that social goods and people are not in space, they make it. As Löw (2001, p. 224) states, 'Raum ist eine relationale (An)Ordnung sozialer Güter und Menschen (Lebwewesen) an Orten' (Space is a relational ordering of social goods and people (living beings) in place). Individuals act therefore as social agents that constitute space. At the same time, however, their action depends on economic, legal, social, cultural and also spatial structures. This means that space can both enable and constrain action. Löw (2001) speaks about the 'duality of space', following the concept of the 'duality of structure' proposed by Giddens (1984).

Representations of Space

Space and place are, however, not only experienced, but also represented, for example on maps. As MacEachren (1995, p. 1) states, 'cartography is about representation'; things that stand in for and take the place of something else. However, 'the concept of 'representation' is one of the most ambiguous in the cognitive sciences, and as a consequence it is ambiguous in the theory of vision as well' (Albertazzi 2006, p. 14). According to Albertazzi (2006) there are two reasons for this ambiguity. First, the term refers to the taken-for-granted external independently existing object to which our acts are directed and second, to the more or less accurate image of the object which exists internally in our mind. This means that most cognitive (and also visual) research makes two theoretical assumptions: first, that a physical world exists and second, that its existence can be observed (Realism).

The idea that the external world can be accessed through an independent observer was brought to the attention of urban planners in the 1960s and 1970s. The concept of cognitive map (see, for example, Kitchin 1994; Kitchin and Freundschuh 2000; Kitchin and Blades 2002) refers to a person's internal image of the environment. This image depends not only on the information perceived through the five senses (seeing, hearing, smelling, tasting and touching), but also on the way this information is stored and evaluated. As a consequence, 'no two persons see the same reality' (Tuan 1990, p. 5). The images in our head are subjective. Nevertheless, there are some similarities between our inner images. 'People everywhere tend to structure space—geographical and cosmological—with themselves at the centre and with concentric zones (more or less well defined) of decreasing value beyond' (Tuan 1990, p. 27). In addition, most people have an understanding of spatial categories based on the human body such as 'front and back', 'open and closed' and 'vertical and horizontal' (Tuan 1990). In addition, certain colours (particularly red, black and white) acquire symbolic meaning that oversteps cultural boundaries (Tuan 1990). This means that, although each person's worldview is unique, all humans share certain perspectives and attitudes.

Architects and planners working with the concept of cognitive (or mental) maps use these characteristics to understand how people navigate through cities. A famous example in this context is The Image of the City published by Kevin A. Lynch (1960), an American urban planner. Lynch (1960) explored (over a period of five years) how people perceive and organize spatial information as they navigate through cities (Boston, Jersey City, Los Angeles). Lynch (1960) concluded that the citizens understood their surroundings in consistent and predictable ways. He identified five elements that the maps had in common and could be used to describe urban cities: paths (the streets, walkways, trails, and other channels in which people travel); edges (perceived boundaries such as walls, buildings and shorelines); districts (relatively large sections of the city distinguished by some identity or character); nodes (focal points, intersections or loci) and landmarks (readily identifiable objects which serve as reference points).

Others have tried to map social relations and processes for marketing purposes. Sinus Sociovision, for example, has developed a marketing tool called Sinus-Milieus, which groups people according to their attributes towards specific topics such as work, family, leisure, money and consumption and their life-style (Sinus Sociovision n.d.). The tool is oriented on the concept of social milieu (or le milieu social), which is associated with the French sociologist Emilie Durkheim (15 April 1858–15 November 1917)[2]. The idea of the Sinus-Milieus is that societies can be divided into groups which possess coherent moral and aesthetic concepts so that they form, consciously or unconsciously, a unit. The aim of the Sinus-Milieus is to make these units visible. However, as Diaz-Bone (2009) states, social milieu research in the context of market research, is theoretically and methodologically problematic as the models used for marketing themselves underlie the rules of marketing. Market research companies are interested in maximizing the distribution and acceptance of their milieu model. As Diaz-Bone (2009) argues, this strategy questions the validity of such models and certainly restricts their use in academic contexts.

---

[2] An overiew of Durkheims's work can, for example, be found by Giddens (1978), Thompson (1982) and Morrison (2006).

Conclusion

To sum up, space is often experienced as having room to move. Place, on the other hand, is experienced as permanent and stable. It has the quality of familiarity, support and nostalgia. Place can therefore acquire a deep meaning for people. They feel attached to their home, city or country. Therefore, not only physical constraints but also cultural values influence the perception of space. In addition, space is not static. It is constantly created and recreated. In other words, it is a simultaneity of stories-so-far (Massey 2005). However, space is not only an on-going process, but it is strongly connected to people. As Löw (2001) states it is a social phenomenon or as Lefebvre (1991) formulated it, a (social) product. In this sense, space is both a product and a process, which is connected to the human and non-human world.

However, space is not only created and experienced but also represented on maps. But maps do not represent reality. They are two-dimensional representations of a three-dimensional world. In other words, they are (socially and technically constructed) abstractions. Nevertheless, maps help us to navigate through the world. They also help us to explore people's perception of the world. The concept of cognitive maps is therefore used in a wide range of fields as it allows us not only to understand people's relationship with their built environment, but also with their social network. Nevertheless, the approach of exploreing people's worldview through visual representations is ambitious as our perception of the world underlies complex physiological, psychological and social processes. This means that 'we are confronted not by one social space but by many—indeed, by an unlimited multiplicity or uncountable set of social spaces which we refer to generically as 'social space'' (Lefebvre 1991, p. 86). Space is therefore not a thing, but rather a set of relations between things or as Massey (2005) states, it is 'the dimension of a dynamic simultaneous multiplicity'. Nevertheless, as Tuan (1977) argues, certain similarities exist. We are individuals, but nevertheless embedded in a broader culture. We could therefore say that space is individual and collective at the same time. It is constantly created and recreated—physically, mentally and socially. It is, similar to our body, continuously moving.

References

Albertazzi L (ed) (2006) Visual thought: the depictive space of perception. John Benjamins, Amsterdam

Diaz-Bone R (2004) Milieu models and milieu instruments in market research. Forum qualitative sozialforschung/forum qualitative social research, [Online]. 5(2). Available at: http://www.qualitative-research.net/index.php/fqs/article/view/595. Accessed 12 July 2009

Giddens A (1978) Durkheim. Harvester Press, Hassocks

Giddens A (1984) The constitution of society: outline of the theory of structuration. Polity Press, Cambridge

Kitchin R, Blades M (2002) The cognition of geographic space. I. B. Tauris, London

Kitchin R, Freundschuh S (2000) Cognitive mapping: past, present, and future. Routledge, London

Kitchin RM (1994) Cognitive maps: what are they and why study them? J Environ Psychol 14(1):1–19

Lefebvre H (1991) The production of space. Blackwell, Oxford

Löw M (2001) Raumsoziologie. Suhrkamp Taschenbuch Wissenschaft, Frankfurt am Main

Lynch K (1960) The image of the city. MIT Press, Cambridge

MacEachren AM (1995) How maps work: representation, visualisation, and design. Guilford Press, New York

Massey DB (2005) For space. Sage Publications, London

Morrison K (2006) Marx, durkheim, weber: formations of modern social thought. Sage Publications, London

Pfrunder M (2002) Neotopia: Atlas zur gerechten Verteilung der Welt. Limmat Verlag, Zürich

Piaget J (1952) The origins of intelligence in children. International Universities Press, New York

Sinus Sociovision (n.d.) Available at: http://www.sociovision.de/. Accessed 12 July 2009

Thompson K (1982) Emile durkheim. Ellis Horwood, Chichester

Tuan Y (1977) Space and place: the perspective of experience. University of Minnesota Press, Minneapolis

Tuan Y (1990) Topophilia: a study of environmental perception, attitudes, and values. Columbia University Press, New York

bodySpace

Fabian Neuhaus

38 *GPS TRACKS PLYMOUTH 2008/09*[1] While in Plymouth, I was recording my personal movement on a daily basis with a simple Garmin Handheld GPS device. It is a collection of tracks over the period of one year and it visualises my interaction with the built environment. Two characteristics can clearly be explained on the image produced. One is that the movement was almost solely purpose orientated. It usually draws a straight line (as direct as possible respecting the built form and the topography) between point A (initial position) and point B (destination). Furthermore, I can say that also the numbers of destinations are rather limited. Although recorded over the period of one year the movement is restricted and highly predictable. There seems to be only a handful of important locations that are worth going to. Obviously there are the three main destinations, home, work, and essentials (Fig. 1).

The second characteristic is closely related to the first one. The routes stay the same; the movement between the points is repetitive. At the beginning there might be some optimising going on, but after two three times it seem to lock in and stay how it is. Overall it is a very personal record of my time in Plymouth. It could be called a diary, a spatial diary. It definitely helps to bring up memories from activities and experiences through recapturing the spatial configuration. I am wondering how long this will last. Will it prove to be as good as a photograph to help me remember certain anecdotes in twenty years time?

39 *GPS TRACKS BASEL 2007*[2] For a three month period I tracked my journey while living in Basel, Switzerland. In this example the modes of transport are bicycle, bus, tram and as a pedestrian. There are a number of lines leaving the image down in to the rest of Switzerland. (Towards north there is Germany and in the West its France).

---

[1] *GPS TRACKS PLYMOUTH 2008/09*, 7 October 2008 16:37, bodySpace, Plymouth, GPS tracks
[2] *GPS TRACKS BASEL 2007*, 12 October 2008 22:44, bodySpace, GPS tracks, Basel

---

F. Neuhaus (✉)
Centre for Advanced Spatial Analysis, University College London, London, UK
e-mail: fabian.neuhaus@ucl.ac.uk

F. Neuhaus (ed.), *Studies in Temporal Urbanism,*
DOI 10.1007/978-94-007-0937-9_6, © Springer Science+Business Media B.V. 2011

Fig. 1 Image by urbanTick /
Plymouth 365, GPS tracks
over one year

This is probably down to the fact that Basel as a city is quite small compared to Plymouth or London. Another aspect, especially compared to Plymouth is that the public transport is very good. Even though one does not have a car, it is simple and quick to go somewhere, this probably motivates to make trips to other places. The pattern that usually shows where I live and where I work appears surprisingly less obvious than expected. The knot where I lived is somehow visible, but apart from this is rather unclear. Strong lines also appear along the train line Basel-Olten and there is a strongly visible mark leading towards the Laufental (Fig. 2).

The following are notes just after I recorded the tracks in 07-02-15. "...it is again the graph with the plotted tracks that show how I move around the city. The pattern stayed the same it became just denser. I stopped this record at the end of the year. So I do now have three month of records, guess that's enough as there are no changes in sight for the near future. The pattern develops around a few hotspots and connects them within and with some points of interest or necessity. As it is basically a movement pattern and not an activity pattern there is not much to find about my behav-

Fig. 2 Image by urbanTick /
the straight lines occur where
the GPS device had a weak
satellite signal or lost the
connection

iour in the city. It is talking about the city structure and tells the story of how one can move about this particular area. Maybe more interesting is what I do in between. One could say this is closer to some kind of space-syntax research, but maybe in terms of how activities are structuring the movement within the settlement this is not very useful. It is too close to the physical reality to tell a richer story. There is a lot of information missing. For example it would be very interesting to actually see where and how long I stopped somewhere. There are breaks in between the lines, at my workplace, where I go for lunch… these events could tell a totally different story. It is actually recorded in most of the daily data on the GPS device, I just do not know how to visualise this…!

I have already been working for a few months with this device and I am still impressed by the output. The drawing shown is very simple but it visualises very clear how much of the city structure I actually know, in terms of physically experienced, and how much I have left out. But still, I would claim to know the city as a whole. Despite the fact I haven't seen large areas I create a mental image of the city and its network of connections. …"

40   *THE LONDON TRACKS*[3] Here is another image of a collection of tracks recorded over a longer period of time. This time it is in London. This record was set up as part of my research for my masters' thesis.

In this project the focus lay on my personal diary. I wanted to find out, or better visualise, the spatial extent of my routines. Although it is a record over a relatively short period of two months, it shows a very clear pattern. It could be described as a bunch of north-south back and forward lines. This is the form and to home respectively, to and from the Bartlett School of Architecture (Fig. 3).

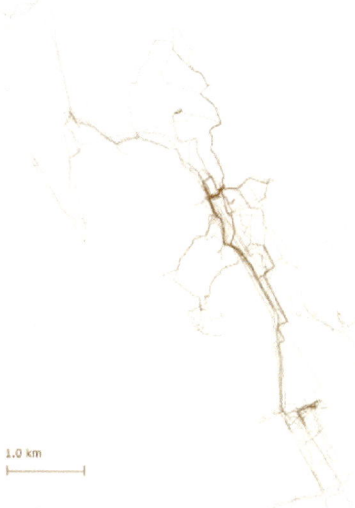

1.0 km

Fig. 3 Image by urbanTick / GPS track in London during 2006 for the period of two month

---

[3] *THE LONDON TRACKS*, 21 October 2008 15:35, bodySpace, GPS tracks, London

Fig. 4 Image by
urbanTick / Plymouth
365 shown at larger scale
including Devon and /
Cornwall

There are some occasional trips leaving this pattern. They are very distinct from the everyday pattern and I can still remember most of them in some detail, although this is two years back. A trip to the Barbican to see the Future City exhibition, the great walk through Hampstead Heath, kicking the ball on a hot day in Regents Park. Those sorts of trips just stand out. This is somehow a different way to memorize spatial activity. The exception stands out from the crowd.

41   *PLYMOUTH365*[4] I have been working with the collected track data from my Plymouth pool. 365 track records represent my interaction with the built environment. Some "landmarks" are drawn out quite well, especially the rigid street structure of the city centre, designed by Abercrombie in 1944 (A Plan for Plymouth) (Fig. 4).

But also the crossings over the river Tamar are visible (only three ways to cross, Tamar Bridge, Torpoint Ferry and Mount Edgecombe Ferry). Other infrastructure features like the train line (especially Plymouth to Exeter) and the A38. The image is just another visualisation, can't keep my hands off, it looks just great.

42   *GPS TRACKS LONDON 2008*[5] A first image of the emerging tracks in London. This record starts in September 2008 (Fig. 5).

The two hotspots already emerge. UCL and Tufnell Park connected via the 390 bus line. I do really badly in crossing the Thames. Maybe I should start deliberately crossing the river. If only for the purpose of this image.

43   *TRACK VISUALISATION*[6] I have been working with the data material Plymouth365. Different approaches have now been tested and it looks promising that this could lead to something (Fig. 6).

I have been focusing on the analysis of the data in the context of a 24 h day. Basically what I did is squeezed all the days into one sample day and plot it. In other

[4] *PLYMOUTH365*, 29 October 2008 16:44, plymouth365, Plymouth, GPS tracks, bodySpace

[5] *GPS TRACKS LONDON 2008*, 18 November 2008 16:54, bodySpace, GPS tracks, London

[6] *TRACK VISUALISATION*, 21 November 2008 00:39, visualisation, bodySpace, space-time Diagram, GPS tracks, analysis, aquarium

Fig. 5 Image by urbanTick /
London, generated 2008-11-
18/three month of data

Fig. 6 Image by urbanTick /
activity graph generated from
GPS track points

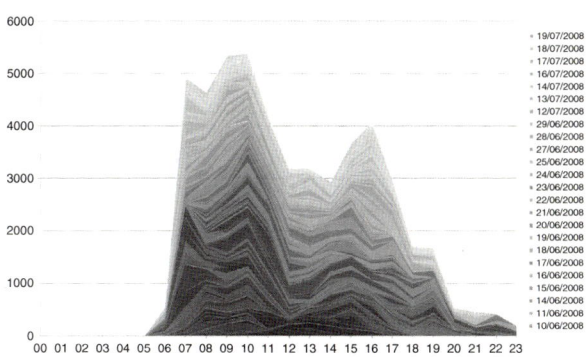

words, all the days are superimposed onto one day. See a clip on Youtube[7] visualising the data. Or in another version see clip here on Youtube[8] (These are screenshot movies and shows Google Earth playing the tracks over 24 h. It is a first shot at it, so needs some cleaning and tweaking) (Fig. 7).

(This data represents are the new London tracks from October and November in 2008.)

---

[7] http://www.youtube.com/v/bPpgVgBamOo&hl=en&fs=1&

[8] http://www.youtube.com/v/gPV7k05wduA&hl=en&fs=1&

Fig. 7 Image by urbanTick / London aquarium, time space diagram referred to as the aquarium. After Kwan (2004)

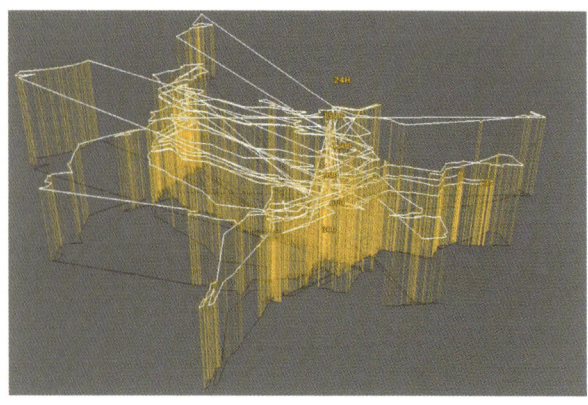

44   *COMPARISON*[9] What is now possible is to compare three different cities. I have a track record from Plymouth, Basel and London.

The following three screenshots are taken from Google Earth at an altitude of 9 km. So they are comparable in scale.

What they all have in common is the fixed points. The main structural elements of how my days work in terms of space and time are the same. Leaving home, going to the same workplace every day, and returning back home. Between those fixed points there build up quite intense tracks lines. This base layer gets extended by some secondary points, e.g. location for the weekly shopping, favourite spots, friends location, … The third element is the trips: journeys that are usually going out of the daily routine to a further destination or just a stroll. This then is represented in the London track log. It is strongly linear and this represents exactly this centrality as the line is pointing towards the centre.

They occur characteristically on days off or weekends. Depending on how familiar I am with the surrounding they are of more focused or of more explorative nature. It is interesting to compare how I respond to the urban surrounding. The three cities have very distinct urban patterns. Take Plymouth, a city (Fig. 8) completely planned almost from scratch after it was destroyed in the Second World War (Fig. 9).

The planner was (Fig. 10) Patrick Abercrombie[10] who also presented ideas for the reconstruction or better new construction of London after the Blitz. Basel on the other hand is a similar size city (Fig. 11) in a very different setting with its growth patterns structuring very much its appearance (Fig. 12).

Or London as the third example, the world city with its single centre core. To explore how those characteristics influence my interaction with the built environment in terms of routes I choose I overlay my tracks onto maps that capture the

[9] *COMPARISON*, 4 December 2008 14:04, interaction, Plymouth, GPS tracks, morphology, London, Basel, bodySpace, urban form

[10] http://en.wikipedia.org/wiki/Patrick_Abercrombie

Fig. 8 Image by urbanTick / Basel city centre with track overlay and historic growth from ca 1860 to ca 1875 and after ca 1926

characteristics of the three cities. Surprisingly, or maybe not so surprisingly, the tracks redraw quite exactly the characteristics of the Abercrombie Plan.

Note in Fig. 8 on page 71 area A (dark brown) is the old medieval town surrounded by walls dated ca 1860. Area B (beige) is the extension, ca 1875, but still surrounded by a wall. Area C is the extension of the city ca 1926, but is also mainly the present extent. It is important to know that after the walls were demolished, the freed up space has been used for major infrastructure projects such as roads, but also open spaces. This means that additionally to the link roads that from the centre outwards there is also a number of ring roads (on the ground of the former walls) that tie in very well with the rest of the network. Moving radially is quite simply in therefore and the use of it is represented through the number of tracks.

Compared to this in London it's quite tricky to travel radially as it has a strong centralized structure, roads mainly leading into or out of the city centre.

Fig. 9 Image by urbanTick / Plymouth Abercrombie Plan with Plymouth 365 track overlay

Fig. 10 Image by
urbanTick / Plymouth with
personal GPS tracks

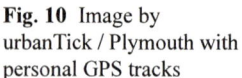

45   *PLYMOUTH AQUARIUM*[11] I have been playing around with the Plymouth365
data set and managed to produce a collaged GPS file. The track data that was collected over the period of one year is displayed simultaneously.

---

[11] *PLYMOUTH AQUARIUM*, 26 November 2008 22:57, visualisation, Plymouth, bodySpace,
aquarium

Fig. 11 Image by urbanTick / Basel with personal GPS tracks

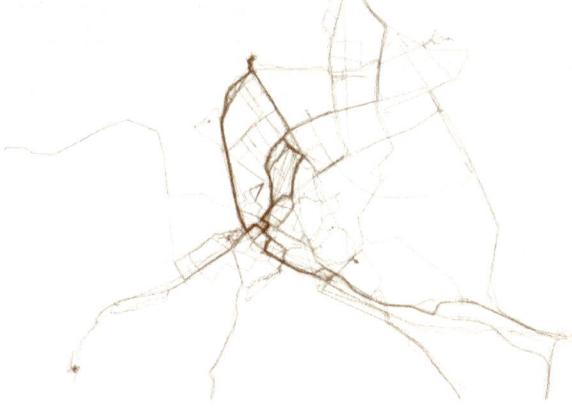

Fig. 12 Image by urbanTick / London with personal GPS tracks

1.0 km

It is an aquarium again where I recalculated the height according to the time. As time passes the track rises up. This has been done with simple spreadsheet calculation and then re-pasting into the GPX file. The new altitude is now the indication of process.

This image uses the simple transformation of the time into seconds as the height. In this example the altitude is between 32,000 m and 85,000 m. It is very difficult to read on the level of everyday Plymouth activities, but it draws nice progress lines from long distance and day trips.

The second image here has the height reduced by 50%. Much more detail is visible on smaller scale where long distance trips lose their quality. An interesting feature is the "wall" that emerges between the place where I lived and my work place. Along the path I used to take emerges a vertical mess of lines at all times/ heights. I must have used this route pretty much at any time in the day during this one year period.

Although I have tried to "clean" the data today, there are still a large number of error lines showing up. Also seem there to be new error lines occurring because of the method I used to collage the GPX file. The problem is that I pasted it as one track and not as a set of tracks. This would involve some more computing, but it's probably worth a try. With such a method some more specific queries would be possible.

46 *INTERACTION WITH THE URBAN FORM—PLYMOUTH CITY CENTRE*[12] Plymouth city centre is a very specific area. It has a very distinct character arising from the strong postwar design by Patrick Abercrombie[13]. It has a truly mono functional use, it is a shopping centre in the most literal sense of the word possible. There are no offices, no restaurants, no pubs or bars, no housing, just shops and on the first or second floors storage space for the shops.

The shops open at 10h00 and close at 18h00. These hours then basically determine the "opening" of the city centre. Outside of those the centre is dead, again literally. There is a very special phenomenon attached to this. Although the opening hours are as described above, shoppers vanish around 17h00. So approximately 1 h before closing the shops are already empty and so is the centre. Being in HMV at half five is like a scene out of "I am Legend"—hello is there someone? (I have written a longer article about this topic on JLF urban research[14].)

See clip on Vimeo[15]/Zoom onto the city centre with GPS tracks overlayed.

To my surprise this pattern shows up dramatically in my records. Although I was aware of this pattern and could have behaved differently, but I didn't. There is no reason to walk through this area, as there is nothing happening and on top of this it becomes rather scary to be on your own in this vast outdoor shopping centre at night. This short clip shows the activities within 24 h. It is zoomed right into Plymouth centre. The activities start around 10h00 and end exactly at 17h00. There is the odd crossing outside of these hours, but the characteristic shows clearly.

47 *CAB SPOTTING SAN FRANCISCO—3D VISUALISATION*[16] A visualisation of the cab traffic in the San Francisco bay area combined with information of the shuttle rada topography mission (Fig. 13).

See also some stills on flickr here[17]. Thanks to Kons for the link.

---

[12] *INTERACTION WITH THE URBAN FORM—PLYMOUTH CITY CENTRE*, 5 December 2008 12:32, visualisation, Plymouth, GPS tracks, bodySpace, morphology, interaction

[13] http://en.wikipedia.org/wiki/Patrick_Abercrombie

[14] http://jlf-urbanresearch.blogspot.com/2007/10/weekfan41071024_24.html

[15] http://vimeo.com/2436298

[16] *CAB SPOTTING SAN FRANCISCO—3D VISUALISATION*, 6 February 2009 09:57, bodySpace, GPS tracks, animation, tracking, cabspotting

[17] http://flickr.com/photos/84796927@N00/3187843440/

Fig. 13 Clip by Kns von
Rhein on Vimeo. (http://
vimeo.com/2780984)

Fig. 14 Image animation
still by Sean Dockray / See
clip on Vimeo. (http://vimeo.
com/3068855)

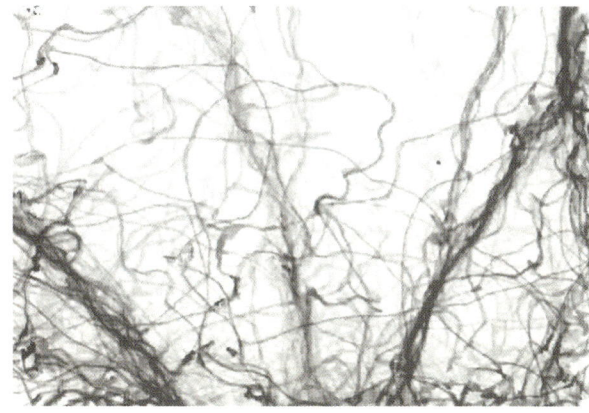

48   *ANT TRAILS*[18] Ants use pheromones to mark their trail and guide following ants.
They mark the path as they go along ant leave tiny little messages. If the trail is successful and more and more ants follow up the guidance becomes more intense and
denser, whereas other trails fade out. Exactly this was visualised by Sean Dockray
in his animation Ameising1[19].See the ant clip on Vimeo[20] (Fig. 14).

The ants movement was recorded in a 45 min shot and then retraced with software support each ant, frame by frame (would probably be quite simple nowadays
with the new After Effects functions). The emerging output might not be the collective memory, as it is called by the author, but some kind of selective evolution of
spatial organization. To read more about ants, the new ant bible has only recently
been published: The Super-organism: The Beauty, Elegance, and Strangeness of Insect Societies, by B Holldobler, Edward O. Wilson, on Amazon for some £ 30.00[21].

---

[18] *ANT TRAILS*, 2 March 2009 22:38, trail, animals, orientation, visualisation, tracking, bodySpace

[19] http://spd.e-rat.org/ameising-1

[20] http://vimeo.com/3444096

[21] http://www.amazon.co.uk/Super-organism-Beauty-Elegance-Strangeness-Societies/
dp/0393067041/ref=sr_1_1?ie=UTF8&s=books&qid=1236035233&sr=8-1

49   *CITY ISLANDS—ON THE LINKAGE OF EVERYDAY LOCATIONS*[22] Debord's psychogeographical map The Naked City (1957) challenged traditional ideas of mapping relating to scale, location, and fixity, and drew on the work of urban social geographer Paul-Henri Chombart de Lauwe's concept of the city as a conglomeration of distinct quarters, each with its own special function, class divisions, and "physiognomy," which linked the idea of the urban plan to the body. An important strategy of the pyschogeographical was the dérive, "a technique of transient passage through varied ambiences".

The image of the Naked City has help visualizing the fragmented experience we all have of the urban environment we live in. The mode of transport plays an important role, but so does usage, distance and function.

As an example for the differences in experiencing and linking the city spaces, two participants from the UrbanDiary project have been chosen. It happened to be a couple and the way they "use" the city could not be more different. Within the pattern of everyday activities, the main vehicle to create the structure of the experienced space is the mode of transport. In this case, the female uses the bus to travel to work and has therefore a continuous space between the home location and the work location (top diagram). The male in the example on the other hand uses the tube to travel between home, work and pub. The result is a number of very local islands scattered over the city, leaving him with no means to connect them spatially (Fig. 15).

The link between the urban plan and the body is not obvious on a daily basis but becomes more apparent over time through the routine. The daily rhythm allows one to connect the physical experience with the memory of the activity.

50   *TRAVEL PATTERNS OVER GENERATIONS*[23] Over generations and time, the travel behaviour has changed, especially in term of distance. From looking at travel patterns on a city scale for this blog post we are looking at a global level. It has become normal to travel around the world and any location on this planet is now to be reached in a day or two. Within only four generations, or one century, the covered land by life time tracks has grown from a regional are to a national to a continental and finally to a global area. The ways in which travel patterns have changed for the host population over recent generations have been shown in an interesting way by the distinguished epidemiologist, David Bradley, when he was at the London School of Hygiene and Tropical Medicine. Bradley compared the travel patterns of his great-grandfather, his grandfather, his father and himself (see Fig. 16). The life-time travel track of his great-grandfather around a village in Northamptonshire could be contained within a square of only 40 km side. His grandfather's map was still limited to southern England, but it now reached as far as London and could be contained within a square of 400 km (Fig. 16).

If we compare these maps with those of Bradley's father (who travelled widely in Europe) and Bradley's own sphere of travel, which is worldwide, then the enclosing square has to be widened to sides of 4000 km and 40,000 km respectively.

---

[22] *CITY ISLANDS—ON THE LINKAGE OF EVERYDAY LOCATIONS*, 24 March 2009 14:57, body, bodySpace, London, cycles, rhythm, psychogeography
[23] *TRAVEL PATTERNS OVER GENERATIONS*, 30 March 2009 12:48, generation, time, bodySpace, travel pattern, mapping

Fig. 15 Image by urbanTick for UrbanDiary / Two different phsychogeographies of London

Fig. 16 Image taken from British Medical Journal / Travel patterns over generations. (http://bmb.oxford-journals.org/cgi/content/full/69/1/87)

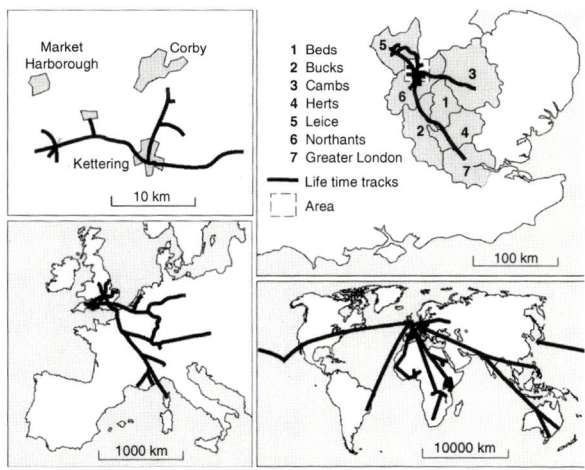

In broad terms, the spatial range of travel has increased tenfold in each generation so that Bradley's own range is 1000 times wider than that of his great-grandfather. (British Medical Bulletin 69:87–99 (2004)) Bradley's record of increasing travel over four male generations of the same family. (A) Great-grandfather. (B) Grandfather. (C) Father. (D) Son. Each map shows in a simplified manner the individual's 'life-time tracks' in a widening spatial context, with the linear scale increasing by a factor of 10 between each generation.

Fig. 17 Participant 01
'Blurb' for the frog tracking
project on first of April

51   *ANIMAL TRACKING—FROGS*[24] First results of a fine scale GPS tracking study
in London's private gardens show amazing results (Fig. 17).

Spring arrived in London and the frogs started to come out of their winter quarters about three weeks ago. They were tagged with GPS devices and have ever
since collected data on their daily routines in the local gardens. GPS accuracy is
somewhere between 3 and 15 m but still, this study shows it is possible to get some
results on very local scale as this back garden tracking shows (Fig. 18).

The two participants 'Blurb' and 'Rosi' where very collaborative and willing to
be tracked. Fortunately the GPS devices are waterproof as the frogs like the wet!
The many gaps refer to their habit jumping from spot to spot rather than walk.

52   *ANIMAL TRACKING—FROGS SECOND*[25] I have found online some more info
on frog tracking. A real tracking device for frogs exists and has been tested in a number

Fig. 18 Participant 02 'Rosi'
with her 'backpack' for the
first of April tracking project

[24] *ANIMAL TRACKING—FROGS*, 1 April 2009 13:04, animals, London, GPS tracks, tracking,
bodySpace

[25] *ANIMAL TRACKING—FROGS SECOND*, 2 April 2009 21:29, animals, GPS tracks, bodySpace,
tracking

Fig. 19 Image by urbanTick / Screenshot showing a time-space aquarium

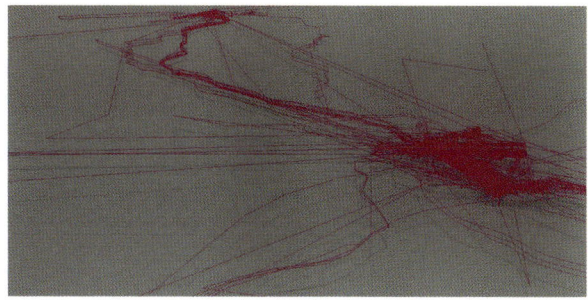

of studies already. It is more of a belt rather than a backpack. I am not sure how much it affects the swim performance but it definitely looks much cooler than the pack!

There is more to this topic about amphibians and reptiles in our gardens though. Apparently no one really knows what is happening at dawn, dusk or throughout the night at the back in the grass. An online article on BBC.co.uk[26] describes with the title 'Stock-take' of garden creatures and calls out "Whether it is frogs in your ferns, or toads in your tulips, a coalition of wildlife charities is asking for volunteers to carry out a national 'stock-take' of the reptiles and amphibians in the UK's gardens." So if you are a proud user of a back garden, report the activity you observe. Actually, the two frogs 'Blurb' and 'Rosi' are now out and about the garden again, but without the GPS devices. No need to worry about them they are fine and probably remember the first of April!

ONE YEAR OF TRAVEL DATA—AQUARIUM[27] Using the travel data from the art project The Location of I[28], by Martin J Callanan[29] this aquarium below was generated. Again the Google Earth Plug-In is used to visualise the KML file. The file can be downloaded here[30], on the website of the artist, tweaking is done in excel (Fig. 19).

The time data is recalculated as the height information. Therefore the altitude represents the time. Other visualisations of this type have been tested here before and can be found here[31].

BiCi_N—MAPPING BARCELONA BY BIKE[32] A project to map Barcelona by bike by Martha Skinner[33] has caught our attention. BiCi_N[34] is a project based on the GPS tracks collected by riders of the new Barcelona rental bikes. Barcelona

---

[26] http://news.bbc.co.uk/1/hi/sci/tech/7977971.stm

[27] *ONE YEAR OF TRAVEL DATA—AQUARIUM*, 10 April 2009 21:33, movement, routine, GPS tracks, bodySpace, tracking, aquarium

[28] http://location.e-2.org/

[29] http://greyisgood.eu/location/

[30] http://greyisgood.eu/location/location_of_i.kml

[31] http://urbantick.blogspot.com/search/label/aquarium

[32] *BiCi_N—MAPPING BARCELONA BY BIKE*, 5 May 2009 09:57, body, Barcelona, crowd sourcing, bodySpace, GPS, mapping

[33] http://avmapping.blogspot.com/

[34] http://www.field-office.com/BICIN/?page_id=32

Fig. 20 Image taken from Wikimedia / Estacio bicing bcn.jpg. (http://en.wikipedia. org/wiki/File:Estacio_bic-ing_bcn.jpg)

has this great rental scheme called bicing[35], where frequently everywherein the city large bike racks are placed with parked bikes and anyone can just grab a bike and explore the city, return it to any other station you wish (Fig. 20).

The project BiCi_N in still in its test phase at not yet up and running, but some first tests have been under way. A two week trial period took place last year and some material of this is now online. See clip on Vimeo[36]

55   *MOBILE AUTOMATIC PEDESTRIAN DETECTION—ETH ZURICH*[37] At ETH Zurich a mobile version of pedestrian detection was developed. It is demonstrated in a clip that featured in a blog post over at technology review[38]. It is stunning how accurate the software is able to distinguish between individuals in these rather crowded scenes. Plus, all is mobile, the camera is mounted in a car and presumably the software runs the analysis live, including these nice little trails the pedestrians leave behind. Technology was developed by researches from the Computer Vision Laboratory[39] at ETH Zurich in a collaboration with Toyota (Fig. 21).

Two papers related to the project above are available online: Coupled Object Detection and Tracking from Static Cameras and Moving Vehicles[40], by Bastian Leibe, Konrad Schindler, Nico Cornelis, and Luc Van Gool A Mobile Vision System for Robust Multi-Person Tracking[41], by Andreas Ess1 Bastian Leibe Konrad Schindler Luc Van Gool1, ETH Zurich, Switzerland 2KU Leuven, Belgium.

---

[35] http://www.bicing.com/home/home.php?TU5fTE9DQUxJWkFDDSU9ORVM%3D&MQ%3D%3D&Y2E%3D

[36] http://vimeo.com/4065048

[37] *MOBILE AUTOMATIC PEDESTRIAN DETECTION—ETH ZURICH*, 19 May 2009 10:43, movement, mobile, bodySpace, tracking, pedestrians, mapping

[38] http://www.technologyreview.com/video/?vid=338

[39] http://www.vision.ee.ethz.ch/

[40] http://www.vision.ee.ethz.ch/~bleibe/papers/leibe-detectiontracking-pami08final.pdf

[41] http://www.vision.ee.ethz.ch/~bleibe/papers/ess-mobilevisionsystem-cvpr08.pdf

Fig. 21 Image taken from the paper Coupled Object Detection and Tracking from Static Camera and Moving Vehicles by Bastian Leibe, Konrad Schindler, Nico Cornelis and Luc Van Gool / Screenshots showing the tracking of pedestrians. 3D localization and tracking results from inside a moving vehicle. (http://www.vision.ee.ethz.ch/~bleibe/papers/leibe-detectiontracking-pami08final.pdf)

56
MAPPING PARTY—OSM[42] The open source online street atlas Open Street Map[43] is produced by volunteers uploading GPS tracks and adding names and features. To get specific areas mapped, mapping parties are organized. A number of interested people meet up to map the area. It's a lot of fun and provides a social aspect to the all so lonely occupation of the mapper. The latest mapping party[44] took place in Milton Keynes in the UK and is very well documented on the web (Fig. 22).

A number of people have participated and they covered quite a lot in a previously for Open Street Map (OSM) unmapped area. Each participant is assigned an individual colour. This trace shows what she/he has been mapping. The very nice example also comes as an animation[45]. A Python script makes this possible (Fig. 23).

Instructions can be found here[46]. Thanks for the link go to Andrew Crooks[47] from GISagent[48]. Open Street Map has provided us with nice animations of GPS traces before. There was the breath taking clip about OSM worldwide earlier this year.

---

[42] MAPPING PARTY—OSM, 26 May 2009 10:00, animation, GPS tracks, Open Street Map, crowd sourcing, data handling, mapping, GPS, bodySpace

[43] http://www.openstreetmap.org/

[44] http://wiki.openstreetmap.org/w/images/2/29/MK_party_render.png

[45] http://splintdev.geog.ucl.ac.uk/misc/obrien/mk_mapping_party.mpg

[46] http://wiki.openstreetmap.org/wiki/Party_render

[47] http://www.casa.ucl.ac.uk/people/person.asp?ID=6

[48] http://gisagents.blogspot.com/

Fig. 22 Image taken from wiki.openstreetmap.org. (http://wiki.openstreetmap.org/wiki/MK_Mapping_Party) / Tracking record by individual from an OSM mapping party

Fig. 23 Clip by Ito World on Vimeo / The growth of OSM to date across the planet. (http://vimeo.com/2598878)

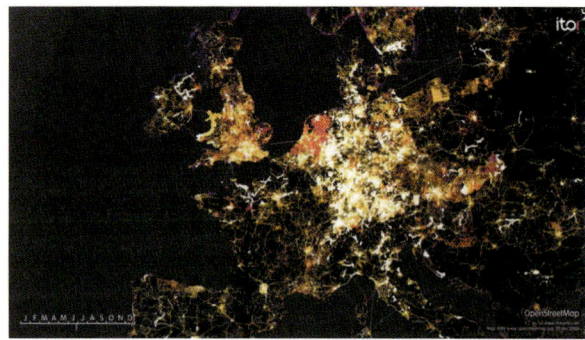

57 *36 H CITY—PROJECTION*[49] A beautiful clip documenting a video installation about the city. 36 h city is multi layered, but also a multi-dimensional projection merging different aspects of the city in order to paint a more comprehensive picture (Fig. 24).

The very interesting point here is how time can be integrated in a spatial representation. The narrative is simple and only concerned with the city but very complex on how it can be told. This work was produced by dottodot[50] as a design for an exhibition. They use one projector for this and it was put together in a software called vvvv[51]. See clip on Vimeo[52]

---

[49] *36 H CITY—PROJECTION*, 2 June 2009 10:00, city, mapping, beat, time, bodySpace, urban, art

[50] http://www.dotdotdot.it

[51] http://vvvv.org/tiki-index.php

[52] http://vimeo.com/628081

Fig. 24 Clip by Ankit
Shekhawat on Vimeo. (http://
vimeo.com/383174)

Fig. 24 Clip by Ankit Shekhawat on Vimeo. (http://vimeo.com/383174)

And just because this is so beautiful, I put in a second clip from the same producers using the same technique. This time it is built around a hotel room. dottodot[53] have also produced lots of other nice interactive exhibition designs such a Sky-Walker[54] or Valcucine's skyscraper[55].

MOVEMENT MAPPING USING FLICKR[56] As a by-product of a research project called "Mapping the World's Photos[57]" a very interesting movement map was generated. The work, by Davis Crandall, Lars Backstrom, Daniel Huttenlocher and Jon Kleinberg from the Department of Computer Science, Cornell University, is looking at organizing a large collection of geotagged photos. Large in this context means something around 35 million images, collected from Flickr[58] via the public API. The main hypothesis of the project is "that geospatial information provides an important source of structure that can be directly integrated with visual and textual-tag content for organizing global-scale photo collections". They were using image recognition software to locate the photos together with the interpretation of the photo tags. In this context the computation bit behind this is not the focus of the interest, although it sounds very impressive. If you are interested in this bit, have a look at their paper directly, which is published online here[59]. The bit I am interested for this post is the bit where they plot the geospatial information. As they describe it in their paper it was more of a by-product that came with the project, but nevertheless it generated interesting visuals. By using the time stamp and the geolocation the movement of the photographer can be

---

[53] http://www.dotdotdot.it

[54] http://www.dotdotdot.it/newdot/?p=398

[55] http://www.dotdotdot.it/en/?p=35

[56] *MOVEMENT MAPPING USING FLICKR*, 3 June 2009 09:30, movement, bodySpace, tracking, flickr, mapping

[57] http://www.cs.cornell.edu/~crandall/photomap/

[58] http://www.flickr.com/

[59] http://www.cs.cornell.edu/~crandall/photomap/

Fig. 25 Image courtesy of David Crandall / London mapped along locations of photographs

traced. Similar to a rough GPS track the different locations in which a photo is taken can be mapped as a sequence in space and time. Crandall et al. were plotting this information and the result was a series of urban tourists' movement maps. In the paper they published two of them one of Manhattan, New York and the other one of the San Francisco Bay area.

A great way to collect data is by mining the existing and continuously growing, as they call it, "global photo library", by using the public API and the published image information. It is a project very similar to the recently posted project "Just landed"[60], where the Twitter API was used together with a tweet analysis regarding phrases containing "just landed" to map global movement. The selection of the image generators, the photographers and sharers is again, just as it was with twitter, a critical point. Who does this represent, who is this group and what can we learn from this group's data? (Fig. 25).

Quoted paper: David Crandall, Lars Backstrom, Daniel Huttenlocher and Jon Kleinberg, 2009. Mapping the World's Photos. www[61] Found through 7.5th Floor[62] by Fabien Girardin—As he points out in his blog post, there are a number of related projects including Currid and Williams' work on Mapping the Cultural Buzz[63]. Another city mapped by the photos taken is London.

59 *DOG DRAWING*[64] A series of video tracking clips by Jeremy Wood. Great visuals, however I am not sure how it is done and processed. It says GPS but it looks more like video tracking, by Jeremy Wood and Hugh Pryor. Jeremy Wood has been

---

[60] http://urbantick.blogspot.com/2009/05/just-landed-global-movement-using.html

[61] http://www.cs.cornell.edu/~crandall/photomap/

[62] http://liftlab.com/think/fabien/2009/04/27/mapping-the-worlds-photos/

[63] http://www.nytimes.com/2009/04/07/arts/design/07buzz.html?_r=1

[64] *DOG DRAWING*, 16 June 2009 10:05, bodySpace, animals, GPS drawing, tracking, GPS

Fig. 26 Image by Jeremy Wood—Location: N51° 52′ 14.3″ W3° 27′ 36.4″ Brecon Beacons (2.1 km SW from Pen Y Fan), Wales, Time: 16/07/02 (09:41:07–10:29:14), Track length: 4.169 km, Average speed: 3.5 kph, Method: foot. I lost the fight to finish off the dragon in the time available, it remains half emerged from the side of a hill. (http://www.gpsdrawing.com/gallery/land/dragon.htm)

working with GPS for a long time and on his website GPSdrawing.com[65] he shows an extensive archive of his personal records and works using GPS. There are some great drawings and writing to be checked out. Also see clip on Vimeo[66] (Fig. 26).

SPACE-TIME—RICHARD LONG[67] Currently there is a Richard Long exhibition[68] on at the Tate Britain[69] in London with the "Heaven and Earth" exhibition until September 2009. It is the first large exhibition of the British artist in eighteen years. The exhibition features sculptures, large scale mud wall works and old and new photographic and text works. Also important to mention is the addition room with a large collection of his books, where some real jewels of publication can be seen. Why feature a landscape artist here in the context of rhythms and movement? There are several reasons ranging from aspects of time, use of space and movement to aspects of mapping and visualisation. On the Tate Britain website the work is introduced and traced back to Long's love of nature and environmental experience. A lot of his works are temporal, maybe most of them. While working with the landscape obviously the method of documenting the work becomes central, especially in Long's work as a lot of his landscape works derive from the interaction of body and landscape or the reaction of the artist to the landscape. The methods he uses to document this interaction range from taking a picture of

---

[65] http://www.gpsdrawing.com/gallery.html

[66] http://vimeo.com/4692371

[67] *SPACE-TIME—RICHARD LONG*, 7 July 2009 08:45, art, time, space-time Diagram, exhibition, bodySpace

[68] http://www.tate.org.uk/britain/exhibitions/richardlong/default.shtm

[69] http://www.tate.org.uk/britain/

his interventions to mapping his activities. His installations of large scale stone circles and mud wall drawings can also be seen in the context of documenting. Long brings elements of the nature into the exhibition spaces being totally aware of the transformation related to context. The aspect of time plays a major role in all works but is particularly present in the photographs that document works he has produced/performed in remote places, like for example "a line made by walking". Long appears in most of his works as the actor and a driven personality. It seems like he just can't stop doing this. Particularly in his works of walks he is restless and eager to move. Also here the time plays a major role as a defining element, maybe even a tool to stop Long from simply keep on walking. Works such as "One Hour— a sixty minute walk on Dartmoor" or "A five day walk".

The mapping of his walks covers a number of additional topics including the aspect of space and space limitation. The geometry of the circle is Long's main element and features in his sculptures and installations, but also his walks as confining or excluding boundaries. In a sense some of his maps can be read as a different type of space-time diagrams.

61   *NATURE'S CLOCK—THE RHYTHM OF LIFE*[70] For now, I am looking to biology to find out about how this field is approaching the topic of cycles and rhythms. Your garden tells you the time[71], if you look closely. First observations on the biological clocks in plants where made in the fourth century B.C. by Androsthenes of Thasos. He participated in the expeditions by Alexander the Great in Asia. He described the daily movement of the tamarind tree (Tamarindus indica). Its leaves move up during the day and down during the night. A similar movement can be observed in the common bean plant. (Refinetti R. 2006. Circadian Physiology 2nd ed., Boca Raton: Taylor & Francis.) In 1745 Carl Linnaeus[72], a Swedish biologist described in his Philosophia Botanica (1751) that different flower species open their flowers at different times of the day. He distinguished between three groups of flowers: Meteorici—flowers which change their opening and closing times according to the weather conditions. Tropici—flowers which change their times for opening and closing according to the length of the day (Fig. 27).

Aequinoctales—flowers which have fixed times for opening and closing. (Note that these are unaffected by the weather conditions.) Only Aequinoctales are suitable for use in a flower clock. (After BBC h2g2[73]) The floral clock[74] would be starting from 3 am with the Goatsbeard, followed by a Dwarf Morning Glory at 5am to a Scarlet Pimpernel at around 9 am to a Day lily at 8 pm you can get flowers to open around the clock. For a full list have a look at Linneaus' Flower Clock[75] or on Wiki-

---

[70] *NATURE'S CLOCK—THE RHYTHM OF LIFE*, 15 July 2009 09:30, clock, biology, nature, shapingCities, cycle, bodySpace, rhythm

[71] http://www.zimbio.com/Carolus+Linnaeus/articles/2/Your+garden+tells+you+the+time

[72] http://en.wikipedia.org/wiki/Carl_Linnaeus

[73] http://www.bbc.co.uk/dna/h2g2/A5170024

[74] http://en.wikipedia.org/wiki/Floral_clock

[75] http://www.users.globalnet.co.uk/~sykesm/aboutFlowerClock.html

pedia[76]. The bees and many other insects must be well aware of such patterns. This might even translate into a busy working schedule inside the beehive as certain dependencies arise. Bees seem to have a clever "dance" to inform other about sources and maybe the time is an important aspect related to this communication? Anyway what I have not found so far is a clever interpretation of why flowers only open at certain times, but maybe the insects are otherwise just too busy? Also Michael Jackson had a floral clock[77] on his Neverland Ranch. It was not a real floral clock in the sense of a biological clock: rather it is a mechanical clock decorated with flowers. Maybe in flowers and plants you would have guessed that they respond to the rhythm of the sun, as they directly depend on it for energy and growth. Most of us would also have heard about the flowers that follow the path of the sun, such as the sunflowers, so not much of a surprise. But if looking at mammals, including humans it might come of more of a surprise that similar patterns can be studied. The key word here is circadian clock. A definition from medterms.com[78] "Circadian: Refers to events occurring within a 24-h period, in the span of a full (24-hour) day, as in a circadian rhythm. Circadian rhythmicity is a fundamental property possessed by all organisms. These rhythms are driven by an internal time-keeping system: a clock. Changes in the external environment, particularly in the light-dark cycle, entrain this biologic clock. Under constant environmental conditions devoid of time cues, rhythms driven by the clock show a period near, but usually not exactly equal to, 24 h." The word "circadian" is a twentieth century invention. It was coined by Franz Halberger[79] in 1959 from the Latin "circa" (around) + "diem" (a day). Halberger was the founder of modern chronobiology and the chronobiology centre[80] and a scientist at University of Minnesota (Fig. 28).

In the 1980s, the circadian rhythm was mainly studied in relation to sleep and sleep disorder. Scientists were looking at how newborn babies need time to grow into the grown up cycle of sleeping at night and being awake during the day, or

---

[76] http://en.wikipedia.org/wiki/Linnaeus%27_flower_clock

[77] http://www.nytimes.com/slideshow/2009/07/02/us/20090702-NEVERLAND_17.html

[78] http://www.medterms.com/script/main/art.asp?articlekey=6766

[79] http://en.wikipedia.org/wiki/Franz_Halberg

[80] http://www.msi.umn.edu/~halberg/

Fig. 28 Image taken from Franz Halberger / Book cover "Introduction to Chronobiology" by Franz Halberger, 1994. (http://www.msi.umn. edu/~halberg/introd/index. html)

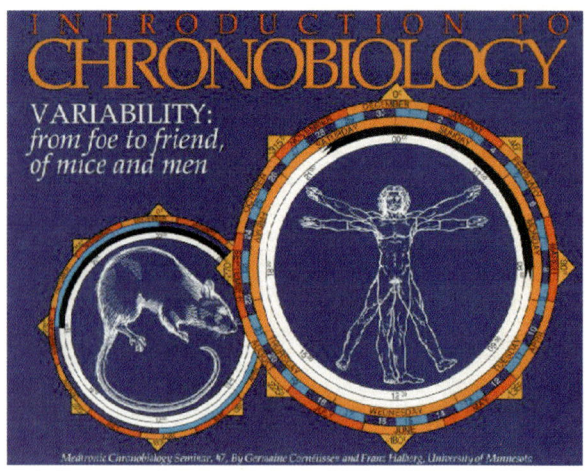

why teens stay up late and have difficulties getting up in the morning and why elderly people often wake up when it is still pitch black outside but can't go back to sleep. Extended research, including experiments with people spending weeks in the dark, has shown that the daylight plays a big part in normal sleep pattern. The human body seems to be capable of synchronising with the light-dark rhythm of the planet. The suprachiasmatic nuclei (SCN), a bundle of nerves located in the brain's hypothalamus (see Kim Kiser Minn Med, Nov 2005[81]), is responsible for keeping track of the time. This region does not tell the time, it simply keeps track of it. The clock is not centralized but distributed and inherent in all cells, but is regulated to stay in sync. Steven Strogatz describes in his book Sync three different levels of 'sync' related to the human body. The first is on the level of cells that are mutually synchronized. On the next level it is the organs that stay in sync. This does not mean that they are all active at the same time, but they each keep their allocated rhythm within the system. As the third level Strogatz describes the synchronization between the bodies and the environment around us. On this third level he does no go into detail about what this might be and how this might manifest. But logically it must have real life consequences in social space, and also physical space. A gene for the biological clock in a mouse was identified and cloned in 1997, the first such gene to be identified at the molecular level in a mammal. New research on the circadian clock's role in the organism suggests that the process controls almost all behaviours and physiology. In a surprising revelation, a new study suggests that the function of ALL genes in mammals is based on circadian rhythms. Up to now scientists believed that about 10% only are influenced by the body clock. The importance of the daily rhythm is only now uncovered. Scientists believe that the main means of orchestrating the vast number of independent elements that follow this rhythm is the daylight cycle. A number of studies have shown that if not exposed to the cycle of day and night, e.g. stay in the dark for a longer period of time, the synchronisation

---

[81] http://www.msi.umn.edu/~halberg/FaTime.pdf

slowly drifts off. It will automatically reestablish itself once back to exposure. (See article at the dailygalaxy[82].) New research has now also tried to explain the differences in life span in connection with the circadian rhythm. NYU dental professor Dr. Timothy Bromage was doing research on the growth of tooth enamel when he discovered these cycles of tooth and bone growth. The rhythm seems to vary from organism to organism and seems to have a direct impact on lifespan. For example, rats have a one-day interval, chimpanzees six, and humans eight. During the 37th Annual Meeting of the American Association for Dental Research, Bromage said, "The same biological rhythm that controls incremental tooth and bone growth also affects bone and body size and many metabolic processes, including heart and respiration rates. In fact, the rhythm affects an organism's overall pace of life, and its life span. So, a rat that grows teeth and bone in one-eighth the time of a human also lives faster and dies younger." (See article at Physorg[83].) A very interesting field I tapped in to here and this short introduction is certainly not covering all the crucial points of circadian rhythms in biology. There is a lot more to discover especially in relation to the third level of sync as described above, where it is about the sync between bodies and the immediate or wider environment. This exactly where my UrbanDiary research should plug in. In this context I see the GPS traces, together with the mental perception of the rhythms and the geographical/physical surrounding.

ANTS—THE YEARLY EFFORT TO CREATE A NEW COLONY[84] In my earlier masters thesis on cycles, I wrote about different kinds of natural cycles. One of the examples was the yearly event, when ant colonies release the drones. Today was this day again, at least in our garden and around the house here in London. Hundreds of ants (black garden ant (*Lasius niger*)) winged individuals flying in the air in search of a mating partner. Then the female ants lose their wings and find a place to start a new colony, the males die. Both female and male winged ants are produced by the colony as reproducers in a big effort. For the colony to bring up this large number of individuals that will once ready leave the nest. The date and time they leave the nest depends heavily on the conditions. It is mainly the temperature that is important. This is to ensure that the ants can fly (not raining) and that after the female ants lose their wings they have enough time to find a new nesting place. "Disparities between local weather conditions can cause nuptial flights to be out of phase amongst widespread populations. During hot summers, flights take place simultaneously across the country, but overcast weather with local patches of sunshine results in a far less synchronised emergence of alates (winged individuals)." (taken from wikipedia[85]) See clip on Youtube[86] (Fig. 29).

---

[82] http://www.dailygalaxy.com/my_weblog/2007/06/circadian_clock.html

[83] http://www.physorg.com/news126712217.html

[84] *ANTS—THE YEARLY EFFORT TO CREATE A NEW COLONY*, 17 July 2009 09:20, animals, cycle, nature, bodySpace

[85] http://en.wikipedia.org/wiki/Black_garden_ant

[86] http://www.youtube.com/v/1Xhdy9zBEws&hl=en&fs=1&

Fig. 29 Image by urbanTick/
Ant discarding the wings

Great information on ants on antblog[87] or The Kurt Kuene Antpage[88]. The ant bible would be The Superorganism[89] by Bert Hoelldobler and E.O. Wilson. They do not agree on everything, but they make a great team. They have published a number of books including The Ants[90] in 1997. Ants have featured earlier this year in a blog post[91], in relation with tracking and how they leave informations on their trail for fellow ants.

63   *OUT AND ABOUT—VR TIMELAPSE*[92] I am out again today. This time with a new add-on to the camera. A 360 VR lens that we managed to fit on the G9. It takes a few steps to mount it. The Canon adapter for the G9 that will provide 58 mm ring, on to this I found a step up ring in one of the Tottenham Court Road shops that takes it from 58 mm to 67 mm. The diameter for the VR module. I have to say the Canon adapter is plastic and is not very stable, especially because the VR is quite long. It is about twice the size of the camera body! (Fig. 30).

It creates these beautiful small world images through the central perspective, very much a visualisation for the mental map, individual perception[93] topic, but better than the gas advert[94]. A first test shot from this morning within CASA.

64   *LONDON SMALL WORLD—TIMELAPSE*[95] Finally the new timeLapse animation is here. It was shot quite quickly in two days, while having reasonable August weather. The editing process was more of a problem, though. It is

[87] http://www.antblog.co.uk

[88] http://krungkuene.org/ameisen_page/

[89] http://www.amazon.com/Superorganism-Beauty-Elegance-Strangeness-Societies/dp/0393067041/ref=pd_bxgy_b_img_b

[90] http://www.amazon.com/Ants-Bert-H%C3%B6lldobler/dp/0674040759

[91] http://urbantick.blogspot.com/2009/03/ant-trails.html

[92] *OUT AND ABOUT—VR TIMELAPSE*, 12 August 2009 13:33, timeLapse, smallWorld, bodySpace, panorama

[93] http://urbantick.blogspot.com/2009/07/space-perception-and-mental-maps.html

[94] http://urbantick.blogspot.com/2009/08/british-gas-subjective-world-view.html

[95] *LONDON SMALL WORLD—TIMELAPSE*, 19 August 2009 10:06, stop motion, animation, timeLapse, London, bodySpace, visualisation, smallWorld

Fig. 30 Clip by urbanTick on Vimeo. (http://vimeo.com/6065296)

shot with a G9, some 1480 stills. While using the 360 VR this was quite an installation and there are issues with the zoom level. Because this has to be done manually it is different in each scene and this proved a problem in the editing process. Photoshop is a helpful tool and without the batch function there would be no timeLapse, but for synchronizing the frame over different scenes it is quite tricky. I know video editing software would do the trick, but the rendering process would consume the same amount of time (Fig. 31).

Anyway here it is, eleven scenes around central London (Any suggestions for places?) Funny enough, I spent two days sitting underneath the tripod and studying the scenes (Fig. 32).

The angle of the VR mirror allows for sitting underneath so I don't appear in all the scenes, but still in a couple of them. In the empty Gordon Square I had to use some bread to attract pigeons to get movement in the shot. In other locations, like the Millennium Bridge, it was too crowded: no need for intervention. Sorry for the shaking in this particular scene, the bridge is in motion because of the crowd. If you sit or stand there for a while, you can feel it. So the little worlds are up now, and

Fig. 31 Image by urbanTick/
StoryBoard detail developed
for arranging the sequences

Fig. 32 Clip by urbanTick on
Vimeo / Shot as a timeLapse
with special lense at different locations. (http://vimeo.
com/6177425)

maybe you spot yourself in the clip somewhere. Music by bradsparky[96] at m3un-
signed.com[97].

65   *GPS TRACKS RUNNING IN 3DS MAX*[98] The visualisation of the UrbanDiary[99]
GPS tracks was a big topic earlier this year. So far Google Earth was used as a
rendering engine and the videos where screen grabs. A rather crude and straight
forward way of creating an animation. However the process seemed to make sense
as the Globe is working well with GPS data. Now, a new tool for visualizing the
tracks has been developed here at CASA. Richard Milton[100] has written little script
to import GPS tracks directly into 3D Studio Max (Fig. 33).

It reads the GPX file and creates a spline for the path, a marker object and time
frames for each point. There is still some tweaking to be done with the time interpretation, especially regarding multiple tracks, but as a proof of concept it works.
See clip on vimeo[101]/with some old school stile filters on top for the fun of it.

[96] http://www.mp3unsigned.com/showmp3.asp?mp3ID=1660&aid=773

[97] http://www.mp3unsigned.com

[98] *GPS TRACKS RUNNING IN 3DS MAX*, 30 September 2009 10:07, visualisation, bodySpace,
GPS tracks, GPS

[99] http://urbantick.blogspot.com/search/label/urbanDiary

[100] http://www.casa.ucl.ac.uk/people/person.asp?ID=28

[101] http://vimeo.com/6830243

Fig. 33 Image by urbanTick / A week as GPS tracks in 3D Studio Max

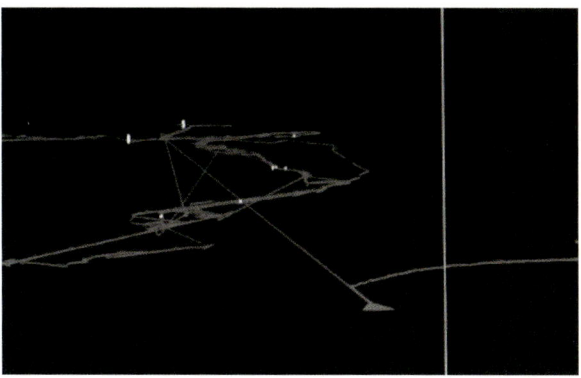

I have only just put out a crappy clip with 10 tracks, but the machine is working on a better version and I will update the post.

In a next step the idea would be to also import the Virtual London model and start visualizing the use of the urban form. Music by watermeron on mp3unsigned.com[102].

IDENTITY AND THE MOVEMENT OF STARS[103] On the news today is the newly discovered rotating dining room built by the roman ruler Nero about 2000 years ago. He reigned from AD 54 to 68. It seems to be an extraordinary discovery in terms of architecture, as archeologists have not seen pillars of similar size in any other ancient Roman structure before. The newly discovered structural pillars are about 4 m in diameter, the BBC reports[104]. The Telegraph[105] has details of the interior, writing "The hall is said to have had a revolving wooden floor which allowed guests to survey a ceiling painted with stars and equipped with panels from which flower petals and perfume would shower onto the tables below." The use of the structure was interpreted with the help of written sources describing such a rotating room. The dining area was described by the ancient historian Suetonius in his Lives of the Caesars. He wrote, "The chief banqueting room was circular and revolved perpetually, night and day, in imitation of the motion of the celestial bodies." See clip on Youtube[106]. The rotation mechanism is imagined to have been powered by streams of water to achieve the continuous movement. Observing the characteristics and the movement of stars and the moon has a long tradition. A lot of this has influenced human culture from the beginning and the identification with these elements has gone as far the assignment of the zodiac signs to periods of the year. In a lot of cultures the rules, king or Pharaoh are identified as godlike and to demonstrate such a relationship this dining room must have impressed the guests (Fig. 34).

The close relationship of these influential objects were a source of power, but also firmness, a great way to shape the desired identity. In an earlier post on the

---

[102] http://www.mp3unsigned.com/showmp3.asp?mp3ID=8095&aid=4172

[103] *IDENTITY AND THE MOVEMENT OF STARS*, 30 September 2009 20:50, movement, bodySpace, cycle, nature, identity

[104] http://news.bbc.co.uk/1/hi/world/europe/8282007.stm

[105] http://www.telegraph.co.uk/news/worldnews/europe/italy/6243961/Emperor-Neros-rotating-dining-room-discovered.html

[106] http://www.youtube.com/v/UR1pEWX68c4&color1=0xb1b1b1&color2=0xcfcfcf&feature=player_embedded&fs=1

Fig. 34 Image by
minasodaboy on flickr /
The panorama on the
Schlithorn. (http://
www.flickr.com/photos/
sawmillsergio/478097277/)

early Egyptian concept of the rebirth[107] this subject was explored. However, as we know from our experience the movement of these bodies is rather slow in comparison to the speed of human activity. Often we have difficulties adapting to such large scale movement. It is too slow to be recognized. To imitate the movement of stars or to be in sync with the rhythm of day and night the mechanism would need to be rather sophisticated, slowing down with the use of gears or similar. I believe it was rather a conceptual imitation and therefore would require the guests to understand the concept. Today a number of similar dining rooms exist all over the world mainly in famous locations, such as on top of the mountain—the Schilthorn restaurant Piz Gloria[108] in Switzerland location for the James Bond movie On Her Majesty's Secret Service[109]—the Space Needle's[110] restaurant in Seattle, or the restaurant on the CN Tower[111] in Toronto, As an element of identity it was and still is a great feature.

67   *BODY MORPHIC—THE CREATION OF SPACE*[112] It is tight in the morning in many senses, body and time are only two examples. Commuting is the result of this (Fig. 35).

Fig. 35 Clip by Indelible
Dance on Vimeo. (http://
vimeo.com/6523546)

---

[107] http://urbantick.blogspot.com/2009/07/birth-and-death-of-sun-daily-cycle-in.html

[108] http://en.wikipedia.org/wiki/Piz_Gloria

[109] http://en.wikipedia.org/wiki/On_Her_Majesty%27s_Secret_Service_%28film%29

[110] http://www.spaceneedle.com/restaurant/

[111] http://www.cntower.ca/

[112] *BODY MORPHIC—THE CREATION OF SPACE*, 5 October 2009 09:31, movement, time, bodySpace, commuting

The motion plays a big part on this as a summary of both time and body. Space could then be described as the movement, meaning that commuting actually creates space. Yi-Fu Tuan describes this nicely in his book Space and Place (1977), he distinguishes between space and place as motion and rest. I am currently writing on this topic for my upgrade and have come a cross a really nice movie clip to visualise some aspects of this discussion. Amazingly this video is very popular and I don't think all these fans are enthusiastic modern dancers, but commuters who feel represented.

DER MENSCH ALS INDUSTRIE PALAST—BODY MACHINES BY FRITZ KAHN [113] The late nineteenth century was the time of the machines and the industrial revolution was in full swing. Machines were everything and adored by a great number of people, including scientists (guess they are still today), architects and artists. Le Corbusier was a big fan of the automobile and the ocean liner. The fascination was very strong and in many of his projects references to these machines can be found. He even wrote: "A house is a machine for living in" (Times[114]). The phrase "Form follows function[115]", coined by Louis Sullivan, could also be seen in this context. Others were looking at the city, for example Antonio Sant'Elia[116], the Italian artist with his machine dreams of the city. Several movies pick up this topic, from Fritz Lang's Metropolis[117] to Ridley Scott's Blade Runner[118]. The idea of the city as a machine has replaced the image of a medieval city, that is dark, narrow, alive but out of control. The industrial city as a machine had an internal function and each piece was understood to be fulfilling a role, there is a very strong sense of control. To some extent this is still how the city is imagined, as a huge interlinked machine that someone is in charge of. Only in the very late century did new descriptions of the city emerge linking it to organic structures (Fig. 36).

During the machine period also the human body was subject to imagination as being a machine. It is the time when sport and sport competition became important and the training of the human, mostly male body, as a machine was convenient.

The artwork of Fritz Kahn falls into this period and illustrates the ideas beautifully. Metaphors have probably always been used to explain human body events. Phrases like "Butterflies in our stomach", "eardrums", "and eyeballs", the heart is "broken" or our "mind's eye". These mental visualisations can illustrate feelings to help make them better understandable for others, since they are very personal and experienced individually. The era was all about efficiency and industrial production was reaching very high levels of production. In this context is easier to understand how people have tried to push the human body. Suddenly, in context of the machine, the unpredictable aspects of the human body became a threat that medical science tried to overcome. But some other aspects of understanding of the body were important at the same time. The industrial revolution also introduced the human body

---

[113] *DER MENSCH ALS INDUSTRIE PALAST—BODY MACHINES BY FRITZ KAHN*, 6 October 2009 23:36, bodySpace, body, machine

[114] http://www.time.com/time/time100/artists/profile/lecorbusier.html

[115] http://en.wikipedia.org/wiki/Form_follows_function

[116] http://en.wikipedia.org/wiki/Antonio_Sant%27Elia

[117] http://en.wikipedia.org/wiki/Metropolis_%28film%29

[118] http://en.wikipedia.org/wiki/Blade_runner

Fig. 36 Image by Antonio
Sant'Elia, taken from wikimedia / perspective drawing
from La Citta Nuova, 1914.
(http://en.wikipedia.org/wiki/
File:Santelia03.jpg)

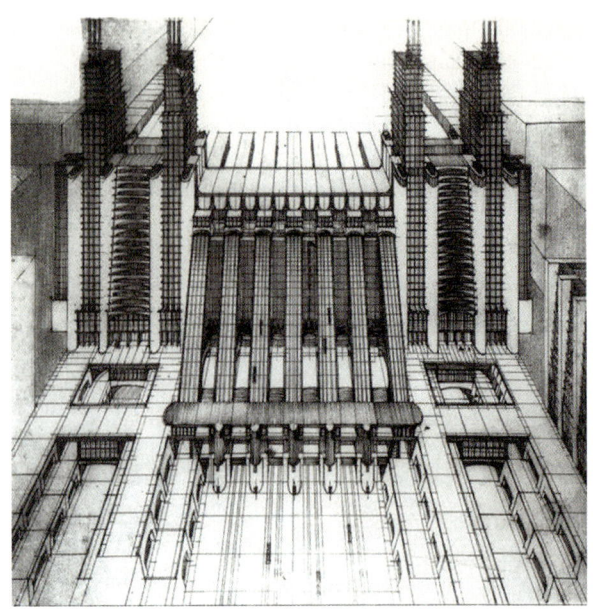

to new forms of movement. The train and the car meant that dramatically different speeds could be experienced and time and distance in relation to the body had to be newly defined. The big change was the fact that flying was now possible. The human body was able, with the help of machines, to fly in the air, just like birds.

69   *GPS TO 3D MAX—UPDATE*[119] In the 3D Max post[120] I wrote about a script to import GPS data directly into 3D studio Max. It was developed here in CASA with a focus on using it in the UK. Due to the interest of people in the code we decided to release it for you to use. It is now available to download HERE[121]. Richard, who developed the code, had to make a few changes for the released version. It has mainly to do with the transformation. As mentioned earlier it was developed with a focus on the UK, so the implemented transformation was from WGS to OS GB. For a general release this might not make much sense. So for now the released code is a simple factor multiplication on the Lat Long GPS information (Fig. 37).

For the quick import that should work fine, as long as you are not working on a Max model dealing with large geographical areas like the whole of Africa. For small scale models this should be OK. However, let us know how it works and what you like or what you'd wanted changed. We are also aware of a problem related to time interpretation. For example if you are using GPS Babel to write the GPX file it will have milliseconds in the format and that might cause the script to report a time interpretation error. You can change it manually in the code, two formats are imple-mented. I have just tested the new script with a rather large GPX file of some three month of tracking data, Max really has to work but it comes up with all the points.

---

[119] *GPS TO 3D MAX—UPDATE*, 23 October 2009 10:15, GPS, bodySpace, visualisation

[120] http://urbantick.blogspot.com/2009/09/gps-tracks-running-in-3ds-max.html

[121] http://www.casa.ucl.ac.uk/richard/maxscript/readgpx-wgs84-1.ms

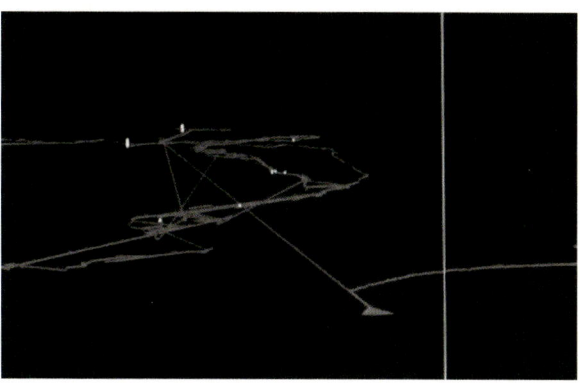

Fig. 37 Image by urbanTick / GPS track rendered in 3D Studio Max

70 *DER MENSCH ALS INDUSTRIE PALAST—ANIMATION*[122] I am currently very fascinated by everything machine. Well as you can guess or experience yourself there is very little that would not fall into this category, in terms of conception. However this might also simply be a preconditioned view through the glasses of the ticking ticking ticking blog topic with the idea of cycles and rhythms. Whatever it is, here is an update to an other post[123] on the human machine, referring to concepts picturing the body as a machine. Famously Fritz Kahn[124] stands for the most complete work of this idea.

However there is a beautiful project by Henning Lederer to animate the drawings of Fritz Kahn and bring them to life. It was produced as an university masters project, details on HERE[125]. Detailed project information can be downloaded as a PDF[126]. Henning also writes a very fascinating blog[127] on everything related to the topic of machines and animation with a string of beautiful examples. See clip on Vimeo[128].

---

[122] *DER MENSCH ALS INDUSTRIEPALAST—ANIMATION*, 28 October 2009 13:19, body, bodySpace, animation, machine

[123] http://urbantick.blogspot.com/2009/10/der-mensch-als-industrie-palast-body.html

[124] http://www.fritz-kahn.com/

[125] http://www.industriepalast.com/

[126] http://www.industriepalast.com/IP_Documentation.pdf

[127] http://machinatorium.wordpress.com/

[128] http://vimeo.com/6505158

Part IV
urbanNarrative

Urban Narratives of Time Images or the Drift of Alienation

Ana McMillin

The contemporary urban experience is constituted by time-images that are related and arranged spatially and temporally in a non-linear way. Defined as descriptions that include actions (Deleuze 1989), these fictional and non-fictional time-images are organized by the urban inhabitant as narratives.

Through experience, the dweller builds the narratives of the urban space, as events are reconstructed and put together by means of imagination and memory according to each individual. It is by means of sound and visual dreams, memory and fantasies that we build our urban narratives.

The map of the "Naked City" (Fig. 1) by The International Situationist group, published in 1957, introduced the individual's movement in the city as a collection of 'constructed situations', the Drift, and was the basis for an establishment of a psychogeography of cities. The group proposed strategies of wandering and travelling, without direction, between the "situations" in the city, for achieving individual freedom. The possibility of individual drifting is a characteristic of all unforgettable cities.

However, these strategies of individual drifting were used many times to create urban environments that 'appear to be public' and only aim to alienate the individual to the goal of seducing to purchase. Creating urban environments where individual freedom can happen and where urban narratives will flourish, but that are truly public and inclusive, is fundamental for urban regeneration and cities expansion.

In such urban environments a sense of place can be found and shared by a community formed of free self-conscious individuals.

We live in a world that is "not restricted to the experience of our motivity" (Deleuze 1989), and, in addition, it is influenced by the virtual experiences where we constantly blur the dimensions of space and time.

The public realm is the tangible space where urban life happens and where public and political actions have always taken place. But, because of our enhanced experiences, the spaces for actions have extended beyond the physical sets and the

A. McMillin (✉)
ACGRM, London, UK
e-mail: ana.mcmillin@gmail.com

F. Neuhaus (ed.), *Studies in Temporal Urbanism,*
DOI 10.1007/978-94-007-0937-9_7, © Springer Science+Business Media B.V. 2011

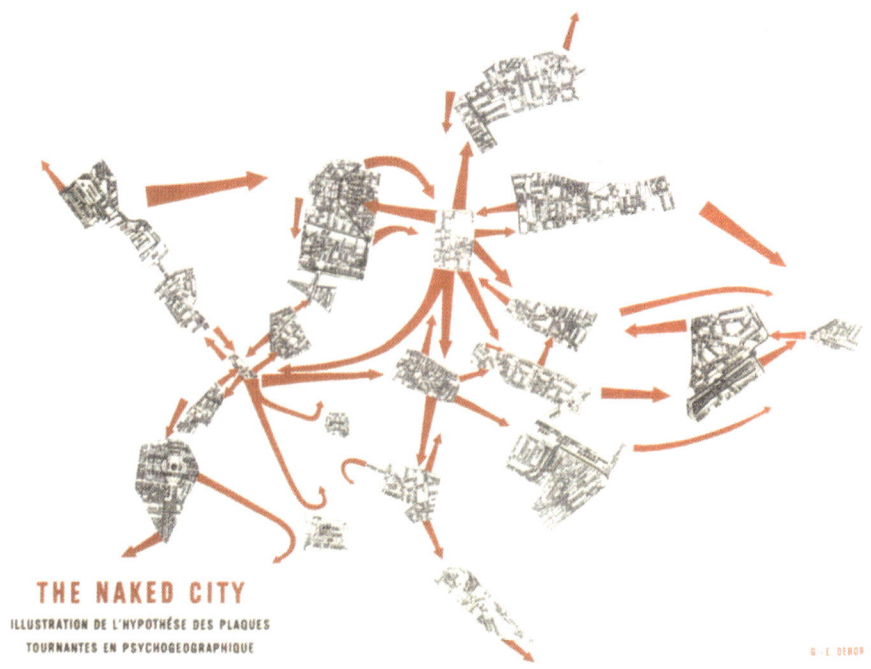

THE NAKED CITY
ILLUSTRATION DE L'HYPOTHÉSE DES PLAQUES
TOURNANTES EN PSYCHOGEOGRAPHIQUE

Fig. 1 Image by Guy Deboard, 1957 / The Naked City

actions themselves have also gone beyond motion, and therefore are no longer con-
strained by time and physical barriers. Urban life, as public life, has extended into
the virtual domain, influencing the individual experiences of the urban environment
and the mental construction of urban narratives.

Lynch's investigation in "The Image of the City", 1960, examined the mental
image that inhabitants construct in the course of their journeys through cities. He
concluded that people remembered "the sculpted" spaces rather then the undiffer-
entiated areas, and the detail or a special incident (Lynch 1960). The time-images
included in the contemporary urban narratives are the experiences of specific spaces
and those with the same meaning that happen in the comparable virtual public life.
These are spaces where the inhabitant can find a happening of place, in a Heidegge-
rian sense. This 'place' is defined as the nature of transcendental, unifying, limited,
enclosed and as the "place of being" (Heidegger 1951). In these places the Event
happens, as set and action become one entity, meaning that the happening can be
born from the set itself—many times the public realm becomes, in fact, the entry
point for a parallel city that only makes sense in an individual's narrative.

Places—urban places—are where we find ourselves as individuals and with
other persons and things. These are places from where we build our narratives, and
from where we appear to the world, and the world to us: a happening of place, an
experience in time.

Design of public space emerges as the creation of identifiable sets, where actions take place and time-images are recorded. In a moment of history where the ordinary is identified with the spectacular: a once banal coffee kiosk becomes a celebrated event.

Allowing for different individual experiences in an urban space is fundamental for the emergence of freedom, critical thinking and a common play. But the physical experience is no longer separated from the fantastic. As the media, advertising and signage invade the public domain and we travel through streets with music in our ears, that we individually choose, the experience of actually drifting is constant through the public sets. Paradoxically, drifting emerges as an experience similar to the alienation proposed in pseudo-public spaces of shopping areas, where music is also played to enhance the experience.

There are possibly no limits for acquiring happenings of place for the urban narratives. In today's urban life the connections between set, as the space, and the actions, as what happens in the space, are striking. The real and the imaginary are interwoven and "happenings of place" exist in a purely mental domain. The fanatical construction of urban narratives, by the contemporary urban dweller, is often an escape from the linear route from home to workplace. The virtual public life experience plays a key role in generating mental actions to animate the repetitive experience of the physical suburban sets that compose contemporary cities.

The design of urban spaces, as creation of physical sets for events, implies the actions that will be recorded there, whether real or imaginary. Functionally and socially mixed urban spaces are more capable of providing the "happenings of place" that will be remembered and from where the urban narratives are constructed.

But in the urban narratives, the individual no longer knows if the time-images are real or implicit, or if the set is physical or imaginary. Happenings are interwoven and mediated by dreams and fantasy to construct the urban narratives. But the narratives that liberate the individual are now the same that will detach him from the reality. Such is the drift of alienation.

References

Gilles D (1989) Cinema II – The Time-Image. The Athlone Press, London
Martin H (1951) Building, Dwelling, Thinking from Poetry, Language, Thought. Harper Colophon Books, New York
Kevin L (1960) The Image of the City. MIT Press, Cambridge MA

urbanNarrative

Fabian Neuhaus

71   *CYCLES IN URBAN ENVIRONMENTS*[1] This is an introduction to what URBAN-TICK is meant to look into. The topic has grown from my Masters thesis and is based on the AKA project—www.jafud.com[2]. It has since evolved into a research topic on its own. The following gives a short introduction. Cycles, rhythms and patterns exist in everyday urban life. There is something that gets us out of the bed in the morning, lets us squeeze into the tube at the same time as so many other citizens do, gives us a sense of time—lets us remember a past event and brings us back to bed after all. The same rhythm brings goods into town, exports products and consumes entertainment. It also scratches on the facade of buildings, changes usages and sets up trends. The city ticks somehow. Cycles appear in any part of life. Examples can be found in time, economics, and the environment and could be seasons, days, technology, events, life cycles, or even particular phenomena like rush hour or basic needs such as breathing, eating and sleeping. They are celebrated through rituals and used as a tool for categorization. In the first place, the main characteristics are, that it is continuous along a time axis, e.g. it could be described as the manifestation of time passing by. In the second place, its characteristic is that some sort or repetition occurs. The repetition is a tool for feedback. 'From the study of living systems and the science of cybernetics, we learnt about the importance of feedback loops to maintain a system. This information is processed along any cycle and constantly leads to an assessment. The continuum of the cycle in its repetitions gives a rhythm or a pattern to life' (Capra 1997, p. 155). This pattern is the subject of this research work with the focus on the urban environment. How do these cycles move people and goods through the city and how its rhythm interacts with the built surrounding? Many different cycles overlap at any point in the city. They are not synchronized and they interfere and disturb one another. This can be the source of movement and activity in urban life.

---

[1] *CYCLES IN URBAN ENVIRONMENTS*, 7 October 2008 12:23, topic, urbanNarrative.

[2] http://www.jafud.com.

F. Neuhaus (✉)
Centre for Advanced Spatial Analysis, University College London, London, UK
e-mail: fabian.neuhaus@ucl.ac.uk

F. Neuhaus (ed.), *Studies in Temporal Urbanism,*
DOI 10.1007/978-94-007-0937-9_8, © Springer Science+Business Media B.V. 2011

In order to understand this, I will try to find out where these cycles come from, how they build up and whether and how they transform into urban form. In my Masters thesis developed at the Bartlett School of Architecture in 2005, I started researching cycles in urban environments. The cycles I identified were grouped into three categories. The first group was natural cycles, containing rhythms such as day and night, seasons and basic human needs. The second group was activity cycles, working hours, weekend, rush hour and it also includes economical cycles, trends and so on. The third group is material cycles, containing everything from material life cycle to building life cycle and containing technical aspects such as refurbishment and concepts of revitalizing. As an overall aspect, cycles touch all fields relating to sustainability, from object to lifestyle to townscape. Referring to the three previously named categories, the second, on activity cycles, will be the main focus of the research. This leads to a focus on the interaction of humans and the built environment.

72   *EVERYTRAIL—TEST TRACK*[3] A new tool for the apple iPhone was released by the popular Everytrail[4] website. This free tool to track movement can be downloaded from the iTunes store[5]. It uses the GPS[6] technology built in to the iPhone 3G[7], but it also uses the cell information and Wi-Fi to record its position. The tracks can be saved locally on the device including pictures. It is possible to take pictures directly from within the application and they get included in the track data. There is the option to upload the recorded data directly, but even better is the option to store it locally and upload all at once. This saves battery power and therefore extends recording time. Developers suggest also to set the screen brightness very low. The main problem for tracking with the iPhone really is that the tracking application has to run in the foreground and it cannot be interrupted with the Home button or the Lock button. The Everytrail software does cleverly offer a "fake" lock option that prevents any input and disruption while the iPhone is in the pocked. This "fake" lock option looks the same as the normal iPhone Lock screen with a slider to unlock, but it is basically just from within this application and therefore means that neither of the two buttons (Home or Lock) on the iPhone can be pressed. Otherwise the "fake" lock will be interrupted. It only prevents touch screen input. I tested it on a shopping trip down Tottenham Court Road in London. Although the device was an old iPhone without GPS the record is pretty accurate and can almost keep up with my Garmin Foretrex 201[8] that I normally use (Fig. 1).

Once the track is uploaded to your personal area on the website (it is free to sign up here too) it is then possible to download the track as either KML, to view/use in Google Earth or as a GPX for use with any GPS software. This is a great option that not many other such products offer.

---

[3] *EVERYTRAIL—TEST TRACK*, 18 December 2008 11:37, London, urbanNarrative, tracking, GPS tracks, iPhone.

[4] http://www.everytrail.com/.

[5] http://itunes.apple.com/WebObjects/MZStore.woa/wa/viewSoftware?id=290954446&mt=8.

[6] http://en.wikipedia.org/wiki/Global_Positioning_System.

[7] http://www.apple.com/uk/iphone/.

[8] https://buy.garmin.com/shop/shop.do?cID=144&pID=257.

Fig. 1 Image taken of Everytrail webpage / Showing the uploaded track

NOKIA NSERIES VINE—THE WEB NOW MADE BY HAND[9] To introduce and advertise the Nokia Nseries, the company sent out four bloggers equipped with N82s, obviously, and tracks them on their website.

They blog and upload pictures and all the information accessible on the website. Visitors can closely follow the four participant's journeys. Their journeys are logged by the device internal GPS and accompanied by a mobile blog. There are also images and videos added. Examples from Jen in India. The project is called The Urbanista Diaries[10]. When accessing it now the project seems to have come to an end. It must have taken place about a year ago (very late blogging). It appears to be technically based on the Nokia SportTracker[11] application. A quick look at this application gives the impression of a not-so-much used offer. It should be online for quite some time now but in the London area there is only one publicly visible track log to find. Not much for an area of 8 m with at least 40% Nokia market share[12]. But the diaries are interesting because built on the experience Nokia has later in 2008 finalized their development for a public location-based-content-sharing platform Nokia ViNe[13]. Nokia offers its own maps, pre-installed, to be used on the device. The Maps contain way-finding options and can guide users through the environment. The developers at Nokia (maybe the marketing guys) must have come up with the idea to also add information but not only to receive. This is what the cool slogan refers to: THE WEB. NOW MADE BY HAND. So it is a manual job again! Nokia has created a web platform called Nokia ViNe where users can upload their journeys to share with others. It was introduced in late 2008 after a rename from Nokia LiveViNe to Nokia ViNe. For anyone wondering what ViNe might bear in meaning

---

[9] *NOKIA NSERIES VINE—THE WEB NOW MADE BY HAND*, 29 January 2009 12:02, mobile phone, GPS tracks, mapping, ViNe, Nokia, N82, tracking, urbanNarrative, Nseries.

[10] http://www.nseries.com/index.html?l=campaigns,n82,urbanistadiaries,home.

[11] http://www.nseries.com/index.html?l=campaigns,n82,urbanistadiaries,home.

[12] http://www.pocket-lint.co.uk/news/news.phtml/16715/17739/nokia-43-uk-market-share.phtml.

[13] http://vine.nokia.com/.

check this out: "A ViNe is any plant of genus[14] Vitis[15] (the grape plants) or, by extension, any similar climbing or trailing plant." Wikipedia[16]. The remaining question could be whether the name derives from the graphics for the product, ranking line with styled leaves, or the other way round? I would say this is good marketing!

The trip data is displayed on a (Nokia) map. The track data can also contain additional information such as images (the Nseries models are equipped with state of the art mobile phone cameras), video (the devices are capable of capturing videos—hello iPhone) and music (well they can play music too) played during the trip I assume. After clicking in to the ViNe page (it takes some time to load with my seemingly slow broadband connection) the first task is fiddling with the map and zooming in to a level that actually unveils some useful information. This appears to be a rather local level. But at the same time this level is not detailed enough and one would like to zoom in as we are used to from Google Earth or Google Maps. The level of detail is probably adjusted by the Nokia technicians and has to do with privacy and exact location identification.

I am surprised that the London area again (as with SportTracker above) is not densely cluttered with lines and colour (the project colours appear to be Pink, Blue, Green) "leaves" It really is surprising that there seem to be not a single track around Bloomsbury. UCL campus about 15,000 students and not a single Nokia Nseries ViNe user?

Images show up as "green leaves", videos are shown in pink and tunes in blue. Images are great to look at, video buffering is not very good and this make it horrible to look at. Very annoying to me was that the blue leaves, music tracks do not play the music. How boring is this? I am one of these persons who cannot memorize words, names have no meaning to me. I want to look at things or in the case of music listen to it. (This is most likely a copyright problem, I know, but what is the point of showing the information then?) Exploring the map is fun though! There are some points I think do not work very well but actually I think the whole project is pretty cool and stylish as Nokia graphics usually are! (Here used to be a ViNe widget, but it looks like Nokia is not supporting this any longer. Was a nice little app to display data from ViNe.)

74   *GEOTIME—FIRST STEPS*[17] Today I have finally got round to installing and trying the software GeoTime[18] on my computer here. Oculus[19] kindly offered a license to run some trials on with my data. It installed all very smoothly and the process is straightforward. I had to click through a few pages of the tutorial files to get the data to appear in GeoTime, but here it is (Figs. 2, 3).

---

[14] http://en.wikipedia.org/wiki/Genus.

[15] http://en.wikipedia.org/wiki/Grape.

[16] http://en.wikipedia.org/wiki/Vine.

[17] *GEOTIME—FIRST STEPS*, 10 February 2009 16:49, Plymouth, analysis, GPS tracks, plymouth365, time, GeoTime, urbanNarrative.

[18] http://www.oculusinfo.com/SoftwareProducts/GeoTime.html.

[19] http://www.oculusinfo.com/whatwedo.html.

Fig. 2 Image by urbanTick / Data Plymouth365, full extend using GeoTime

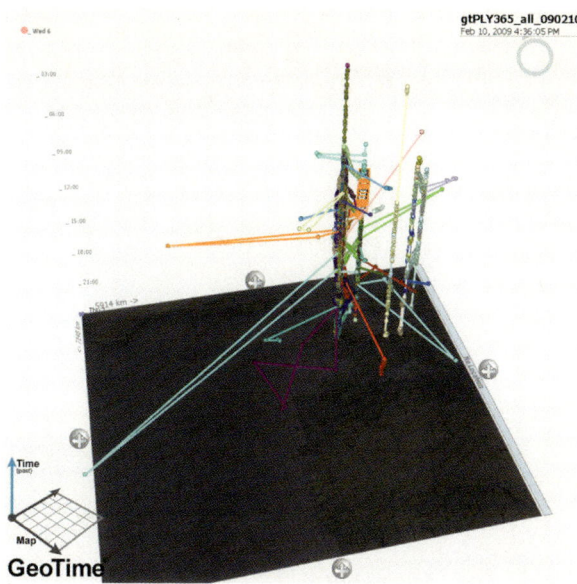

Fig. 3 Image by urbanTick / Data Plymouth365, zoomed in on the city, using GeoTime

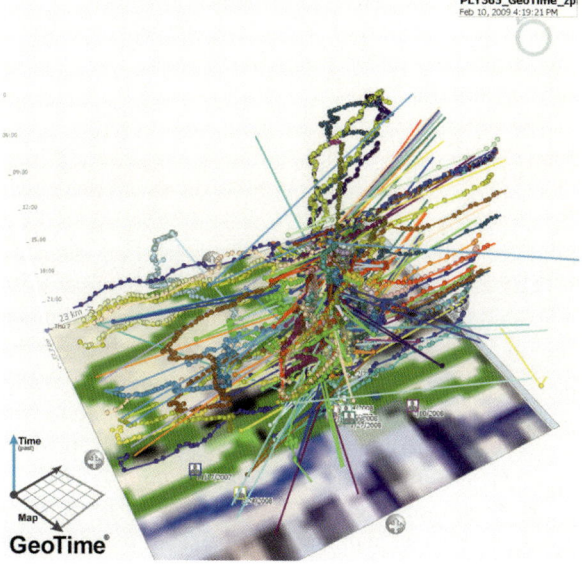

It is the same data set used in visualisations earlier, as in Plymouth aquarium[20]. The data was imported using Excel by following some advice from the tutorial pages. GeoTime seems to be very picky importing the KML files. I didn't get one of those to show. Exporting to KMZ works fine and looks good in Google Earth.

---

[20] http://urbantick.blogspot.com/2008/11/plymouth-aquarium.html.

Fig. 4 Image by urbanTick /
A slice of the day, data Plym-
outh365 between 10 am and
11 am using GeoTime

GeoTime®

The exported file is truly time tagged, this means the time feature can be used and the data can be replayed. Some analysis functions sound really interesting. I finally got the meeting analysis function to work. This would be very interesting, have to work on this (Fig. 4).

The isolating features are great, it is possible to only display data with certain characteristics, for example a time frame. There is more to come, this will occupy the next weeks to work through my data with this new tool.

75   *LOCATION OF I—TRACKING ART PROJECT*[21] Location of I[22] is an art project by Martin John Callanah. The artist is tracking himself live daily.

On the internet we can follow his moves and see what he is up to and where he is going. The website also has an archive and makes the past two years accessible to retrace the artist's movements. Commercial companies have only recently discovered that this sort of service could be interesting for customers, e.g. Google Latitude[23] or Brightkite[24]. The artist's motivation to work on the Location of I project was to be findable in both, the virtual world and the real world. He concludes: "I have become so findable and so contactable: I hide."

The technology he uses is purpose-built software running on Windows mobile on a mobile device with built in GPS. I am wondering how he manages the gadget's

---

[21] *LOCATION OF I—TRACKING ART PROJECT*, 13 March 2009 10:07, art, urbanNarrative, GPS tracks.

[22] http://greyisgood.eu/.

[23] http://urbantick.blogspot.com/2009/02/google-longitude-tracking-service.html.

[24] http://brightkite.com/.

Fig. 5 Image by Guy Debord
1957, taken from The Naked
City / The diagram showing
Paris as a series of islands

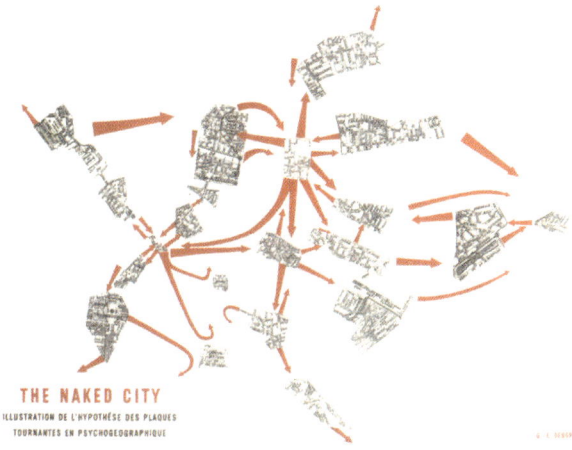

THE NAKED CITY
ILLUSTRATION DE L'HYPOTHÈSE DES PLAQUES
TOURNANTES EN PSYCHOGÉOGRAPHIQUE

battery life. The iPhone for example would not be capable of tracking for longer than a couple of hours without recharging….

So let's try to find out what the artist has done on the start day of the UrbanDiary project, that is 2009-02-05. On Saturday the 28th of February, I only hope he was not walking down that road!

DERIVE[25] The situationists aimed at developing a different method to explore the city. With phrases like "We are bored in the city, there is no longer any Temple of the Sun." (Ivan 1953 in McDonough, T. ed., 2002. *Guy Debord and the Situationist International*, no 1) they set out to explore the daily urban environment by "cruising" it (Fig. 5).

Guy Debord describes the technique of exploring in his "Theory of the derive" like this: "Among the various situationist methods is the derive (literally: 'drifting'), a technique of transient passage through varied ambiances. The derive entails playful-constructive behaviour and awareness of phsychogeographical effects; which completely distinguishes it from the classical notions of the journey and the stroll." (Debord 1956 in McDonough, T. ed., 2002. *Guy Debord and the Situationist International*). The illustration "The Naked City" was developed with these ideas in mind and represents bits and pieces of a map of Paris hold together by a number of arrows indicating connections. This view of islands within the fabric of the city not only represents random walks but also general daily experience we all make. The places we visit are very often not linked through experienced space, but rather through a spatially disconnected mode of transport, e.g. the tube or a busy bus.

MOTION DAY—CLIP SELECTION[26] The life-cycle is a concept to include parts of what this blog is about. There is a limitation to each subject and each activity. In

---

[25] *DERIVE*, 17 March 2009 09:54, psychogeography, memory, rhythm, identity, morphology, mapping, urbanNarrative, Paris.

[26] *MOTION DAY—CLIP SELECTION*, 29 March 2009 14:05, map, urbanNarrative, cycles, mapping.

Fig. 6 Clip by Johnny Kelly on Vimeo / The life cycle of a piece of apple (fruit). (http://vimeo.com/3715286)

many areas the cycle is something that spans over generations and as such an element of integration and continuity (Fig. 6).

The following clip gives an idea of this life-cycle with a great graphical language: In a web 2.0 society Google has taken over the world of location and mapping. With its free online map service and Google Earth application, most of the visualisations and animations of the UrbanDiary project are based on these tools. It is not only the context, the information, but also the style and the graphics that are dominated by the Google giant (Fig. 7).

We are more familiar with the graphical language of the Google Maps than with any local guide and special elements of this language are entering our daily lives. Just as the following clip visualizes, see Fig. 7.

78 *SPAIN GEOTAGED*[27] The MIT SENSEABLEcity lab produced a clip of a visualisation of geotagged Flickr photographs located in Spain. The visualisation covers

Fig. 7 Clip by Aram Bartholl on Vimeo / Real life Google Maps style placemark. (http://vimeo.com/1179879)

[27] *SPAIN GEOTAGED*, 1 April 2009 09:29, memory, tags, flickr, travel pattern, mapping, location, urbanNarrative, visualization.

Fig. 8 Clip by MIT Sensable City Lab on Vimeo. (http://vimeo.com/2614180)

a time period of one year and gives a good impression of which spots get photographed by digital and web enthusiasts (Fig. 8).

"(Un)photographed Spain maps thousands of these public, digital footprints over one year. As photos overlap in certain locations, they expose the places that attract the photographer's gaze. In contrast, the absence of images in other locations reveal the unphotographed spaces of a more introverted Spain." (by SENSEABLECity on vimeo) Through digitalurban.blogspot.com.

STOP MOTION MEETS MOVING[28] A really nice stop motion clip by mustardcuffins[29] on vimeo. It is titled "Still Moving" and described as "Stop motion Tilt shift meets tracking. What fun! Lots of photos…. this technique is an extension of my other video The Persistence of Vision. Shot in London with a Canon G9—no I didn't film it from a train or bike—no roller skates!" (Fig. 9).

Tracking here is not in the sense of location tracking as in the UrbanDiary project, but rather in the sense of tracking elements of orientation and navigation. This is

Fig. 9 Clip by mustardcuffins on Vimeo. (http://vimeo.com/3619284)

---

[28] *STOP MOTION MEETS MOVING*, 3 April 2009 16:50, stop motion, urbanNarrative, London.

[29] http://vimeo.com/user306916.

shown lovely by keeping an element in the focus while moving around it or passing by. It could be read literally as a visualisation of how a person perceives the city while moving through and in this sense it could be titled as a subjective (Google) Street View.

80   *ROUTINE AND TRACKING IN ADVERTISEMENT*[30] This week I came across two campaigns that caught my interest because of their language of communication. I thought, wow, the topic has now become very popular, if it is being used in ad campaigns. One is an article on men's clothes in the latest edition of the GQ magazine, German edition[31] (GQ 2009, April) and it plays with the daily routine of working people in the city.

The suite changes every day, but the location is everyday approximately the same. The story over five spreads implies that the guy is following a working week routine and passes this yellow hydrant in the morning on his way to work just before nine. It is a brilliant setting for fashion and works very well. Although I think the photographer could have played a bit more with light and weather. See clip on Youtube[32].

It somehow reminds me of this 1990s hair conditioner ad on TV, where the blond woman was portrayed on three different locations in three different weather conditions, but her hair stayed the same. I think it was a product by Schwarzkopf. A clip can be found here[33].

The second campaign is by enjoyEngland.com[34], advertising UK holiday locations employing Google Earth style location data representation (found in the Guardian, Saturday 2009-04-04). The story here is told on a satellite image sowing a costal town, presumably in the UK. Specific locations are marked with information on activity and duration, very much like the UrbanDiary project. The arrangement is used to tell the story of one particular weekend trip, but stands for what you could do with your next weekend. It then also points out that there are 112 weekend and bank holiday days a year, presumably enough time for one or two such experiences… How did they calculate the amount of days off?

81   *DAILY ROUTINE—COMMUTING ON THE BUS*[35] Most of us travel to work daily and most likely we travel in a mass of fellow travellers towards a destination likely in a inner city location. This collective daily migration also known as the rush hour is part of the city beat and pumps through the city's veins of streets like a liquid (Fig. 10).

The public transport plays a major role in this choreographed migration. Here in London its the tube and the big red buses that take the lot. The daily trip on a London bus as seen from the back, in a time laps animation by urbanTick for Ur-

---

[30] *ROUTINE AND TRACKING IN ADVERTISEMENT*, 7 April 2009 14:35, routine, urbanNarrative, location, advertisement.

[31] http://www.gq-magazin.de/coverfinder/0/0/0.

[32] http://www.youtube.com/v/fFVkkQ8x_cM&hl=en&fs=1.

[33] http://www.uralt-fernsehserien.de/Sound/Drei-Wetter-Taft.htm.

[34] http://www.enjoyengland.com/.

[35] *DAILY ROUTINE—COMMUTING ON THE BUS*, 11 May 2009 22:53, bus, transport, London, routine, cycle, timeLapse, urbanNarrative, rhythm.

Fig. 10 Clip by urbanTick on Vimeo. (http://vimeo.com/4610154)

banDiary. Shot with an iPhone using timeLapse[36], processed in Quick Time. Music "If You Are the One to Take Me Home" by thinkstandard[37] at mp3unsigned.com[38].

> Queen_Btch: just landed in London heading to the pub for a drink then im of to bed...so tired who knew hooking up on an airplane would be so tiring =S
> jvirgin: Just landed in Maui and I feel better already ... Four days here then off to vegas
> jchecrothers: Just landed in Dakar, Senegal... Another 9 hours n I'll be in South Africa two entire days after I left ... Doodles (*JUST LANDED—GLOBAL MOVEMENT USING TWITTER*, 13 May 2009 09:59, movement, twitter, urbanNarrative, animation, global, mapping)

Just landed... Twitter tweets like this are sent out to let the world know what one is doing. Previously the phrase was I'll call you mum, when I'm there...

Tweets with this phrase have been used in project by blprnt[39], to map global movement. Simply by searching the twitter posts and combining them with the home location from this person's twitter home page the path are generated. It is done by using the twitter API and MetaCarta[40] for Lat/Long information. To put everything together processing[41] is used. See clip on Vimeo[42].

The result is very intuitive and beautiful, global movement is this simple. It turns out that there is a lot of movement from the United States in this animation and this makes one wonder, large areas on the world map are not flown to it seems. Twitter movement is not equal to representative movement; the technology is not avail-

---

[36] http://www.xyster.net/timelapse/index.php.

[37] http://www.thinkstandard.com/.

[38] http://www.mp3unsigned.com/showmp3.asp?mp3ID=1949&aid=884.

[39] http://blog.blprnt.com/.

[40] http://www.metacarta.com/.

[41] http://processing.org/.

[42] http://vimeo.com/4600351.

Fig. 11 Clip by Eirik
Solheim on Vimeo. (http://
vimeo.com/2639782)

able to everyone. Old stats[43] from last year (twitter is not very open with its user numbers) show 40% of usage in the states and 60 in the rest of the world. Japan has a share of 36% and the rest of the 60% are divided almost equally by the western European countries. Nevertheless this animation is a great usage of this informal, I let the world know, tool.

83   *ONE YEAR IN 40 S—NATURAL CYCLE*[44] A one year project by Eirik Solheim[45] produced this nice time Lapse. It shows a nature scene over the period of one year, from winter to winter, including snow! A tutorial on how this was shot and processed is available on his blog[46] (Fig. 11).

84   *24 H WORLD AIR TRAFFIC*[47] A visualisation of world wide air traffic over a 24 h period. Amazing, how all these yellow dots swirl over the world map. The expected hotspots, the states and Europe as destinations show up. Although one would expect that we live in a 24 h society especially regarding air traffic, the day/night rhythm directs the number of flights. Flight activities pick up in the early morning hours and dies out in the late night hours. At the beginning one can observe how the flight traffic in the states slowly calms down and at the same time with the rise of the morning in Europe the number of flights picks up, enjoy! See clip on Youtube.[48] The animation was produced to be shown on the high definition 3D-Globe "Orbitarium" in Technorama—The Swiss Science Centre in collaboration with Institute of Applied Information Technology InIT, Zurich University of Applied Sciences, Winterthur. The data used is from 2008. There are plenty of versions of this animation; another one can be found here on vimeo[49].

---

[43] http://blog.twitter.com/search/label/stats.

[44] *ONE YEAR IN 40 S—NATURAL CYCLE*, 21 May 2009 10:44, nature, stop motion, year, snow, timeLapse, cycle, urbanNarrative, season.

[45] http://eirikso.com/about/.

[46] http://eirikso.com/2008/12/27/one-year-worth-of-images-give-some-amazing-videos/.

[47] *24 H WORLD AIR TRAFFIC*, 22 May 2009 20:56, rhythm, traffic, day, world, air traffic, cycle, urbanNarrative, night.

[48] http://www.youtube.com/v/ue8XXSQYyoQ&hl=en&fs=1.

[49] http://www.vimeo.com/1841471.

85   *BREATHING EARTH—LIVING AND DYING ON THE PLANET*[50] The beat as
a driving force has been used on this blog already a number of times. It refers to
a constant that imposes a rhythm on activities. There is the beat of the drums, the
scheduled beat of trains, tubes and buses, the beat of events and shows or the beat
of the shopping street with opening times and new trends. In all this we, as individuals, are swirled around in a big buzz but still we have and keep our own beat.
On to level of our personal body a number of elements beat in sync. There is the
heartbeat, the blink of an eye and the breath that keep us going. In the visualisation
breathingearth[51], these body functions are taken onto a global level. Not individually but collectively and in the form of births and deaths. By visualizing the starting
beats of the births and the ending beats of the deaths, a global picture of how the
earth beats individually might be drawn. How ever sad the death of an individual
and however joyous the birth of a new life, the striking thing in this is how continuity emerges. Animated as flashing dots the map visualizes births and death on the
planet in "real time". Every country on the map features with information on population, birth and death rates. In addition the amount of CO_2 produced by country is
displayed in black and red. Where does the data come from for this visualisation?
According to the producers, all data used on Breathing Earth is the latest available,
as of December 2008. Birth and death rates: 2008 estimates, from the CIA World
Factbook. Population data is based on July 2008 estimates from the CIA World
Factbook. When Breathing Earth was started, it used each country's birth and death
rates to calculate how much its population had changed since July 2008, and adjusts
its population figure accordingly. To calculate the total world population, Breathing
Earth adds up the population figures of all countries. It continues adjusting the various population figures as you watch it, each time a person is born or a person dies.
CO_2 emission rates are 2004 figures from the United Nations Statistics Division.

86   *LONDON DAY*[52] I have been out with the cameras last week to capture some of
the daily motion of the city. The result is a massive amount of pictures and a time
lapse movie. Taking time lapse pictures all day long can seem boring, but actually it
was rather interesting. I was using three cameras, a Canon G9 with a ChDK script[53]
to allow automated capturing and two iPhones with the timeLapse[54] application
installed. This setting already kept me busy looking after the three cameras in the
public realm. But I guess more interesting was for once just to stand there and watch
the scenery unfold and develop. Usually we are in a hurry and going from A to B,
where B is the focus (Fig. 12).

Very seldom we are strolling and enjoying the moment. While doing this I had
some time to just look at the places and the events and I never felt bored. I have

---

[50] *BREATHING EARTH—LIVING AND DYING ON THE PLANET*, 29 May 2009 09:30, generation, nature, personal, global, analysis, pulse, beat, world, cycle, urbanNarrative, rhythm.

[51] http://www.breathingearth.net/.

[52] *LONDON DAY*, 29 July 2009 12:31, timeLapse, stop motion, London, animation, urbanNarrative.

[53] http://chdk.wikia.com/wiki/CHDK.

[54] http://www.xyster.net/timeLapse/.

Fig. 12 Clip by urbanTick on Vimeo / London Day, a day in London shot as a timeLapse. (http://vimeo.com/5820181)

to admit that I went to some very exciting places. One location is around Waterloo Bridge and the London Eye and an other one is St. Paul's Cathedral. Both are busy places and offer great views. But both places are windy and a great lesson in time lapse photography is, always bring a raincoat. At the location you're standing it is always going to be windy and in the case of London (for once) it will be raining sooner or later. The point is you don't wana miss out on these dramatic clouds moving across the sky as they pour the rain over the city. Music Summer Hill by DANGSTA[55] on akmusicvideo.com.[56] And apparently there is a real story board to the movie above….

87 *MENTAL MAPS—AN OVERVIEW*[57] In the UrbanDiary Interview I am using mental maps to get participants to express how they navigate the space in the city. Mental map in this context means that participants are asked to draw a sketch of how they remember and would describe the space they are using on a daily bases. In addition to the technical GPS record this personal view has the focus on perception of space based on memory, experience, personal circumstances and current concerns. The sheet is prepared with a title and a box, but is otherwise blank. Participants are given complete freedom on how to draw a "map". The only rule is not to copy it from a street map or image. In addition they are asked to comment on what they draw, to record the sequence the sketch of their mental images of space is drawn. See earlier posts on the UrbanDiary mental maps here[58] and here[59]. On of the very famous studies using mental maps is "The Image of the City" by Kevin Lynch. It was carried out over five years and summarized in this 1960 book. Lynch says: "Every citizen has had long associations with some parts of his city, and his image is soaked in memories and meanings" (Lynch 1960, p. 1). It is a fairly sweet and stereotypical description with a lot of implicit hints to society but expresses

---

[55] http://www.akmusicvideo.com/profile/DANGSTA.

[56] http://www.akmusicvideo.com/audio/Summer_Hill.

[57] *MENTAL MAPS—AN OVERVIEW*, 6 August 2009 11:30, mentalMap, memory, identity, emotional cartography, flickr, visualisation, urbanNarrative, psychogeography.

[58] http://urbantick.blogspot.com/2009/06/ud-interviews-maps-and-schedules.html.

[59] http://urbantick.blogspot.com/2009/05/routine-part-01-mental-maps-of-daily.html.

that there is some knowledge and meaning in each one of us about the environment we live in and have to navigate through. It is something that is not about North or South, exact distance measurements or overarching, objective descriptions. Rather it is about personal experience, judgment and what is physically and psychically important to the subject. Lynch said, "Most often our perception of the city is not sustained, but rather partial, fragmentary, mixed with other concerns. Nearly every sense is in operation, and the image is the composite of them all" (Lynch 1960, p. 2). As early as 1913, Charles Trowbridge commented on how people have different sense of orientation. He concluded that there are two groups of navigators. Some people have imaginary maps in their heads centred upon the location of their homes. They are able to navigate a certain distance on familiar ground, but they would lose orientation in unfamiliar ground. The other group was more described as "egocentric" and orientated to their own position at the moment, with a better ability to navigate in unfamiliar territory. The map is just one form of expression of these personal memories and descriptions. But although it is called a map, it has two fundamental differences. It has no scale and no objective direction assigned to it. The drawing lives off its elements and may only stand in this context, e.g. there is no assumed direction pointing towards north unless the author of the map assigns it with an arrow. Nevertheless some features of a map can be borrowed by the participant, such as top down view, symbols, and so on (Fig. 13).

Other methods can be a description in words, both as a text or an interview. The Lego Serious Play[60] is another creative way to expressing memories and perception and a more hand on approach. David Gauntlett[61] from Westminster University is a researcher working with this method. The instructions to draw a mental map are simple. The focus lies on the content and not the beauty of the sketch, there is no right or wrong. The key is that the sketch is not copied from a map or image but rather drawn from memory. Lynch introduces the mental map to the participants as follows: "We would like you to make a quick map of … Make it just as if you were making a rapid description of the city to a stranger, covering all the main features. We don't expect an accurate drawing—just a rough sketch." (Lynch 1960, p. 141) (Fig. 14).

It is a rather quick exercise and does not require a lot of planning and thinking. In fact from my experience with mental map-making, there are three phases to the creation of the sketch. First is the skeleton phase, it contains most of the important information, objects, direction, names and paths. The second phase puts the flesh on by linking between memories with information and description. This will often trigger some more memories and makes the map rich and representative. The third and last phase is the beauty process, where no more important information is added, but rather the sketch is adjusted and critiqued. Mental maps have been used in a variety of spatial research. On one hand there are studies such as Lynch's with a focus on the built environment and a rather detailed perception description. On the other hand there are studies to focus on the quality of the environment more in terms

---

[60] http://www.seriousplay.com/.

[61] http://theory.org.uk/david/index.htm.

Fig. 13 Clip by David
Gauntlett on Youtube /
David Gauntlett explains
and illustrates his technique.
(http://www.youtube.com/v/
lLGQahsXjVM&hl=en&fs
=1&)

Fig. 14 Image by Maira
Kalman and Rick Meyerow-
itz / New Yorkistan, a New
Yorker mental map © "New
Yorkistan" Kalman and Rick
Meyerowitz, 2010

of feelings such as desire, stress, fear or happiness. Such a study has been done by David Ley[62] in Philadelphia in 1972 or a current similar project on fear in Los Angeles by Matei[63] (2003). From participants responds he was able to create a three dimensional surface to represent the amount of fear in the Los Angeles region. This is indicated with red and green colours. While working with children mental maps are also often used as a method of expression. For example in "Environmental fears and dislikes of children in Berlin and Paris" (2008) Olga Nikitina-den Besten looks at the absence of children in today's cities and investigates the highly specialized urban environment from a child's perspective of safety, fear and joy. The aspect of drawing should not be underestimated. With children, the reaction will ultimately be ok they like drawing so the method is appropriate, but adults often have more difficulties drawing even a simple sketch. Drawing is not something adults necessarily do very often, but children are expected to do some drawing (Fig 15).

An investigation into people's desire using mental maps is summarized in the book "Mental Maps" by Peter Gould and Rodney White. They are looking at where people would like to live. They asked people: "Suppose you were suddenly given the chance to choose where you would like to live—an entirely free choice that you could make quite independently of the usual constraints of income or job availability. Where would you choose to go?" (Gould 1974, p. 15). From the responses they generated a surface of desire for different areas in the world. Here an example of a 3D model of the UK, where the height indicates the desire. Clearly there is an increase from north to south (model viewpoint is in the north looking south).

To a great extent there is a lot of information contained within the mental maps on how people perceive space and ultimately how people create their space. The creation of space is something very personal. We can describe it as a very dynamic concept of temporal perception based on mood, concerns and circumstances. As a very abstract concept it could be compared to the creation of space in the virtual world as an orbit around subject in time and space. Space as in social space or individual space is probably not the same as Euclidean space, the way we think about space generally. If we describe space from personal perception and time point of view, the concept of space might be something very different from a the space as a box concept. To extend and intensify the research on mental maps you are all invited to contribute your own, very personal mental maps of the place you live. For this purpose is the flickr group[64] MENTAL MAP at http://www.flickr.com/groups/mentalmap/. It is an open group and you can add your sketch of the environment you live in. The instructions are outlined above by Kevin Lynch. You can contribute two types of maps, an overall sketch of the city, town or village you live in and a detailed description of your way to work and back home again. For both it would be great if you include a short description and it is necessary to geotag the image before adding to the group. Otherwise it will be rejected by flickr. The geotag is a rough location in the area of your sketch. I am thinking about putting all the mental

---

[62] http://www.geog.ubc.ca/~dley/homepage.html.

[63] http://www.mentalmaps.info/.

[64] http://www.flickr.com/groups/mentalmap/.

Fig. 15 Image taken from
environmental fears and dislikes of children in Berlin and
Paris by Olga Nikitina-den
Besten / Figs. 4 and 6 / A boy,
10 years, from Berlin and a
girl, 12 years, from Paris

maps together in a publication as a summary of worldwide perceptions of people's environments. A map of all the posted Mental Maps can be seen here[65]. There might not be much there at the moment but hopefully it will grow in the next few weeks.

88   *LONDON RUSH HOUR—BY CHRIS SEARSON*[66] Just another London timeLapse, this time with a focus on the London Rush Hour (Fig 16).

Chris Searson[67] has used a shutter speed between 0.3 and 2 s and a neutral density filter. Together this creates a strong sense of movement. It starts off really professional, sadly the ending is a bit of a fade out. But it's beautiful, I especially like the shot on Millennium Bridge towards St. Paul's with the evening sky in the background.

89   *MY WORLD MENTAL MAP POOL ON FLICKR—UPDATE*[68] The mental map pool[69] on flickr is slowly filling (Fig. 17).

It is not like everyone is dying to add a map, but still there are some really good sketches uploaded. On the map[70] it has dots on Europe and North America., and a text map of Dallas[71] by Austrini[72]. It was created for a tourist visiting Dallas and uses words to describe the lines and features literally, combining the thought and spoken about with the shape and physical form of features. There are some sketches of London commuters travelling in central London using mainly public transport, where the main arteries of transport lines clearly start showing up (Fig. 18).

---

[65] http://www.flickr.com/groups/mentalmap/pool/map?&fLat=51.5099&fLon=-.1211&zl=3&order_by=recent.

[66] *LONDON RUSH HOUR—BY CHRIS SEARSON*, 11 August 2009 12:31, movement, rushHour, London, urbanNarrative, timeLapse.

[67] http://vimeo.com/chrissearson.

[68] *MY WORLD MENTAL MAP POOL ON FLICKR—UPDATE*, 25 August 2009 08:10, flickr, urbanNarrative, mentalMap.

[69] http://www.flickr.com/groups/mentalmap/pool/.

[70] http://www.flickr.com/groups/mentalmap/pool/map?&fLat=42.157&fLon=-8.4582&zl=15&order_by=recent.

[71] http://farm3.static.flickr.com/2480/3740702592_623a674e98_b.jpg.

[72] http://www.flickr.com/photos/fatguyinalittlecoat/.

Fig. 16 Clip by Chris Searson on Vimeo. (http://vimeo.com/6017188)

Fig. 17 Image by Austrini / Dallas as a word map, unveiling experience and history. (http://www.flickr.com/photos/fatguyinalittlecoat/)

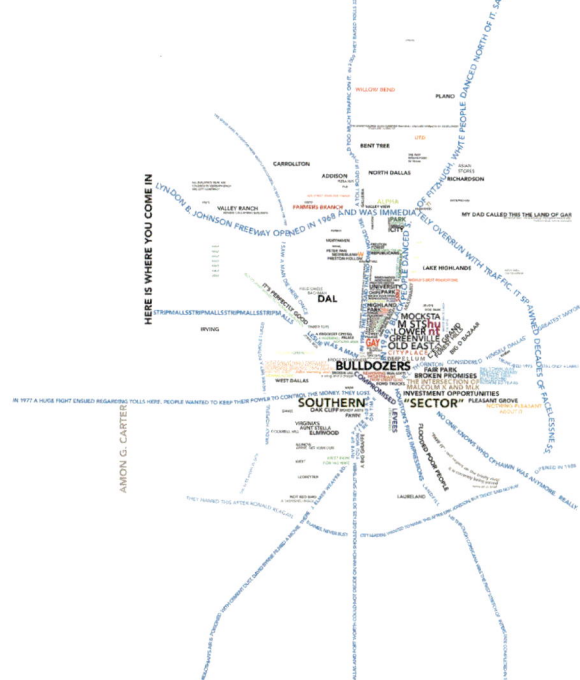

Fig. 18 Image by Sung-Hyun Jang from GISplusAR / Mental map of London. (http://www.gisplusar.blogspot.com/)

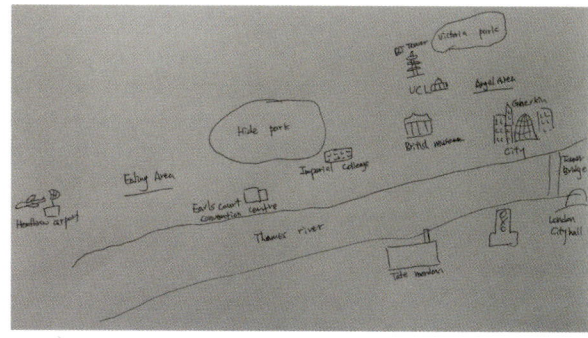

Fig. 19 Clip by Matthew Dance from Wiser Path / Mental map drawn on a tablet. (http://wiserpath. blogspot.com/)

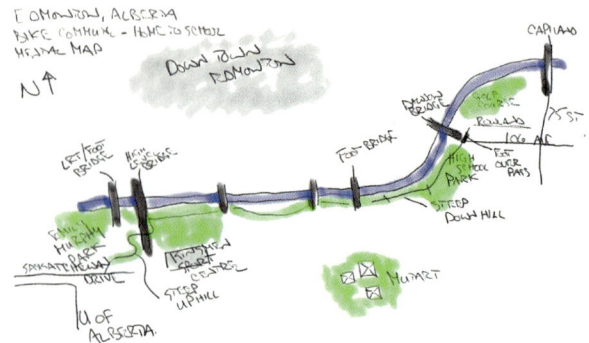

On the overall city sketches it is very interesting how the personal focus and experience shows through and information about individual memory is revealed. A cool clip of a map being drawn is put to the pool by Matthew Dance[73] (Fig. 19).

It is the view of his journey[74] from home to school in Edmonton, Alberta, Canada, captures with a tablet as he was sketching it. It obviously gives a nice sequence that would speak about how he is remembering the space. Just to showcase a few. Hopefully the pool will be growing a lot more and new examples from a lot of different places will be added. Why don't you add your city sketch and journey sketch NOW?

90   *SMALL WORLD—THE MAKING OF*[75] London Small World[76] was posted last week here on the blog. The 360 VR timeLapse processing has been very tricky. Some results were on the blog earlier this month, but it was a complicated workflow and the result has raised some questions and eyebrows (Fig. 20).

The main problem arises from shooting scenes with different zoom settings. At first the idea was to zoom right in to the mirror to allow for as much resolution of the focused 360 area as possible. This has become less and less important because of the fact that there are enough pixels anyway for HD use with 5 mp capture settings and I also realized that the frame and the background, usually the sky around the mirror make for a good backdrop. The first trial was run on the bases of a cutout version of the mirror set in a white space. The HD dimensions did not really matter, later with the requirements of the background the dimensions and the proportions became important or rather defining (Fig. 21).

Having this variety of zooms makes it virtually impossible to get an in sync version out, using the current scenes. Solution, going out a shoot some more. It has to be seen as an ongoing experiment and some conclusions have to be drawn from it. For me, this means, think about the workflow and requirements of each step of the work flow first! And then go out and take pictures. Well it wouldn't be fun anymore

[73] http://www.flickr.com/photos/gpmarsh/.

[74] http://www.flickr.com/photos/gpmarsh/3841799916/in/pool-mentalmap.

[75] *SMALL WORLD—THE MAKING OF*, 28 August 2009 07:10, visualisation, stop motion, London, urbanNarrative, smallWorld, timeLapse.

[76] http://urbantick.blogspot.com/2009/08/London-small-world-timeLapse.html.

Fig. 20 Image by urbanTick / Story board for the London Small World clip

Fig. 21 Clip by urbanTick on Vimeo / The London Small World clip as a timeLapse animation. (http://vimeo. com/6310201)

if we'd known everything beforehand, would it. The experiment is the exciting bit, isn't it. Anyway some more tests with a more elaborated workflow using Final Cut or After Effects to adjust and align the image content. The conclusion is basically that I will go out again and capture some more material. I will be using a stricter set of camera settings to make sure the raw material is easier to compile.

LONDON 365—ONE YEAR OF GPS TRACKS IN LONDON[77] This month I've already been in ondon for one year. So it is time to look back at my personal track record and see where I have been. Of course this goes in comparison with last year's PLY365—One Year Plymouth[78] (Fig. 22).

It is the same time span, but the amount of data has increased dramatically due to the use of the new device. Plymouth has been recorded with the Garmin Foretrex 201, whereas London has been partially collected with the Garmin Forerunner 405. The 405 records about a third more points, meaning that the data volume is at around 150,000 location points compared to only 60,000 in Plymouth. The drawing that appears on top of the London urban fabric is my interaction with the urban fabric by finding my way. Interesting how it acts as a memory trigger. By following the line I can bring up images in my mind about what happened there (Fig. 23).

---

[77] *LONDON 365—ONE YEAR OF GPS TRACKS IN LONDON*, 4 September 2009 11:58, movement, memory, personal, GPS drawing, GPS tracks, mapping, morphology, London, GPS, urban form, urbanNarrative.

[78] http://urbantick.blogspot.com/2008/10/plymouth365.html.

Fig. 22 Image by urbanTick / One year of tracking data recorded in London

Fig. 23 Image by urbanTick / Zoom in on the London Zoo ZSL, a frequently visited place

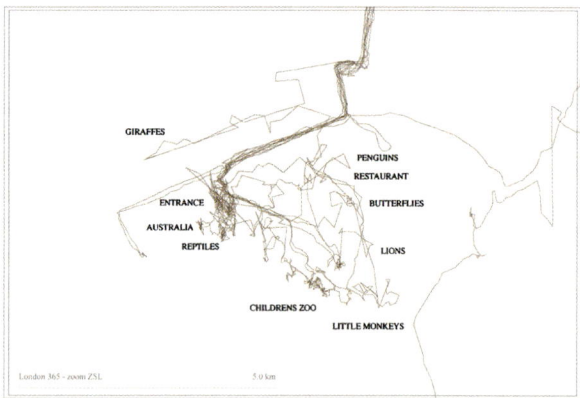

Interesting that I have only been on the north side of the river. There are visits to the Tate Modern, Waterloo Train Station or the South Bank, but that's about it. Already in my previous London record[79] the pattern was very much the same travelling between Kentish Town and Bloomsbury. By looking at the collection and comparing it to Greater London, I haven't exactly managed to see the whole lot. But I don't remember my year as being boring at all. It is more or less the same pattern that also has shown up in the UrbanDiary records, although they are recorded over the period of two month only. This longer period suggests that the emerging pattern is rather stable. Just updated the map, I have to confess that I missed part of the beginning dated late 2008. Other than me probably no one would have noticed anyway, because it is really hard to spot what is what. There are some particularly interesting areas on the map. One is Regents Park and London Zoo. I have been quite often to ZSL and those visits draw nicely on the map.

---

[79] http://urbantick.blogspot.com/2008/10/London-tracks.html.

Fig. 24 Clip by urban team on Youtube. (http://www.youtube.com/v/qWo9Cv6QOu8&hl=en&fs=1&)

GPS REAL WORLD GAMING[80] The urban environment has become a playground. Not only recently but together with the availability of mobile technology and location based information there was a steep rise of digitally supported large scale urban games. Since the mid nineties those sort of games have been developed.

First by geeks and small communities, then together with universities that had a computer science department. Nowadays the games slowly become commercialized. Only this week there was a large event on the South Bank here in London organized by Hasbro[81]. They unveiled a new Monopoly game called "Monopoly City Streets[82]" and uses the whole world as a play board. For this Hasbro has teamed up with Google (Fig. 24).

It is based on Google Maps and any road can be clicked and bought, provided you have enough money. A lot of the roads here in London have already been bought up and their value is rising. The road I live in is already at 1,600,000 something. Players can then also start building on the roads they own (it is a bit strange to build on the road, but I assume it is more of a technical problem).

So you get these castles, energy plants and high-rises blocking the road. But it looks funny. The task is to become the richest developer by the end of January 2010.

A more interactive game in the real world is fast foot[83]. It has won this year's best mobile gaming award. It is built around GPS tracking and rather simple. It is for four to five players and played in a 1 km radius. One guy is X and the rest of the players are the runners trying to catch X. One of the most popular eighties games Pacman has also a real world version called Pacmanhattan[84].

MAPPING THE EVERYDAY—MAPPING WORKSHOP[85] I have been invited for a workshop at University of Plymouth, Faculty of Art, School of Architecture. The topic is mapping and the aim is to introduce the students in a one-day workshop

---

[80] *GPS REAL WORLD GAMING*, 11 September 2009 10:30, game, urbanNarrative.

[81] http://www.hasbro.com/en_GB/monopoly/search.cfm?N=191&Ntk=All&Ntx=mode+matchall.

[82] http://www.monopolycitystreets.com/.

[83] http://www.fastfoot.mobi/.

[84] http://www.pacmanhattan.com/.

[85] *MAPPING THE EVERYDAY—MAPPING WORKSHOP*, 24 September 2009 08:00, Plymouth, urbanNarrative, presentation, mapping.

to various techniques. We are a team of four guest tutors; the series is organized by Bob Brown, Master of Architecture Program Leader. My contribution is under the subject of the narrative in the city and entitled "Mapping the Everyday—The Spatial Extension of Routines". This workshop provides an opportunity to test the ideas and concepts in the context of the UrbanDiary[86] project. One of the key concepts developed from the UD tracking project is the idea of individual space creation resulting in a continuous, spatial narrative[87]. Through the movement and experience of the body[88] one creates a story, which in turn is creating memory and identity, not on only for the individual, but for the city as a collective. As an introduction I will be giving a short presentation about the research work I have been doing over the past year.

94   *PLYMOUTH MAPPING WORKSHOP—PROGRAM*[89] To day we'll be mapping Plymouth. Well Plymouth has been mapped before, but I think it is a great location for this sort of exercise. It has such a complicated history with twists and beds and its identity is still strong. A large part of this identity is directly derived from its residents' self-image. Plymouth has always been a very strong-minded region and it still is. This has also something cheeky and irrational, which results in a weird place with lovely people. It is the end of the world, though, geographically, also economically and fashionably. I have to stress that this is not only to be understood in a negative sense. There are some very beautiful aspects to it. Take the great 1960s, 1970s, and 1980s buildings. These ugly grey monsters in the identity-lacking city make a great collection. Or take the hopeless reinvention of Plymouth with the Abercrombie Plan[90], a great piece of late modernist urban planning that was already dated, but has never really arrived at its location. Plymouth is still trying to implement it, although by now it has lost its head, its arms, its legs … But most of all you have to be there and feel for yourself. The atmosphere is incredible, it is one of the places with the most spatial misunderstandings and the result is literally breathtaking. I am looking forward to the results. Find the input slides that summarize the topics we will be working on Google Docs[91].

95   *THE URBAN NARRATIVE AS A TOOL—MAPPING WORKSHOP*[92] The mapping workshop down in Plymouth was structured roughly into four sections. The first three in the beginning were to explore the topic of urban stories and the fourth to actually invent an urbanNarrative (Fig. 25).

The first part was about lost and found objects. The participants were asked to bring in an object they had found on the familiar commute between home and university. It had to be something small enough to bring to university and something

---

[86] http://urbantick.blogspot.com/search/label/urbanDiary.

[87] http://urbantick.blogspot.com/search/label/urbanNarrative.

[88] http://urbantick.blogspot.com/search/label/bodySpace.

[89] *PLYMOUTH MAPPING WORKSHOP—PROGRAM*, 25 September 2009 09:30, mentalMap, Plymouth, mapping, time, urbanNarrative, presentation, body.

[90] http://www.plymouthdata.info/Plan for Plymouth.htm.

[91] http://docs.google.com/present/edit?id=0Aef57LqFKnJFZGZ6cDM4NThfODVkdzJkZm5nOA&hl=en.

[92] *THE URBAN NARRATIVE AS A TOOL—MAPPING WORKSHOP*, 2 October 2009 09:50, body, mentalMap, urbanNarrative, mapping.

Fig. 25 Image by urbanTick /
Selection of objects trouve
found by participants of the
workshop

that obviously did not belong to the surrounding it was found, an 'objet trouvé'. Everyone brought in something, wondering what we might do with this. Even though they did not know what I had in mind everyone had already formed some kind of relationship with the object. Already the fact that it was found on the familiar, individual commute created a sense of ownership supported by a curiosity. We got together and put all the objects in the middle and I asked them to speak about the found object and explain where it was found, speculate about who might have lost it and what its value is. This quickly got out of hand. The stories became lively and very creative. They even started to interlink as people quickly realized that the area the objects were found in is rather small and invented characters could have met on another occation. There where stories about lost shopping baskets, lottery tickets, loaves of bread, bits of wood and many more. Without intending to, we spent a good hour talking about Plymouth as a city and the everyday life (Fig. 26).

The main characteristics started to come through, such as the relationship to the water with the story of the lost lottery ticket combined with the sailor who was connected to the wooden plank. Or the aspect of university life and students in Plymouth as love stories over a bracelet, alcohol and a brick wedged under a railing. But also the social problems involving different classes and characterizing areas played an important role around the Marks and Spencer bottle. We continued by drawing and sketching the commute, introducing mental maps. While discussing the sketches, again participants realized that they actually described similar section of the city and started comparing their personal perception with some one else's description of the same space. Differences in time and mode of transport were identified.

After discussing Kevin Lynch's Image of the City we quickly mapped Plymouth as a whole using Lynch's five elements of path, node, edge, district and landmark. The third element was directly aimed at the real body experience, to actually go to

Fig. 26 Image by Colin
V. / Mental map of skating
between home and university

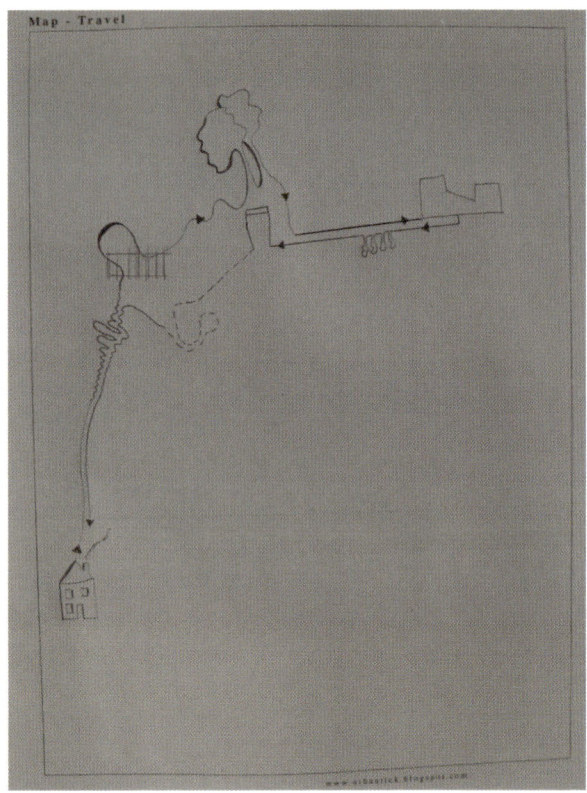

the city and physically experience it. The Plymouth After Life tour was perfect for
this. I took the students on a walk through the car parks of the city centre.

The design of the urban plan by Abercrombie is intended to welcome the visitors and residents with the big axis, either north south or east west. But in reality
everyone sneaks in through a little back door from the car park inside a block into
the shopping street. We walked up and down raw concrete staircases, across large
decks of car parking and through long tunnels or bridges. Because these service
spaces are normally not experienced in sequence it generated a strong impression.
This divide between back and front of the "modern" layout became apparent and
discussion sparked among the way. For the urbanNarrative part of the afternoon the
participants were sent of in groups to find the location of their story with the help of
a GPS device. In a visualized short story they had to reveal the location. The story
was made up of the objects from the morning and the invented characters. It was a
great day and good fun. I was myself surprised by the power of stories once more.
This playful approach to describing and mapping the spatial aspects of the environment proofed valuable in many ways. Not only in the aspect of character, body and
location, but also in terms of time, atmosphere and sequence.

Fig. 27 Image by devine74 / Mapping his commute from home to work

MENTAL MAP—FLICKR POOL[93] The online pool at flickr collecting mental maps from all over the world is starting to take shape. I have just added some examples drawn at the mapping workshop[94] down in Plymouth (Fig. 27).

The pool has grown quite a bit and it is featuring mental maps from China, Canada, America, United Kingdom and Belgium.

I would also like to showcase some examples here. First there is the sketch by devine74[95] with very detailed drawn landscape and building features. And then there is also the beautiful map of a commute focusing on sound with the audio experience along the way (Fig. 28).

There is a big difference between the morning and the evening journey. This is illustrated through two sets with each a slightly different focus.

As before you can also join in and share you map sketch on: http://www.flickr.com/groups/mentalmap/.

---

[93] MENTAL MAP—FLICKR POOL, 9 October 2009 09:20, flickr, urbanNarrative, mentalMap.

[94] http://urbantick.blogspot.com/2009/09/plymouth-mapping-workshop-program.html.

[95] http://www.flickr.com/photos/43255270@N07/.

Fig. 28 Image by Tommy
B / Mapping the way in and
back out

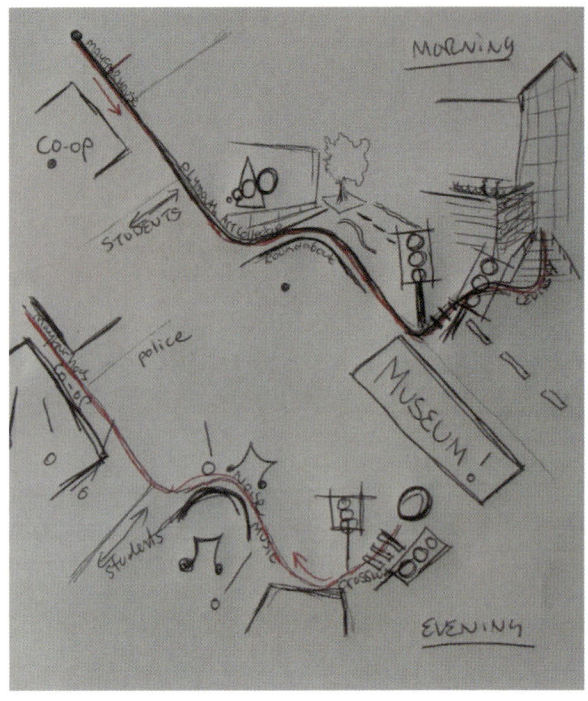

97   *MOUSE IN MATRIX—HOW MENTAL MAPS ARE MADE*[96] How do we create
mental maps? In a story the New Scientist[97] reports new development in the area of
brain studies. The research was presented in nature[98] in September 2009.

Scientist have long speculated even though he involved brain areas have long
been identified, but how it happens was still subject for debate. Apparently the region in the brain is called the hippocampus. The problem so far was that recording
the activity required the subject's head/brain needed to remain fairly stable and this
is not possible for normal navigation. The New Scientist[99] reported earlier initial
findings related to the brain's spatial navigation activities. Reportedly after playing
Quake II researchers came up with the idea of using a virtual reality surrounding
for the experiment to record brain activity while navigating. Researchers at Princeton University developed a Quake based VR environment for rodents as well as a
special navigation ball on which the rodents could run (in a stabilizing harness to
keep them relatively still) and navigate the VR maze. Basically they created a mini

---

[96] *MOUSE IN MATRIX—HOW MENTAL MAPS ARE MADE*, 20 October 2009 09:01, navigation, orientation, urbanNarrative, mentalMap, virtual world.

[97] http://www.newscientist.com/article/mg20427304.900-matrix-for-mice-probes-how-mental-
maps-are-made.html.

[98] http://www.nature.com/nature/journal/v461/n7266/full/nature08499.html.

[99] http://www.newscientist.com/article/dn16751-brain-scan-reveals-memories-of-where-youve-
been.html.

IMAX for the mouse, reports wired.com[100]. They were the able to scan the mouse's brain activity as it learned to navigate the maze. Some treats along the way helped I guess. However, there is little information on what they have actually found. At the moment the main interest seems to be the technique how they used to record the brain activity, so mainly the VR for mice set-up. It looks fancy though. See clip on the New Scientist webpage[101]

In these experiments scientists are not really interested in how and what the brain records and how participants (in this case mice) actually understand the maze or the environment they have navigated. Here they simply assume that this is taking place. They are talking about a mental map but are just looking at activity as 'space' is navigated. To some extent this is only implicit looking at how the memory and sense of place is building up. History is always biased by the fact that it is in the past and it is remembered back from a present state that might be rather different from the past and this influences the way the memory is recalled. Some sort of processing is taking place and the result is a weighted remembering. Through this history has a present relevance, but is not 'true'. In this respect the mental map as a review of the maze experience is probably a rather different case than the activity of navigating it. Let's wait and see how scientist interpret the rodent's sketch of the maze….

98   *APOCALYPTICA AND THE NEW CITY OF SPACE*[102] Last weeks the most disturbing science news headline was "How the city hurts your brain[103]" circulating as new research that proves the evil of cities. The original article can be found at the Boston Globe[104]. It all starts with a very innocent introduction where the author says: "The City has always been an engine of intellectual life, from the eighteenth-century coffeehouses of London, where citizens gathered to discuss chemistry and radical politics, to the Left Bank bars of modern Paris, where Pablo Picasso held forth on modern art. Without the metropolis, we might not have had the great art of Shakespeare or James Joyce; even Einstein was inspired by commuter trains." From this point it goes downhill. From spreading cholera to the argument that the before named artists eventually moved out of the city, concluding " … (the city) it's also a deeply unnatural and overwhelming place" Well that is a statement, DEEPLY UN-NATURAL! However, as we try to grasp the extend of the devastating news, the authors are quick with analysis and of course solution. It is all down to the city affecting the brain and a few minutes on the busy street will blow your memory and you start suffering from reduced self control (what does that mean?). Again with a very pointed argument, "that's why Picasso left Paris". The excuse comes in the form of

---

[100] http://www.wired.com/wiredscience/2009/10/mouse-virtual-reality/.

[101] http://brightcove.newscientist.com/services/player/bcpid2227271001?bctid=44892629001.

[102] *APOCALYPTICA AND THE NEW CITY OF SPACE*, 30 October 2009 10:09, sustainability, history, city, analysis, morphology, shapingCities, urbanNarrative, culture, theory.

[103] http://www.boston.com/bostonglobe/ideas/articles/2009/01/04/how_the_city_hurts_your_brain/.

[104] http://www.boston.com/bostonglobe/ideas/articles/2009/01/04/how_the_city_hurts_your_brain/.

the acceptance that "The mind is a limited machine" while still concluding this, the first solution comes in the form of "One of the main forces at work is a stark lack of nature". I am aware that this is not actually a solution, but rather another analysis or hypothesis, but in its tone directly implies to be a solution. And it does not stop there it goes straight through the wall with the sledgehammer solving ALL! the problems: "...that hospital patients recover more quickly when they can see trees from their windows, and that women living in public housing are better able to focus when their apartment overlooks a grassy courtyard". WOW, now I feel much better and I am convinced we live in a better world. I do actually very much agree with the authors on the first point. The fact that this kind of research comes exactly in time with the news (and of course the media coverage and interpretation) that now over 50% of the world's population live in cities. Unfortunately it dives right back down with a sweet but unrealistic naive world view of: "For a species that evolved to live in small, primate tribes on the African savannah, such a migration marks a dramatic shift. Instead of inhabiting wide-open spaces, we're crowded into concrete jungles, surrounded by taxis, traffic, and millions of strangers." I think I stop here, because the article goes on for another four pages, I hope I have missed the point of the article and if some of you read it all through, please let me know what I missed. The 'leave a comment' field can be found at the end of the post. But actually there is another reason to stop at this point, because this one point is very interesting and important. We are living in a mainly urbanised world. Most of us live in urban areas and rising. The UN predicts some 70–80% by 2050. "The United Nation Population Fund, UN agency, says in a new report that humanity will have to undergo a 'revolution in thinking' to deal with a doubling of urban populations in Africa and Asia. The UN continues to say that the number of people in African and Asian cities will grow by 1.7 billion by the year 2030. And worldwide, the number of city dwellers will reach five billion or 60 per cent of the world's population (citymayors[105])" 'Revolution in thinking' is probably a more appropriate suggestion than to point out how bad our (western) cities are. To call them Western city is important, because this is what I believe the above article is referring to. Conditions in other 'urban' areas in the world are dramatically different from what Westerners call 'a city'. And I mean, to dig out a cholera example is pathetic. According to Wikipedia[106] the first cholera pandemic reached London and Paris in 1832, a second one in 1849, the third Europe skipped, fourth in 1854 and a fifth in 1866 that was locally very much condemned as by then London was just about to finish its new water and sewage system (I guess it is still the same, but that is another topic). However you can see that since 1866 dramatic chances in the urban environment were introduced. I am aware that I also imply a lot here, but to bring it across in a similar style: the city was a much worse place. (We all know that this is a very difficult way to express thought about historical events and while being aware of the implications of the distorted and constructed past as seen from the present. It might be much more complex, but we'll keep things simple here for today.) To come back to the new challenge of the dramatic growth in urban population—a doubling of

---

[105] http://www.citymayors.com/society/urban-population.html.

[106] http://en.wikipedia.org/wiki/Cholera#History.

the city population in Asia and Africa—another example might be of interest. Thinking back to the last urban crisis this latest and now upcoming reaction very much reminds me of Haussmann's[107] renovation of in Paris or Ebenezer Howard with the Garden City. In fact both came after the cholera pandemics. I am pretty sure, actually I was only waiting for the first such news to appear, that we will see a lot of reactions to the 'city problem' coming down a similar route as the article quoted in the beginning of this post. It is all bad and we have to reinvent to solve it. Urban designers will be very quick to jump to Howard's idea of the Garden City to have a ready made solution. Someone will dig it out (Fig. 29).

However to make it clear, I am not playing down the urgent and extend of the raising question. In the contrary, it is an urgent matter, especially because the urban planning profession in general and urban design and architecture (I add them here because they all think they can do both anyway) in particular is in an identity crisis with no consistent concepts available at present. The only thing that buzzes around is sustainability, but it's got no content to it. In an article on io9[108] Chanda Phelan[109] presents how apocalyptic stories have changed in the past 200 years. She explains "It's not the idea of Ending itself that has faded—that will be around until we are actually mopped off the face of the Earth. It's the actual moment of disaster, the blood and guts and fire, that has been

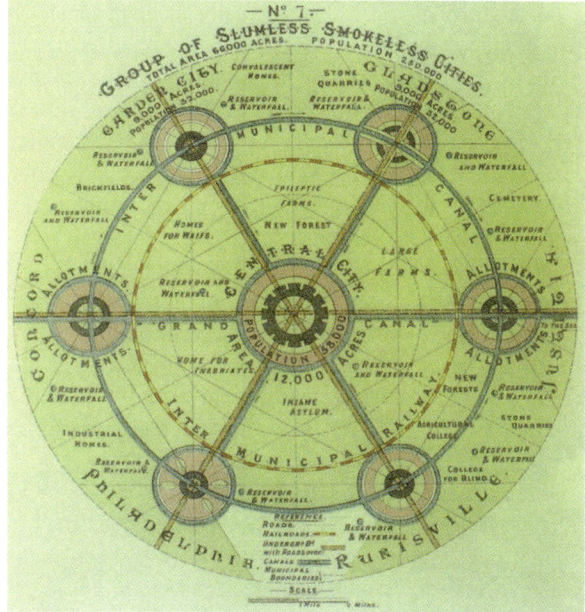

Fig. 29 Image by Ebenezer Howard (1850–1928) via Wikimedia commons / As published in "Garden Cities of tomorrow", Sonnenschein publishing, 1902. (http://commons.wikimedia.org/wiki/File:Garden_City_Concept_by_Howard.jpg#filelinks)

---

[107] http://en.wikipedia.org/wiki/Haussmann%27s_renovation_of_Paris.

[108] http://io9.com/5392430/research-reveals-that-apocalyptic-stories-changed-dramatically-20-years-ago.

[109] http://phnuggle.wordpress.com/.

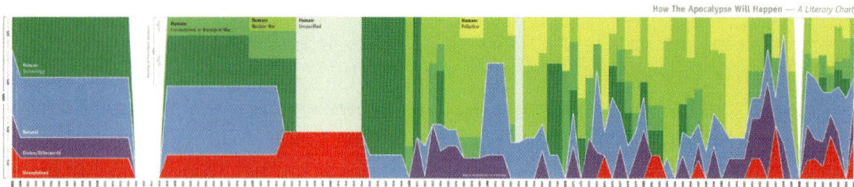

Fig. 30 Image by Stephanie Fox / How the apocalypse will happen—a literary chart

losing ground in stories of the End. Post-apocalyptic fiction is a 200-year-old trend, and for 170 of those years, the ways writers imagined the end were pretty transparently a reflection of whatever was going on around them—nuclear war, environmental concerns, etc. In the mid-1990s, though, everything just turned into a big muddle. Suddenly, we'd get a post-apocalyptic world whose demise was never explained. It was just a big question mark." And she also points out that actually it was never about the end, but the new beginning. However she analyses that in the last 30 years there has been a decreasing interest in the why and how of the end, very often simply assuming that there was an end. Presumably, from my reading of it, the apocalypse was never about, it actually ends, but about narrating a sin or something stylised 'problematic' to actually urge people to change something in the present. Implying "if you don't behave now, something disastrous might, could possibly, eventually, maybe happen". And in this sense skipping this part of the apocalypse is indeed a very dramatic change (Fig. 30).

In this sense the attitude to the posed urban growth question would be, let's skip the growth, the infrastructure demand, logistics, flows, identity, morphology, material, organisation, atmosphere, form, transport, colour, work, resource, governing, social, knowledge, communication, finance, and so on question and just build a New Cities for some 80 million people or maybe better a set of Garden cities, each with some 58,246.1 residents? So what to do?

99   *RELOCATION OF CONCEPTS AND IDENTITY*[110] A beautiful short film by Peter Kidger and ex Bartlett students—'the Berlin infection'—is a mixture of high resolution still photographs and 3D animation. It is an intriguing tale of identity and the assigning of it to particular objects of the urban context. He produced it as part of his postgraduate diploma in architecture in the unit 15 at the Bartlett School of Architecture in 2006. On his youtube page you can find some more animations of this kind (Fig. 31).

100   *THE SNAIL ON THE SLOPE—A NARRATIVE IN STRUCTURES AND LINES*[111] The narrative is currently a big topic in the construction of my research project. The creation of the narrative through activity as a constant process, currently guides the conception of the study. The idea really is to get to grips with the creation of time and space as temporal phenomena. If we employ the narrative as the structural element this might become possible.

---

[110] *RELOCATION OF CONCEPTS AND IDENTITY*, 3 November 2009 09:15, animation, identity, architecture, London, urbanNarrative, culture, urban.
[111] *THE SNAIL ON THE SLOPE—A NARRATIVE IN STRUCTURES AND LINES*, 5 November 2009 09:23, animation, urbanNarrative.

Fig. 31 Clip by Peter Kidger on Youtube. (http://www. youtube.com/v/LrTzSwU1rw 4&hl=en&fs=1&)

This has to be seen in the context of the UrbanDiary tracking project and the time-space aquarium as the approach in time geography. The narrative here describes the time-space aquarium as a whole, containing similar trajectories. But since a number of narratives can fit in to a story it allows for the combination of multiple time-space aquariums with different time and space parameters. The narrative in a sense is purely structural and simply describing the way the body of content is organised. It is organised along an inner coherence. See clip on Vimeo[112]

As a visualisation of the concept 'the snail on the slope' is very interesting, since it works with a strong focus on the form aspect of the narrative. The movie is actually based on a novel and the sequences of processes are generate for each chapter. The novel was initially written by the Strugatsky brothers. For the visualisation, processing was used.

THE ORIGIN OF ARCHITECTURE—NEST BUILDING[113] Architectural anthropology[114] is described as: "At the end of the sixties, in the course of the so-called 'crisis of modern architecture' a movement of architectural theoreticians greatly stimulated by Amos Rapoport's 'Built Form and Culture' (1969) began to widen their horizon into the ethnology of architecture" (Egentre[115] 1990). In this sense it is research into the history of architecture. Together with an illustration of five lines of architectural evolution it is presented as a comprehensive body of work into the understanding of how architecture developed into a technological sophisticated science. But essentially it argues that humans (even great apes do) always had an urge to adjust the environment to suit specific needs. Interesting to me seems the argument that architecture can be traced back to the nest building of great apes. However this will definitely be challenged with questions around design and the idea of a discipline of architecture as opposed to individual temporal structures. However this is probably an argumentation of modernist understanding of the 'plan'. Nevertheless I would argue that between temporal structures of 'night beds' constructed by apes and a detailed concept of space and time lies a big gap. It might

---

[112] http://vimeo.com/6654322.

[113] *THE ORIGIN OF ARCHITECTURE—NEST BUILDING*, 15 November 2009 23:52, animals, architecture, biology, shapingCities, urbanNarrative.

[114] http://en.wikipedia.org/wiki/Anthropology.

[115] http://home.worldcom.ch/~negenter/031AA_Tx_E.html.

Fig. 32 Image taken from creative class / The bird nest by Herzog and de Meuron at night. (http://www.creative-class.com/creative_class/tag/olympic-stadium/)

be down to a few million years of evolution, I don't know. The argument is logical, however I would point out that a lot of species build nests[116] or construct temporal structures. Even more beyond the nest usually animals have a clear concept of space and the idea of 'owned space' in the sense of a territorial behaviour. This territory[117] is marked for example by a blackbird singing or a cat spraying. In this context the argument might look different. For the argumentation and presentation of architectural projects a lot of leaps a crazy combinations are undertaken. And recently nests have seen a rise in popularity, but I have not heard H&dM arguing for their Olympic stadium that the shape is the origin of architecture. However it would fit (Fig. 32).

---

[116] http://en.wikipedia.org/wiki/Nest.

[117] http://en.wikipedia.org/wiki/Territory_%28animal%29.

Part V
LocationInformation

Mental Maps: The Expression of Memories and Meanings

Matthew Dance

What did the first maps look like? Were they created by a nomadic people out of found materials and left on the ground when the people moved on? Or, were these maps found only in the heads and imaginations of those travelling over a landscape? One way to imagine how ancient peoples navigated and experienced a landscape is to reflect on how we understand and communicate geographic space in our day-to-day lives. How do we navigate from point 'A' to 'B'? How do we communicate that knowledge and understanding; and to whom do we communicate?

Nomadic societies had a social network that was most likely small, consisting of those few people encountered on a day-to-day basis. Oral communications within this small group, coupled with found objects, enabled a mapping exercise to occur where individual experience was disseminated to the group. Over generations their maps developed a rich depth of history where locations became associated with events, and inaccuracies were weeded out by fresh eyes telling the story of location, describing the sense of a place with time and space fusing into one meaning. A complex tapestry of events and locations permeated the collective memories of those who relied on the land for everything.

The maps that were held within a community represented a collective mental map disseminated through "…oral traditions with all knowledge stored in memory transmitted generation to generation" (Davis 2009). Individuals possessed an understanding of the landscape as a reflection of their unique experience. By communicating that meaning to the community, and across generations, the individual meaning of place was fused with all other individual experiences and understanding. The aggregate map that resulted from this process represented a collective experience and interaction with an environment. For instance, Inuit hunters are able to draw detailed maps of their travels and hunting locations. Each important location has layers of understanding, including what species can be found there and when they were caught, and under what conditions. Each location is connected to the other through a web of routes that vary depending on the weather, and time of year. Furthermore, each hunter posses this knowledge, and contributes to the pool of un-

M. Dance (✉)
WEB Mapping Consultant, Edmonton, CA
e-mail: matt@matthewdance.ca

F. Neuhaus (ed.), *Studies in Temporal Urbanism,*
DOI 10.1007/978-94-007-0937-9_9, © Springer Science+Business Media B.V. 2011

derstanding by talking about their individual experiences. As such, the map creation process encompasses three vital tools—a social network, a collaboration process, and a cartography—a way of representing a cultural or physical attributes on a map.

Fast forward several millennia to find a generation of people who need physical maps to navigate a manufactured landscape. The process of map creation has shifted from a cultural need to a professional activity; the domain of mapping is no longer the occupation of everyday people. As with farming and many other activities, the production of maps is completed by someone who has a technical understanding—cartographers and GIS technicians. They act as our interpreters, defining how a road, a building, a lake or mountain is represented on a map. We still have a mental map, and a social network, but we have lost the collaboration and mapping tools to those who have specific training. Our mental maps have become secondary source of information to professional, authoritative, maps; something to be drawn on a napkin or envelope to communicate directions to a friend or someone asking on the street.

Over the preceding millennia, difficult navigation problems have been solved, and time has been rendered linear. We can calculate, not just longitude, but our exact position to within centimeters, using a complex system of satellites perpetually orbiting. We communicate with those satellites via a watch or a phone, and can broadcast our real-time location to our friends. Arguably, these technical advancements represent a powerful way for people to understand and interact with each other and their local environment. In addition, new mapping techniques have enabled the creation of more accurate maps, as well as a NeoGeography, where everyday people engage in the creation and communication of geographic knowledge though their Garmin watch or iPhone.

Empowered by these exotic technologies, we are emerging from the phase where only experts manufacture maps. We are actively engaged in the democratization of the map-making process via technical innovations linked through the Internet. In a way, after all this time, mental maps are still key to our collective understanding of our local and global environment. Mental maps have not gone away, but have been with us all along, shelved in the offices of academics and armchair geographers, hidden deep within our daily navigation. Kevin Lynch is one such academic, and stated in his seminal book, The Image of the City, "Every citizen has had long associations with some parts of his city, and his image is soaked in memories and meanings" (Lynch 1960). Time is linear by our watch, but not within our experience or memories of place. I can delve back in time to the first time that I rode a bicycle in New Brunswick, or remember the look of snow in my Alberta backyard while sitting on a plane to Paris.

Mental maps are maps of the past. They represent the meaning a place has to us based on our cumulative individual experiences with that place. When this complex network of meaning is linked, place-to-place, a mental map for one person emerges. A happy place is linked to a melancholy place, is linked back to another happy place—creating a tapestry of personal experience defining the past use of a landscape, urban or otherwise. But, the meaning of place can give a place meaning. With the right technologies and a collaborative effort, one's tapestry of meaning can be connected to many others, defining the places that have meaning, and why they have meaning. In such a way, we can understand what elements, in combination, define the best places for people. This local knowledge is not currently easily accessible to those who plan our neighbourhoods and communities. But the Social Internet is about to change that.

The Social Internet defines a means of interaction between people that is characterized by a rich user experience including an exchange of multimedia information and the development of cumulative and combined knowledge based on that exchange (Parameswaran and Whinston 2007). Within this context, the development of new technologies is enabling citizens to collaborate in an online environment around place, or places. Specifically, there are three technologies (tools) that define the line in the sand, collective understanding and group knowledge: Mapping tools, Collaboration tools, and Social Networks.

Mapping tools are best explored via Google Mapmaker. Mapmaker has enabled point, line, and polygon drawing on top of aerial photos and the result can be saved as 'my maps', an individually customised map. This enables individuals to represent their personal experience and interactions within their local geography—mapping points of interest, favourite routes, and places. And, more importantly, people can also add detailed descriptions of these features, including their experience and why a place has meaning. While it is possible to share maps with your friends, Google Map Maker lacks the option to collaborate with your social network on the creation of a map, or in defining why a place has a collective meaning to the members of your network.

For collaboration, other tools exist on the Internet. A wiki, for example, is a collaboration tool that enables all users to edit any page or to create new pages within the defined structure. Wiki promotes meaningful topic associations between different pages by making page link creation intuitively easy, it seeks to involve the visitor in an ongoing process of creation and collaboration that constantly changes the website landscape (http://en.wikipedia.org/wiki/Wiki). If we interpret 'topic association' and 'website landscape' within a mapping context, we establish a tool set that can build a collaborative geography of meaning within a wiki-enabled online map. Topic associations become locations linked by individual and community meaning within a website landscape that is allegorical to the physical landscape.

Current technologies are supporting the emergence of a small handful of applications that combine social networks with a geographical wiki (GeoWiki). This amalgamation empowers individuals to access a collective intelligence by way of their friends and associations within their social circle. Layers of 'social' can be built via interactions at the personal, community and geographic level. For instance, you may contribute your experience to a friend's GeoWiki while collaborating on a description of place with someone you have not met in person. In this way, connections between places can be explored with those you personally know, and those whom you have not met.

Coming full circle, today's technologically mediated social networks broaden the discussion beyond those small nomadic communities. In distant past mental maps were the result of an individual's and communities' reflection on place—past use, past experience, and past significance—that were created through a discrete tool set with a social network of family, friends and community at its core. The expression of these old tools are being recast by a socially and location aware Internet. Social Networks, coupled with mapping and collaboration tools are enabling an ancient form of understanding to emerge as people connect through the Internet in a discussion centered on the meaning of place.

References

Davis, Wade (2009) The Wayfinders: Why Ancient Wisdom Matters in the Modern World. House of Anansi Press Inc, Toronto
Lynch K (1960) The Image of the City. MIT Press, Cambridge, MA
Parameswaran M, & Whinston AB (2007) Social computing: An overview. Commun Assoc Inf Syst 19:762–780
Wiki was accessed on Wikipedia and can be found at: http://en.wikipedia.org/wiki/Wiki

LocationInformation

Fabian Neuhaus

BLUETOOTH TRACKING[1] Someone in Apeldoorn, the Netherlands has set up a small network of five Bluetooth sensors. The sensors are placed in different locations in the city, as said on the projects homepage "with friends and family", to keep it a low budget project. Each location has a simple USB Bluetooth adaptor connected to the internet. All the information is then stored in one location in a database. The sensor will pick up mobile devices with Bluetooth turned on. They are identified by a unique MAC address. Through the network of sensors within Apeldoorn it is then possible to roughly track individual devices. The amount of data collected from just five locations is quite a lot. Within the first four weeks the network registered 15,000 unique devices. As it occurs, some devices are picked up by two or more sensors and therefore reveal information about movement within Apeldoorn of individual devices. Data from one sensor over a period of time reveals a picture of the usage pattern of the area it covers. An example from the project homepage at bluetoothtracking.org (Fig. 1).

Below you see the statistics of the Apeldoorn Driehuizen Bluetooth scanner. The location of this scanner is near a couple of office buildings. You can clearly see the early morning and late afternoon traffic: it even shows that they usually go for a walk after lunch. One afternoon peaks at 12, Friday afternoon, and this is because many people take Friday afternoon off. Dutch people like to enjoy long weekends and often take Friday afternoon off. This simple chart visualises how working hours create a pattern in everyday movement. The chart only represents one week, but every week is most likely the same as the pattern is repetitive. The University of Bath, it was revealed by a Guardian article on Monday July 21, 2008, has undertaken a very similar study. For this study the university, three years ago, installed ten

---

[1] *BLUETOOTH TRACKING,* 5 November 2008 12:14, locationInformation, citySensing, bluetooth, tracking.

F. Neuhaus (✉)
Centre for Advanced Spatial Analysis, University College London, London, UK
e-mail: fabian.neuhaus@ucl.ac.uk

F. Neuhaus (ed.), *Studies in Temporal Urbanism,*
DOI 10.1007/978-94-007-0937-9_10, © Springer Science+Business Media B.V. 2011

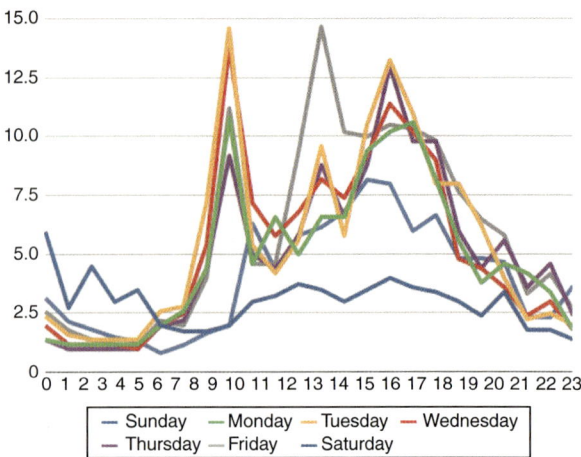

Fig. 1 Image taken from Bluetooth tracking / Showing weekday activity according to number of bluetooth devices recorded

Bluetooth scanners to capture signals from mobile devices. The data is used to study how people move around cities. The project is called Cityware and, similar to the previously mentioned example based in the Netherlands, stores the data centrally to allow analysis. On the Cityware project home page[2] the team publishes a map of data collected back in 2007. During a day on 9 different locations, 6 time sessions have been scanned.

103   *TRACKING IN VIRTUAL WORLDS—TOOL FOR SECOND LIFE*[3], SlogBase[4] is an open source tool to track the movement of avatars in Second Life. The code offers a database that can be attached to objects in Second Life and sends sensor data to an external database. It was developed with a marketing focus in mind. It is advertised by saying how important it is to know what visitors do and what they are interested in. By monitoring the movement on one's own land the offers can be adjusted or exchanged based on the analysis of the logged data. A lot of information can be logged with this tool. Beside the location, speed and direction other additional data can also be logged. This can be age or mode of transport.

104   *GADGET*[5] Well, actually this is Google Earth (GoEa) right in my blog! Great, I'm loving it. Just three years back, I could not believe it, when I got my first, unofficial Google Earth version on my mac.

It was amazing to explore the world in this new way all from the comfort of my personal keyboard or mouse respectively. Now GoEa is everywhere, on my phone (yes I have an iPhone) and now on my blog too! What do I need my desktop for these days? It is fixed… rather it was never broken. There seems to be an issue with safari. If you can't see any content try Firefox instead. It seems to work, for both

---

[2] http://www.cityware.org.uk/index.php?option=com_content&task=view&id=75&Itemid=35.

[3] *TRACKING IN VIRTUAL WORLDS—TOOL FOR SECOND LIFE,* 12 November 2008 14:51, tracking, locationInformation, virtual world.

[4] http://slogbase.com/.

[5] *GADGET,* 15 January 2009 10:00, locationInformation, visualisation, Google Earth, GPS tracks.

maps and GoEa. This gadget was found at Google, where else? Click link[6] to get your own. There is no need for an API it seems.

GOOGLE LATITUDE—TRACKING SERVICE AND SOCIAL NETWORK A LA GOOGLE[7] Google officially started a new Location based service today called Google Latitude[8]. It is kind of a location based social network and capable of showing the location of friends and family members. "See where your friends are in real time!" is the phrase Google uses to introduce it. Users need to download software to their mobile device. From the mobile browser, one has to visit google.com/latitude and follow the instructions. There is a list of devices[9] that work with the new service, but basically it is the Android powered T-Mobile G1, Blackberry, Windows 5.0 and Symbian S60 devices. iPhone and iPod touch will be coming soon and so will Java-enabled phones. See clip on youtube[10].

The network can also be accessed through the Google page. In case you are not on the go you can still follow your friends' location updates from the computer after logging in to your Google account. It is also possible to share the computers (presumably laptop) location through the Wi-Fi access point. The service is said to work in 27 countries and will be free but most likely involve some cost from your mobile phone provider. Picking up from the online discussion going on about these kinds of services, there are privacy concerns regarding this type of service/information. An other similar project called Loopt[11] has introduced an "override" feature that allows users to put in their location manually and basically "lie" about the location they are at. A similar option should be in Google Latitude. (from www.ft.com, by Richard Waters[12]) Other companies that offer location based social networking services are Brightkite[13], Loopt[14] or Pocket Life[15] by Vodafone. They all seem to be in their beta stage, but it looks like are fairly busy. The devices they work with vary a lot. So if your device is not supported by one service just try another one. Particularly Brightkite seems to accept basically any mobile phone.

MINI TRACKER AS TINY BACKPACKS[16] So far research on bird travel and migration behaviour is largely guesswork, especially the actual bit of travelling. It

---

[6] href=%22http://www.gmodules.com/ig/creator?synd=open&url=http://code.google.com/apis/KML/embed/embedkmlgadget.xml.

[7] *GOOGLE LATITUDE—TRACKING SERVICE AND SOCIAL NETWORK A LA GOOGLE,* 4 February 2009 12:41, locationInformation, social network, tracking, Google Latitude.

[8] http://www.google.com/latitude/intro.html.

[9] http://www.google.com/support/mobile/bin/answer.py?answer=136640.

[10] http://www.youtube.com/v/Q-Oq-9enE-k&color1=0xb1b1b1&color2=0xcfcfcf&hl=en&feature=player_embedded&fs=1.

[11] http://www.loopt.com/.

[12] http://www.ft.com/cms/s/0/5e734478-f24f-11dd-9678-0000779fd2ac,dwp_uuid=e8477cc4-c820-11db-b0dc-000b5df10621.html?nclick_check=1.

[13] http://brightkite.com/.

[14] https://www.loopt.com/.

[15] http://www.pocketlife.com/index.html.

[16] *MINI TRACKER AS TINY BACKPACKS,* 15 February 2009 19:52, locationInformation, animals, GPS tracks, tracking.

is well known where they live and what their destination of migration is over the course of the seasons. What is largely unknown is the bit in between. What is their exact route of travel, how fast do they travel and how often do they rest, these are the main questions regarding bird migration behaviour. Scientists have tested many techniques, from banding a bird's legs (which was until recently the most successful of the methods), to tracking flocks with radar to even using satellites, all without much success writes scienceno.sciencemag[17]. It is known that birds can fly at a rather fast speed of around 60 miles and hour and that they do travel almost half way around the globe during their migration. Biologists are interested in the details of this knowledge but to receive new data they had to find a new method of observing the birds' movement.

A new mini tracking device has enabled researchers at York University in Toronto to tag rather small songbirds. The main problem here is the weight. Engineers at the British Antarctica Survey have developed a small light weight tracker to follow the trips of albatrosses, rather large birds. The scientists at York were able to minimize the technology to a total weight of 1.5 g. It sits on the bird's back and is held in place with two straps around their legs, just like a miniature backpack. The sensor is not exactly a GPS, it is a solar geolocator. It collects and stores data in relation to the sun. A total of 34 purple martin birds were tagged in summer 2007. Only seven of them could be recaptured a year later. Nevertheless the data was exciting. The data showed that the birds flew two to six times faster going north, than going south. Researchers also discovered that they actually flew much faster than initially guessed. Information about the stopover points will help to protect birds, especially songbirds that are in steep decline.

107   *PROTESTS IN IRAN—EARLY MAP MASHUPS*[18] Following the election results from last Friday large-scale protests are under way in Iran since the weekend. On BBC journalists are guessing that they are the biggest demonstration since the 1979 revolution. They can only guess, because journalists are no longer allowed to work and cover stories related to election and protests. The Government seems to have restricted services on telephones, SMS and internet. Protesters and Iranians from all over the world have taken to Twitter to communicate and report on what is happening. Also on youtube the videos documenting scenes and rallies are huge. Twitter has reportedly delayed its maintenance, which would have meant for the site being down during the day for Iranians, as found on ITworld[19]. It appears that Twitter is down in the UK at the moment at 2009-06-16 22h05. This might not mean that it is down in Iran. We'll hear about it in the news. It is amazing how quick location based information is generated and within almost the last year it has become normal on the internet to have all the information georeferenced on a map. Some first mashups, found on programmable web[20] and googlemapMania[21], have emerged: others will

---

[17] http://sciencenow.sciencemag.org/cgi/content/full/2009/212/1.

[18] *PROTESTS IN IRAN—EARLY MAP MASHUPS,* 17 June 2009 09:00, locationInformation, twitter, mapping, mashup.

[19] http://www.itworld.com/internet/69322/iran-all-twitter-service-maintenance-pushed-back.

[20] http://www.programmableweb.com/mapping.

[21] http://googlemapsmania.blogspot.com/.

definitely follow, when the newspapers get round to actually starting to mapping some information. Similar mashup also by 20 min.fr[22].

If you know nothing about Iran, the BBC has put together some helpful information, in maps[23] and in text[24] on latest events and in text[25] on historical events.

CITYSENSING—ENVIRONMENTAL SENSORS AVAILABLE[26] Together with the GPS tracking technology also a whole bunch of other sensors are now available in rather small format and a price: and they can easily be combined. So sensing the environment in a small scale is becoming possible, even popular. A number of projects are under way. Here I put together some examples. This sort of information is especially interesting for learning more about micro climates. The knowledge regarding fine scale environmental information in cities is relatively low. With the now widely available technology it becomes possible to sense and record the environment as a pedestrian, or a cyclist. This in turn could allow the collection of data to generate a better picture of micro climates. Mobile phones as electronic devices that a large number of people are carrying around daily could potentially become sensors and record and transmit environmental related information on a large scale. Research that develops prototypes for this kind of data collection has been undertaken at Carnegie Mellon's Human-Computer Interaction Institute by Eric Paulos. "How would it change your ideas about moving around in the world, if you could suddenly sense things you couldn't see?", he asks. As a response to this work some phone manufacturer have already expressed interest, as he reports in the seed magazine[27]. Probably a good element for DIY made sensors is the Ardurino[28] open source platform, software and hardware. "Arduino is an open-source electronics prototyping platform based on flexible, easy-to-use hardware and software. It's intended for artists, designers, hobbyists, and anyone interested in creating interactive objects or environments" (from Ardurino.cc).

An environmental sensing project runs in Paris. It is called "la montre verte[29]" and is so far about a "green watch". It grew out of the idea to mobilize the 1,000 fixed environmental sensors around Paris and generate more accurate real time data. So far 30 prototypes of the green watch have been produced and are tested at the moment in Paris. The team has produced some beautiful visualisation[30] from the collected data. It is built on a Google Map with a detailed interactive interface to select and replay the collected data.

CamMobSens (Cambridge Mobile Urban Sensing) also works on a sensing project similar to the Paris project. So far they have collected data around Cambridge. A

---

[22] http://cartes.20minutes-blogs.fr/archive/2009/06/16/la-twitter-map-des-elections-en-iran.html.

[23] http://news.bbc.co.uk/1/hi/world/middle_east/8051660.stm.

[24] http://news.bbc.co.uk/1/hi/world/middle_east/8102465.stm.

[25] http://news.bbc.co.uk/1/hi/world/middle_east/country_profiles/806268.stm.

[26] *CITYSENSING—ENVIRONMENTAL SENSORS AVAILABLE,* 20 July 2009 09:3, senses, city, environment, citySensing, shapingCities, locationInformation, tracking.

[27] http://seedmagazine.com/content/article/the_tricorder_arrives/.

[28] http://arduino.cc/.

[29] http://lamontreverte.org/en/.

[30] http://lamontreverte.org/vis/.

short clip of the data can be seen here[31], a paper has been published[32] on the project. Nokia is very active and always experimenting with new technologies.

Of course they are also developing something related to the topic of extended environmental sensors. They have a dedicated project webpage on Nokia[33]. And of course there are also products, not yet ready. It is on the Nokia page described as: "The concept consists of two parts—a wearable sensor unit which can sense and analyse your environment, health, and local weather conditions, and a dedicated mobile phone. The sensor unit will be worn on a wrist or neck strap made from solar cells that provide power to the sensors. See clip on Vimeo[34]. NFC (near field communication) technology will relay information by touch from the sensors to the phone or to other devices that support NFC technology." Nokia's eco sensor concept.

Integrating environmental live data into further digital development on the computer, the people from pachub[35] are working on this. They have developed a plug in for Sketch up to use live sensor information to feed into the SketchUp platform. Information on it is on their blog[36].

109   *CITYSENSING—FROM HIGH-TECH LAB TO EVERYDAY GADGET*[37] I recently put up a blog post about CitySensing[38] and ever since the topic is following me around town. Not only because of all the potential sensors I'm carrying around with me, but probably also because I am more aware of the topic. I think the topic in general is closely related to the perception of space and in this sense to the mental map[39] we all construct of the space we navigate. Our body senses are usually on high alert while walking down the road and the environment is constantly assessed. Because of the uneven pavement we adjust our balance, with our ears we can hear the squirrel in the tree above us, we can smell the oil and dust from the building site on the road, we see the red van on the crossroads ahead. This only lists the senses that are "official" senses. Probably there is also a sense of some more embodied information such as muscles providing a sense of force and speed, the breath and the heart beat as an indicator of effort or the information about balance and body parts orientation. In short there is a lot of information. For now I guess the technical sensing is probably simpler to describe, as the processing of the data into information is done by a chip and we can tell the chip what the output should be so it looks like a more straightforward exercise. The Economist[40] has put together an extensive list of

---

[31] http://www.escience.cam.ac.uk/~mcal00/MESSAGE/try2c.mov.

[32] http://emeraldinsight.com/Insight/viewContentItem.do;jsessionid=54F8B2FD61208D220009 42D68C998AFB?contentType=NonArticle&hdAction=lnkhtml&contentId=1733163.

[33] http://www.nokia.com/corporate-responsibility/environment.

[34] http://vimeo.com/5490631.

[35] http://www.pachube.com/.

[36] http://blog.pachube.com/2009/07/pachube2sketchup-realtime-sensor-data.html.

[37] *CITYSENSING—FROM HIGH-TECH LAB TO EVERYDAY GADGET,* 10 August 2009 08:30, locationInformation, shapingCities, environment, citySensing, tracking, senses.

[38] http://urbantick.blogspot.com/2009/07/citysensing-environmental-sensors.html.

[39] http://urbantick.blogspot.com/2009/07/space-perception-and-mental-maps.html.

[40] http://www.economist.com/sciencetechnology/tq/displaystory.cfm?story_id=13725679.

sensing projects and their potential. There are some really exciting technical City-Sensing projects out there. For example a cooperation of five Universities (Imperial College, Cambridge[41], Leeds, Newcastle and Southampton) on the MESSAGE[42] project has investigated the use of mobile sensors in urban environments and a variety of applications. A short clip[43] shows a visualisation of the collected data. In an interview for "The Naked Scientist" on BBC the researchers explain about the potential of the project and podcast transcript can be found here[44]. In Berlin, Germany scientists are testing a network of sensors that are installed in buses. A BBC report can be found here[45]. The sensors cover the usual air and road temperature as well as humidity, pollution indicators, some cameras and of course GPS. So traffic information can be calculated. The data is wirelessly transmitted to a processing centre. A project website can be found here[46].

As a more everyday gadget based project the pathintelligence project is quite interesting. It is developed to locate the users of mobile phones and aimed at retail and shopping centres. The system detects the unique signal of each phone and can locate it with about 1–2 m accuracy. The shoppers are tracked with a number of static sensors and the data is then used to derive information about flows and preferences of visitors. A demo can be seen here[47]. For shopping centres there is a lot of pressure and competition so they are probably very willing customers for this kind of information. It is partly about offering a better service, but also about internal competition between the brands. For example the tenancy mix but also the optimization of rental costs are listed as benefits. Surprisingly this is only discussed in research circles and shoppers are largely unaware of the monitoring process. The Times had an article[48] on the topic, which was then picked up by the spy blog[49].

A pretty amazing CitySensing project is the sensity[50] work by Stanza[51]. The artist himself describes the project as "An artwork and visualisation using data from around the environment. A wireless sensor network showing emergent space as social sculpture". The sensors used can monitor temperature, sound, noise, light, vibration, humidity, and have a built in GPS unit (Fig. 2).

These dynamic visualisation scapes have been on show around the world and usually each show leads to another record, as the artist never travels without his

---

[41] http://www.escience.cam.ac.uk/mobiledata/.

[42] http://bioinf.ncl.ac.uk/message/.

[43] http://www.escience.cam.ac.uk/~mcal00/MESSAGE/try2c.mov.

[44] http://www.thenakedscientists.com/HTML/content/interviews/interview/1107/.

[45] http://news.bbc.co.uk/1/hi/sci/tech/7423535.stm.

[46] http://www.fp6-moryne.org/.

[47] http://www.pathintelligence.com/en/products/footpath/footpath-technology

[48] http://technology.timesonline.co.uk/tol/news/tech_and_web/article3945496.ece.

[49] http://p10.hostingprod.com/@spyblog.org.uk/blog/2008/05/path-intelligence-phorm-for-shopping-centres.html.

[50] http://www.stanza.co.uk/sensity/index.html.

[51] http://www.stanza.co.uk/.

Fig. 2 Image by stanza /
Sensing Copenhagen

equipment. So from London[52] over Copenhagen[53] to Paris[54] and Texas[55] to Sao
Paulo[56] the cities are sensed by stanza.

A more of a web 2.0 project relying on crowd sourcing is the lhrNOISEmap[57]
project by Ian Tout[58]. He is currently finishing his masters in Geographical Information Science (GISc) at Birkbeck College. He is mapping the aircraft noise produced
by an aeroplane approaching or leaving London Heathrow Airport.

For this he has built an online map based on Open Street Map and uses the web
platform AudioBoo[59] and their free iPhone application to record aeroplane noise
in London. The short clips can then be mapped, as they are automatically georeferenced. In a second step the data will be aggregated and the noise levels should
appear on the map as a layer. So if you have an iPhone and are somewhere under
the flight path of London Heathrow give it a try and participate[60] in this mapping
project. A simple step-by-step guide can be found here.[61] You can also follow the
project on Twitter.[62]

---

[52] http://www.soundcities.com/sensity_London_runtime/index.html.

[53] http://www.soundcities.com/sensity_copenhagen_runtime/index.html.

[54] http://www.soundcities.com/sensity_paris_runtime/index.html.

[55] http://www.soundcities.com/plutopia/index.html.

[56] http://www.soundcities.com/sao_paulo_310/index.html.

[57] http://www.lhrnoisemap.org/.

[58] http://www.lhrnoisemap.org/contact.html.

[59] http://audioboo.fm/.

[60] http://www.lhrnoisemap.org/takepart.html.

[61] http://www.lhrnoisemap.org/takepart.html.

[62] http://twitter.com/lhrnoisemap.

10   *VIRTUAL NOTES IN THE REAL WORLD—IPHONE*[63] As promised with the
last post on Google's Latitude, I spent some more time on other options. And actually it can be said up front; Latitude is boring whereas other applications can be very
exciting. Sorry, I had to mention this. As discussed in a comment last week Latitude
is probably not meant to be cool. I now understand it more as an additional data
service Google provides. A service that especially targets a new market of location
based information. I assume Google plans to get people to use it, but then to involve
third party companies to "use" the location data to target them specifically. This will
most probably include Google itself, for ad placements for example. Anyway this
is only speculation and others might be more expert in this field. There is a huge
discussion on this topic, including some horrific stories about privacy and stuff. But
this was about other options for location based interaction. From the iPhone based
tracking, the step towards web based tracking is not far off and the set of additional
options is enormous, starting from a simple message or chat tool right up to location based tags and content such as photographs. The limitations of gadget based
tracking are obvious, it is as if you are talking to yourself, a rather introverted and
singular recording of spatial movement. The web based option on the other hand
offers instant updated and interaction. I have been testing Brightkite[64] and MapMe[65]
the last few days and I am just blown away. Not necessarily with the interface, the
options or the features, but more by what a location based social networking tool
could be. Facebook[66] is so 1957[67] compared to this. The exciting thing is probably
that you can take it with you and that where you are actually influences what you
see, on the little screen of course. On the other end the information you add to the
network has this same dimension too. So you can get quite easily in touch with
new people, if used on a mobile device, because you constantly come across in real
space other people's digital junk (positive).

But to start from the beginning, how does it work, what can you do on how does
it feel? First we look at the MapMe application. It is developed by John McKer-
rell[68]. It is a place to store your location and share it with friends. Like Latitude it
has a main page on which it shows your location on a map. This map is based on
Open Street Map[69] data. A big awful yellow marker has written on it "I am here".
Maybe "ME" would do it as the service is called MapMe? The big problem is the
colour approach of the open street map. It makes it really hard, if not impossible,
to actually see the location dots other than the big yellow box. Have a try on the
image above, can you spot the greenish-brown dots? At least in London this is the

---

[63] *VIRTUAL NOTES IN THE REAL WORLD—IPHONE,* 11 August 2009 13:49, timemap, mobile, tracking, tags, virtual world, iPhone, mapping, Open Street Map, locationInformation, Flickr,
Google Latitude, social network.

[64] http://brightkite.com/.

[65] http://mapme.at/.

[66] http://www.facebook.com/.

[67] http://en.wikipedia.org/wiki/1957.

[68] http://blog.johnmckerrell.com/.

[69] http://www.openstreetmap.org/.

case, because it is so dense. Somehow the colours on MapMe appear brighter than on the original OSM page. A number of sources can be used to feed the location into the application. Through email with FireEagle, Twitter, Latitude, RSS feed or InstaMapper.[70] This variety is great, although some seem rather crude. Like email, but then you think, there might be some devices that update positions via SMS or email, if they are not based on the rather new concept of free unlimited data access, so yes, great option. The second cool add-on here is the timeline, hidden in the history tab. It makes the past locations accessible in a timeline. It is based on the Smile timeline code on Google Code. It is an interface based on horizontal bands that each are based on time units. One is the year, then the month and then the day, even the hour can be added. By pulling the bands one can navigate in time. The location points are then displayed on both, the band (as dots or lines) and on the map. The two stay in sync while moving through time. Brilliant feature. This is probably the first feature you will miss on Latitude!

That's about it on MapMe. Unfortunately I have not been able to find any of my friends on this network, as it only allows you to search by username and if you don't know, you don't know. So if you are on MapMe please add me as a contact! Was just looking for a direct link to my profile, but could not find anything so search for urbanTick. The link page is actually the history page. So here is my link then—urbanTick[71]. It is really not so much of a socializing tool as a personal recorder, for which it works brilliantly. It actually offers a developer API to add to the existing application and also lets you access the recorded data. Information about this is on the mapme blog[72]. If we move over to Brightkite this is completely different. It is a fully grown social networking tool. It is like facebook having attached a different design. Surprisingly there is no map! Not that facebook would have one, but if the service is location based the first thing to think about probably is a map. In the discussion board, what a surprise, there is a thread about this and the reply by Martin May[73] one year ago was "That's coming...the map is kinda clunky right now. We have great plans for it, but it will take us some time to get everything in... it's beta, after all." So there is still no map and it is still Beta, but it is still cool. You know, maybe not having a map makes it more interesting. On the iPhone I have to say, there is the option to click on things and it would open the location in the maps application. There is actually the same button for the web tool. A map can be accessed through an individual post or location. It even embeds Google Street View[74] to give you an image of the location beside the post. Having said that there is one really cool feature that almost makes up for the missing map. It is possible to export the posted contents as a KML file to Google Earth or link it as a RSS feed. And it includes not only your stuff, but your friends' posts as well, great. Guess you

---

[70] http://www.instamapper.com/.

[71] http://mapme.at/where/urbantick#/200908131045/48.

[72] http://blog.mapme.at/developer-api/.

[73] http://getsatisfaction.com/brightkite/topics/all_friends_on_one_map?utm_medium=widget&utm_source=widget_brightkite.

[74] http://maps.google.com/maps?ll=51.523760,-0.134040&cbll=51.523760,-0.134040&layer=c&cbp=1,319.4420600858369,,0,7.703862660944213&hl=en.

Fig. 3 Image by urbanTick /
Screenshot Brightkite web
app distance filter

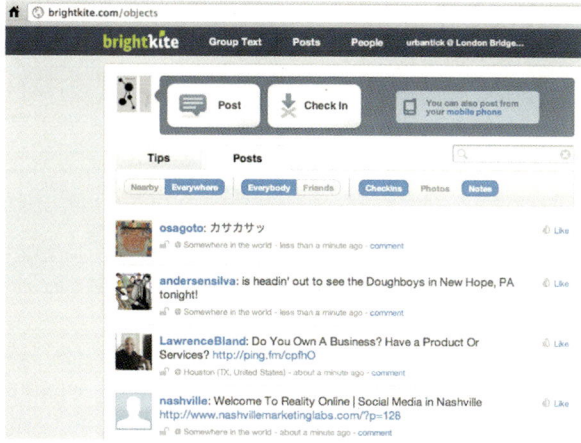

could simply put that feed into the yahoo pipes and have it on a map. The really big thing here is it the location based information that you can access content through. You can literally run into a comment or an image! The information filter is not only based on your friends' network but also on the location, close 920 m), block (200 m), neighbourhood (2 km), area (4 km), city (10 km), metro (50 km), region (100 km) (Fig. 3).

This becomes really interesting if we take the aspect of time into account. I thought about this when I posted a random picture of something I simply had in front of my lens, a construction site on the road. Now I am able to look at images other people have posted in the same location from before the construction started and people will pass by this location in the future and see my image of the building site even though the construction has long finished. Meaning that it builds up an immensely rich database of location based everyday information over location and time. A similar thing is the mobile flickr[75] "around me" service. If you use flickr on a mobile device it will give you the option to filter contend based on your location, it is cool, but does not offer the control of Brightkite. A specification of this is the save a location tool, where you can mark a location as special. It is a place mark and can be used to tag a restaurant for example. If you write a review or only leave a note about how the meal was others can pick it up (Fig. 4).

The iPhone app can be downloaded for free and is a must have. It is simple but offers a lot of features. There seems to be an issue with the bottom line links. On my phone the first option shows two icons on top of each other but only one can be accessed. The "request" button is somehow behind the "I am …" button after I clicked on the "more" tab. So again if you are on Brightkite give me a shout[76]! The only problem with these tools, applications and software really is the real space experience. I found myself in the last few days sunk into my iPhone and being kind of

---

[75] http://flickr.com.

[76] http://brightkite.com/people/urbantick.

Fig. 4 Image by urbanTick /
Brightkite for iPhone application screen shorts

absent from the environment around me. Although I was in a way deeply involved
in the here and now, the past and other users' experience at the same places. My
experience was not too different from looking at Google Street View from a remote
location. A rather dull and emotionless consumption of something that is being sold
to me as a real location while being a bunch of pixels. It has a lot of qualities and
interesting aspects that are not yet explored to the limit, but there is a downside to it,
as that the mobile use takes you out of the real world into the pixel world and vice
versa while the benefit is not quite clear.

111   *IPHONE—TRAFFIC UPDATE USER GENERATED IN REAL TIME*[77] A new
application is available for the iPhone and other mobile devices that provides traffic
information (mainly aiming at individual car traffic) and at the same time records
traffic conditions to update the information. This commercial application is called
WAZE[78] and is at the moment only available in the states and Israel[79] it seems. It is
developed by Ehud Shabtai, Uri Levine and Amir Shinar[80]. It is one of the first truly
crowd sourced applications. The user data from GPS will automatically generate a
live map. If the user moves slowly it will show as a red trail on the road and others
can see that there might be a traffic jam. See clip on youtube[81].

In addition users can also upload detailed information such a speed cam or accident and even record additional roads that do not yet appear on the map. A guided
tour with comments[82] can be found here. The WAZE fan page on facebook[83] is here.
There are two questions that I allow to ask. One is the obvious question of how to
verify the user generated data. Who can be trusted and who might just play with the
application. For example if I would be using it (I don't own a car) and log data while
walking there would be red roads wherever I go. So is there some sort of filtering
and overriding feature built into the automatic live mapping? The second question
is one that I already ask myself while reading about the MIT user and especially

---

[77] *IPHONE—TRAFFIC UPDATE USER GENERATED IN REAL TIME*, 17 August 2009 08:30,
locationInformation, citySensing, traffic, iPhone.

[78] http://www.waze.com/.

[79] http://www.waze.co.il/.

[80] http://www.waze.com/about/about_us/.

[81] http://www.youtube.com/v/NU9hVdb-rp8&hl=en&fs=1&.

[82] http://www.waze.com/guided_tour/.

[83] http://www.facebook.com/pages/Waze/86232932633.

Fig. 5 Image taken from WAZE.
com / Screenshot of the live map

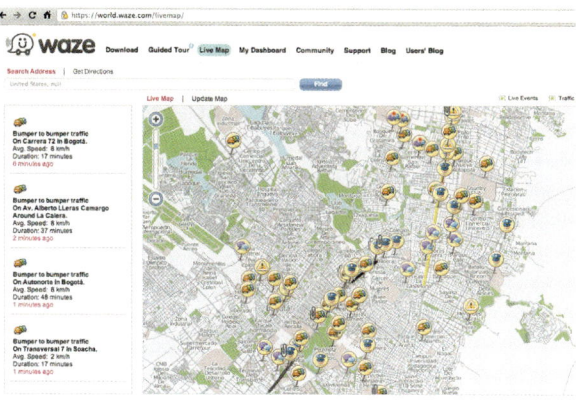

mobile phone focused research in Carlo Ratti's SENSABLECity team where they
also discuss products that help individual car drivers to find better ways through the
city. Why would we want to develop and use something as old fashioned as this? Individual car traffic is so 1920. And in this century still being trapped in this discussion about being fast and powerful and independent and so on is a bit sad actually.
I don't believe this can provide us with a global solution: it is just another attempt
to strengthen individual needs in a struggling urban environment. But in this case a
technologically advanced cool gadget for the cool gadget you already own so why
not use it! (Fig. 5).

The MIT project[84] is a bit older and called CarTel[85]. It is a bit more complicated
but essentially works the same way. The iPhone and Android option obviously is
pretty hot. The graphic is a bit too playful and childlike for my test and could be a
touch more formal ad serious but there you go. Thanks to gisagents[86].

360 VR PANORAMIC LONDON VIEW[87] Looking back at the London Small
World clip I produced a few weeks ago, there is some contextual stuff that should be
published alongside. One such project is the London Monument View[88]. It is quite
simply what the title suggest and in short the 365/24/7 version of London Small
World. It is a camera with a 360° lens, installed on the Monument in London. It
gives a live webcam image and also a previous day time lapse[89] (Fig. 6).

It is an art project by Chris Meigh-Andrews[90] installed in 2008 during the renovation of the Monument. The idea is to process the images according to environmental data. In detail this means the orientation of the images corresponds with the

---

[84] http://web.mit.edu/newsoffice/2008/car-sensors-tt1008.html.

[85] http://cartel.csail.mit.edu/doku.php.

[86] http://gisagents.blogspot.com/.

[87] *360 VR PANORAMIC LONDON VIEW*, 8 September 2009 16:46, senses, timeLapse, environment, London, citySensing, locationInformation, photography, smallWorld.

[88] http://www.themonumentview.net/index.php.

[89] http://www.themonumentview.net/index.php.

[90] http://www.meigh-andrews.com/.

Fig. 6 Images by the monument view project / Screenshots taken on 2009-08-11

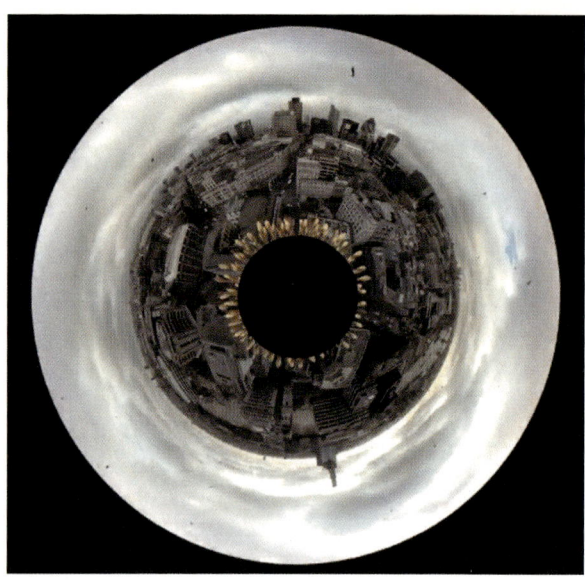

wind direction, the air temperature influences the colour tone and the wind speed
the speed of the image stream.

The construction on top of the monument looks like this; funnily enough the
glass jar in the middle is the actual lens case, so it is quite small and the weather
station takes up a lot of space. The environmental sensing equipment is the same as
Andy Hudson-Smith over at digitalurban[91] uses. He has a live page that also works
on the iPhone[92]. To see today's Monument panorama go here:[93] there is also a log
book where you can access any data in 2009. If you are interested in today's time
lapse click here:[94] you probably have to wait a second for the clip to load.

113   *360 PHOTOGRAPHY—BOROUGHS GO FOR GOOGLE STREET VIEW*[95] In
the context of the Small World[96] time Lapse series I was obviously interested in
what else is going on in this field of panoramic photography. Just by chance I also
came across new smart camera cars in the neighbourhood. I approached them and
we had a chat about their work. They were expecting me to ask about Google Street
View. They responded by apologizing for not working for Google and it turned out
they work for the London based company 360viewmax[97] (it was printed in rather
big letters all over the small car) and they are doing a job for Islington council. It
appears that the council has discovered the value of Street View for their purpose.

---

[91] http://digitalurban.blogspot.com/search?q=weather+station.

[92] http://digitalurban.blogspot.com/2009/07/iphone-live-weather-app.html.

[93] http://www.themonumentview.net/panorama.php.

[94] http://www.themonumentview.net/index.php.

[95] *360 PHOTOGRAPHY—BOROUGHS GO FOR GOOGLE STREET VIEW,* 10 September 2009
10:13, photography, mapping, citySensing, locationInformation, digital, orientation, smallWorld.

[96] http://urbantick.blogspot.com/2009/08/London-small-world-timeLapse.html.

[97] http://www.360viewmax.com/.

They want to use it for maintenance surveys. What that is I haven't really figured out. How it works is quite complicated at it involves two people in the car. There is a secondary, quite big writing on the back of the small car: "Caution: this vehicle stops frequently". Meaning what it says, the car stops every 20 m or so to take a picture. It is kind of done manually. Beside the driver the second person in the car has a laptop with GIS information on a map. The location of the image is, I believe manually input into the GIS system. GPS as they have told me is only used for rough navigation as they say it is not accurate enough. Compared to this the Google cars just drive along the road and take photographs on the go. The argument of 360viewmax is that they want to deliver high quality images with a lot of detail. The installation on the roof of the car is three Nikon p6000 cameras. Funny enough the cameras have a built in GPS module but it is not used. However, there is a cool demonstration[98] of it on the 360viewmax webpage (I had some issues with Firefox this morning when I tried it, but it worked on Safari). You can click into an Islington neighbourhood and down to street level to jump into bubbles of 360 panoramas. The interface is rather crude and located somewhere in a GIS technical engineer kind of world. Maybe they will develop at some point a neat designed consumer interface.

There has been this huge debate about privacy around Google Street View and they where forced to blur faces and number plates. In this council version of Street View however these elements are not blurred and number plates can be read for example. In terms of Google Street View, it has sparked a lot of controversy, especially around the launch of it in a new area. I remember the fuss about it in London for a week, when it launched earlier this year. And just a month ago the launch in Switzerland sparked the same discussion. Now in London there is hardly any comment on it in the news, apart from the odd use of the service to visualise a location. Also in everyday conversation the fear of loosing privacy has been replaced by curiosity and acknowledgment. People speak about it as a useful tool, mainly saying: it is great to see a location that you are not at. Then they bring the excuse of planning for a journey and it would help to orientate in unfamiliar surrounding. Well it might do but come on, it does not really replace being there. It is related to the phenomenon of the photograph and the discussion of truth. In general photographs are believed to be a true image of reality and therefore Google Street View is in this view a digital replication of the actual scenery at this location. So it urges the question whether it is live and people can be seen, because people identify with it so intensely that it becomes a virtual reality. However if you are interested to know where the real Google Street View cars drive at the moment Google has finally disclosed this information. Not in detail, but you get an idea what areas are getting mapped at the moment and the chances are that you come across a Google camera car. You can click here[99].

---

[98] http://www.360viewmax.com/revised_demo/website demo/map0/map_0_0.htm.

[99] http://maps.google.com/help/maps/streetview/where-is-street-view.html.

Fig. 7 Clip by Dust Films on Vimeo. (http://vimeo. com/6671301)

114   *GETTING LOST WITH THE GPS*[100] When did you last get lost? It must have been a while ago. The art of getting lost has got lost itself nowadays. The sense of not knowing the exact direction to a familiar object, place or location can be very unpleasant. On the other hand it can be very relieving. If you are prepared to accept that you have lost control over the situation or at least the location you might find yourself enjoying it. The idea of strolling through the city, not directed by a specific destination is a concept introduced by the Situationists. The aimless wandering or derive,[101] as it is called in the Situationist writing, can even be a method to observe the city. However, people also get lost by accident. The marketing campaign of a number of companies make us aware of a lot of possibilities of how we could get lost and with this fuel a lot of people's fears of the immediate surrounding. In-car navigation is now the number one gadget in car sales, it has overtaken the air condition feature or the CD player.

People seem to enjoy being talked through the environment, and then it all depends on the voice. I assume gadget developers put a lot of thought into the voices they offer as the direction instructor. Even how it is said must be important. In a recent interview Bob Dylan has announced that he is in talks with GPS manufacturers to lend his voice for a next generation of Gadget. Click here[102] for a sample of his voice. I am still waiting for the voice over that starts shouting at someone who just missed the turn for the fourth time. "You twat, can't you follow instructions! I said turn LEFT!" (Fig. 7).

The other way round, people shouting at the in-car navigation system are probably quite common. The BBC[103] has recently collected a number of stories of people getting lost with the GPS. Due to a software fault, the GPS will not correct your spelling mistakes. And it seems that people quite often misspell their destination. And a little knowledge is still needed to distinguish between Capri and Capri, as

---

[100] *GETTING LOST WITH THE GPS,* 29 September 2009 09:38, locationInformation, navigation, orientation, GPS.

[101] http://urbantick.blogspot.com/2009/03/derive.html.

[102] http://news.bbc.co.uk/1/hi/entertainment/8219651.stm.

[103] http://news.bbc.co.uk/1/hi/talking_point/8174216.stm.

a Swedish couple have learned after they arrived in the Industrial Town of Capri instead of the island Capri in Italy. Via GPSCity[104].

15   *COMOB—COLLABORATIVE TRACKING WITH THE IPHON*[105] CoMob[106] is an iPhone GPS tracking application developed at Edinburgh College of Art in collaboration with Edinburgh University. "The CoMob iPhone Application was developed as part of a research project exploring the creative use of collaborative GPS mapping."

It is a simple tracking application that sends the location to a customised server. It was designed for an art project presented at ISEA2009. Some images of the event can be seen on flickr here[107] by jensouthern. The application determines the position and sends the information to a pre-configured server. The update frequency is customisable as well as the server. You can change the server and for example send the location to your own server. It does not give you a visual feedback, all you can see is numbers. The interesting data is saved on the server.

The CoMob (in red) application has only recently received a sister application CoMob Net (in blue). It is built on the base of CoMob, but adds some group functionality and a visualisation using Google Maps. A group of iPhone users can use the application simultaneously and see the location of each group member on the screen. Locations are shown with a connection line between them producing shapes across the urban fabric. Usage is really simple, all you have to do is put in a user name and choose a name for the group. If joining an existing group simply type the name in the box provided and you're linked up. Here too it is possible to customise the server to store the data. So get your iPhone friends to come out into the streets and start mapping… Download CoMob[108] or CoMob Net[109] directly from iTunes here. You can then join our CASA group by entering the name of the group to the settings page (lowercase and you have to hit return to verify the entry).

16   *LAYAR—AR AT LARGE FOR THE IPHONE*[110] It is here, finally for the iPhone. Layar[111] is available and with it a whole series of information packages. There is nothing new on it, but the way it is visualised is new. You get familiar stuff like Wikipedia[112], Open Street Map[113], ArchINFORM[114], Twitter[115], Panoramio[116],

---

[104] http://www.facebook.com/pages/GPS-City/24852380666?ref=nf.

[105] *COMOB—COLLABORATIVE TRACKING WITH THE IPHONE,* 13 October 2009 09:32, locationInformation, iPhone, application, tracking, software, GPS.

[106] http://www.comob.org.uk/.

[107] http://www.flickr.com/photos/jensouthern/3536809270/.

[108] http://itunes.apple.com/WebObjects/MZStore.woa/wa/viewSoftware?id=313374071&mt=8.

[109] http://itunes.apple.com/WebObjects/MZStore.woa/wa/viewSoftware?id=326303438&mt=8.

[110] *LAYAR—AR AT LARGE FOR THE IPHONE,* 15 October 2009 10:24, augmented reality, locationInformation, virtual world.

[111] http://layar.com/.

[112] http://en.wikipedia.org/wiki/Layar.

[113] http://www.openstreetmap.org/.

[114] http://eng.archinform.net/index.htm.

[115] http://twitter.com/.

[116] http://www.panoramio.com/.

Fig. 8 Image by urbanTick /
Screenshots, depending on the
angle, Layar adjusts the horizon line of the overlaid plane
that serves as a reference for
the displayed data

Fig. 9 Image by urbanTick /
Screenshots, Brightkite layer
on Layar

flickr[117], Brightkite[118] plus a lot more. There is a high chance that the library will grow dramatically in the next few months. Currently there are a lot of services from Japan as layers available, as well as from the Netherlands. An up to date list of Layar layers can be found HERE[119] (Fig. 8).

Layar is basically the browser that visualises the data provided by individual companies offering a specific service. Download the app for your iPhone here.[120] Let's have a look at how it looks and feels, by testing some services around CASA[121].

The reference information is drawn from the GPS/Wi-Fi/Network to establish the current location. The compass built in to the iPhone give the direction of the phone. Layar provides a grid plane to locate the information and presumably give a better sense of depth. The icons used to represent the information are rather simple, a circle, a square, ... The interaction with these objects is limited to select them. It turns out that this is a difficult task at times. One, because it is a rather small area of the screen that is available for the actual AR display (the rest is cluttered with backup information) and two because the icons are overlapping one another and are obviously displayed even smaller if they are further away from the present location. However there is an automatic selection that works fine if there are only one or two items on the screen and by moving the iPhone you can alter between them, but as soon as you get more items the sensitivity of the compass can not keep up with the millimetre differences between the items (Fig. 9).

---

[117] http://www.flickr.com/groups/mentalmap/.

[118] http://brightkite.com/people/urbantick.

[119] http://layar.com/layers/.

[120] http://itunes.apple.com/WebObjects/MZStore.woa/wa/viewSoftware?id=334404207&mt=8.

[121] http://www.CASA.ucl.ac.uk/.

Fig. 10 Image by urbanTick / Screenshots, London Tube, not as nice as nearest tube, but with additional information that it links to

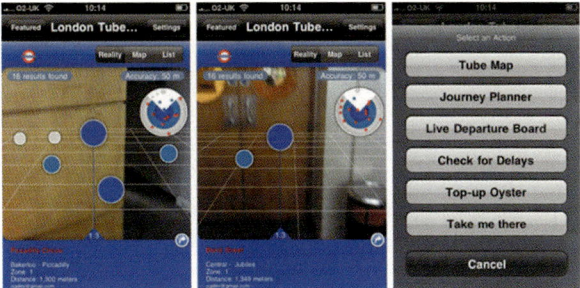

Fig. 11 Image by urbanTick / Screenshots, Panoramio as the Layar layer, link page and panorama on the web

The top bar holds a setting button that contains a number of options related to the service. For example the range/distance within results are displayed can be adjusted. The second bar on the top allows to switch between a map, a list and the AR mode, here called reality, WOW! Additional information for each selected item is displayed in the box below (Fig. 10).

It also provides a link to the displayed contend at its original location on the web. Meaning, Layar is really just a window to search for stuff (Fig. 11).

In this respect it could increasingly compete with Google and this raises the question why Google has not yet developed their own service or when they will buy Layar? Well at this point is still a very crude application with a rather cluttered and ugly interface, crappy icons and not very intuitive handling. See clip on Youtube[122].

But you know it is a first stab at a commercial platform to display location based information projected onto reality though the lens of a camera and this is exciting enough. How beautiful and simple this could look like was shown by acrossair[123], it was reviewed in an earlier post HERE[124].

---

[122] http://www.youtube.com/v/nkPHDMVxKn0&rel=0&color1=0xb1b1b1&color2=0xcfcfcf&hl =en&feature=player_embedded&fs=1.

[123] http://www.acrossair.com/acrossair_app_augmented_reality_nearesttube_London_for_ iPhone_3GS.htm.

[124] http://urbantick.blogspot.com/2009/09/nearest-tube-augmented-reality.html.

117   *INTEGRATED VIDEOS AND MAPS FOR DRIVING DIRECTIONS—MICRO-SOFT*[125] New development on the navigation gadget front. This time it comes from Microsoft[126] and that is in itself a bit surprising. So far the company has not been closely linked with navigation. In general they are trailing behind everyone, generally trying to improve the stuff others have developed and promoted. In this sense this 'new' development has to be looked at. The research featured as an article on Technology review[127] this week where its chef researcher Billy Chen[128] introduces us to the concept. They are using video for driving directions. Instead of Google Street View, they are playing video recordings of the route in Microsoft Virtual Earth. The research is partly about the recording and synchronising of the map as a video, but partly also about the influence of this method for direction instructions. The results of course claim that the animated instructions enable participants to find the route easier, with 60–70% for participants who were instructed only with image (Google images I presume).

However, the paper written about the project can be found HERE[129]. It has to be noted, that it is not simply a replayed clip. An important feature of the software is the way it focuses on landmarks and guides the users view field. It is not a passive record that has just followed the movement. Rather it is a carefully calculated section of the 360-degree recording. See clip on Youtube[130].

Through this movement, emphasis is put on certain aspect along the route, say a landmark. This means that the route somehow has to be processed and interpreted. How quickly and with what kind of system the software can be rolled out is not clear.

118   *RECORD YOUR LIFE—WITH THIS?*[131] TimeLapse has featured here extensively before and I am always interested to hear about new projects in stop motion. One of the aspects of time lapse is the 'compression' of time as opposed to the 'real time' video recording at 25/30 frames a second. TimeLapse can be any frame rate per second, minute or year. In post processing the images are then output as a clip at the video frame rate. This then is a video with dropped frames, skipping sections, but thus compressing an event in to a much smaller time frame. There are brilliant examples of year-long projects, capturing the change of the seasons[132]. For a lifelong project a couple of difficulties have to be overcome. One is the readiness of the photographer. In order not to miss the opportunity to get the good shot, one has to be constantly on the trigger.

---

[125] *INTEGRATED VIDEOS AND MAPS FOR DRIVING DIRECTIONS—MICROSOFT,* 19 October 2009 09:01, orientation, citySensing, navigation.

[126] http://research.microsoft.com/en-us/.

[127] http://www.technologyreview.com/computing/23711/page1/.

[128] http://research.microsoft.com/en-us/um/people/bilchen/.

[129] http://research.microsoft.com/en-us/um/people/cohen/vdd_webpage/paper/integrated_videos_and_maps_for_driving_directions.pdf.

[130] http://www.youtube.com/v/FjR3of9jKxw&rel=0&border=1&color1=0xb1b1b1&color2=0xcfcfcf&hl=en&feature=player_embedded&fs=1.

[131] *RECORD YOUR LIFE—WITH THIS?,* 21 October 2009 09:30, routine, timeLapse, gadget, photography, citySensing, diary.

[132] http://urbantick.blogspot.com/2009/05/one-year-in-40-seconds-natural-cycle.html.

Fig. 12 Images by
Microsoft / Example shots
taken with a SenseCam

This is not possible over a longer period while 'living' the lead role in the soap opera project. Another implication is the storage capacity, even though it is a compressed version of filming it quickly generates a lot of data. A new product is about to enter the market to take on exactly the customers that are interested in that kind of stuff, somehow that would consequently include me too. However, the product was initially developed by Microsoft[133] in one of the research centres, actually in the Cambridge research centre. In short it is a camera that can be worn as a bracelet and it takes, as the name suggests, images triggered by a bunch of sensors. These sensors are light-intensity and light-colour sensors, a passive infrared (body heat) detector, a temperature sensor, and a multiple-axis accelerometer. The camera processor controls the sensors and will, if there is a change in sensed environment, take a picture. Every thing is automatic, hands-free photography so to say. Cleverly the developers got rid of the viewfinder, to save on unnecessary elements, and probably to stop customers using the device as a normal camera. Whether the device has an actual release button to manually shoot an important scene is not reported (Fig. 12).

Reading the specs does not necessarily make you jump for joy, the cam spots a VGA 640 × 480 pixels resolution receiver. I am not a big fan of massive resolution, but having at least the option for a timeLapse on vimeo in HD[134] should probably be standard. That's only some 1,080 × 720 pix what even a first generation iPhone will do! But it goes on, the camera is capable of taking a picture every 30 s only and there is only a 1 GB flash memory available. Microsoft suggests this will give you room for 30,000 pictures (Fig. 13).

As a life log this is, as gizmodo[135] points out, only a record of 10 days at a 30 s rate, not exactly a lifetime. Again there is currently no data regarding the power supply available but this is likely to have additional implications. It is unlikely that

[133] http://research.microsoft.com/en-us/um/cambridge/projects/sensecam/.

[134] http://vimeo.com/hd.

[135] http://gizmodo.com/5383272/camera-records-your-life-10-days-at-a-time.

Fig. 13 Images by Microsoft / Vicon the SenseCam

the cam will manage a 10 day session. Microsoft has now licensed the product to Vicon[136], based in Oxford, UK, a specialist for motion capturing. The reason named for this move is demand. So far some 500 devices have been produced. The new producer is prepared to launch the product in the next few months according to the New Scientist[137]. But at a price of £ 500.00, not cheap eh, you might think now, me too. See clip on Youtube[138].

However the blogging community has taken this announcement to test a few funny slogans. They came up with a couple of funny titles for the device: Sense-Cam—the Black Box Flight Recorder for human beings, by gizmag.com[139], 'Black box' cam for total recall, by the BBC[140]. And here an example of the cam in use.

119 *ARE WE LOOSING OUR SENSE OF DIRECTION?*[141] Are we losing our Sense of Direction? What a rhetoric question. Without the context this does not really make sense, or does it? Usually as things are starting to be fun, someone comes over to tell you how bad this is and that you should not do it because of this or this or even this reason. At least it was like this when you were a teen, battling for independence with beloved ones. However this is long gone and things have changed since. And still situation is the same. But now we are wiser and think twice, maybe it is true, or at least partially, there might be something about this other opinion I have not thought of in this way. Here we are with the news, finally, GPS is BAD! Yes, you are right, your SatNav is doing harm to you as you drive. At least this is what the headlines of the news on the New York Times blog[142]

---

[136] http://www.vicon.com/.

[137] http://www.newscientist.com/article/dn17992-new-camera-promises-to-capture-your-whole-life.html?DCMP=OTC-rss&nsref=tech.

[138] http://www.youtube.com/v/V0iqj27LKGA&color1=0xb1b1b1&color2=0xcfcfcf&hl=en&feature=player_embedded&fs=1.

[139] http://www.gizmag.com/go/2694/.

[140] http://news.bbc.co.uk/1/hi/technology/3797581.stm.

[141] *ARE WE LOOSING OUR SENSE OF DIRECTION?*, 22 October 2009 09:21, locationInformation, navigation, orientation, virtual world, GPS.

[142] http://ideas.blogs.nytimes.com/a2009/10/19/can-gps-help-your-brain-get-lost/.

and the walrus magazine[143] suggest Actually it is all based on an article by Alex Hutchinson. We actually have another SatNav article[144] here on urbanTick, that addresses the problem of arriving at the desired location but in this case it was about spelling the destination name correctly. In general Alex Hutchinson points out in his article that navigating is a learning process that is a dual relationship between brain and action. The more we use it the better we are at it, but it needs to be maintained. Scientists have identified an area in the brain, the hippocampus, which is responsible for this sort of navigation task. "The brains of London cabbies have out sized rear hippocampuses, because they are required to painstakingly learn the byzantine lanes and byways of the Old World city." (NYblog[145]) Most of us will not attempt to learn the apparently 25,000 street names and thousands of landmarks required for becoming a cabbie. However navigating and orientating do not necessarily require you to know all the names of the streets. Other elements are important in day-to-day navigation. Hutchinson refers to Veronique Bohbot[146] a researcher at McConnell Brain Imaging Center: "Bohbot demonstrated in a widely cited 2003 study that our mapping strategies fall into two basic categories. One is a spatial strategy that involves learning the relationships between various landmarks—creating a cognitive map in your head. The other is a stimulus-response approach that encodes specific routes by memorizing a series of cues, as in: get off the bus when you see the glass skyscraper, then walk toward the big park. For their study, Bohbot created a virtual maze that tested both methods; they found that about half of us prefer spatial strategies, while the other half prefer stimulus-response" (walrus magazine). We probably use both of these techniques depending on the situation, but most likely we prefer one over the other. What navigation type are you?

20 *GAMING AT LARGE SCALE*[147] Real world gaming with the help of mobile gadgets with GPS are high up this week. This weekend's Saturday Guardian Guide points to a gaming event that will take place over the next weekend simultaneously in three locations across the UK.

It is once more a sign of the upcoming section of location-interactive-real-world-games. Those are popular, together with the availability of gadgets, popular and they also develop into more mass compatible storyboards and technologies. In an other post on real-world games HERE[148], for reinterpreted old classics. The announced event 'greatstreetgames[149]' will take place between 29 October and the 1 November simultaneously in Gateshead, Sunderland[150] and Middlesbrough[151]. It is set up as a competition between the three places, but anyone can join any team, it is open to the public (Fig. 14).

---

[143] http://www.walrusmagazine.com/articles/2009.11-health-global-impositioning-systems/.

[144] http://urbantick.blogspot.com/2009/09/getting-lost-with-gps.html.

[145] http://ideas.blogs.nytimes.com/2009/10/19/can-gps-help-your-brain-get-lost/.

[146] http://www.bic.mni.mcgill.ca/~vero/.

[147] *GAMING AT LARGE SCALE,* 26 October 2009 09:45, game, interaction, locationInformation.

[148] http://urbantick.blogspot.com/2009/09/gps-real-world-gaming.html.

[149] http://www.greatstreetgames.org.uk/.

[150] http://www.sunderlandevents.co.uk/event-detail.asp?EventID=3389.

[151] http://www.visitmiddlesbrough.com/site/whats-on/products/great-street-games-p413731.

Fig. 14 Image by KMA via Pruned / A visual of the upcoming game project

Basically it will consist of a large playing field projected in each location where players collect points by collecting 'virtual' balls. It will be a best of five series each game lasting 90 s. The city with the most points wins. Surprisingly the official web pages do not make a very big deal out of it. There is very little information to be found outside the world of techies and geeks. It is designed by KMA[152], collaboration between Kit Monkman and Tom Wexler. They introduce their work as follows: "KMA's work creates large, immersive, sometimes networked, 'digital playgrounds', in which distinctions between audiences and performers disappear. The resulting social engagements reaffirm the urban community through embodied, rather than verbal, discourse." The project has already featured on Pruned[153] and was embedded in a lovely story envisioning the encounter with the projected game field as something one might stumble across in the darkness of the vast city, something that might be a discovery. However this game is locally very confined to a rather small space as the visualisations suggest. You won't need the GPS to play, maybe to find it, if you were texted the latest location for today's game. Nevertheless, it does connect over a large distance the three cities. From the available descriptions it is difficult to grasp how much interaction is possible between the locations, but this definitely would be the most interesting aspect. Maybe someone in Sunderland will snatch your virtual ball and drop it in their own box. To some extent the game proposal reminds me of the 'Where's Wally' scene with the six team football.

---

[152] http://www.kma.co.uk/.

[153] http://pruned.blogspot.com/2009/10/great-street-games.html.

As it looks, Hollywood also has realized that there is something changing in the world of gamers and games. They have implemented the aspect of real people in a virtual game for quite a while, probably because it makes for simple plots. The latest version is the 'Gamer[154]' movie directed by Mark Neveldine and Brian Taylor. What they haven't yet realised is the spatial aspect of the emergent street games and with it the importance of the location. But probably this is the point, a game is not a movie, you are not entertained, you are entertaining as you play the game.

21   *WORLD RACER*[155] Gaming in the real world is currently the big thing and interactive technologies do support these activities. However there is on the other side similar effort to make games more realistic, see game engines on digitalurban[156]. In between the two extremes, you could say, there sits Google Maps and Google Earth. Of course not as an official game but in terms of reality vs. virtual, as it virtually represents the reality. Google has so far had little aspiration to take on the games market, apart from the flight simulator in Google Earth together with release 4. There are now, with the release of the new flash version, some new options. Not Google, but independent developers, have started to merge some gaming interaction with Google's virtual real world platforms. A very early one was the Monster Milk Truck[157] that could be driven in Google Earth. I love that one, with its nice effective jumps. It was made possible by the release of the Plug-In to run Google Earth in a browser.

Earlier this year we saw the launch of Monopoly[158] based on Google Maps and there are new racing games out. One is RealWorldRacer[159] by Tom Scott. Here you can enter a destination in Google Maps as you would to find a route you are planning and off you go. There are four cars to compete with, plus along the track check points, you have to drive relatively close by, to deactivate. This is to make sure you are not driving off somewhere on the map, as there are currently no other bounding elements implemented. Another tool is googleDrive[160] developed in conjunction with the MIT by Samuel Birch[161], this one is said to have limitations where you can only drive on the actual roads, however it did not work on my machine so let me know what you think of it. See clip on Youtube[162].

The third is Driving Simulator on geoquake and here you can choose between four different vehicles. A beta version was just released featuring different perspective, HERE[163].

---

[154] http://www.apple.com/trailers/lions_gate/gamer/.

[155] *WORLD RACER,* 28 October 2009 09:10, game, locationInformation, Google Earth, Google Maps.

[156] http://digitalurban.blogspot.com/search?q=game+engine.

[157] http://earth-api-samples.googlecode.com/svn/trunk/demos/milktruck/index.html.

[158] http://urbantick.blogspot.com/2009/09/gps-real-world-gaming.html.

[159] http://www.tomscott.com/realworldracer/#.

[160] http://www.phatfusion.net/googleDrive/.

[161] http://www.samuelbirch.com/.

[162] http://www.youtube.com/v/iMB5gzUtiM4&color1=0xb1b1b1&color2=0xcfcfcf&hl=en&feature=player_embedded&fs=1.

[163] http://geoquake.jp/en/webgame/DrivingSimulatorPerspective/.

Fig. 15 Image taken from Wikipedia / Satellite path orbiting the earth. (http://upload.wikimedia.org/wiki-pedia/commons/9/9c/Constel-lationGPS.gif)

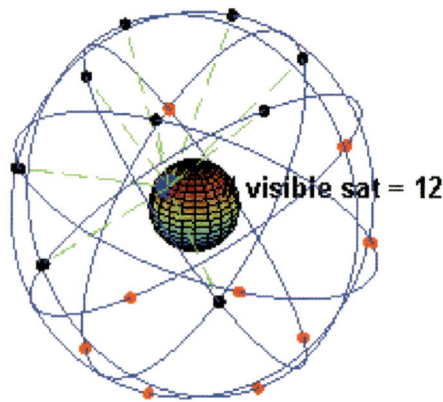

122   *GPS SIGNAL JAMMED BY THE PENTAGON*[164] Actually the GPS signal can be manipulated, who would have guessed otherwise? The system being an American Military Defence innovation, this is one of the strategies implemented to prevent enemies using the system against US targets. The system implemented was the selective availability (SA) restriction imposed on the signal for civil, e.g. non-military, use. Today a large variety of digital gadgets are equipped with GPS receivers, ranging from in car navigation systems to mobile phones. This was kicked of by the former president Bill Clinton's decision to lift the imposed SA restriction in 2000. Following the SA removal, civil and commercial GPS accuracy increased from around 100 m to between 3 and 15 m (Pendleton 2002 as cited in Spencer 2003, p. 56) (Fig. 15).

To come back to the temporal and local jamming of the GPS signal holds still an important status in the strategy of US military action. The European system Galileo is still under construction and its partial launch will not be until 2012 or beyond. The other functioning system is the Russian Glonas. However this is not covering the entire planet with a signal as it only operates on 18 satellites (2008) focusing on Russia. In this sense, the US holds a monopoly. The jamming of the signal is normally not known to the public and only speculated over. However it is very likely that it is used in current war zones, like Iraq and Afghanistan. There are reports over this jamming to be found on the internet. Computerworld[165] has an article on the subject quoting some GPS experts on the matter. "Sam Wormley, a researcher at Iowa State University in Ames and manager of an authoritative GPS resources and accuracy Web site, said that the Pentagon 'definitely' has the capability to jam civilian GPS signals in a given area without interfering with more precise military signals. Wormley said that's because the military signals occupy a different and smaller slice of the GPS frequency band than that used by the civilian signals." The jamming most likely is achieved through a slight desynchronisation of the clocks.

---

[164] *GPS SIGNAL JAMMED BY THE PENTAGON,* 29 October 2009 09:31, GPS device, location-Information, navigation, global, GPS.

[165] http://www.computerworld.com/s/article/65096/Pentagon_is_probably_jamming_GPS_in_Afghanistan_experts_say.

For military purposes this can easily be decoded. There are very funny discussions going on out there on the web around the possibility of jamming the satellite signal. A good one[166] is on yahoo.answers.com, where some guy accuses his neighbour 'Joe' of jamming his satellite dish, because whenever Joe is home the guy thinks his TV signal is disrupted. Thinking this further, how do we know that the actual position is correct? As we have seen in the introduction of this post, as well as in last week's new Argos catalogue, consumer GPS products have become immensely popular and everyone needs to know where they are. Whether this is true or not in this case is probably not that important. Therefore, we don't know if the represented location on Google Earth is actually the true position as in Lat Long, yes we can see that this image shows the street we're in, but the structural framework of the Lat Long coordinate is not necessarily the 'right' one. But I guess this is the question of the artificially imposed grid that we can only virtually refer to and believe in as a convention. So next time you end up in New York, rather than the planned Newark because of a spelling mistake[167] while typing it into the gadget, you can blame the US for temporarily jamming your specific satellite. But if you are after your neighbour here are some web stores[168] where you can purchase your own satellite jammer to annoy your 'Joe'. However I wanted to link a creepy James Bond extract, where the space craft swallows the satellite, but you guessed it, it is not out there yet. So if anyone has this sequence lying around please upload and link it here. However I therefore link to a very boring but scientific clip that actually visualises the GPS signal availability in Kabul during the course of one day. See the video by Richard Langley 'Kabul.GPS.Visibility.mov'[169].

The scientist, Richard Langley, a professor of geodesy and precision navigation at the University of New Brunswick has observed the predicted position of the satellite versus the actual signal strength in the area and there seems to be clearly a jam. However, that was recorded back in 2001, but most certainly this has taken place before and after, as well as in other places than Kabul too.

---

[166] http://answers.yahoo.com/question/index?qid=20070327041132AAEfQFD.

[167] http://urbantick.blogspot.com/2009/09/getting-lost-with-gps.html.

[168] http://www.globalsources.com/manufacturers/GPS-Signal-Jammer.html.

[169] http://gauss.gge.unb.ca/kabul/Kabul.GPS.Visibility.mov.

Part VI
UrbanDiary

From urbanTick to UrbanDiary

Fabian Neuhaus

Traditionally the city is mapped as a network of streets and large numbers of buildings and blocks. This given space is generally taken as universal and true. The aspect of change, movement and time are often ignored, because they have not one state, but many. The urbanTick[1] research aims to address this problem by looking at ways to observe and map these processes. By tracking activities and actions it starts to evolve a new perspective on how to define and interpret the city as a collective product of pattern in time.

In this context the UrbanDiary[2] project collects data on the spatial extend of individuals' routines in the wider London region. The project records the movement of participants with the help of GPS devices[3] and aims to capture the beat of the city[4]. The output is a collection of personal statements on how individuals "use" and experience the city. The pattern represents the occurring repetition in the participant's behaviour. Thick lines start to accumulate on the daily routes and draw out the very personal arteries of the city. To the surprise of most participants the individual activities are rather confined.

The London trajectory map produces a star shape. Compared to records of other cities[5] this characteristic is individual to each city and is determined by the morphology, transport network and citizen behaviour (Fig. 1).

Depending on the preferences of transport by the participant the emerging patter of activity draws a continuous track or starts to build up isolated and spatially disconnected areas of activity[6] reassembling Guy Debord's Naked City (1957).

---

[1] http://urbantick.blogspot.com/.

[2] http://www.facebook.com/pages/Urban-Diary/67812788988.

[3] http://urbantick.blogspot.com/search/label/GPS.

[4] http://urbantick.blogspot.com/2009/01/transport-rhythm.html.

[5] http://urbantick.blogspot.com/2008/12/comparison.html.

[6] http://urbantick.blogspot.com/2009/03/city-islands-on-linkage-of-everyday.html.

F. Neuhaus (✉)
Centre for Advanced Spatial Analysis, University College London, London, UK
e-mail: fabian.neuhaus@ucl.ac.uk

F. Neuhaus (ed.), *Studies in Temporal Urbanism,*
DOI 10.1007/978-94-007-0937-9_11, © Springer Science+Business Media B.V. 2011

Fig. 1 Image by urbanTick
for UrbanDiary / UrbanDiary
map showing 15 participants'
records / UDall_090417.
(http://www.casa.ucl.ac.uk/
urbantick/ut/blogImage/
UDtracks_map_090415.jpg)

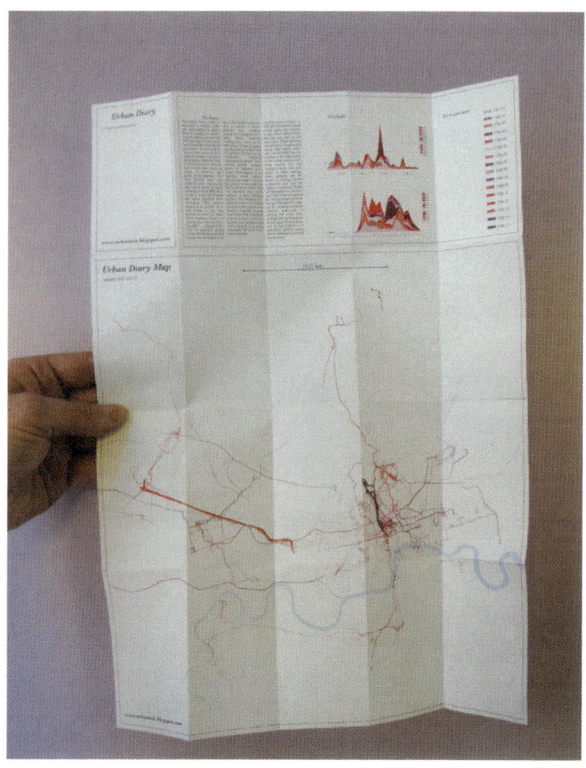

A number of clips have been using Google Earth as the rendering engine to
visualise the GPS data. The CASA Virtual London Model has been used to set the
recorded locations into a spatial context (Fig. 3).

This setting is regarded as a first step to combine the time based information
and the morphological data[7]. Regarding the findings, there are two main levels of
interest; one is the level of the individual and the context of the personal routine and
activity. The other one is the collective level looking at overall patterns and rhythms
that point towards a spatial society. The first one is ultimately present for the participants and mainly the context they each perceive themselves in. The second, collective level is something that has to be constructed from the individual data (Fig. 3).

What shape are you?[8] It emerged from the recorded data, that each participant
has her/his unique pattern of tracks. Almost like an individual fingerprint the shape
created by daily movement is unique. The urbanTick project will continue on the individual level with interviews, directed towards understanding participant's perception and memory using mental maps. This will be connected to the body experience,
looking at morphology as a product of rhythmic processes (Fig. 4).

---

[7] http://urbantick.blogspot.com/search/label/morphology.

[8] http://urbantick.blogspot.com/2009/04/what-shape-are-you.html.

Fig. 2 Image by urbanTick
for UrbanDiary / Space-Time
Aquarium showing a 24 hour
period in the live of three
individuals. (http://www.
casa.ucl.ac.uk/urbantick/ut/
blogImage/UDaquarium_07-
09-UT_0221Final02_090319.
jpg)

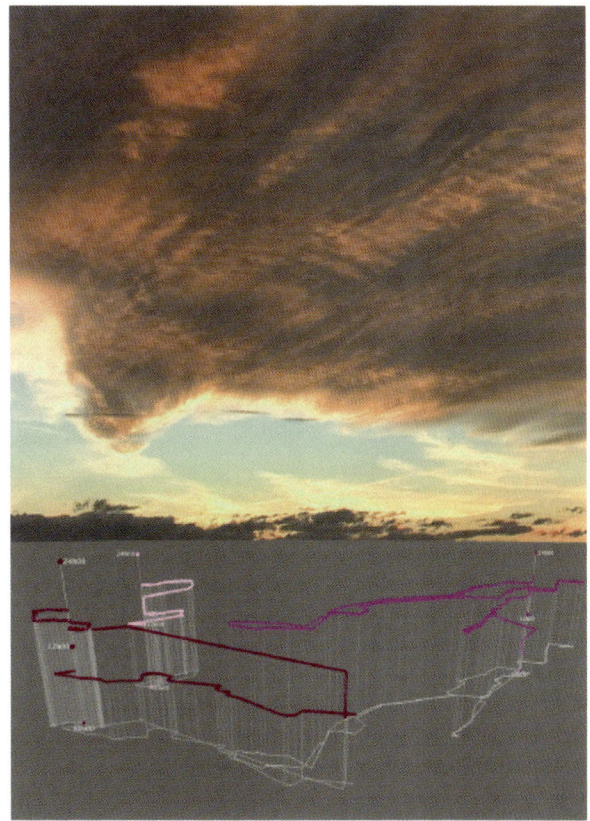

Fig. 3 Clip by urbanTick
on Vimeo / UrbanDiary two
month of records. (http://
vimeo.com/4277201)

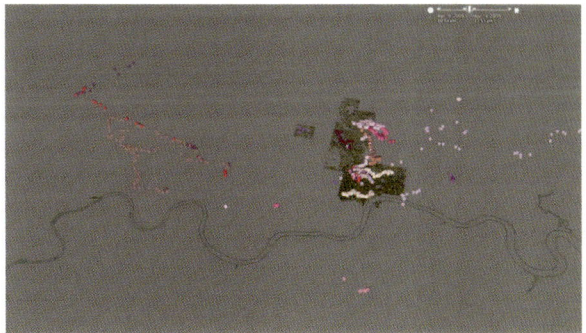

Fig. 4 Image by urbanTick
for UrbanDiary / Individual
track records all shown at the
same scale and over the same
period of time

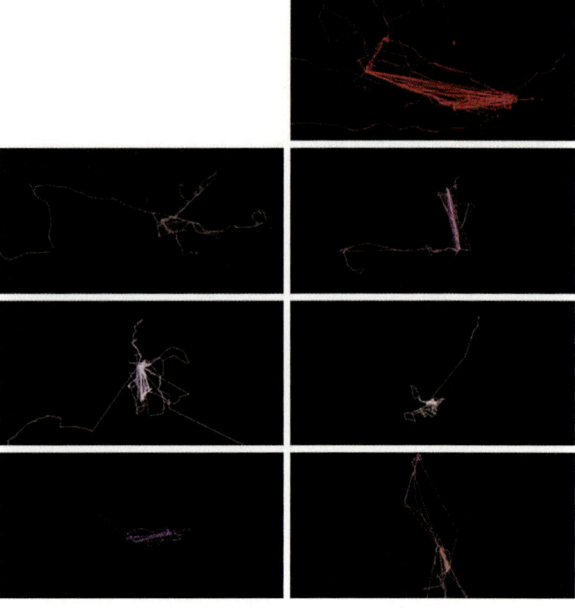

UrbanDiary

Fabian Neuhaus

23 *LONDON DIARY—WEEK ONE*[1] A short clip to visualise different people's movement over the period of one week in London. It is a first test with a number of participants using Garmin GPS devices. The data returned is actually better than expected, although there are a lot of errors, even in the city centre there is often a signal. For a better visualisation the day and night feature of Google Earth was used to clearly mark the passage of time. It's sweet how they all rest in their place when it is dark, and then start off early in the morning.

See clip on Vimeo[2]/One week of movement, animation produced in Excel and with a converter by Bill Clark[3] brought to Google Earth[4]. The weekend has been used by a number of participants to make trips, sometimes quite far, in most cases to visit relatives or friends. Looking forward to get to work with the data from next week.

24 *LONDON DIARY—WEEK TWO*[5] It has been a busy week, as always. The data collection this week was again good, with some nice tracks. To the disappointment of some participants, the pattern has been VERY similar to last weeks. See clip on Vimeo[6]/Movement of ten individuals over two weeks. Unfortunately our lives do not

---

[1] *LONDON DIARY—WEEK ONE,* 13 February 2009 00:09, animation, Google Earth, GPS tracks, UrbanDiary, London, rhythms, routine, cycles.

[2] http://vimeo.com/3193950.

[3] http://www.earthpoint.us/ExcelToKml.aspx.

[4] http://earth.google.com/.

[5] *LONDON DIARY—WEEK TWO,* 20 February 2009 10:51, rhythm, animation, GPS tracks, UrbanDiary, London, visualisation, cycles.

[6] http://vimeo.com/3281700.

F. Neuhaus (✉)
Centre for Advanced Spatial Analysis, University College London, London, UK
e-mail: fabian.neuhaus@ucl.ac.uk

F. Neuhaus (ed.), *Studies in Temporal Urbanism,*   179
DOI 10.1007/978-94-007-0937-9_12, © Springer Science+Business Media B.V. 2011

quite cover as much ground in the city as we might like to think, the routines we follow are rather strong. Nevertheless, to find that the perception is different is already a good finding. But have a look yourself, here is a clip generated from the data. A different view gives the following clip. Here, the data is replayed in 24 h, so all the records played in one day. The coverage shows that there is activity throughout the day, except the early morning hours. Between 02 h00 and 07 h00 there is a big gap in activity. The rest of the time 07 h00 to midnight and beyond is very active. See clip on Vimeo[7]/the two week data replayed as a 24 h summary.

What is a bit misleading here is that the weekend activities are squeezed in together with the weekday activities. From the clip above we have seen that the activity pattern between the two varies a lot. The next step would be to find a visualisation that clearly focuses on this problem. You can see last week's visuals here[8].

125   URBANDIARY LONDON MAP[9] The map of the last three weeks keyed by participants. The dotted lines indicate connections within a trip sequence but without proper GPS signal (Fig. 1).

There are a number of patterns showing up now. On of the main ones is the difference between workweek and weekend. The workdays are back and forward movement between home and the work place. The London characteristic here is a sort of a star shape. People live outside and travel linear into the centre and back out. For some participants the workweek tracks are only two little islands on the map, connected through a dotted line, as a lot of travelling is underground. The weekend travel pattern on the other hand is mainly around the home location and tends to be directed outwards. Very often this is directed by the location of friends and family.

126   LONDON DIARY—WEEK THREE[10] An update on the collected data from the UrbanDiary project. It is already three weeks now and it is still going. The collected data is good, the main problems lie in the handling and processing. I tend to focus on the 24 h time frame visualisation, where the data is replayed all in one day, rather than visualizing it day by day over three weeks. It is much denser in this way and patterns show up more clearly. On the other hand the danger is that one off activities have a very strong influence on the visualisation. Each participant is represented by an individual colour. For this weeks visualisation I again used the Google Earth but without the satellite imagery. So it is visually simpler and there is more control regarding the colours. I am also using the 3D Virtual London model developed here at CASA to provide some context. Having this background moving into analysing the connections between the activity pattern and the morphology is one step closer. The 24 h cycle I have also changed this week (Fig. 2).

I have noticed that altogether there are activities roughly between 06 h00 and 02 h00 in the morning. The default duration on Google Earth is obviously 00 h00 to 24 h00. The recorded animation now starts at 04 h00 in the morning and continues

---

[7] http://vimeo.com/3303322.

[8] http://urbantick.blogspot.com/2009/02/London-diary-week-one.html.

[9] URBANDIARY LONDON MAP, 25 February 2009 15:04, visualisation, map, GPS tracks, mapping, UrbanDiary.

[10] LONDON DIARY—WEEK THREE, 3 March 2009 14:53, visualisation, rhythm, animation, GPS tracks, UrbanDiary.

Fig. 1 Image by urbanTick
for UrbanDiary using gpsvi-
sualiser.com to convert the
data / Track map showing the
London traces. (http://www.
gpsvisualiser.com/)

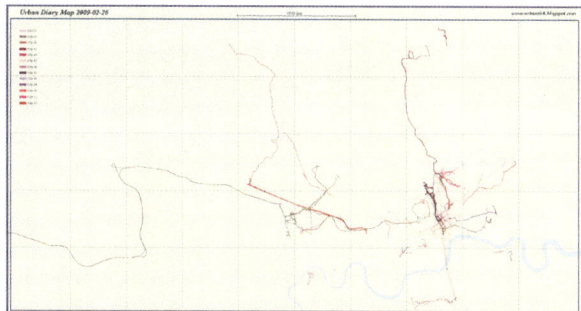

Fig. 2 Clip by urbanTick on
Vimeo / Visualising week
three including bits of the 3D
London Model. (http://vimeo.
com/3453387)

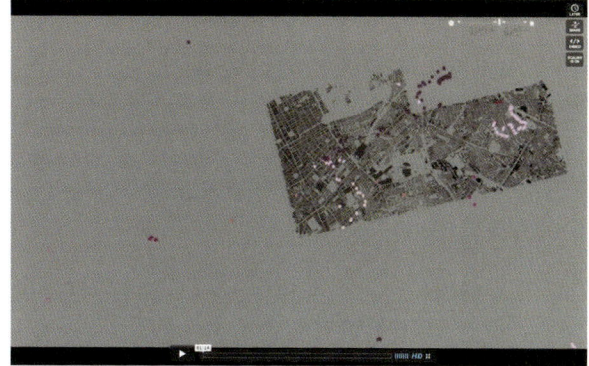

Fig. 3 Clip by urbanTick
on Vimeo / The clip shows
a zoomed area around UCL.
(http://vimeo.com/3453468)

until 03 h00 the next morning. A zoomed in version of the animation visualises the
area around UCL. It is again replayed within a 24 h time frame and representing the
different participants with different colours (Fig. 3).

The normal workday pattern starts showing up again, 09 h00 to 17 h00, outside
this frame there is very little activity. The third zoom is looking at a neighbourhood
area where participants live. In this case the colours used in this visualisation are
not based on individuals but they represent weekdays and weekend days. The dark-

Fig. 4 Clip by urbanTick on
Vimeo / A zoom into a neighbourhood area. (http://vimeo.
com/3453430)

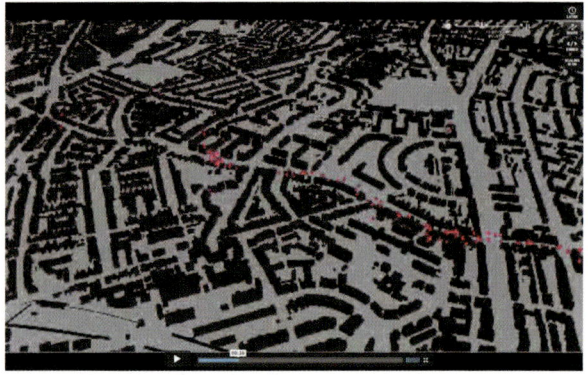

er purple is the weekdays, whereas the lighter pink is the weekend activities. The
emerging pattern tends to be focused on the main transport axis for bus travel and
tube stations as locations. On the other hand the weekend pattern shows activities
within the neighbourhood and local streets rather than the main streets. So weekday
activity tends to be towards the south in two time frames, one in the morning and
one in the evening. The weekend activity, in this case, tends to be towards the north
and throughout the day (Fig. 4).

127   *THE DIARY IN GRAPHS*[11] Some first graphs analyse the tracking data in some
other ways. It is now almost one month (I have not yet got the data from all the
participants for this time period) of tracking and I think this is going to be the first
milestone in the project. At the moment I think that one month could make a pretty
good unit as a base to start analysing the data. A cycle of four week patterns could
provide enough data to paint a rough picture of the activities and range. As it is the
first month I'm only guessing here and will have to check this assumption as more
data will be coming in over the next couple of weeks. The graph visualisation focuses on the quantitative aspect of the data together with the time information over the
location information. The idea is to look at the schedule information contained in
the record. This is of interest as the project is interested in enhancing knowledge on
personal, spatial routines. The graphs are visualizing the amount of activity over a
specific time period. The periods are one day—24-h, one week and one month. Using these units of general time frames helps to establish an appropriate framework
for the data. Participants are all understood to use these time frames. More specific
units could relate to religion, culture or specific responsibility or job. These will be
respected on a more individual level of analysis. In the graphs the x-axis represents
time whereas the y-axis refers to amount of activity. This is measured by the number
of log points the GPS device has stored for the time period in question. The graphs
do not give information about time spent in one location: they solely focus on travel
time between destinations.

    One month analysed by day and participant. In total there are four peaks over
four weekends. They generally do match, although one peak has slightly moved
into week three. This was the UK midterm week, a holiday brake. Participants who

---

[11] *THE DIARY IN GRAPHS,* 6 March 2009 00:16, graphs, visualisation, UrbanDiary.

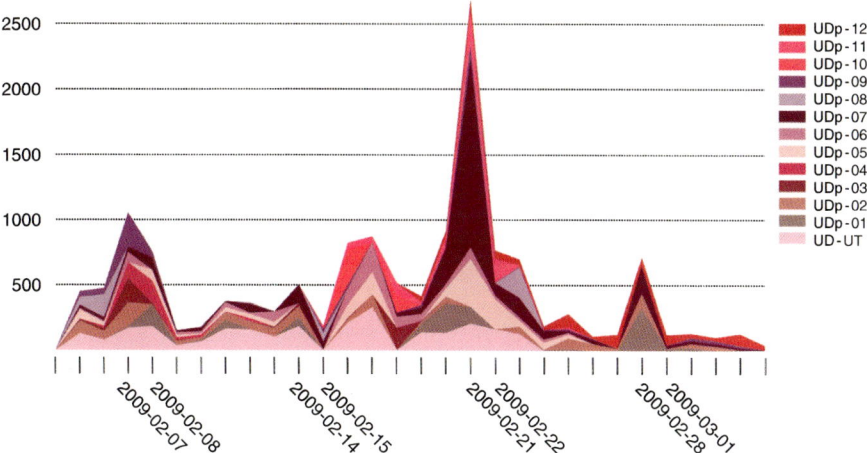

Fig. 5 Image by urbanTick for UrbanDiary / Graph of GPS data collected as part of the UD project during the first month

have children or work in a school have spent more time travelling during the normal weekdays. Surprisingly the Sunday at the start of this mid term week is very low. All of the participants have recorded little activity. It must have been really bad weather and people stayed indoors. On the contrary, one Saturday pops out extensively. It turns out that one of the participants had an intensive outdoor sports day, during that he generated a large number of points (Fig. 5).

There is an activity accumulation on Saturdays. This shows up in particular in the week's graph. Saturday has more than double the amount of points of other days of the week. Not only this one participant who is doing intense sports activity on Saturday, but all of the participants tend to have significantly more activity on Saturdays. Other than that the weekdays are fairly equal in terms of activity with a tendency to a low point midweek (Fig. 6).

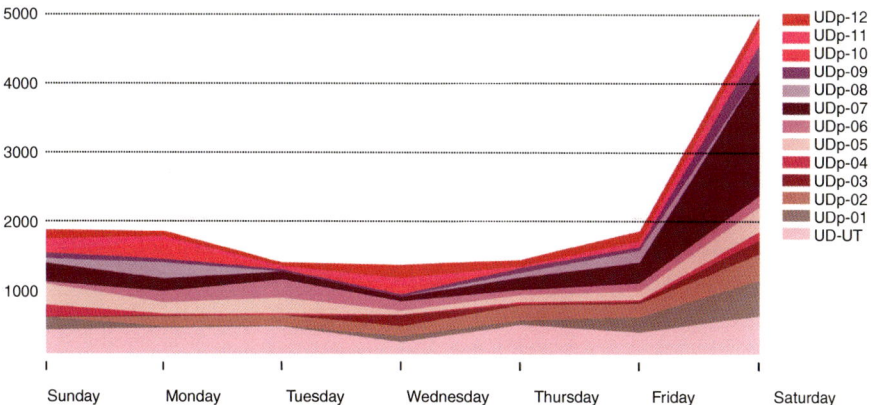

Fig. 6 Image by urbanTick for UrbanDiary / Graph showing participant activity over the week based on GPS records

Compared to the regularity of the week, the 24 h graph shows a number of peaks. The graph starts at midnight with an expected flat bit representing few activities. In the first hours of the day there is some activity but it reduces to virtually zero in the early hours of the morning. The day then starts with a first peak of the morning rush hour. Around seven participants start leaving the house, but it then really takes off from eight, peaking around nine and coming to a first low point around ten. From this low the second peak starts rising immediately. By looking closely at the participants involved in these first two peaks one can see that actually there is two groups, one generating the first "rush hour peak" and the second group mainly contribute to the second similar peak about 1 h later. The second peak has a twin peak with a first high point around 10 h00 and a second one just before lunch around 13 h00. After lunch around two o'clock there is the low point of the day with the least activity during this 24-h day apart from the early morning hours. After the lunch break, there is a fat afternoon/evening peak. This is representing a number of weekend afternoon activities like the outdoor sport that was mentioned above. Included into this fat peak are a first evening rush hour high point between five and six and a smaller second peak around eight, probably pointing to the visit of the pub after work (Fig. 7).

Colour correspond with the key on the map here[12]. Generally this resembles the expected daily routine pattern of a western city. What is more surprising is accuracy the pattern shows up, rather than any unexpected results. Although the sample is not representative it was not expected to show this regularity.

128 *UD RECORD—MAPPING BY WEEKDAY*[13] I have quickly generated a track map coded according to weekdays (Fig. 8).

It is coded in orange for the weekend tracks and in brownish for the week days.

A comment on analysis of the pattern will follow… Check online for the image to see a higher resolution version.

129 *UD AQUARIUMEXAMPLE*[14] A refreshed visualisation of the space-time diagram, called the aquarium. This time with the all new UrbanDiary project data.

Schematic representation of a Saturday track record of three participants of the UrbanDiary project recorded in London. The data is plotted with the z-axis representing time of the day. The time frame in this case is 24 h and starts from the bottom at 00 h00 passing the time upwards to 24 h00. Each participant has a time reference icon over the home location, where the journey starts and ends. There are three participants: two male, one female, of whom the female and one male participant have family (Fig. 9).

The single male goes in to work just as normal although it is a Saturday and returns home in the afternoon to do some sport activity locally where he lives. His journey starts at 08 h23, ends at 17 h19 and travels around 15 km. The woman does some local activities with her family and travels in to her workplace briefly later on. She starts her day at 07 h01, ends at 20 h09, and covers 30 km while travelling.

---

[12] http://urbantick.blogspot.com/2009/02/urban-diary-London-map.html.

[13] *UD RECORD—MAPPING BY WEEKDAY*, 11 March 2009 23:37, GPS tracks, tracking, mapping, UrbanDiary.

[14] *UD AQUARIUMEXAMPLE*, 17 March 2009 21:01, aquarium, GPS tracks, UrbanDiary.

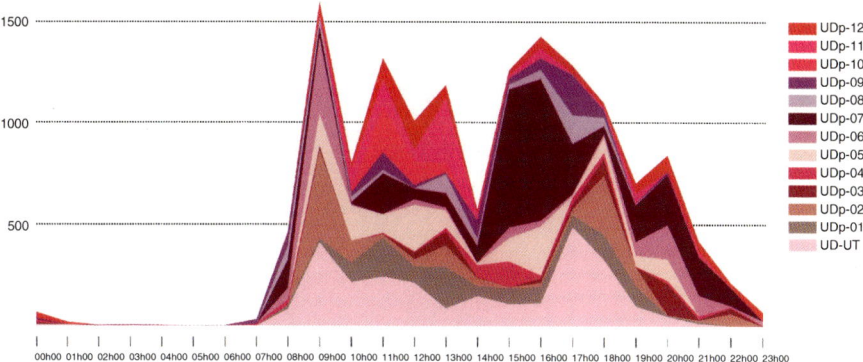

Fig. 7 Image by urbanTick for UrbanDiary / Graph showing the participant activity over a 24 hour period based on GPS records

Fig. 8 Image by urbanTick for UrbanDiary / Track map for London coloured by day of the week

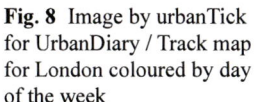

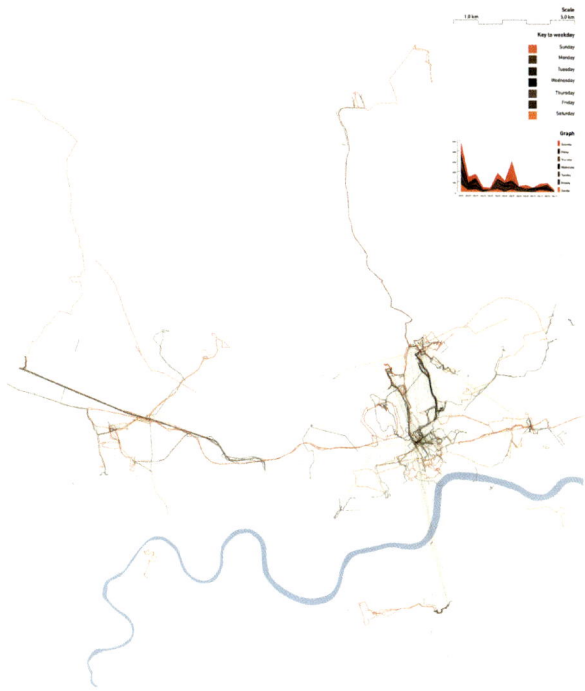

The second male participant spends his day in the local area. This journey starts at 11 h45, ends at 18 h53, and measures 5 km.

30   *PRESENTATION CASA SEMINAR*[15] Presentation of the PhD work that I have been doing so far. The presentation was given in the context of the CASA Seminar series. Wednesday, March 25, 2009, Galton Lecture Theatre, with the title: UrbanDiary—Cycles, rhythms and pattern in everyday life. This PhD research project focuses on

---

[15] *PRESENTATION CASA SEMINAR*, 26 March 2009 14:11, presentation, UrbanDiary.

Fig. 9 Image by urbanTick
for UrbanDiary / Time-Space
aquarium showing three
individuals over the period of
24 hours

the cycles and rhythms in the urban environment. Like day and night or the rush-hour, there are a number of repetitive patterns occurring in the city. Maybe they are the result of spatial and social organization methods, but probably they are involved in the organization of the city as a system. With the use of GPS technology I research patterns in people's everyday activities. The main interest is the spatial extension of these routines. Findings are expected to be useful for planning and urban design in particular. The slides are here.[16] Of course there were some clips integrated with the slides for the presentation, I just haven't found the clever way to combine the two for the web presentation. Any good ideas? The clips are somewhere on the blog if you are interested.

131   *THE NEW URBANDIARY MAP IS HERE—TWO MONTH OF TRACKING*[17]
The new and updated UrbanDiary Map is here! Bigger, bolder and with even more tracks! (Fig. 10).

It contains now two months of tracking data of 16 different participants. The collection is still growing and will be updated continuously. After this period of

---

[16] http://picasaweb.google.com/s/c/bin/slideshow.swf.

[17] *THE NEW URBANDIARY MAP IS HERE—TWO MONTH OF TRACKING*, 15 April 2009 17:11, movement, GPS tracks, mapping, UrbanDiary, London, tracking, visualisation.

Fig. 10 Image by urbanTick for UrbanDiary / Track map for London

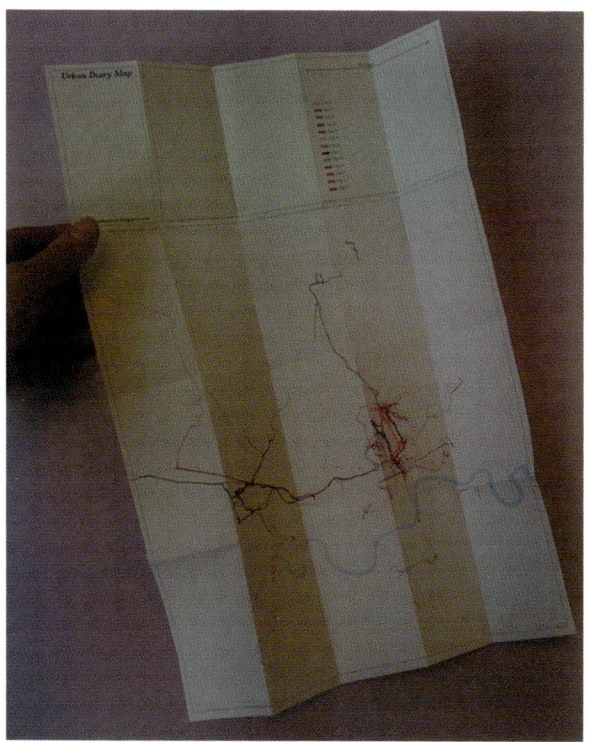

Fig. 11 Clip by urbanTick on Vimeo. (http://vimeo. com/4277201)

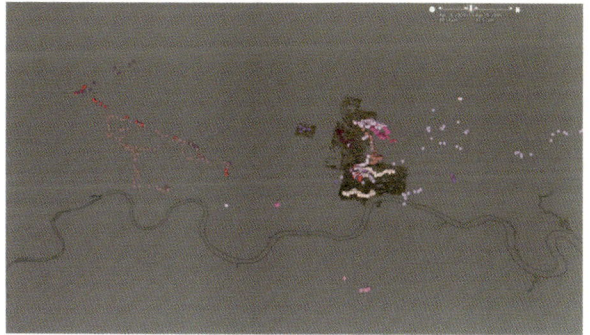

two months the participants' routes have mainly established and show up bold on the map. Nevertheless some oneoff routes continue to appear and they could be of much interest.

TWO MONTH OF TRACK RECORDS—URBANDIARY UPDATE[18], The Urban-Diary [19] project has been tracking participants for over two months (Fig. 11).

---

[18] *TWO MONTH OF TRACK RECORDS—URBANDIARY UPDATE,* 22 April 2009 15:33, routine, London, GPS tracks, UrbanDiary.

[19] *http://www.facebook.com/pages/Urban-Diary/67812788988#/.*

Fig. 12 Clip by urbanTick on Vimeo. (http://vimeo. com/4469668)

Fig. 13 Images by urbanTick for UrbanDiary / What Shape are You? Individual tracking pattern over a period of two month

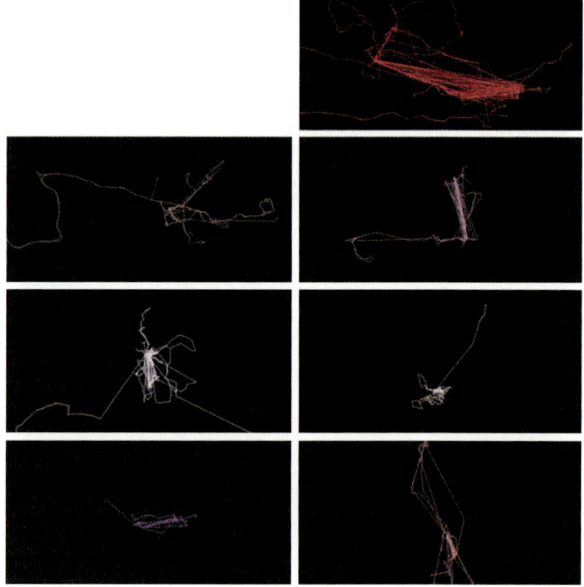

The data is now used to render a set of new animations. It is a general setting, superimposing all participants' days on top of one day, including weekdays and weekends (Fig. 12).

The radial transport structure in the city really starts showing up now and the corridors are highlighted. The daily beat of moving from the outside to the inside in the morning and back out in the evening is a strong characteristic.

The trips that do not follow this rule can be identified as weekend activities or days off. The colours correspond to the map[20] posted earlier.

---

[20] http://www.casa.ucl.ac.uk/urbantick/ut/blogImage/UDtracks_map_090415.jpg.

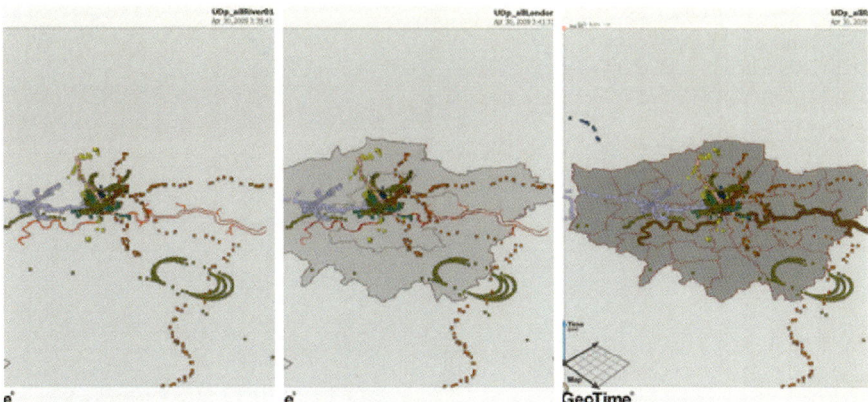

Fig. 14 Image by urbanTick for UrbanDiary / Location points with river Thames (*far left*), inner and outer London (*centre*), London regions (*right*)

33   *WHAT SHAPE ARE YOU?*[21] While working with the GPS track data of the UrbanDiary project, in connection with the series of interviews I am conducting, I suddenly recognized the different shapes and patterns that are being produced by the participants (Fig. 13).

Really funny shapes and forms, but always with a number of strong fixed points. The shape is determined by a number of factors such as the spatial relationship of destinations, the distances travelled, the amount of travel and the intensity of repetition. The first point, relationship of destinations, makes for the overall shape and the last point, the intensity of repetition, makes for the character of the shape. The images are all generated from data of participants who have a track record of two month and the drawings are the same scale.

34   *HAVING THE MAP—BASE MAPPING IN GEOTIME*[22] Finally I managed to get some kind of data from ArcMap linked into GeoTime[23] as a base map. The projection that works is only WGS84, but most of the data we have here obviously is in British national grid. So some transformation is required. This very often results in some funny shapes and suddenly you go, wow, I haven't seen greater London as this kind of squashed tomato shape yet. Another problem is to get the transformed files to match up, and so on. It is confusing. But here we are at least the Greater London area is there and the river Thames (Fig. 14).

And then even the buildings appear, imported from the Virtual London Model[24], developed here at CASA. They are slightly out of place but there they are (Fig. 15).

Next step will be to add some detailed information to the GeoTime data. At the moment it only represents track point location data. But with the series of inter-

---

[21] *WHAT SHAPE ARE YOU?* 23 April 2009 23:19, psychogeography, personal, GPS tracks, UrbanDiary, London, routine, rhythm.

[22] *HAVING THE MAP—BASE MAPPING IN GEOTIME*, 30 April 2009 14:31, visualisation, GeoTime, UrbanDiary.

[23] http://www.oculusinfo.com/SoftwareProducts/GeoTime.html.

[24] http://www.casa.ucl.ac.uk/projects/projectDetail.asp?ID=55.

Fig. 15 Image by urbanTick
for UrbanDiary / Zoom Kings
Cross with location spots

Fig. 16 Image by urbanTick
for UrbanDiary / Lines of
activity, zoom Kings Cross

views that are under way at the moment, some more detailed data about the participants' activities are available (Fig. 16).

GeoTime could be quite helpful in relating these different types of information. These images are screen shots taken from GeoTime with the software's internal screen grabber. The top view was used to get the displayed GPS data to match properly with the imported base map. For visualisation purposes this was seen to be the easiest way to understand what was going on. By switching into 3D view things get complicated and it is difficult to make sense of the combination of data that moves up and down in time and a base layer with a static maps -especially when zooming in to see details. The feature to replay the data can be helpful in this situation though (Fig. 17).

Fig. 17 Image by urbanTick
for UrbanDiary / 3D view in
GeoTime

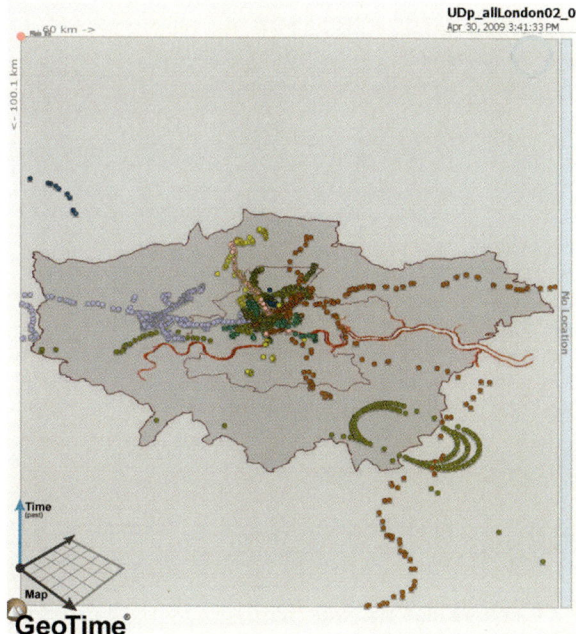

The map then acts as the division between past and future, basically the present. A location dot is used to mark this position. 2009-05-02/An update on this mapping topic./The issues where something I talked about with Curtis from GeoTime.

He suggested that a very quick fix is a available through the recourses in ESRI ArcGIS. They actually offer a number of base maps as free resources in 9.3 the world street network works quite good for the London location. And after I found the slider to adjust the map transparency I was quite happy with the result.

ROUTINE PART 01—MENTAL MAPS OF DAILY COMMUTING[25] As a second phase of the UrbanDiary project, the data collection focuses on the participants' perception of their routine and activity. During semi structured interviews detailed information is collected to accompany and extend the data recorded via the GPS device. The topics selected for the interview are personal information such as work status and family status, routine, schedule, spatial knowledge, contextual knowledge, transport, memory of routes and GPS device usage. During the interview the participants are also asked to write down information about their daily, weekly and yearly schedule and also to draw a mental map of their travel from home to work and back. Some preliminary observations from one of the first sketches drawn by a UD participant, looking at mode of transport, sequence of noting down descriptive elements and a comparison to the GPS record of the route (Fig. 18).

---

[25] *ROUTINE PART 01—MENTAL MAPS OF DAILY COMMUTING*, 14 May 2009 23:38, Urban-Diary, mentalMap, mapping, psychogeography.

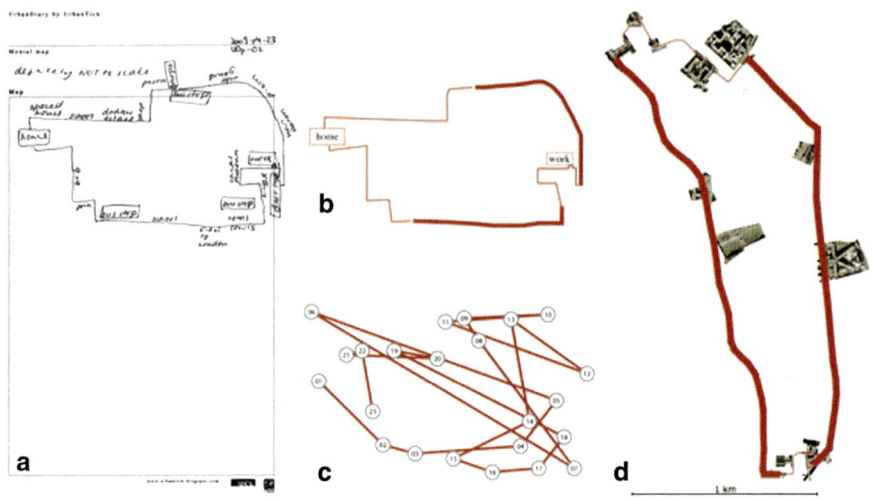

Fig. 18 Image by urbanTick for UrbanDiary / Comparison with GPS tracks

Of course also the way participants use the space given to work on is already very interesting and in this case only the very top of the sheet was used. Participants are asked to comment on what they draw and the transcript of this helps to interpret the drawing, for example regarding the sequence or comments they have made about their feelings in connection with a certain element. The first two analysis diagrams look at relationship of mode of transports (top) and sequence of map creation (bottom), both based on the participants' meal map. What looks like another of the GPS records is more of a dot-to-dot doodle. The mode of transport in this example is bus journeys and walking. Comparing this to the GPS record (left) it is clearly visible that the length of the bus journey is different. In the mental map the walked part is represented in much more detail than the bus journey. This is only to give a quick update on the UD project. The amount of data that these interviews provide for the project will keep me busy for a while. The next update will be on a comparison of schedules.

136   *ROUTINE PART 02—PERSONAL SCHEDULES*[26] Another look at the recent interviews does focus on the personal schedule. Part one on mental maps can be found here[27]. To complement the GPS records, the individual information regarding the daily program participants have set up, is an important aid to drawing a more comprehensive picture. During the interview participants are asked to note down what their schedule is on a daily, weekly or yearly basis. The daily schedule is an obvious unit, but to put it in a more meaningful context additional units have been chosen. It turned out that this is usually the longest

---

[26] *ROUTINE PART 02—PERSONAL SCHEDULES*, 27 May 2009 10:06, schedule, memory, personal, psychogeography, experience, analysis, GPS tracks, UrbanDiary, routine, mentalMap, rhythm.

[27] Routine Part 02—Personal Schedules.

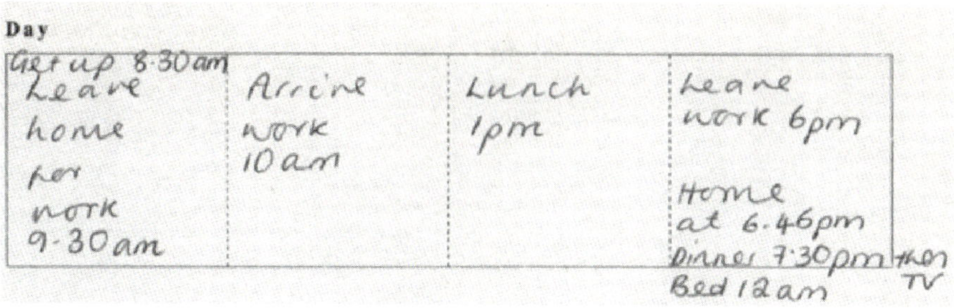

Day

Get up 8.30am Leave home for work 9.30am	Arrive work 10am	Lunch 1pm	Leave work 6pm Home at 6.46pm Dinner 7.30pm then Bed 12am TV

Fig. 19 Image by urbanTick for UrbanDiary / The daily schedule in an example by one participant

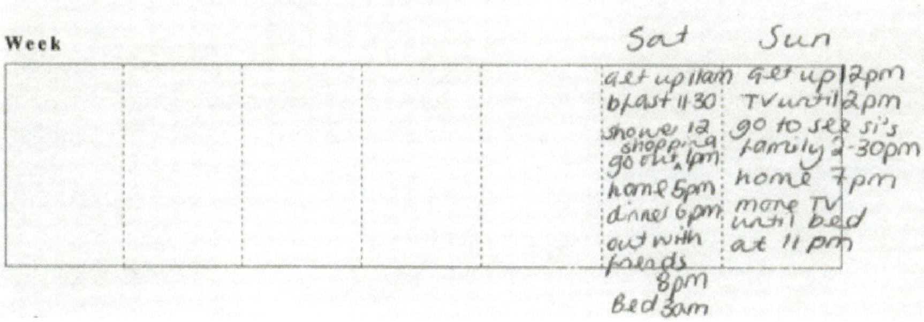

Week

				Sat get up 11am bfast 11.30 shower 12 shopping go this 1pm home 5pm dinner 6pm out with friends 8pm Bed 3am	Sun get up 12pm TV until 2pm go to see sis's family 2-30pm home 7pm more TV until bed at 11pm

Fig. 20 Image by urbanTick for UrbanDiary / The weekly schedule with a focus on the weekend, referring back to Fig. 19 for the weekdays

and most complicated bit of the interview. It seems to be not as simple to explain one's daily schedule. There are a lot of Ifs, and ors together with thens and woulds. In short it is presented as a dynamic string of decisions with numerous dependencies. Nevertheless there are strong elements of direction within this pool of fluid decision making. Again the major element is the working week versus the weekend. It is very easy to simplify all this information and boil it down to a few catchy phrases. Too often in the past personal schedules have been described as work, leisure, home. I don't think this can capture the richness with which participants have talked about their personal routines. Even if on first sight a story sounds simple and organized the perception of it for the individual might be different. To illustrate this, here is an extract of one record (Fig. 19).

To put it in a context the weekly time frame can help to understand that there are variations to this. In the example the changes are mainly between working week and weekend. The focus does represent the personal situation. There are big differences between participants that have dependent children and those that have none (Fig. 20).

Taking the two time frames together it represents the participant's "mind map" of weekly activities. Regarding the information one might think there could be large gaps between plans and activities. But actually the two are pretty close. The "mental

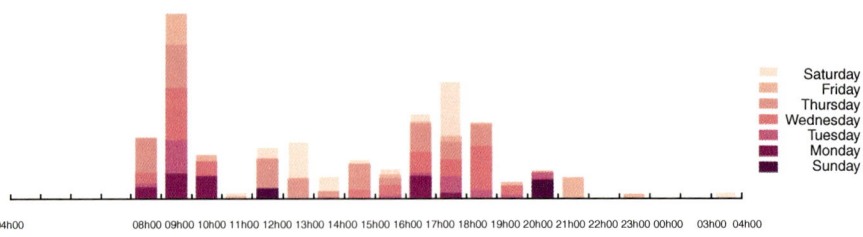

Fig. 21 Image by urbanTick for UrbanDiary / Weekly schedule generated from GPS records

picture" of our routines is pretty good. Comparing this to participants' perception of their spatial activities this is surprising. In spatial terms people often think their activities are much more flexible, and they are travelling more, than they actually are. This has lead to a lot of disappointment during the GPS tracking. (See UrbanDiary week 2[28]) By generating a schedule from the GPS data we have another record of when activities take place and are able to compare the two. They are pretty similar. The generated schedule plots data per hour and is coloured by weekday. Vertically the amount of activity at the time is shown and is derived from the number of recorded log points. The two peaks represent the rush hour. The very light colour on top is the activities that took place on Saturdays. Sunday on the other hand is the darkest colour on the bottom (Fig. 21).

Regarding how the time frame interaction with the urban form takes place an abstract version of the schedule can help. The following representation has only four units over 24 h to simplify and make clear where activity takes place, the units are morning, midday, afternoon and evening. Activity that involves spatial interaction on weekdays is basically during the rush hour in the morning and the evening. Other than this there is little activity. The weekend pattern is different in terms that there is afternoon and evening activity, with Saturday being the most active day (See also the detailed analysis of the daily weekly and monthly pattern of UD participants.)[29] (Fig. 22).

The information from the time frame of one year has not proved to be too interesting. For most of the participants this was too wide a category. It seems not be a unit that a lot of people plan in, although in professional life this is definitely important and annual planning is key. In terms of personal activity few have had planned activities other than the expected Christmas and Easter breaks. Birthdays and holiday were among the other named activities on a yearly scale. Regarding the city and spatial morphology, the longer term is of course interesting, but the connections have probably to be found elsewhere.

---

[28] http://urbantick.blogspot.com/2009/02/London-diary-week-two.html.

[29] http://urbantick.blogspot.com/2009/03/diary-in-graphs.html.

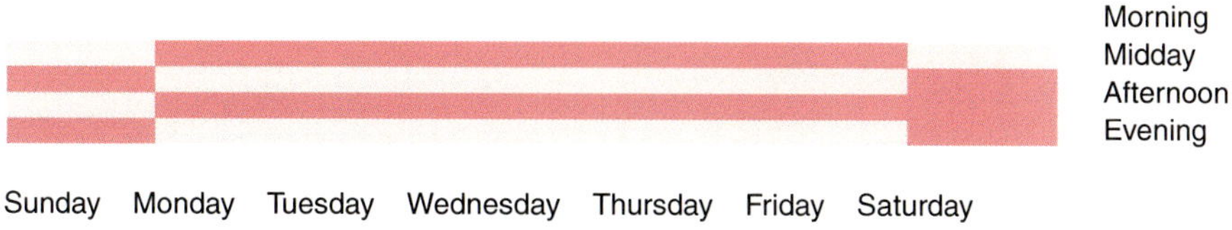

Morning
Midday
Afternoon
Evening

Sunday   Monday   Tuesday   Wednesday   Thursday   Friday   Saturday

Fig. 22 Image by urbanTick for UrbanDiary / The weekly schedule simplified

Fig. 23 Image by urbanTick / Screenshots from map 3D

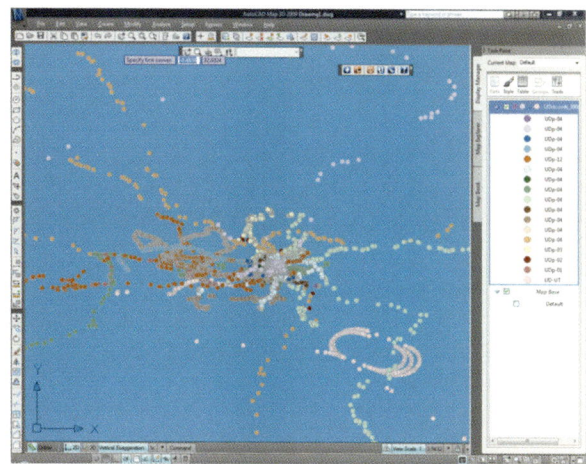

37   *URBANDIARY DATA IN AUTODESK MAP 3D*[30], CASA[31] has recently been awarded "Centre of Excellence" by Autodesk[32], and they provide their software packages. The software is now available in CASA and a few projects are taking shape on them. See a recent post by digitalUrban[33] on the latest project[34] using LandXplorer[35] to map aerial images onto a 3D Lidar London model. An other software of the Autodesk package is the Map 3D[36], a sort of AutoCAD[37] GIS. On their website it is described as "AutoCAD® Map 3D software enables engineers, planners, mapping technicians, surveyors, and GIS professionals to directly access, edit, visualise, and analyse a broad variety of CAD and spatial data in a familiar Auto-CAD® software environment." (Fig. 23).

With the experience from the previous mapping of the UrbanDiary data, this product looked as if it would be worth having a look at. The initial contact came

[30] *URBANDIARY DATA IN AUTODESK MAP 3D*, 3 June 2009 16:06, visualisation, software, data handling, mapping, UrbanDiary.

[31] http://www.casa.ucl.ac.uk/.

[32] http://www.autodesk.co.uk/adsk/servlet/home?siteID=452932&id=779580.

[33] http://www.digitalurban.blogspot.com/.

[34] http://digitalurban.blogspot.com/2009/05/textured-lidar-scan-of-London-150.html.

[35] http://www.3dgeo.de/.

[36] http://www.autodesk.co.uk/adsk/servlet/index?siteID=452932&id=12392181.

[37] http://www.autodesk.co.uk/adsk/servlet/index?siteID=452932&id=12306568.

Fig. 24 Image by
urbanTick / Screenshot
taken from Map 3D, the
attribute box

Fig. 25 Image by
urbanTick / Screenshot from
Map 3D, the generated key

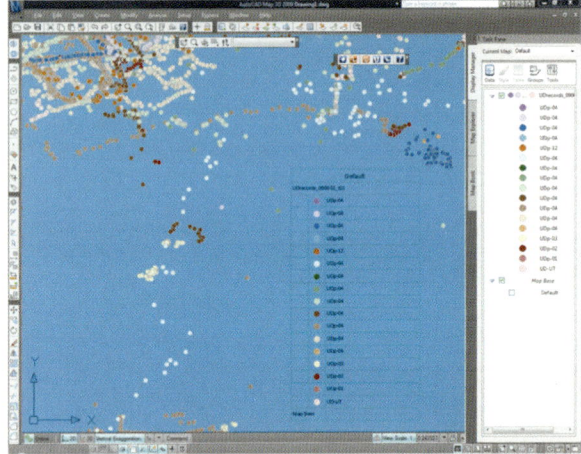

Fig. 26 Image by
urbanTick / Screenshot
from Map 3D, the data
displayed per week day
including a label

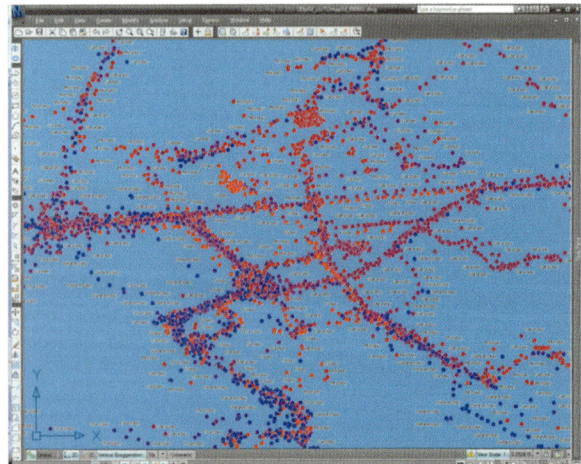

from a link I came a cross on the web while searching for something related to a CSV file. On map3d.wordpress.com[38] I cam a blog post on how to import a CSV file into Map 3D[39] and as the UrbanDiary data was available in CSV I thought I just give it a go (Fig. 24).

It is actually straightforward once I figured out that the data formats in the CSV file have to be set to number rather than text. Anyway, the data can be linked in via the OCDB data base link. This will include all the attributes from the CSV table. So far so good the data is there and can be used (Fig. 25).

With the help of the attribute table, changes in the visualisation are simple. The rule builder is easy to use and produces good results, including an automatically generated key (Fig. 26).

So for not having used the software before I am quite satisfied with the result. Importing the data, sorting it according to the attribute table and apply visualisation characteristics depending on features, not bad. It appears that the program slows down quite quickly. The first run was with a subset of the UrbanDiary data, some 10,000 points and this was fine. Going up to 45,000 points used quite a lot of power and slowed down the machine drastically. Switching from 2D mode into 3D did not really work and it was a struggle to get back without quitting the program. The next thing was the analysing functions. Using the buffer worked ok, again on a subset of points, but the machine got slower again. Meaning it was not responding at times and I would get the funny message by Vista "The program is currently not respond-ing would you like to quit or wait for the program?" Of course I want to wait for the program and eventually it would come back. The first crash was not far and after the importing some aerial imagery of London to give the points some context I gave up. But only for today, because I was impressed by the program's user-friendly approach. Compared to other GIS that are very technical, Map 3D was a little bit more intuitive to me. I am now telling myself that the performance problems are all down to me not being experienced enough and it will be all better next time. The next thing to try is eventually to get the GPS data from Map 3D into Autodesk 3D Studio Max for visualisation purposes. This would be the software way, people here in CASA are currently working on a programming solution for this.

38 *SHAPING CITY PRESENTATION AT ARUP LONDON*[40] I gave a talk today at ARUP London about my research on cycles and rhythms in the city (Fig. 27).

The talk was titled Shaping Cities, from the body rhythm to urban morphology. With this title, it brings together the different aspects of scale in the research, rang-ing from natural body functions to patterns of movement in the city. Along this key terms such as memory, identity, time and orientation are explored and visualised with examples from the work featuring on this blog, ranging from PLY365 to Ur-banDiary.

---

[38] http://map3d.wordpress.com.

[39] http://map3d.wordpress.com/2008/01/02/bring-a-csv-file-into-map-3d-with-data/.

[40] *SHAPING CITY PRESENTATION AT ARUP LONDON*, 15 June 2009 14:56, Plymouth, Urban-Diary, London, plymouth365, cycle, Basel, presentation, rhythm.

Fig. 27 Presentation
by urbanTick at scribd.
(http://d.scribd.com/Scrib-
dViewer.swf?document_
id=16440100&access_
key=key-1ufh9d451gv1httmd
r9m&page=1&version=1&vi
ewMode=)

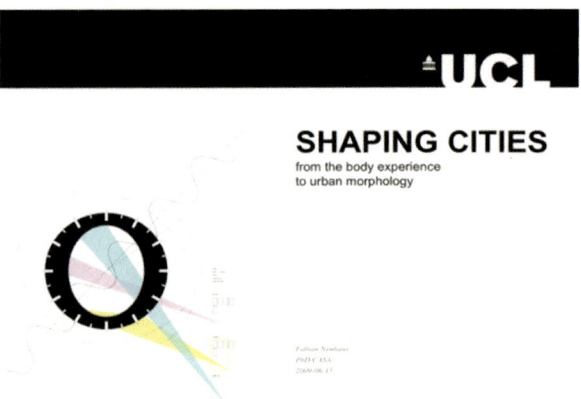

139   *UD INTERVIEWS—MAPS AND SCHEDULES*[41] Interviews—The interviews
are conducted towards the end of the participants tracking period. Designed as a
semi structured interview they are recorded. The aim of the interview is to collect
information on how the participants actually perceive the activities and how he/
she would describe these routines. It is also designed to record additional information about the purpose and the destination of recorded trips. From the GPS data
a schedule can be generated, but this might not reflect the intended plans of the
individual. Through this personal input it is thought that the meaning of the data
analysis will be improved. An additional interest is the participant's memory of their
activities. Around this topic a number of questions are designed. The interview is
structured through key topics; these are demographics, routine, space, movement,
map, memory, and GPS device. The demographics section is aiming to establish the
participant's situation and commitments that influence his/her routines and activities. The next topic is routine, trying to establish the participant's different routines
set within different time frames, over a day a week and the whole year. As part
of this the participants are asked to write this down on a prepared schedule. This
will allow comparison of the schedules participants have given themselves with
the schedule generated from the recorded data. Overall schedules generated from
the data will be discussed in the section graphs further below. The topics of space
and movement are looking into how participants use the space on a daily basis and
how it is perceived in connection to the routines. It will also be interesting to see
how they are able to connect the spaces they frequently visit regarding their mental map. This is especially interesting in this London setting, as for example the
travelling by tube might leave the travellers unable to connect locations spatially.
Movement on the other hand is directed towards how participants travel and how
this is part of the routine. Here again it is interesting to hear from the participants
how they see themselves and how much they think they travel. For the map the
participants are asked to draw the mental map of one journey. It is the journey

---

[41] *UD INTERVIEWS—MAPS AND SCHEDULES*, 18 June 2009 09:50, routine, schedule, mentalMap, personal, interview, UrbanDiary.

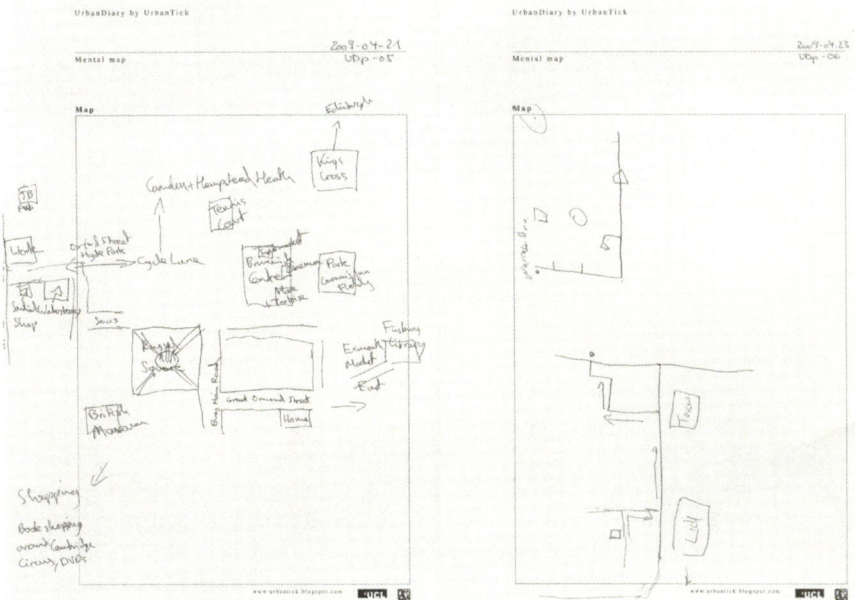

Fig. 28 Images by UrbanDiary / Participants mental map of journey to work

from home to work and back for all participants to allow to compare. To draw the map they are asked to include not only the direction they travel, but also additional elements they use for navigation, orientation or simply remind them about the route. This can be street names, buildings or urban settings. The last topic is to talk to the participants about the usage of the GPS device and their personal experience. This includes general usage, charging, downloading, comfort of wearing and so on.

During the interview interesting aspects of daily activities come up. An interesting one is that a lot of participants do feel the need to explain their activities and explain them. Another aspect is that there is a strong belief that more or stronger is better. In this case it is related to amount of movement, flexibility or distance. Routine seems to have a negative image, whereas flexible and independent seem to be positive. This experiment has been very disappointing for a number of participants in this respect, as the recorded movement unveiled a routine that seemed to be much stronger than the participants have so far realized (Fig. 28).

Mental maps—The participants draw these maps during the interview, without any visual help such as maps or graphics. It is only their memory they can use and therefore they are said to represent the mental image the individual carries in his/her mind. In this setting the mental image of what the participant remembers of their daily trips will be provoked to be visualised. Participants are all asked to draw the same journey, the daily trip from home to their work place and back. This will provide a minimal base they all have in common to let them become comparable.

This large data set is at the moment being processed. Some first analysis of maps[42] and schedules[43] have featured on the blog earlier.

140   *POPFEST 2009 AT LSE—THE SPATIAL EXTENSION OF EVERYDAY LIFE*[44]
I will be at the POPFest 2009[45] tomorrow, presenting elements of my research work under the title UrbanDiary—The Spatial Extension of Everyday Life. I will be focusing on the method and the first trial with the GPS data collection, specifically on the individual level. This will mainly focus then on the mental maps and individual perception of routine and space. The presentation can be seen here as a preview[46]. The POPFest 2009 is this year at LSE in London, from July 2nd to July 4th. It is a platform for mainly postgrad students to show and discuss their work. "POPFest is a population studies conference organised by postgraduates for postgraduates with the aim of providing a relaxed, supportive environment for students to come together to present work and discuss ideas. This is a great opportunity to meet other students studying in the same area, practice your presentation skills and get some useful feedback from your peers. The conference provides a forum for postgraduate students studying any aspect of population in disciplines including Social Sciences, Demography, Human Geography, Social Anthropology, Social Statistics, Health, Development, Social Policy and other related fields. Presenters have an excellent opportunity to discuss their work in front of their peers and have a chance to get feedback and ideas from fellow researchers. Those not wishing to present can get an idea of the sort of research being conducted by their peers and make valuable contacts for the future. POPFest is an ideal spring-board for all postgraduates regardless of their stage of research providing an opportunity to practice ones presentation skills, whether as a paper or poster display, before facing more demanding academic conferences. POPFest has survived over the past 14 years due to the support and good will of the postgraduate community and the BSPS. For POPFest to continue this support and enthusiasm is essential. The BSPS is very keen to ensure the development of postgraduate population research through POPFest and has confirmed its continuing support to the conference." This year's Timetable[47].

141   *MAP 3D VS ARCGIS*[48] Following an earlier post about the UrbanDiary data in Autodesk Map 3D, I would like to talk about further development on this topic. The plan was to generate the UrbanDiary maps using this software and with this move towards a more automated workflow from GPS data to map with maintaining the level of possible graphical intervention (Fig. 29).

---

[42] http://urbantick.blogspot.com/2009/05/routine-part-01-mental-maps-of-daily.html.

[43] http://urbantick.blogspot.com/2009/05/routine-part-02-personal-schedules.html.

[44] *POPFEST 2009 AT LSE—THE SPATIAL EXTENSION OF EVERYDAY LIFE*, 1 July 2009 17:18, urbanTick, presentation, conference, UrbanDiary.

[45] http://www2.lse.ac.uk/socialPolicy/BSPS/postgraduates/PopFest.aspx.

[46] http://docs.google.com/present/edit?id=0Aef57LqFKnJFZGZ6cDM4NThfMTFjNWtocjlnag&hl=en.

[47] http://www2.lse.ac.uk/socialPolicy/BSPS/pdfs/Popfest2009_overview_timetable.pdf.

[48] *MAP 3D VS ARCGIS*, 8 July 2009 10:00, UrbanDiary, software, data handling, analysis, mapping.

Fig. 29 Image by
urbanTick / Using Autodesk
Map 3D to work with the
GPS tracking data from the
UrbanDiary project

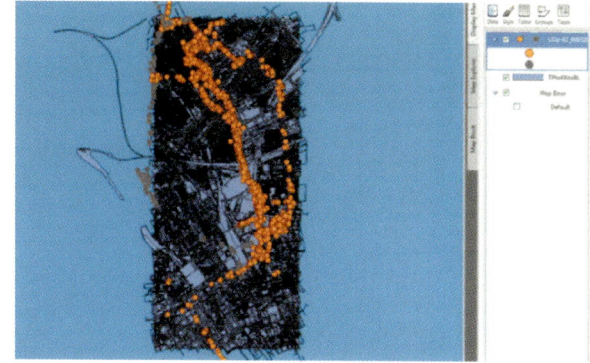

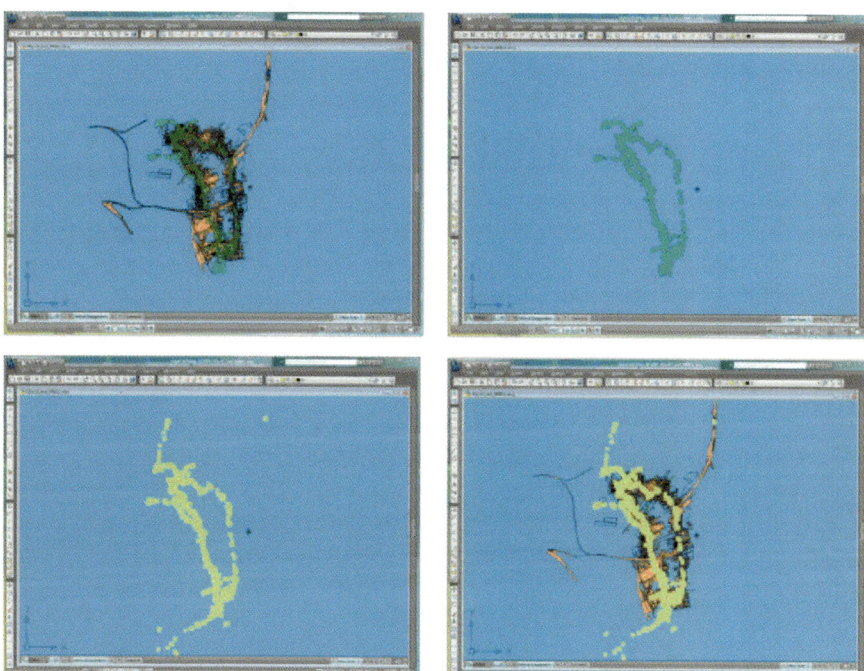

Fig. 30 Image by urbanTick / Using Autodesk Map 3D

As described in the earlier post data from the database could be connected and be represented in the software including context data. Simple manipulations and representations of the data could be made easily in Map 3D and actually I grew a little bit fond of the software although I did not like AutoCAD when I last had to use it. So I was determined to stick to this and work it all through in this one application. Unfortunately, too soon I seemed to exceed the capacity of the software (Fig. 30).

Following the processing of the UrbanDiary interviews the task is to develop a combination of interview/mental map data and the GPS/map data. The idea is to

Fig. 31 Image by
urbanTick / Using ArcGIS to
export the data to Illustrator

look at the work related spatial movement with a special focus on the mental map
features.

It turned out that the number of recorded GPS points per participant combined
with the building, street and land use information is too much for Map 3D to handle.
It started to crash continuously; up to the state I was not possible to open a file. The
method I used was maybe not the most economic one but seem simple to me. From
the GPS points I defined a buffer to establish a zone of "experience", which I inter-
sected with the base map to only be working with relevant information. The issue in
Map3D led to the move across to ArcGIS, which appeared to be comfortable with
the data (Fig. 31).

Fig. 32 Image by urbanTick for UrbanDiary / Poster 'the spatial narrative of Everyday Life'

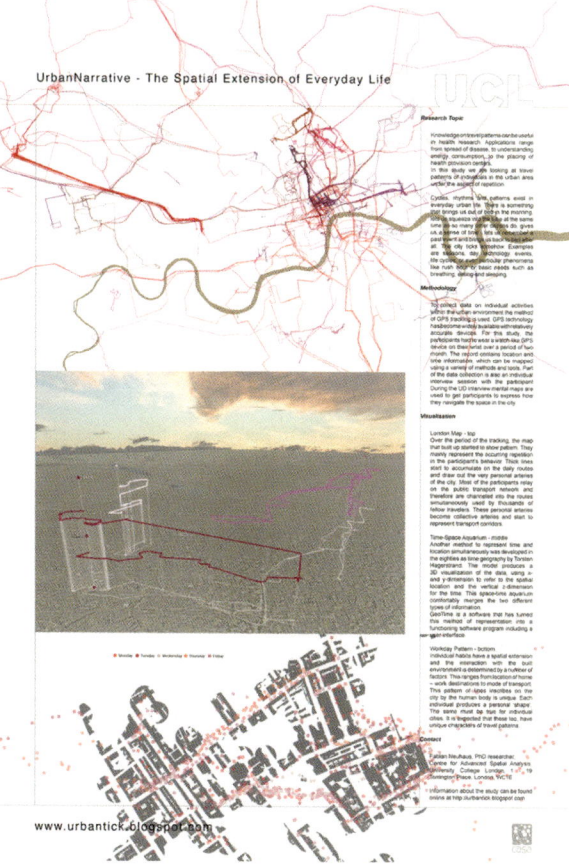

It also turned out that the same steps of work are quite simple achievable, although a little less intuitive. This reaches down to the export for Illustrator. Map 3D translates much simpler into Illustrator with its native DXF format. In ArcGIS, I could not manage to produce a workable file that remained distinct in terms of features. So I had to rely on the map export using about 12,000 dpi. Proper maps will follow as they are processed in Illustrator.

IDRN MAPPING CONFERENCE AT THE ROYAL GEOGRAPHICAL SOCIETY[49] I will be at the IDRN conference[50] tomorrow at the Royal Geographical Society in London. It is under the title of 'The use of mapping software & systems in health and academic research'. Mapping in the area of health research has recently become popular. We have seen some experiments earlier this year using data related to the spread of swine flu. Also there is the Google Flu Trends[51] project, monitoring

---

[49] *IDRN MAPPING CONFERENCE AT THE ROYAL GEOGRAPHICAL SOCIETY*, 3 November 2009 16:29, visualisation, GeoTime, aquarium, mapping, UrbanDiary.

[50] http://idrn.org/events/upcoming/mapping.php.

[51] http://www.google.org/flutrends/intl/en_gb/.

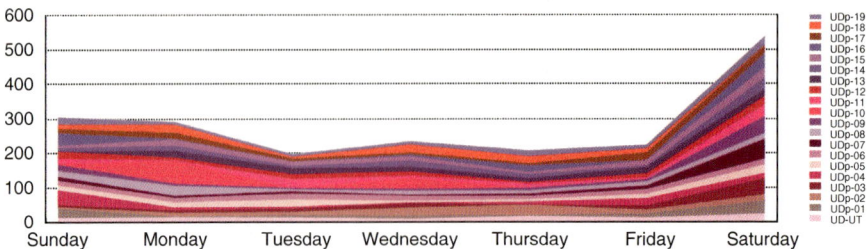

Fig. 33 Image by urbanTick for UrbanDiary / Activity graph per day of the week for 20 participants

flu outbreaks. Apparently they are pretty good, only I think with Swine Flu they had some problems. Interesting that there is no data available for the United Kingdom on the Google page (Fig. 32).

However, I am presenting a poster with the tracking data of the UrbanDiary[52] project, showing different approaches of visualisation techniques. There is the normal map using arcGIS, then there is the time-space aquarium vis, done in either Google Earth or GeoTime;[53] and the last visualisation is individual movement with the context of the built environment, again using ArcGIS.

143 *NEW GRAPHS—THE ACTIVITY DURING THE WEEK*[54] Finally I took the time to reprocess the UrbanDiary graphs. Since the last time the study sample has grown from 12 to 20. This is a good sample size and will give a different picture. However, it must be say, that the sample is not as consistent as it was with the first batch. They have all undertaken the study more or less during the same time frame, where as now the sample is spread over the period of half a year or more. Nevertheless the individual tracking time remains the same at two month intervals. Also, it must be noted, that this time the graphs have been calculated slightly differently. Where as before it was purely on a count basis, this time it is based on the activity percentage per time unit for each participant. This accounts for the effect one particular active event has on the overall picture. The weekly graph remains the same. There is significantly less activity during the week days than there is on Saturdays. Even Sunday remains in line with the rest of the week. Why on Saturday participants record almost twice the amount of activity I don't know at the moment. It has something to do with outdoor activity, probably some sports (Fig. 33).

While looking at the weekly pattern, the peaks remain largely the same. There is the nine o'clock peak for the morning rush hour and the six o'clock peak for the evening rush hour. There is also the after peak hour both for the morning and the evening (Fig. 34).

Clearer in this graph now is the fact that there are more afternoon activities than morning activity. This most likely has to do with the weekend, particularly the Saturday. I suspect that the large chunk of Saturday recordings are based on afternoon activities.

[52] http://urbantick.blogspot.com/search/label/UrbanDiary.

[53] http://urbantick.blogspot.com/search/label/GeoTime.

[54] *NEW GRAPHS—THE ACTIVITY DURING THE WEEK*, 26 November 2009 16:40, analysis, graphs, UrbanDiary.

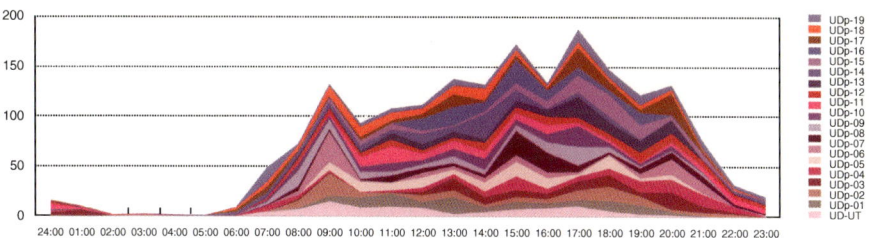

Fig. 34 Image by urbanTick for UrbanDiary / Activity graph per 24 h of one day for 20 participants

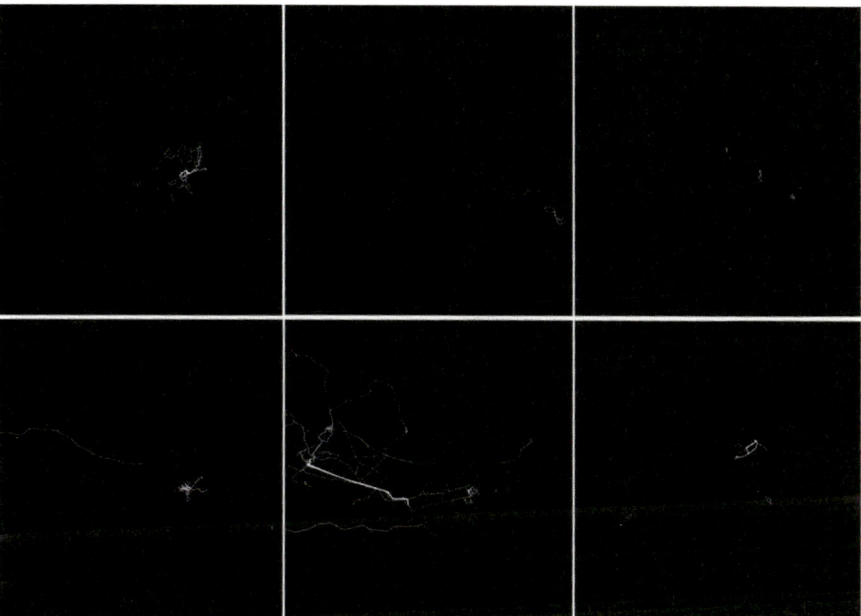

Fig. 35 Image by urbanTick for UrbanDiary / Different shapes produced by participants of the UrbanDiary project over the same period of time

WHAT SHAPE ARE YOU?—UPDATE[55] As an update to the 'what shape are you?'[56] post, here are some new shapes. The Project now counts 20 participants so we also have 20 shapes. All shapes are produced over the period of two month and are represented here at the same scale (Fig. 35).

As previously noted these 'drawings' depend on the location of important destination relative to one another and on mode of transport as well as frequency. The mental picture of the city that each individual builds up while interacting with the urban fabric is tremendously different. Linking back to the visualisation 'The Na-

---

[55] *WHAT SHAPE ARE YOU?—UPDATE*, 27 November 2009 13:07, rhythm, personal, identity, mapping, UrbanDiary, London, routine, psychogeography.

[56] http://urbantick.blogspot.com/2009/04/what-shape-are-you.html.

Fig. 36 Image by urbanTick
for UrbanDiary / Tracking
map showing 20 par-
ticipants by colour, updated
2009-11-27

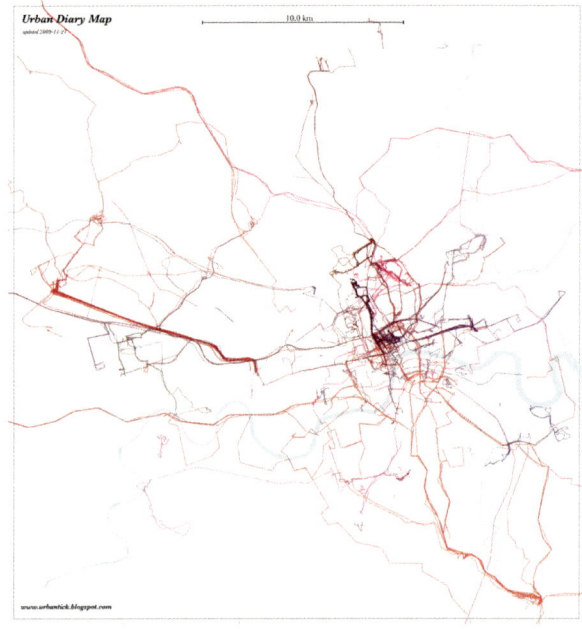

ked City'[57] the psychogeography of the city is very much dependant, or it is a result
of this as produced through the derive[58].

145   *UD TRACK MAP—UPDATE*[59] The latest UrbanDiary map is here, updated
2009-11-27. This now includes 20 participants, each tracked over the period of two
months. It adds a number of new highlighted routes that mark individual routines.
The density of the centre has risen again and strengthens the centralistic structure of
routine trips. However there are now also more one of trips to paint a more detailed
picture of the London network (Fig. 36).

Out of the 20 participants one stands out as not having centric oriented routine.
In this case it is a more radial shape produced, with one-off's leading into the centre.
If you compare it on the 'what shape are you?', it stands out for its orientation—it
is square 2/5[60]. More UrbanDiary updates on the facebook page—become a fan!

146   *URBANDIARY ON LAYAR*[61] Layar featured on the blog before and now I have
been playing around with the augmented reality platform to use it for the visualisation of the UrbanDiary data (Fig. 37).

I have now created an UrbanDiary layer showing track points that are already in
the database. For now this is only a test and it is not yet available as a public layer
(Fig. 38).

---

[57] http://urbantick.blogspot.com/2009/03/city-islands-on-linkage-of-everyday.html.

[58] http://urbantick.blogspot.com/2009/03/derive.html.

[59] *UD TRACK MAP—UPDATE*, 30 November 2009 11:51,mapping, UrbanDiary.

[60] http://www.casa.ucl.ac.uk/urbantick/ut/blogImage/whatShapeAreYou_BW.jpg.

[61] *URBANDIARY ON LAYAR*, 1 December 2009 16:24, visualisation, GPS tracks, augmented
reality, UrbanDiary.

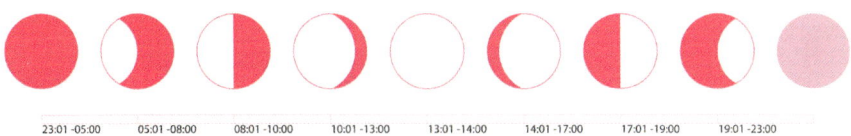

| 23:01 -05:00 | 05:01 -08:00 | 08:01 -10:00 | 10:01 -13:00 | 13:01 -14:00 | 14:01 -17:00 | 17:01 -19:00 | 19:01 -23:00 |

Fig. 37 Image by urbanTick for UrbanDiary / Waxing and waning crescent indicating the time of the day

Fig. 38 Clip by urbanTick on youtube / With a proof of concept displaying the UD data around CASA. (http://www.youtube.com/v/ Keo3fhKGAfE&hl= en&fs=1)

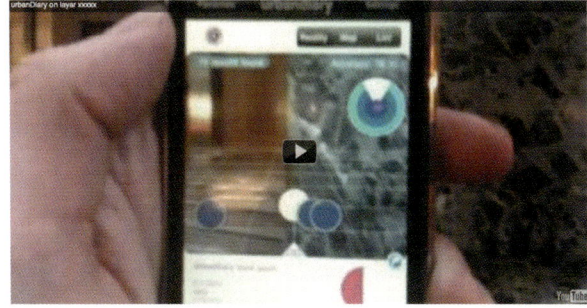

The POIs it displays are all GPS track points collected by participants of the UrbanDiary project. So each dot means someone passed by here earlier. I am however not quite convinced by the Layar platform visually, as I have expressed in previous posts. As a first test to visualise the collected data it serves very well. I am actually thinking about it as an extension to the time-space aquarium. However this is of course only a first stab at it and a lot of information is not yet included. I tried to have a go at the aspect of time. Each point, after it has properly loaded, displays a visual time indication on the bottom right as a waxing or waning crescent. This gives an idea of the time this particular point was recorded. I choose to do this as for now Layar does not allow for individual icons. There is only a set of three icons currently available.

UPGRADE SEMINAR—PRESENTATION[62] I will be giving my upgrade presentation today in the form of a CASA seminar. It is under the title: "UrbanDiary—The Spatial Narrative of Everyday Life or the construction of time and space in the city". The abstract: This PhD research project focuses on cycles and rhythms in the urban environment. Cycles such as day and night or the rush-hour—there are a number of repetitive patterns occurring in the city. These patterns are the result of spatial and social organisation methods, but they are involved in the organisation of the city as a system. The hypothesis is that these rhythms stand in a direct relationship to the urban morphology.

The presentation of posted here is now updated[63].

---

[62] *UPGRADE SEMINAR—PRESENTATION*, 2 December 2009 16:27, body, time, presentation, machine, UrbanDiary.

[63] http://docs.google.com/present/embed?id=dfzp3858_101jmjczqht&size=m" frameborder=.

Fig. 39 Image by urbanTick / Working paper 151 cover (part)

148   *URBANDIARY WORKING PAPER*[64] The UrbanDiary working paper has just been published on the CASA publication page. It is a write-up of the GPS tracking study undertaken during 2009 with 20 participants. Each one was tracked for a period of two months. The paper outlines the methodology, the concepts, such as mental maps, and it also examines technical aspects of GPS. A main focus is on the aspect of visualisation of this kind of temporal data. Thanks for supporting this project go to Garmin for supplying the Forerunner 405 s and especially all the participants of the study. Details on urbanTick can be found on this blog/UrbanDiary[65] or on the UrbanDiary facebook page[66]—become a fan! Now to the content of the paper, abstract: "This working paper investigates aspects of time in an urban environment, specifically the cycles and routines of everyday life in the city" (Fig. 39).

As part of the UrbanDiary project (urbantick.blogspot.com), we explore a preliminary study to trace citizens' spatial habits in individual movement utilising GPS devices with the aim of capturing the beat and rhythm of the city. The data collected includes time and location, to visualise individual activity, along with a series of personal statements on how individuals "use" and experience the city. In this paper, the intent is to explore the context of the UrbanDiary project as well as examine the methodology and technical aspects of tracking with a focus on the comparison of different visualisation techniques. We conclude with a visualisation of the collected data, specifically where the aspect of time is developed and explored so that we might outline a new approach to visualising the city in the sense of a collective, constantly renewed space. The actual paper can be downloaded from HERE[67] and detailed information is on the CASA publication page[68].

---

[64] *URBANDIARY WORKING PAPER*, 10 December 2009 14:22, publication, UrbanDiary.

[65] http://urbantick.blogspot.com/search/label/UrbanDiary.

[66] http://www.facebook.com/pages/Urban-Diary/67812788988.

[67] http://www.casa.ucl.ac.uk/working_papers/paper151.pdf.

[68] http://www.casa.ucl.ac.uk/publications/workingPaperDetail.asp?ID=151.

Part VII
Review

Footprints, a Regeneration Process

Luis Suárez

Sustainable Growth

With booming but volatile economies, cities in Latin America are growing fast. Nevertheless, it seems that we find ourselves in a good position to repair mistakes and make all the right decisions in order to model our future cities.

It is important to study and learn from the great ancient and contemporary urban settlements. Latin American cities are still at an early stage of growth, therefore developing countries often look up towards "developed" countries in search of innovation. The understanding of innovation is always connected to the local environment and its inhabitants, it is not easy to understand, but it must be understood that a well thoughtout sustainable project in south America, as little as it might be seen (e.g.: an indigenous house made with mud layered bricks), is as innovative as any contemporary project in Europe built with state of the art materials and technology.

Rural areas are the natural engines of our Latin nations. There is still a high percentage of inhabitants working outside urban settlements. In order for a country to produce its own food, agricultural production must be recovered, nourished and not forgotten. An intimate connection between region and city, with the penetration of the rural sector into the city (urban farms), reduces energy consumption on the transportation of goods needed to supply the demand of the Latin megalopolis.

Latin cities are unique and spontaneous due to sociocultural behaviour, local environment and politics. Their uniqueness must be understood, after all this is what carves our great cities. Unfortunately in Latin America very few comprehend sustainability. Wise decisions as a response of climate change are far from becoming a priority in the political agenda. This is why cities are growing in despair, some of them like Panamá copying mistaken, excessive unsustainable growth processes, and some others making good but unresolved attempts. In the case of Bogotá, due to political interests, the proposal of an expensive metro railway system has become

L. Suárez (✉)
Estudio ARQ, Bogotá, CO
e-mail: luis@estudio-arq.com

F. Neuhaus (ed.), *Studies in Temporal Urbanism,*
DOI 10.1007/978-94-007-0937-9_13, © Springer Science+Business Media B.V. 2011

an obstacle to the yet to be finished "transmilenio", an efficient articulated bus system accompanied by a cycle path network proposed by Enrique Peñalosa.

Generators

Away from the political endeavours, if the aim is sustainability, Latin American countries could base their growth on productivity, creativity and knowledge generators. A generator should be understood as any project that is able to bring development and innovation by creating activities that are useful to the inhabitants of a certain community. Technological innovation is an environment condition based in two principles:

- concept of uncertainty (probability and unpredictability): the chaos theory can be related for this case
- Necessity to incoporate state of the art practice, this theory demands highly skilled and competitive individuals.

These two theories, combined with continuous process of knowledge and sustainability, will enhance networks at organisational and individual levels. With these premises taken into account, the morphology and the urban path of growth for our cities will be one of regeneration, and/or sustainable growth based on creativity and productivity generators: self sufficient environments with various activities, creating people magnets. Ideally the main purpose of the generator should be one of spreading knowledge among the community by camouflaging it with daily human activities such as business, culture or leisure; meaning that knowledge should be spread in physical and virtual forms among the space and the individual. The rise of new generators should only be the response to a necessity for development, individual entities that mature and learn from others until they are ready to spread their own knowledge.

The Key Player

The inhabitant is the key player for sustainable societies. In order to create sustainable environments we should all follow a similar theory; for a city to become sustainable it must have a "green-citizen". According to St Catherine College director Dr. Richard Shore the Sustainable Individual is characterized by:

- Critical thinking based on both knowledge and values. Commitment to the environment as the matrix of all life.
- Commitment to civic equality and justice. Habits of participation and contribution to the community. Viable skills for employment. Engagement with lifelong learning

Morphology

It is impossible to predict a "finalized" form without expecting the process to be subjective of change. Based on chaos theory, we now know that we can only predict the near future. A city, just like its inhabitants, can only have certain future goals because many factors can alter the final result and sometimes goals must also be flexible for change. Sustainability of the footprint created by human development does not depend on horizontal or vertical growth but on the care taken during the process of growth. If this process is well supported the final outcome will be one of positive feedback for the inhabitant and the environment. Dr. Silvia de Schiller argues that planning codes in South America have promoted a transformation of the urban fabric, producing a change from the continuous street facades of the traditional square Spanish colonial city block to free standing high-rise towers. This alteration in the morphology brings changes in the urban conditions, in order to evaluate this changes she considers three factors:

Microclimate conditions: sun and wind in urban spaces throughout the year. Urban design qualities: using the five qualities (permeability, vitality, variety, legibility and robustness) proposed by Bentley et al. 1985. User behaviour: space use and visual evidence of pedestrian preferences.

Footprints

Zero carbon footprint cities are utopias far from our present era, nevertheless our environmental footprint is not always negative, we are creators protectors, artists and more. Sustainability is the equilibrium between society, economy and environment.

Jaime Lerner the Brazilian architect, mastermind behind the great success of Curitiba in Brazil, is confident that any city can change within two years, if fast and concrete action is taken. He calls this process of space revitalization "urban acupuncture". Revitalizing spaces, by improving urban design quality will improve the footprint that we are leaving behind. Urban fragments already use thousands of square km of land that will never be recovered, a large percentage of this areas are misused or abandoned. Revitalizing, recycling or regenerating the urban fabric will bring opportunities to remodel our future cities, decrease the impact that these stains are causing and improve quality of life. The human footprint is what we call civilization: morphology of a city is only the result of wise or bad decisions. Horizontal or vertical growth is irrelevant; the process is what defines the legacy.

Review

Fabian Neuhaus

49 *GOOGLE EARTH FOR THE IPHONE*[1] Here we go, Google[2] has transferred the application Google Earth[3] to the iPhone. It is possible to carry the earth in one's pocket and have it at one's fingertips. The application can be downloaded from the iTunes store for free. Navigation is simple with the touch screen by using the fingertips to move, zoom in and zoom out. Amazingly the accelerometer of the phone is used to tilt the view. There is a set of layers that can be turned on and off. Google[4] integrated Wikipedia[5] and Panoramio[6] so far. Unfortunately it is not possible to display customized kml files.

Watch a short movie by Google[7] on Youtube[8]/Google Earth on the iPhone.

This would become very interesting if this functionality will be added in the future. The New York Times[9] has put together a good and bad list to summarise first impressions. It can be downloaded through this iTunes link[10].

50 *INTEREST AND SHARING*[11] Tonight we had the 1000th visitor on the blog. It is great that so many people are interested in the work on the topic of everyday cycles and routines. The first entry on the blog dates from the 7th of October 2008. So only 98 days online, with twenty entries featuring seven videos and a number of images (Fig. 1).

---

[1] *GOOGLE EARTH FOR THE IPHONE*, 29 October 2008 09:55, Google Earth, iPhone, review.

[2] http://googleblog.blogspot.com/2008/10/introducing-google-earth-for-iphone.html.

[3] http://earth.google.com.

[4] http://www.google.co.uk.

[5] http://www.wikipedia.org.

[6] http://www.panoramio.com/.

[7] http://www.google.co.uk.

[8] http://www.youtube.com/v/v6BPuKaLel4&hlen&fs1&.

[9] http://www.nytimes.com/external/readwriteweb/2008/10/27/27readwriteweb-google_earth_on_the_iphone.html?sr=hotnews.

[10] http://phobos.apple.com/WebObjects/MZStore.woa/wa/viewSoftware?id293622097&mt8.

[11] *INTEREST AND SHARING*, 13 January 2009 10:45, graphs, links, history, review, analysis, visits.

F. Neuhaus (✉)
Centre for Advanced Spatial Analysis, University College London, London, UK
e-mail: fabian.neuhaus@ucl.ac.uk

F. Neuhaus (ed.), *Studies in Temporal Urbanism,*
DOI 10.1007/978-94-007-0937-9_14, © Springer Science+Business Media B.V. 2011

Fig. 1 Image by urbanTick / Visitor statistics by Sitemeter

urban Tick
Site Summary

VISITS	
Total	1,008
Average Per Day	45
Average Visit Length	1:31
Last Hour	1
Today	11
This Week	318

PAGE VIEWS	
Total	1,492
Average Per Day	65
Average Per Visit	1.4
Last Hour	1
Today	16
This Week	457

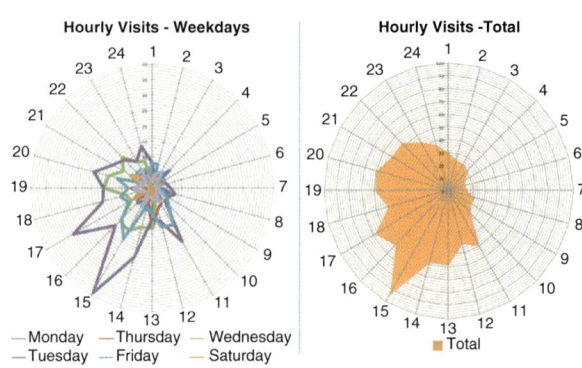

Fig. 2 Images by urbanTick / Graphs by hour and by weekday

The visits so far have developed rapidly and closely related to being referred from by popular blogs. Some analysis of the hit record shows the popularity of the blog over the course of 24 h. It turns out to be very popular on mid weekdays, in mid afternoon… (Fig. 2).

As we started this blog, it was not the aim to attract a lot of attention, rather was the idea was to use it as a diary (in the sense of the project) and logging the work that we are doing here to keep track of things and log some progress. To now see that putting the work online generates such an interest really is a big motivation. The topic of cycles, as it is defined at the moment, puts the focus on everyday routines and habits and this really is what we all experience or rather produce. Anyone experiences it on a daily basis, e.g. rush hour, shop opening hours or meal times, or is involved in longer periodic events such as the now just passed festive season with the busy celebrations. To understand more about these patterns is the aim of the work and obviously makes a lot of people curious. The interest was generated by some big blogs that picked up the work and made it prominently accessible for a wider audience. The DigitalUrban blog[12], then the New Scientist blog[13], the Gearth blog[14], the AllPoints blog, the PlymothianTransit blog[15], andrelemos.info[16] and also

[12] http://digitalurban.blogspot.com/2008/12/gps-city-tracks-1-year-in-24-hours-via.html.

[13] http://www.newscientist.com/blogs/shortsharpscience/2008/12/man-becomes-his-own-big-brothe.html.

[14] http://www.gearthblog.com/blog/archives/2009/01/urban_tick_research_results_in_goog.html.

[15] http://www.plymothiantransit.com/2009/01/urban-tick.html.

[16] http://www.andrelemos.info/2009/01/gps-city-tracks.html.

Fig. 3 Image by urbanTick /
The Garmin Foretrex 201s
being tested

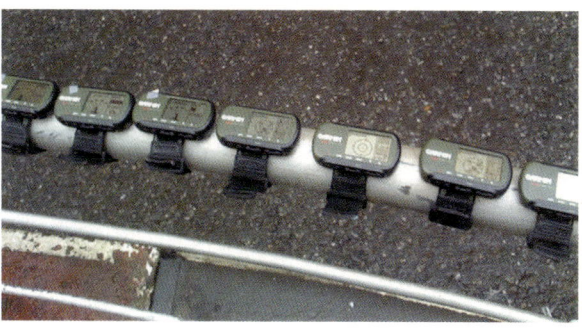

the heomin61 blog[17]. So maybe it become a routine for some visitors to come back and check this spot for new work and of course comments and suggestions on the work are very welcome. For the future progress of the work on cycles and rhythms the aim is to make a broader study based on GPS tracks involving a number of individuals. Maybe even to start an online community who would share individual routines to help painting the bigger picture. Something like "the City Routines", a big drawing that represents the habits of inhabitants. We'll see how it goes.

THE TRACKING—FORETREX TUTORIAL[18] The devices are here, and I can start recording peoples movement. I have a bunch of Garmin Foretrex 201 devices and will give them out to volunteers to track them around the city. The intention is to collect information about the spatial extent of everyday routines (Fig. 3).

This preliminary study will show how useful the data is and what measures I have to take to improve it in the following sets of tracking. Of course I am expecting some problems, especially with signal strength (as it takes place in central London), but I'll see what the returned data is. Here is a quick introduction on how to use the Foretrex 201: The GPS needs a sky view to establish a satellite connection. This can take a few minutes from a cold start. To establish the exact location, signals from four different satellites are required, hence the symbol on page one (see below). The accuracy of the positioning depends on several factors. This includes weather, location, landscape and built environment. It is not easy to receive a proper signal in central London. The main difficulty is to establish a signal, once it is established, the Foretrex is quite good in maintaining it. On public transport a window seat is required to receive a signal. On the tube it will obviously not receive a signal and after leaving the tube station, the device will need to establish a new connection. It will do so automatically. The device does record the track by default. There is no need to save something.

The PAGE button is also used to go out of menus. Whereas the ENTER button is complementary to this, for selecting or entering a menu. The ARROW buttons are used to navigate. In case the device freezes, the PAGE and POWER button have

---

[17] http://heomin61.tistory.com/751.

[18] *THE TRACKING—FORETREX TUTORIAL*, 5 February 2009 13:09, tutorial, review, Foretrex 201, tracking, GPS, Garmin.

Fig. 4 Image by urbanTick / In case the device cannot locate a satellite outdoors, it asks for input. If you are not indoors, you enter no. The following up question will be, whether you have moved a great distance. Here you can say yes and the device will do a more intense satellite check and you should get a signal

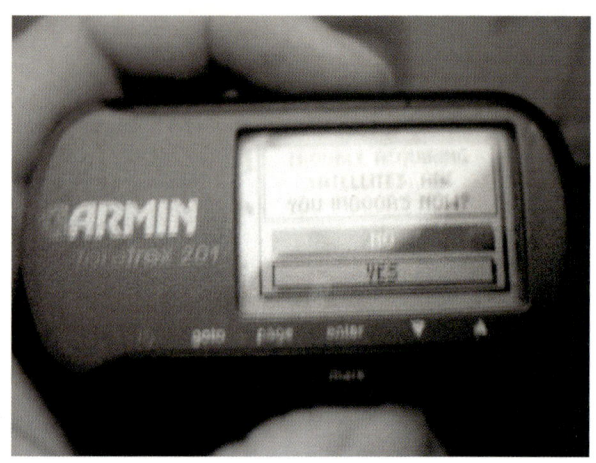

to be pressed continuously for about 5 s to turn off the device. If you stay indoors for some time, the device might recognize and ask you. If you enter yes, the device will turn off the GPS signal receiver in order to save power. To turn the GPS signal receiver back on as you leave the building, just use the POWER button to turn the device off and back on (Fig. 4).

Charging will need about 6 h. It can be left overnight. For charging the device needs to be connected via the Cradle. If the Foretrex is turned off whilst charging it will show a charging symbol on the screen. As it is fully charged it should then display charging complete. According to the manufacture, the battery lasts for about 15 h. This means charging is required about every two days. For further and more detailed information please refer to the official Garmin QuickGuide[19] or the full Handbook[20].

152 *UNDERWATER—GOOGLE EARTH BETA 5.0*[21], Google[22] released this month a new 5.0 Beta[23] version of Google Earth. The main new feature is the water. Before, the oceans were just blue surfaced with little detail. See clip on Youtube[24]/The Google Earth underwater world.

In Google Earth 5.0 the oceans have become part of the (virtual) world and user can explore the "all new" underwater world. This is a great feature and I imagine the beauty of the detail if someone starts implementing the rising water level. Not only on the level of climate change and catastrophes, but more on the level of the daily

[19] http://www8.garmin.com/manuals/Foretrex201_QuickStartGuide.pdf.

[20] http://www.garmin.com/manuals/Foretrex201_OwnersManual.pdf.

[21] *UNDERWATER—GOOGLE EARTH BETA 5.0*, 13 February 2009 10:54, cycles, water level, rhythm, Google Earth, visualisation, review, tide.

[22] http://www.google.com.

[23] http://earth.google.com/index.html.

[24] http://www.youtube.com/v/GSuJq4UzkIA&color10xb1b1b1&color20xcfcfcf&hl=en&feature =player_embedded&fs1.

cycle of the tide. This was kind of the trigger for my research topic in the first place. The project of the floating city[25] in the Thames Estuary, where the ever changing sea level was a research field and had a great impact on the project. To capture this rhythm in Google Earth would be great.

See clip on Youtube[26]/The new Google Earth timeline feature.

There is also a new time line, redesigned and a lot bigger. On the PowerBook screen it takes quite a lot of room, which is annoying. But I'll see how it improves the handling, as I will use it in the next few days. The new timeline makes also a series of older aerial photographs accessible. It is now possible to follow the change of a place over time using a series of older images.

See clip on Youtube[27]/The new Google Earth recording feature.

Recording is now a feature of the free Google Earth version. So far only users who bought a license of the popular visualisation tool had the option to record their trips on the (virtual) planet. Now everyone can record and share recorded trips including sound—live comments. The focus is on recorded TRIPS, it really is only a record of the navigation done within Google Earth and not a real movie. It is not possible to exchange these recordings other than as KML/KMZ files and you need Google Earth to replay these files. You can exchange them though, but not as real movie clips like it is possible in the paid version of Google Earth.

One more new thing is the GPS direct import. Google has now discontinued the $ 20 version of Google Earth and implemented the GPS track importing function in the free version. It covers still the same functions as it did three years back, meaning only Garmin/Magellan and NMEA support. I have not been able to get it to work though so far with my serial to USB connection to read directly from my Garmin Forerunner. I have been doing this back when I still had the paid version, but I remember it to be very difficult and each time a number of attempts to connect to the right port were needed. It would scan through all the available ports one by one and then eventually hook to the right one. I am suspecting that Google decided not to support the serial connection any longer.

53   *INTEREST AND SHARING—UPDATE*[28] Six month into writing this blog it hits the 2500 visitors mark. The last post on this was back in mid January where it hit the 1000 visitors mark and now it is more than double this number. This is very good news. Again there were some very supportive links to the work on this blog and the work was quoted on a number of other blogs including digitalurban[29] and GISagents[30], many thanks to them (Fig. 5).

The graphs with the stats updates from sitemeter[31] show a surprisingly similar picture. There is almost no change in the visitors' pattern in terms of hour of the

---

[25] http://www.jafud.com.

[26] http://www.youtube.com/v/FOR0fPTx-os&hlen&fs1.

[27] http://www.youtube.com/v/jYF3UFmHyNQ&hlen&fs1.

[28] *INTEREST AND SHARING—UPDATE*, 9 March 2009 15:37, graphs, links, history, review, analysis, visits.

[29] http://digitalurban.blogspot.com.

[30] http://gisagents.blogspot.com/.

[31] http://www.sitemeter.com/?astats&ss40urbantick.

Total visits per hour   Total visits per hour per day

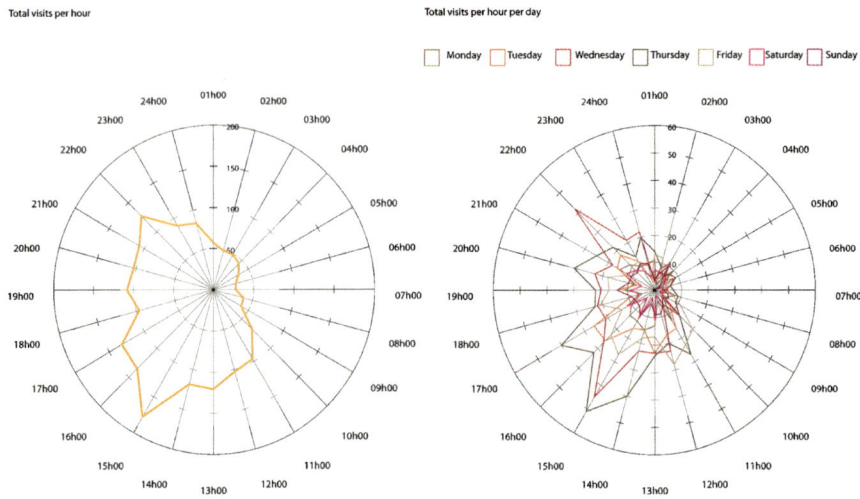

Fig. 5 Image by urbanTick for UrbanDiary / Graphs showing blog visitor per time unit

day looking at the total visits per hour. There is again a peak around three in the afternoon and a second one around ten in the evening. The later one could probably be America with the time difference, so that they also visit around three in the afternoon local time. The visitors per week day look also similar, the mid week days are popular, with Thursday having the lead, whereas the weekend is rather quiet. The last update on this was followed by an outlook for this project. One point was about collecting tracking data of a number of individuals and the other point was regarding an option to build up an online community to collect much more data to quantify the picture of urban cycles. The tracking of participants has started as the UrbanDiary[32] project and fourteen individuals have already been collecting data of their daily activities for one month. This pre-study is going well and the data is very good. For the second point the UrbanDiary project has now a facebook page![33] It is updated with news from this blog, but mainly with news from the UrbanDiary project and enables participants and people being interested in this topic to share information and experience directly. The page is accessible to facebook members and to non-members so you can bookmark it and follow it even if you are not on facebook.

154   *JUST ARRIVED—THE NEW UD TRACKING WATCHES—GARMIN 405*[34] The two test devices supplied by Garmin have just arrived. They are charging now, but will be soon out for first test walks around central London. The main interest is how well they will play in these urban conditions. Garmin kindly sent us two forerunner 405 wristwatch GPS to test. They will be used in the UrbanDiary project to extend the field of participants (Fig. 6).

---

[32] http://urbantick.blogspot.com/search/label/urbaDiary.

[33] http://www.facebook.com/pages/Urban-Diary/67812788988.

[34] *JUST ARRIVED—THE NEW UD TRACKING WATCHES—GARMIN 405,* 16 April 2009 14:32, tool, review, forerunner 405, GPS, Garmin.

Fig. 6 Image by urbanTick / The Foretrex 405 and the up to date UrbanDiary map

First touch, the device is surprisingly responsive through the "Touch Bezel" and one immediately finds oneself attached to the new tool. Simple setup, including a short tour through the device function at startup help to be able to use it straight away from the beginning. Setting up the first of the devices in the court of Torrington Place took no more than an impressive 2 min to get a good Satellite signal and location. Compared to the Foretrex 201 that was used at the same time this is great and the weather conditions were very cloudy. The 201 didn't find a signal for 5 min and we couldn't be bothered to wait in the rain for the device to find a signal. Garmin has supplied a heart rate monitor belt and ant stick as well so this will be in the next phase of testing.

GEOTIME ON THE MAC[35] I have reinstalled the iMac and set up parallels on it (Fig. 7).

This allows to run the Mac osX and Windows Vista in a separate window. And there you go, it allows to install, GeoTime on a Mac. Before now I was running it on a windows machine. I tried a few things, including importing the whole data set from the UrbanDiary project. It works ok, but seems to be slower than the installation on a Windows machine. I will test it some more and see if it is worth working on a Mac. The next step will be to get the ArcGIS integration to work with it on the Mac.

GARMIN FORERUNNER 405—UD TESTED—REVIEW[36] We have been using the Garmin Forerunner 405 now for more than a week and it's time to look at this tool again. An earlier post was all about how great this device feels and looks, but this time we want to go a bit deeper into how it is to actually use it. The two devices we have at the moment were in use pretty much non-stop ever since we got our hands on them. And getting your hands on them or better your finger is one of the highlights of this tool. The Bezal, as it is called by Garmin is the company's answer to Apple's iPod wheel. It works as a touch sensitive ring around the clock face, but unlike the iPod it has no click, only touch. The fact that

---

[35] *GEOTIME ON THE MAC*, 20 April 2009 14:07, visualisation, review, GeoTime, mac.

[36] *GARMIN FORERUNNER 405—UD TESTED—REVIEW*, 28 April 2009 23:39, tool, review, GPS, Garmin.

Fig. 7 Image by
urbanTick / Running Geotime
on the iMac

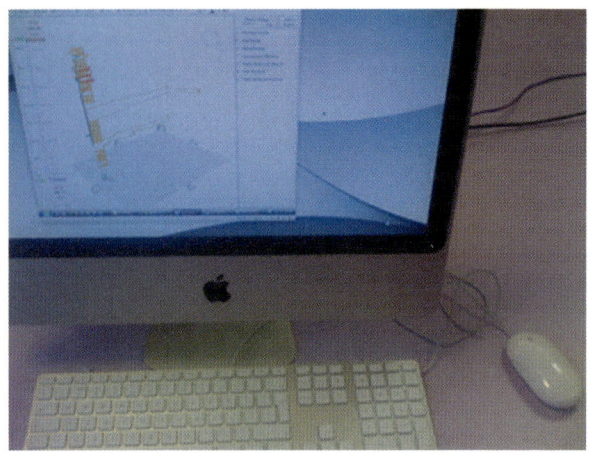

one can actually touch it and communicate through touch makes for a great relationship right from the start, although the device's response is not always as expected. The Bezal does play up and sometimes reads touches as rotations or rotations as touches, I suppose this is what the click wheel is all about. The settings for this input method are great and after testing them one can definitely find a personal best fit. But to get things in a bit more order we'll restart this review with the setup process. Lovely how the device itself actually gives you an introduction. At first startup the 405 introduces itself, as the instructions on screen get you to use all the methods of input. This is very nice and works very well, as one is able to use the device straight away. The first satellite connection then sets the device's date and time and you're ready to go. The first satellite fix the device got really quickly. Something under 2 min, which for a central London location and inside a courtyard, is really good. To start tracking, two settings need to be made. One is to turn the GPS receiver on and the other one, the one I only realized after my first trip around the block was not recorded, the timer needs to be started. This makes it at first glance a bit more complicated than the previous device 201, where to turn on the device was all that was required. Then off you go and you are tracked and this means tracked! Once the signal is established there is hardly anything that causes the 405 to lose it. Again this is tested in central London in narrow streets with high buildings, on buses and so on. The accuracy is generally around 7–9 m. Sometimes it is actually a bit scary, when you are inside the kitchen of your ground floor flat and the device still gives you 9 m accuracy or you're sitting on a double-decker bus on the lower floor in an aisle seat and check your device—7 m! Being used to a 201, the reception of the 405 is a dream! On the other hand, compared to a 201 the information on the 405 is much reduced. The display is obviously smaller, but the information one can access is also reduced. I assume Garmin aims at another target group with the 405 and they decided, that for training, less information is good enough. For example there is no altitude information, no information about actual speed or location. Also, compared to the 201 the compass and the track record map are not a feature of the 405 and so

Fig. 8 Image by
urbanTick / Forerunner 405,
colour black

is all the information's about sunrise, sunset and so on. Further, it is worth noting that one screen usually only gives the user one type of information. Say on the time screen only the time and the date is displayed, but not the satellite connection or any timer information. So if you are interested in what is going on as you are on the go, you find yourself tapping and turning all the way. To get to the input methods from there, the Bezel as much as we have fallen in love with it in the first place is not always one hundred percent accurate, as mentioned before. There are three methods of input on the Bezel itself. One is rotating round the clock to navigate down, clockwise, or up, anti clockwise. To select a menu a tap on the Bezal is all that's needed and in you go. The third method is actually tap twice and this is for confirming messages that pop up on the screen. The 405 does not, unlike the 201, come up with questions, like, are you indoors? There are buttons on the device though, but after discovering that you can tap the Bezal you'll probably find this more convenient and not use the real buttons much. One button is for selecting, enter, the other one is for quit, exit. One major button we do miss is an on/off button, or at least a way to turn off the device (Fig. 8).

There is no way to turn it off; you just let the battery die. A strange thing to do really, if you think of someone doing training, as the developers may have done, who does that twice a week, this person might want to turn the device off for the two days it is not in use. The menus and its content are, overall very clear and simple. A rather big thing is connecting the device to the computer, surprisingly. The device itself has no connection point, it transmits the data wireless via a Garmin made protocol. For this an additional USB stick called Ant-stick is required. Of course for this additional software is required and this software is preferably downloaded from the internet. There is actually no Mac software on the CD that is included in the package; only Windows support is delivered in the pack. Fortunately there is Mac support and apparently we did not get it to work on Windows yet, we are still working on this. So basically Internet is required for the setup, not only to download the software, but also Garmin makes everyone sign up online before they are allowed to use the device. We could not really believe it at first, not even Apple makes you sign up for using the iPod after you have downloaded the software, that comes actually preinstalled if you are on a Mac. So we signed up, and there you go your data gets downloaded and by default is uploaded to the internet and publicly available. The default settings on your online account are set to public, so unless you change this your training or whatever you recorded on the device, including your weight, birth date or your resting heart rate. After all that it is possible to change the settings in the references of the Garmin Ant Agent program, so that it does not upload to the internet directly. There are currently some issues reported and discussed online, with this special USB Ant stick. Older laptops, especially PowerBooks seem to hang up if the USB stick is disconnected without the machine shut down. The MacBook we tested did work fine but just would not enter sleep mode after disconnecting the stick. Garmin seems to be working on these problems. The tracks are saved in a. TCX file format. Apparently this stands for Garmin training centre. That is the Garmin software that goes with all this to actually visualise the recorded data. This is another thing one needs to download and set up, but we won't talk about this here. This. TCX data can be translated with the aid of the brilliant GPSBabel[37] software into any other GPS related format you wish for.

The only thing one has to do is select the input file format, as the.TCX is not automatically recognized as the Garmin training centre format. The right format would be.TCP, as it is called after exporting out of the real training centre, but it works fine. The heart rate monitor data gets lost with most file transformations, as very few formats are intended to incorporate such information, but the standard stuff is there to play on Google Earth.

The 405 has better signal compared to the 201, but it also saves a lot more track points. A trip comparison showed that for the same trip at the same time, the 201 saved 234 location points, but the 405 saved 645 location points. The route both records display does actually not much differ. The recording interval of the 201 is pretty good with few points. On the other hand the 405's storage capacity is much more limited. Similar is the battery life. The 405 needs to be charged every day/night.

It does charge quickly though, 3 h will do it. We managed to get 08h45 tracking time out of the device, while having the GPS on for the whole time. As we are looking at tracking people's daily routines, this is the very least we need. In this respect the 201 was pretty good. It would do during the experiment with participants two or three days before charging. If the user does turn off the GPS when inside, a normal full day out of the house, nine to nine is possible, but not much more. Charging is a funny thing with the 405, much because of the unconventional way Garmin choose to connect the cable to the device. It is not plugged in, it is clipped on. It is a refreshing way to do it as we are used to the boring plugs we daily use on our ten different gadgets that want to be fed, but it makes the device useless during the charging period because the Bezal is partially covered by the clip. The 201 could be used while being plugged in, actually this would even open more options, like external antennas or real time tracking. So the 405 can for example not be used in the car and having it charging while playing with it. Before summing up, some words on the choice of colour. The device is available in two colours only, who would guess it, black, and some green beige, one for males and the other one for females presumably. But actually this green beige weird colour is great looking! Over all, a superb

---

[37] http://www.gpsbabel.org/.

Fig. 9 Image by urbanTick /
Forerunner colour green/
beige

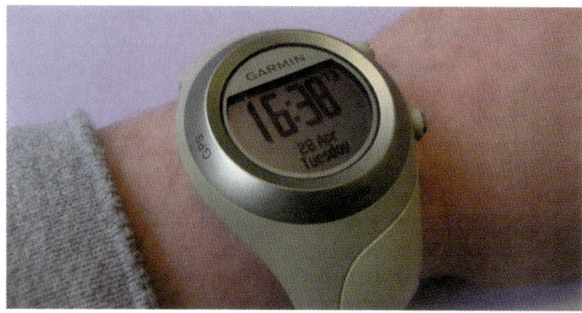

device, it has its clearly specified target group and usage area but within this it is
flexible and very good (Fig. 9).

It is definitely better than the old Foretrex 201, even though not in all areas. This
review has probably been a bit harsh at times, but we loved the device right from the
start and still do. Hmm, actually we have left out the major part of the device. The
training bit, together with the heart rate monitor and some virtual training partners,
pace, laps and that sort of thing. We are not into this and don't understand any of it
so we cannot comment, we haven't even tried to use it, sorry. But apparently it is
great. If you are interested in this sort of use of the device you might want to read
here, Garmin Forerunner 405 review[38].

5000—URBANTICK[39] 5000 visitors so far on urbanTick! Great stuff and thank
you all for the interest in the work that is presented in this spot. 5000 is a good number to look back again at what the number say and how the graph draws this time,
plus looking at the content so far and what will come up for the near future. The
content of this blog was aimed at rhythms and cycles in its description. These topics
have been rather on the sideline and the focus was more on GPS and tracking stuff.
This has mainly to do with the UrbanDiary project that is still ongoing, which generated this interest. For the future the intensity towards GPS and specifically tracking will remain, plus more posts more directly aimed at cycle and rhythm research
as well as the additional topic of the body in relation to rhythm, routine and the
body. Body will relate on one hand to the human body with the physical experience
of space and time and on the other hand directly to the city and the urban morphology as space and time. This addition will enable the research to start evolving a not
so traditional view of the city as a result of motion and change rather than the traditional fixed points and space containers. Regarding blog's visitors, so far the peaks
were at 15h00 and 22h00 with the mid weekdays being most popular (Fig. 10).

There is a slight shift in the days, it not Thursday with the most visitors, but
Wednesday now. It is still at 15h00 in the mid afternoon when it peaks, but then it
basically stays up until 22h00, whereas the late night and the morning stays relatively calm.

---

[38] http://www.google.co.uk/search?q=garmin + 405+review&ieutf-8&oeutf-8&aqt&rlsorg.
mozilla:en-US:official&clientfirefox-a.

[39] *5000—URBANTICK*, 6 May 2009 22:51, graphs, review, history, analysis.

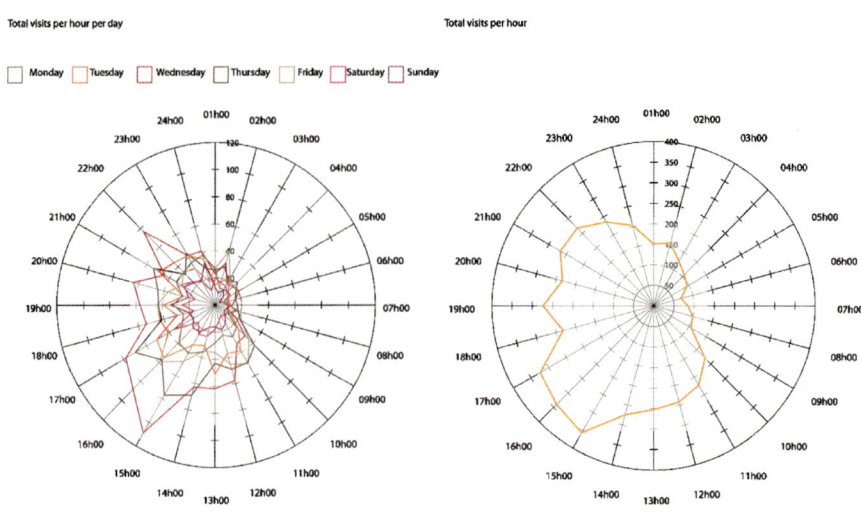

Total visits per hour per day   Total visits per hour

☐ Monday ☐ Tuesday ☐ Wednesday ☐ Thursday ☐ Friday ☐ Saturday ☐ Sunday

Fig. 10 Image by urbanTick / The latest visitor statistics

158   *WANT TO KNOW THE WHEREABOUTS OF YOUR PET?—TRACK IT!*[40] The topic of animal tracking has featured on the blog already a few times, starting with a joke for April 1st. It was a story about tracking frogs[41] in my backyard and it sparkled a number of responses ranging from oh, how are they supposed to mate with this large tracking device, to uh, actually we don't even know how many of these amphibians live in our back gardens[42]. So here is an other one, not a joke, but an animal tracking project, tracking your cat! It makes an interesting combination. Cats are known as very loyal and loving animals; they like routine, show up when you feed them and will lie on your computer keyboard when you try to work. There is another side to this cuddly animal. It is a hunter and predator, kills and eats a large variety of small animals and enjoys strolling around. This second side we, as pet holder know very little about. How far do they stroll, where do they hunt and where do they sleep, are some of the questions we might find ourselves thinking about while on the bus to work. Is Spotty maybe enjoying herself at the neighbours, or does the old lady down the road feed her? The cat wouldn't tell us and we will never know, which is probably good, but there you go here comes the solution. Why not track your cat with GPS? (Found through csendsedesign blog[43]) The solution is Mr. Lee's CatTracker[44]. A simple GPS tracker that you can put on your cat, let it collect some data, and then download to the computer put it on Google Earth and most likely you will get some lines around your house, in your back yard and down the street, great!

---

[40] *WANT TO KNOW THE WHEREABOUTS OF YOUR PET?—TRACK IT!*, 24 May 2009 10:00, animals, review, tracking, GPS.

[41] http://urbantick.blogspot.com/2009/04/animal-tracking-frogs.html.

[42] http://urbantick.blogspot.com/2009/04/animal-tracking-frogs-second.html.

[43] http://csensedesign.co.uk/blog/?p183.

[44] http://www.mr-lee-catcam.de/ct_index.htm.

This is it, the tiny device that can be attached via a harness or collar to the cat and of it goes. It is a small pack, containing receiver, battery and antenna. It connects via USB 1.1 runs for approximately 30 h while saving location points every 30 s and has storage capacity for 64,000 points. That makes for around 530 h of tracking … while charging of course. Anyway, would be fun to test the device.

Of course the company does have some more great ideas for pet owners. There is also the catCam. Put a cam on your cat and you can even see what the cat saw. A clip can be seen here[45]. The page has also lots of tips and trick, including manuals if you are planning to build your own tracking equipment to follow your pet. Bits and pieces are available from their web store. Having said that, there are scientific pet tracking projects. One of them featured not long a go in an article in the Guardian[46] and is looking at cats as predators. Scientist believe that cats "are responsible for the deaths of millions of small wild animals each year" (Guardian from Monday 16th of February[47]) Research is undertaken at the University of Reading and the project including the GPS receivers seems not to have started yet.

BOOK—DATA FLOW[48] Visualisation is part of our daily lives and we are constantly reading, interpreting or producing this kind of communication. In today's book visualisations are described, as "Visual metaphors are a powerful aid to human thinking." It goes on with referring to the modern time and the newly found complexity with "As our experience of the world has become more complex and nuanced, the demands to our thinking aids have increased proportionally." Anyway, the book is about visualizing information and called Data Flow—Visualizing Information in Graphic Design[49]. It is not new, new, but recent, published by Gestalten[50] in late 2008. It brings together a great collection of recent graphic visualisations of information and data. Of course the book itself is highly designed and a real joy to look at (Fig. 11).

The book is structured into six topics, namely Datasphere, Datanet, Datascape, Dataoid, Datalogy, and Datablocks. This is a purely visual characterization of the final products, but formally helpful and of course sexy. Actually everything is pretty much sexy in this book. As these titles already tell you they represent circle, net, surfaces, blocks. Those are the simple ones, the hard ones are Datanoid and Datalogy, here some references are needed to explain what the editor means with the title. Datanoid is deriving from humanoid, meaning "having human characteristics or form".

It describes visualisations humans can easily relate to through different ways, by integrating people, photographs and actions. The Datalogy seems to derive from analogy and refers to "similar to", combining comparison and experience. To make things simper a complex structure is needed. The book certainly achieves this. They seem fairly formal groupings at first, but have some thinking behind them. The introduction to each chapter starts with a quite poetic description of each topic. This

---

[45] http://www.mr-lee-catcam.de/BINARY/catcam_video.wmv.

[46] http://www.guardian.co.uk.

[47] http://www.guardian.co.uk/news/blog/2009/feb/16/catnav-track-killer-pets.

[48] *BOOK—DATA FLOW*, 4 June 2009 11:30, visualisation, review, data handling, book, graphics.

[49] http://www.gestalten.com/books/detail?id=ceaea7651adf9ba0011b78b89b9d0295.

[50] http://www.gestalten.com/.

Fig. 11 Image taken from
Data Flow / Cover of the
book published by Gestalten

makes reading the book fun but is not very helpful if one is interested in details. It is followed by a summary of the chapter again in a fairly superficial manner, but comparing or introducing a few key examples. This gives a good impression of what follows. Each graphic is then described with a short text block of around 60 words. This is very brief and each creator could probably fill pages with contextual information, but the visualisation is designed to speak for itself so it might be a good compromise. This kind of defines the character of the book; it is more of a compendium than a reader, containing a collection and not a description. Between all this there are a few interviews with designers of some of the presented visualisations, they are, Lust, Jessica Hagy, Cybu Richli and Catalogtree. Some of their work also features over a number of pages, whereas normally through out the book, one page is one visual, with 256 pages this might be about 180 different visuals in full colour obviously. The interviews are rather short, around eight questions. The style of the interview is a rather school like question and answer game. A bit more of a flexible chat would probably make the discussion more interesting. In the end one gets the feeling that the questions generally have been rather implicit, which leaves little

Fig. 12 Images taken from
Data Flow / Sample pages

room for surprising answers. Anyway, if you have the patience to read through them there is interesting insight on how the designers approach projects and what they think about the topic of visualisation. There are a number of diagrams we have seen published elsewhere before. One of Christian Nolde's Emotion Maps, the San Francisco Emotion Map is published here. For his book Emotional Cartography see earlier post here[51]. Funny enough this is in the chapter Datascape and not in Datanoid. Other projects are the cab spotting project that features with a graphic (see blog entry[52]), or the "manual" visualisation of mobile phone activity by Nicolas Fischer, maybe something the MIT should be thinking about (upcoming blog post) or the plotting of the 90 min movement of footballers, taken from the Game England vs. Poland in the 2006 World Cup. Who has won 2–1? Some of the other stuff, mainly the Dataspheres recently featured in the Computer Arts 2009 March edition. To conclude on this review, the book is great and very sexy, as mentioned above (Fig. 12).

It is one of the sort of books that give you real inspiration and immediately makes you want to pimp all that recent stuff you have produced. And once more you find yourself saying, I knew for a long time: it is possible to actually produce great visuals! And for a very short moment you forget about all the crap and ugly stuff you are surrounded by, nice!

The book: R. Klanten, N. Bourquin, S. Ehmann, F. van Heerden, T. Tissot, 2008. Data Flow. Berlin: Gestalten Some links to designers featuring in the book[53,54,55]:

EXPLORE, COLLECT, RUN—WITH OPEN STREET MAP[56], Trailrunner[57] is managing software for exercising. It supports a broad variety of exercising forms, ranging from manual records, pulse meters, shoe pods to GPS trackers. The software has been around for a few years and has evolved quite a bit. Especially now with the new 2.0 release that is available now as a beta release. The

---

[51] http://urbantick.blogspot.com/2009/05/emotionalcartography_31.html.

[52] http://urbantick.blogspot.com/search/label/cabspotting.

[53] http://www.jeffreydocherty.com/.

[54] http://www.catalogtree.net/.

[55] http://www.cvanvleck.com/.

[56] *EXPLORE, COLLECT, RUN—WITH OPEN STREET MAP*, 8 June 2009 11:00, review, GPS tracks, software, GPS.

[57] http://www.trailrunnerx.com/.

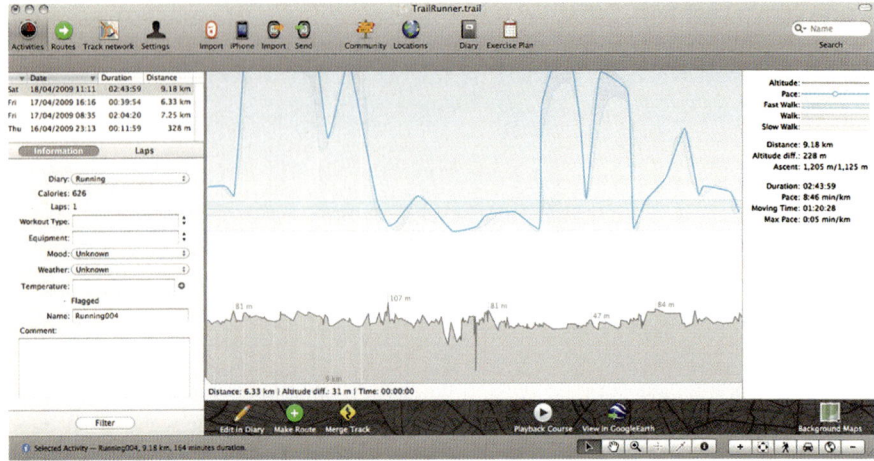

Fig. 13 Image by urbanTick / Trailrunner software interface screenshot

new feature that caught the attention is the integration of Open Street Map[58]. With Trailrunner you would always get a base map. Even in the early days you could choose from different free mapping services. For a free online available software this was something special. Although the maps and aerials have been crude and often in a low resolution it was something that marked Trailrunner out from others. Things have changed dramatically across the internet regarding free mapping services and very detailed and accurate information is available in different forms. Trailrunner managed to develop in sync with this and when you look at the product now, the map integration is probably still the best feature. With the integration of Open Street Map (OSM) the software allows access to the open source platform and ensures a certain independence from Google or Microsoft Virtual Earth. Both other services are available too, but to give the user the choice between the completely different projects is a big plus. Out there in the mapping community is a great divide, or better a number of divisions. Some swear by Google Maps, other only use Microsoft and a third group would only go for open source projects such as OSM. Integrating all of them is a clever move and pleases a wider user group. It is even possible to manually add your own maps. But apart from this, Trailrunner knows to please with a series of other features too. From the range of supported gadget, to the range of file formats and the detail of visualisation and settings, all the way to the customisation there is something for everyone. The software supports directly the import from iPhone/iPod[59], the Nike Pod[60], LoadMyTracks[61], SonicLink[62] and a variety of Garmin formats and software including the Ant Stick. Manually files can be imported from a GPX, TCX, HRM or KML file format (Fig. 13).

---

[58] http://www.openstreetmap.org/.

[59] http://trails.lamouroux.de/.

[60] http://www.apple.com/iPod/Nike/.

[61] http://www.cluetrust.com/LoadMyTracks.html.

[62] http://www.polarelectro.co.uk/uk-en.

The visualisations are on the map or as diagrams and include a nice playback feature. The tracks can be manipulated right in the software by splitting or merging and new tracks can be added also by drawing them directly on the map. For exporting there are options to choose from such as, GPX, TCX, KML, PDF or text available. There are lots to the Trailrunner and elements like diary and exercise plan I haven't discussed here. Compared to other similar services such as the online service Garmin Connect[63] or Nokia's Sports Tracker[64] it demonstrates how much fun managing your exercise can be. For up to date news visit the Trailrunner blog[65]. The latest software version of Trailrunner can be downloaded here[66].

61   *TOMTOM FOR THE IPHONE*[67] At yesterday's WWDC TomTom[68] has announced the release of their in car navigation for the iPhone (also for the new iPhone 3GS[69]) including car kit for secure docking. The docking attaches to the windscreen and allows portrait and landscape mode. The TomTom[70] application including the latest maps will be available from the iTunes store soon they say. See clip on Youtube[71]/TomTom on the iPhone demonstrated. Some first shots from the conference shown at engadget[72]. Let's hope that soon, we can have a look at it. So far we have to enjoy the clip on Youtube: See the TomTom announcement here[73].

62   *NEW GARMIN FORETREX 301/401*[74] Garmin® Announces Rugged, Waterproof Foretrex® 401 and 301, Wearable Navigation that's Easy to Use in Tough Conditions. Garmin has announced this week a new model for its Foretrex family[75]. It has been a really long time since the Foretrex 101 and 201 were first introduced. They were really good devices and probably some of the first handheld GPS that where actually usable. And they still are. The Foretrex is the GPS device I am using so far in the UrbanDiary project and the set of them is still performing quite well. Although I have recently compared it to the new Forerunner 405 that I have two test devices for, it is a lot better in terms of GPS signal reception the 201s still work well. So there are high expectations for the new models and whether the big step forward that the first Foretrex made can

---

[63] http://connect.garmin.com/.

[64] http://sportstracker.nokia.com/.

[65] http://prmac.com/release-id-5796.htm.

[66] http://trailrunnerx.com/en_download/index.html.

[67] *TOMTOM FOR THE IPHONE*, 9 June 2009 10:00, review, software, GPS, iPhone.

[68] http://iphone.tomtom.com/index.html.

[69] http://www.apple.com/iphone/.

[70] http://iphone.tomtom.com/index.html.

[71] http://www.youtube.com/v/YskygegTjAU&rel0&color10xb1b1b1&color20xcfcfcf&hlnl&featureplayer_embedded&fs1.

[72] http://www.engadget.com/2009/06/08/apple-partners-with-tomtom-to-bring-real-navigation-to-iphone/.

[73] http://iphone.tomtom.com/announcement.html.

[74] *NEW GARMIN FORETREX 301/401*, 19 June 2009 10:00, GPS device, review, gadget, GPS, Garmin.

[75] http://garmin.blogs.com/pr/2009/06/garmin-announces-rugged-waterproof-foretrex-401-and-301-wearable-navigation-thats-easy-to-use-in-tou.html?activeBranchIdnewsroom.

be repeated will reminds to be seen. But let's have a look at what Garmin writes about these models. Finally, Garmin builds in a USB connection, so far the 201 still works with a serial connection. It seems to spot all the features that the previous model had, including sunset and sunrise, fishing and hunting times. There are some new features though. These are an electronic compass and a barometric altimeter and of course a new high sensitive GPS receiver. Also the 401 model will allow transferring data wirelessly to other devices. It will hopefully be based on the ant technology so that the device can also communicate with a computer. In terms of storage and capacity the device surprisingly has not improved. It is still the 10,000 points per track and 10 tracks, plus 500 waypoints. It is a lot but since every little gadget is increasing its storage capacity it seems odd that this one doesn't. This is of course not an argument, but a hint. Telling from the images, the screen will be still black and white without the function of adding a contextual map. Which is all right, as the screen quality is good and if you want a coloured feature map you would probably buy another device. Also, reading from the description there will be no longer a model with an internal battery. Both models 301 and 401 will work on two AA batteries, with is a shame. I know there are issues with charging an internal battery whilst you are out and about but having only AA option really has the danger of producing a lot of battery waste. There are solutions to the charging problem out there ranging from solar chargers to tiny wind turbines and pull strings that work for a series of other devices with internal batteries and since this new model now has an USB connection his will make things in this respect much more simple. In term of size and weight the new ones are around 20% smaller while still fitted with the same screen size. This is an improvement, as many of my participants using the 201 have mentioned in the feedback, that the device was "a bit chunky". In terms of weight the new 401 is slightly heavier with 87.3 g compared to 78 g for the old 201. This is surprising, as the overall size has been reduced. The direct comparison on the Garmin website between the 201 and the 401 can be found here[76]. So all in all exciting news but it is a little bit disappointing to see how little the device has improved over at least six years. But as said earlier it remains to be seen how the device actually performs. Prices are on the Garmin page at $ 200.00 for the 301 and $ 260.00 for the 401. There are not yet any prices for the UK.

It is advertised on the Garmin blog[77] as "Versatile new Foretrex units perfect for military use or some family fun". This is a big leap between the two and although we know this is where the technology is coming from the two don't go well together.

163   *IPHONEAPP—OLDMAPAPP*[78] An upcoming very promising application for the iPhone is the oldMapApp[79]. It is a simple application that let you flip through

---

[76] https://buy.garmin.com/shop/compare.do?cID144&compareProduct257&compareProduct30026.

[77] http://garmin.blogs.com/my_weblog/2009/06/versatile-new-foretrex-units-perfect-for-military-use-or-some-family-fun.html.

[78] *IPHONEAPP—OLDMAPAPP*, 30 June 2009 07:30, iPhone, review, memory, application, mapping, identity.

[79] http://www.oldmapapp.com/.

Fig. 14 Clip by Old Map
App on Youtube / A demo
of the Old Map App on
the iPhone. (http://www.
youtube.com/watch?v=VN
3LnCOl9zA&feature=pla
yer_embedded)

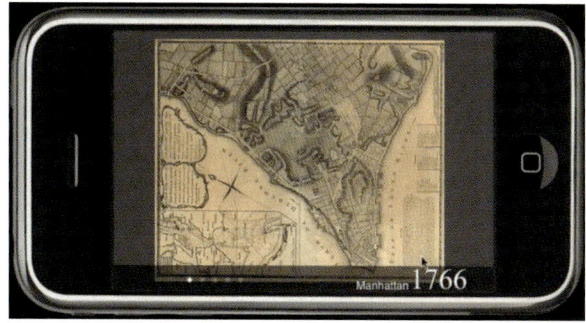

some old maps. But these are not just simple scans, they are all geo-referenced and layered on top of new online maps. The layers' transparency can be adjusted to let your compare now and then. For map freaks and location enthusiasts this will be brilliant. Google does offer a similar thing with the 5.0 version of Google Earth by using the timeline. The oldMapApp[80] does, as the name suggests, offer old historic maps, whereas Google offers only access to old satellite imagery, back from when they started Google Earth. To browse through the history of a place and follow development patterns is very much a detective game and can reveal a lot about the identity of a place. Also elements of collective memory can be found, so keep our eyes open. The application does use the location information from your phone so it knows where you are and can display the information in connection to the historic maps. Using the newly built-in compass in the iPhone 3GS it even knows which direction your are looking. Old Map App uses a modified version of the excellent open-source route-me[81] mapping framework. Modern maps are courtesy of Open Street Map[82], which is creating an open-source map of the world (Fig. 14).

At the moment, this means in the preview, the app offers only scans from the New York region, dated from the seventeenth to the nineteenth centuries. We are of course hoping this will be extended before the release. Found through MapRoom[83].

SOLAR CHARGER—FREELOADERPRO[84] I have been away for a few days, away from the desk and away from the city and away from my computer and away from some power sockets. Away really from quite a lot of the routines I normally repeat daily or even hourly. Although I have been away from quite a lot I did not separate from my GPS and my iPhone. So some solutions regarding the power management had to be found. Great idea, solar chargers are available and not any longer really expensive. So I checked out the options and very soon was able to narrow it down to devices that could probably do the job of powering two iPhones, two GPS

---

[80] http://www.oldmapapp.com/.

[81] http://code.google.com/p/route-me/.

[82] http://www.openstreetmap.org/.

[83] http://www.mcwetboy.net/maproom/.

[84] *SOLAR CHARGER—FREELOADERPRO*, 1 July 2009 09:00, iPhone, review, gadget, GPS, Garmin.

Fig. 15 Image by
urbanTick / Freeloader
Supercharger charging the
FreeloaderPro

both Garmins but different plugs, and Camera. All this over the period of a couple
of days so no big deal one might think. The two options were the powerMonkey[85]
and the Freeloader[86]. I got some advice from Andy over at DigitalUrban[87] and he
was testing the powerMonkey not very successfully a couple of months back, so I
made the decision to go for the Freeloader, mainly because the new FreeloaderPro[88]
comes with a wide range of adapters for all sorts of devices from iPhone/iPod to
mobile phone and PSP on 5.5 V and can now also charge a wide range of Camera
and Camcorder batteries on 9.5 V. Also the option to extend the solar panel with
the FreeloaderSupercharger[89] made a lot of sense. So I went down the road into the
nearest Maplin store and bought both, the FreeloaderPro and the FreeloaderSupercharger. Happy and feeling prepared I left all the routine and habits related to the
stuff mentioned earlier behind me and headed off. To get straight to the point it was
a bit of a disappointment really. I worked out very well in the beginning regarding
the FreeloaderPro as a battery to recharge the devices. The FreeloaderPro works as a
solar collector and charges its internal battery that on the other hand can then charge
the device. Apparently not simultaneously, meaning it has to charge itself first and
can only then recharge. A bit annoying but there you go. Anyway it worked at first
because I did, while following the instructions on the box charge the FreeloaderPro
while still at home straight through its USB port to fill its internal battery (Fig. 15).

Why do I need to charge my iPhone so frequently, it would normally last for
half a week easily you might ask. I just love the little app on my phone that enables timeLapse photography and it basically runs all the time and having photos
taken back to back seems quite power intensive so the battery runs down quick.

---

[85] https://powertraveller.com/.

[86] http://www.freeloaderpro.co.uk/.

[87] http://www.digitalurban.blogspot.com/.

[88] http://www.solartechnology.co.uk/shop/freeloader-pro.htm.

[89] http://www.solartechnology.co.uk/freeloader-superchargers.htm.

Fig. 16 Image by
urbanTick / Freeloader
Supercharger charging an
iPhone

The charging of the GPS, a Garmin Forerunner 405 works all right, is quick and the device full. The iPhone is more of a problem though. It does charge up rather quick through the USB port, but it would only go up to about three-quarters (having the FreeloaderPro full). This was expected, as the explanations on the website already warned about this issue, but on top of this, the battery ran out much quicker. So the iPhone was showing a large green, almost full battery sign, but it would only last for an hour. The even bigger problem occurred as the FreeloaderPro appeared not to charge up properly again. It would not, through out all the sunny days we had it out, charge for more than half. Not with the FreeloaderSupercharger connected via USB to it and not on its own either. I tried it for a number of days and the weather could not have been better! Midweek I had to give in and get my iPhones charged at the normal power socket in the wall. This was probably the low point of it all, as I had really high expectations. Anyway one good thing I discovered afterwards was that the FreeloaderSupercharger works very well on its own for the Garmin Forerunner 405. The 405 come with a USB cable to charge so it can be directly connected and charges up rather quickly to a nearly full 98% with a good 7 h battery live afterwards, This trick does not work for the iPhone, somehow the amount of energy delivered seems not to be high enough for the device to recognize it as being charged. Some side notes on the FreeloaderPro concern issues with the status light. It is nearly impossible to see it in the sunlight and where else would you use it? Not even shading it with my hands made a big difference, I usually had to take it under my T-shirt to be able to see if there were any lights on and what colour they were at. The other issue is with plug holes and robustness. To me such a device should be built for the outdoor use and the FreeloaderPro certainly does not have that feeling to it. I did not test this aspect of it, but it does not have a very robust feeling to it. And being at the beach with sand covers for the plug holes would be nice (Fig. 16).

A better fit for the cables, while having it attached to the backpack often the USB plugs would disconnect with the movement so after a while you find that it did not charge at all because it got disconnected. To sum up it has been a bit disappointing as said before, but I still believe in the concept. It is small, it is light, and it is relatively cheap and it should work. The timeLapse imagery will be ready to be put online soon so you can see what all this struggle was intended to do.—These timeLapse are now online[90]. There will also be an update on the Freeloaders functionality shortly. I have been in contact with the guys producing them and they have sent me a brand new one. I will update you in a post.

165 BOOK—EMOTIONAL CARTOGRAPHY[91], Christian Nold's[92] book Emotional Cartography has featured on this blog earlier, shortly after it has been published online. This time I would like to look back at the book and talk a bit more about the content beside Christians projects.

The book is a collection of essays that tie in with Christian Nold's Biomapping Project. The six elements basically form the main body of the book and are hold together with some of the Biomapping project visualisations. The range of contributions ranges from fictional stories (Marcel van der Drift) to theoretical and practical analysis of participative art (Sophy Hope). This really provides a good context for the project even if you haven't been familiar with Christian's work beforehand. In some contributions the text is reprinted, others are specifically written for this publication, but all try hard to relate to the idea of Emotional Cartography. The striking image that these texts point out about the concept, is how unique, new and innovative this approach is. To begin the book the introduction titled "Emotional Cartography—Technology of the Self", Christian Nold sets out the context, introduces his work and the essays. He is not short of examples and project anecdotes so it is a text that makes you want to know more. The first essay "Machines Made to Measure: on the Technology of Identity and the Manufacture of Difference" has a strong focus on the body it possibilities and contradictions with the possibility to injure or imprisoning. The identity is explored along examples of body parts of uniqueness, such as fingerprints. "A Future Love Story" by Marcel van der Drift, a picture of futuristic usage of location based information and the extent to which the technology could be directly connected to the human body. It is a rather literal and direct story that draws strongly on present development. Steven Boyd Davis writes about the interpretation and the subjective standpoints in his text "Mapping the unseen: Making Sense of the Subjective Image". The concept of engaging with these subjective views of location information is very interesting and funny at times. Surprisingly he manages largely to skip around the obvious example of mental maps. Sophy Hope then brings up the context of the engaging public art in the UK. "Socially Engaged Art: The Conscience of Urban Development" draws out historic and recent examples of this mainly urban phenomenon of participative art projects and how they have come to take on new roles in local community planning. The book concludes with Tom Stafford exploring the possibilities of the human brain in a following up text entitled "Hacking our Tool for Thought" to his book "Mind Hacks" written for O'Reilly together with Matt Webb. Tom explores the possibil-

[90] http://urbantick.blogspot.com/2009/07/natural-cycle-tide-timeLapse.html.
[91] BOOK—EMOTIONAL CARTOGRAPHY, 3 July 2009 01:09, review, emotionalcartography, book, mapping, psychogeography.
[92] http://www.softhook.com/.

ity and limitations of the human brain and how it potentially could be hacked. He is also interestingly very much focusing on the aspect of such possibilities for the group and not the individual. He largely draws directly on the output of some of the Emotional Cartography projects, which provides a good integration and conclusion for the book. Overall an interesting collection and a good read because it is diverse. Apart from the introduction there is very little about the technological aspects of the Emotional Cartography project. This is refreshing and allows for other focuses to be worked out more prominently. Especially the topic of the body enjoys a great focus although I suspect this was not planned to such an extent. The book is freely available on the internet as a full quality colour version at emotionalcartography[93] or as a 2 mb version here[94]. It is all published under a Creative Commons.

66   *BOOK—THE FUNCTIONAL CITY*[95] urbanMachine is a new series on urban-Tick that explores the idea of the city as a machine. It is of course inspired by the topic of cycles and it might be in a sense a literal translation of clockwork. But even so, there are elements that work in such a way like public transport, others like water and electricity are just "available" any time one plugs the plug or opens the tap. What about the waste management or cleaning, maybe public service in general? The aim is to investigate what makes the city tick on the level of very basic, everyday tasks done by regular women and men. It is about infrastructure but also the service that keeps this infrastructure in shape, physically and socially. To start this topic, what better way than to look at the modern city. The modern city has many different faces, but here we are looking at the "real" modern city in the modern sense of the movement of the early twentieth century. Maybe modern city could be replaced with "The Functional City". This term comes even closer to the idea of the urbanMachine, probably this is where the term is derived from. The machine was central to a lot of the modern ideas and admired as the ultimate thing and applicable to any task. Le Corbusier admired the ocean liners as complete entities and of course as a functional triumph. Some of the liners' formal features even play a role in his building designs. This machinist fetish has lead to dramatic constructions in the modern movement. From buildings to urban theories the function was top of the list. Even today, the city would be compared to a machine by a lot of people, when asked. In terms of urban design, the functional approach has a very long tradition. The formalization and rationalization of urban spaces has always been part of planning approaches. From early Chinese cities, to Roman layouts, to garden cities, to new towns, the city was compromised into a single perspective. This approach is tightly interwoven with subjects of power, representation and truth. These aspects are also inherent in the modern movement, although they were able to introduce a shift from a personal focus to a more institutionalized reign of the plan as the central holder of truth. Together with this the architect/planner as the creator of the plan slipped into a unique position. Within this context the term functional city could

---

[93] http://emotionalcartography.net/EmotionalCartography.pdf.

[94] http://emotionalcartography.net/EmotionalCartographyLow.pdf.

[95] *BOOK—THE FUNCTIONAL CITY*, 13 July 2009 08:21, city, review, architecture, machine, book, urban.

have a slightly different meaning. It is a more scientific meaning that imposes a great deal of rationality and logic.

The book "The Functional City—The CIAM and Cornelius van Eesteren, 1928—1960[96]" edited by Kees Somer brings together the history of the CIAM from 1928 to 1960 with a specific focus on Cornelius van Eesteren as a member of the movement. It is published by NAi Publishers in early 2007. Before talking about the content, some words on the physical book. It is a large and thick book, one of the category A4+. The design and layout is brilliant, from the font palette to the implementation and instrumentalisation of images. It is one of these books that you just buy after seeing the cover and having read the title you are on the way to the till, where you get a chance to flip your thumb through the pages while you pay. Coming back to the content, I can't really read the introduction as in my copy it is, together with the book's table of contents, in Dutch. It is only written in English from the first chapter onwards, don't know why. Anyway, the story starts with the first CIAM congress in La Sarraz, June 1928. From there the forming of the CIAM in relation to other movements of the time is described. It all begins with a chaotic struggle to hold the opposition and find a position. In fact the book show and highlights through out the story that in fact the struggle was part of the CIAM. Things were always rushed and different opinions made it difficult for the group to unfold their impact. But one of the first actual manifestations of the CIAM ideas is probably the "Siedlung am Weissenhof" der Werkbundausstellung Stuttgart in 1927. The CIAM went through phases, starting from the public housing (Weissenhof) and working through different steps to the urban structure and implied a methodological link between the smallest and the largest spatial unit: the house unit and the city. This led to the catchy triad 'home-neighborhood-city' (Somer) In this sense the focus on the city has grown. This makes sense as the members were all architects and the discipline of urban planner and urban designer had only just been invented. The book is structured into five steps ordered as topics of content and objectives of the group. This is, as mentioned before, from public housing to urban planning, but on the other hand from CIAM the working group to the limits of collectivity. In a sense the struggle with cooperation and compromises is the line that runs through the book. Along this the different developments on theorization of urban planning, especially in chapter four "Comparative Urban Planning", is developed. That the actual representation, mapping, cartography and visual statistics were actual topics of the CIAM was new to me. This is beautifully illustrated with plans and drawings from CIAM members. The term functional city is part of this "newly developed" approach and consists of four topic. The simple division between the group of housing, recreation, work and traffic. "The structure reflected the situation of scientific urban planning at that moment. ... This modern vision of urban planning was based on the insight hat the most important aspects of social life could be summed up in a nutshell as housing, work and recreation, all linked by traffic" (Van der Would 1983, p. 131). Throughout the book photographs are used as documentation and evidence of activities and persons. This has a beautiful side effect, it illustrates through the course of the book

---

[96] http://www.naipublishers.nl/architecture/functional_city_e.html.

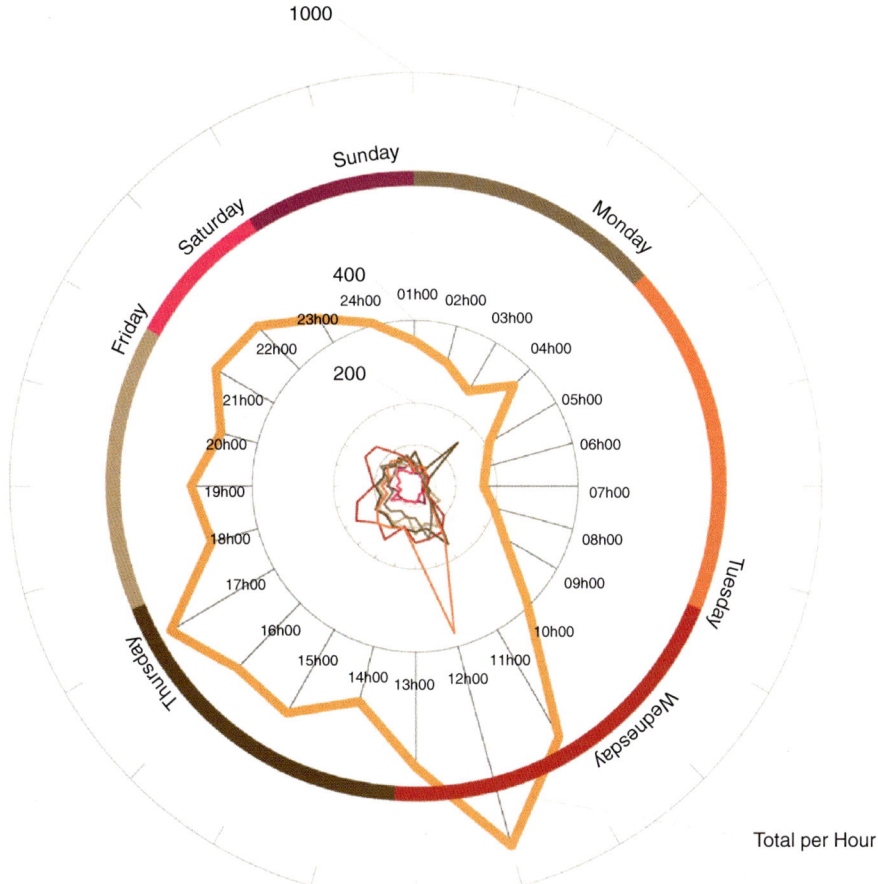

Fig. 17 Image by urbanTick / Visualising the visitor statistics per hour, day and overall

how the members grow old. Not in a voyeuristic sense, but in a more natural sense. This give the course of the CIAM as a movement even more weight in terms of its development and achievement. The young founding members feature on page 18, including Le Corbusier, have visually aged on page 227, Le Corbusier and Corne-lius van Eesteren. This beautiful human portrait makes it a great read beside all the historic facts it redraws the course of drama with real characters.

10,000–URBANTICK[97] Some 10,000 visitors on urban tick … over actually (Fig. 17).

urbanTick has become more popular and from 5,000 visits in just two month the 10,000 visitors mark was reached. I have to confess, that I have done a lot more promotion for the blog during this time, including writing more regular posts. I am aiming at one post a day, not strictly but more or less. The graphs look a bit different

---

[97] *10,000–URBANTICK*, 14 July 2009 10:02, graphs, review, history, analysis.

Fig. 18 Image by
urbanTick / The newly
designed plug to charge the
iPhone 3GS

this time. I merged all three graphs into one. Looks better and is more complicated to read. So for those who'd rather have it in short, the data itself has changed. There is a much bigger peak over lunch now. The big peak at noon is largely influenced by I a one off event, where the blog has over 160 hits within 1 h. At least this shows the record from sitemeter[98]. I cannot remember having seen this, but there you are. This also brings the Tuesday high up, although Wednesday remains the most popular day. Tuesday, Wednesday and Thursday are within a difference of 100 visitors the leading days of the week. The weekend is pretty low compared to the week-days, less than half the visitors. During the course of the day, it is the morning for European visitors and after four for the US visitors. I usually used this post to talk about the direction the research will be going in the next few month, but this time the period was so short, I have hardly started the stuff I proposed last time. So, the direction will stay the same, towards a city of body experience. And a note about the blog, I have lost the comment link in the html of my site at some point. Sorry about that, I will try to put it back anytime soon, as I am very interested to hear about your comments!

168   Brilliant—new Apple iPhone 3GS[99] The new iPhone 3GS has just arrive on my desk today, this is very exciting! I bought my first generation iPhone back in 2007 on the day it was introduced in the UK not only because it was my birthday. I was really happy with it and to be honest I think I have to get used to this new shape, it looks different. So what am I going to do with this new toy then? (Fig. 18).

There are a lot of new feature compared to the iPhone first generation. The GPS and the compass, the cut and paste, but also the increased speed and better transfer rates. A lot is new and this is reflected in the applications. There are a lot of applications already out there that deal with space, time, tracking, visualisation and so on. I will feature them on the blog, as I go along. So if you are interested in this kind of

---

[98] http://www.sitemeter.com/?a=stats&s=s40urbantick.

[99] Brilliant—new Apple iPhone 3GS, 15 July 2009 15:20, review, gadget, iPhone.

Fig. 19 Image by
urbanTick / Screenshot
street view on the iPhone

updates watch this space. It is nothing new, the iPhone has been introduced a few weeks ago, but it's always nice to get something new isn't it?

REVIEW APPLE IPHONE[100], The new iPhone arrived last week[101], so it is time to look at the new features[102] and of course discuss some first applications. To say something about the physical design of the device is probably rather personal, but I really liked the shape and feel of the first generation. The new curves have already been introduced with the second generation, but I never really grew to like it. It is all right if you are holding the iPhone in your hand, but if you are using it on a flat surface it is rather annoying. Say it lies beside your computer keyboard on the desk, as mine usually does and you want to have a quick look at something. What you do is you press the home button to light up the screen and...The new power plug is amazing. That lovely little knob is exactly what it should be. What I am not sure is, if this still works with the older models. My first generation iPhone still had the little transformer with the plug, any experiences? The material seems very sensitive to scratches. First thing I did is put on a screen shield. The back I left uncovered so far and the result of only six days is a fairly scratched back. Compared to the metal back the plastic is not very tough. A first thing to note is the keyboard[103], it is very responsive and now available in landscape. This makes typing texts easier and together with the new cut and paste[104] feature you have a full text editing functionality, it even works for images and web content. Who needs more, all the Word crap? You feel free and light with such a simple method of typing (Fig. 19).

The other important feature is the navigation and the maps. To now have GPS, Maps and the Compass[105] in the phone is very exciting. It works all right and Google maps do a good job. Even very basic navigation from A to B is possible, together

---

[100] *REVIEW APPLE IPHONE*, 21 July 2009 10:54, iPhone, review, gadget, GPS, apple.

[101] http://urbantick.blogspot.com/2009/07/brilliant-new-apple-iphone-3gs.html.

[102] http://www.apple.com/iphone/iphone-3gs/.

[103] http://www.apple.com/iphone/iphone-3gs/keyboard.html.

[104] http://www.apple.com/iphone/iphone-3gs/cut-copy-paste.html.

[105] http://www.apple.com/iphone/iphone-3gs/maps-compass.html.

Fig. 20 Image by urbanTick / Some of my iPhone screens

with on screen instructions. The instructions are not location based and steps have to be switched manually, but nevertheless it is built in. The TomTom[106] navigation was announced earlier this year at the WWDC, see earlier post[107] and will definitely make a big difference. But this will be a paid app. The street view feature full screen is just incredible. Even if you work with the technology in the web and computer daily this is exciting! (Fig. 20).

A quick look at some London focused applications for the iPhone. Of course we all are only waiting for the augmented reality tube direction application that is developed by acrossair[108]. They are waiting for approval through Apple and for them to make it available in the iTunes store. Should be soon they say. Find the clip on Youtube[109]/The demo for the Nearest Tube App on the iPhone.

But in the mean time, there are some basic applications for tube use. There is a lot of free stuff out there so before you pay have a look in the free section and this is exactly what I do for now. Although the apps are usually on £ 0.50 to about £ 2.00, not much. Some research on app usage has shown that additional apps downloaded from the app store are used for a couple of days, regardless whether free or paid for. So back to the tube applications for London. I am looking at both, for travel and navigation, but even for journey optimization, TubeExits[110], if you are not a frequent commuter. It basically tells you to board which carriage in order to be in a good position at arrival. Most appealing tube map comes with iTrans Tube[111]. It is free and features a tube map that can be navigated, zoomed and a click on the station will bring up information about train times from this particular station. General tube

---

[106] http://iphone.tomtom.com/index.html.

[107] http://urbantick.blogspot.com/2009/06/tomtom-for-iphone.html.

[108] http://www.acrossair.com/apps_nearesttube.htm.

[109] http://www.youtube.com/v/U2uH-jrsSxs&hlen&fs1&.

[110] http://www.tubeexits.co.uk/.

[111] http://www.newmediaetc.com/link.php?link315261043.

line information is also available from Tube Status[112] or Tube Info. Tube Info[113] lets you access every single station on the line concerned, where as Tube Status only lists information about closures or maintenance. The TubeMap application combines all the above features, but is not very appealing graphically. So to conclude there are a number of "get around London" applications for free available for the iPhone. I am sure there are more out there and if I come across some additional ones I will ad them. They suit commuters and visitors alike and are a must for everyone in the London area. Of course for the work related to the blog here, the GPS and tracking applications are the most interesting bit. I have been testing some of them too and will review them later this week. For now I think Everytrail[114] still is in the top league. I am using it since the beginning of the year[115] and it works well.

GPS TRACKING APPLICATION FOR THE IPHONE[116] Since the GPS module in the iPhone[117] was introduced in the second generation, a lot of applications have been developed and still are. With the new third generation the software development continues and there are a number of GPS tracking applications that are established and maintained. There are two elements to these tracking apps. One is the application on the iPhone and the other one is some computer software or online solution to display and manipulate the data collected through the mobile device. In short, the iPhone app is only to collect the data: visualisation and manipulation mainly has to be done on the computer. I will be discussing three applications for the iPhone. They are Trails by Felix Alamouroux[118], iTrail by Justin Davis[119] and Everytrail[120]. All of them are compatible with the TrailRunner[121] computer software that has been discussed here earlier and the Everytrail online platform[122]. The first tracking application that has been reviewed here was the Everytrail application for the iPhone. It is a FREE, simple software that is connected to an online platform for visualizing and sharing tracks. Two screens are offered, one is for data information, e.g. time, speed, location, and the other one is a map view based on Google Maps. The map view shows your position with a red square and the location of photos taken on the way (Fig. 21).

Although it is a very simple application there are a few neat features to it. If you have a login for the Everytrail website you can upload the recorded track directly, including settings like public/private and having it published to twitter (recent feature). The app allows taking pictures that are automatically geotagged and treated

---

[112] http://itunes.apple.com/WebObjects/MZStore.woa/wa/viewSoftware?id296883812&mt8.

[113] http://www.mxdata.co.uk/products/tube_map.aspx.

[114] http://www.everytrail.com/.

[115] http://urbantick.blogspot.com/2008/12/everytrail-test-track_18.html.

[116] *GPS TRACKING APPLICATION FOR THE IPHONE*, 27 July 2009 11:01, review, application, tracking, GPS, iPhone.

[117] http://www.apple.com/iphone/.

[118] http://trails.lamouroux.de/.

[119] http://sites.google.com/site/iphoneitrail/.

[120] http://www.everytrail.com/iphone.php.

[121] http://urbantick.blogspot.com/2009/05/explore-collect-run-on-open-street-map.html.

[122] http://www.everytrail.com/.

Fig. 21 Image by urbanTick / Screenshot / Everytrail screen, map and settings

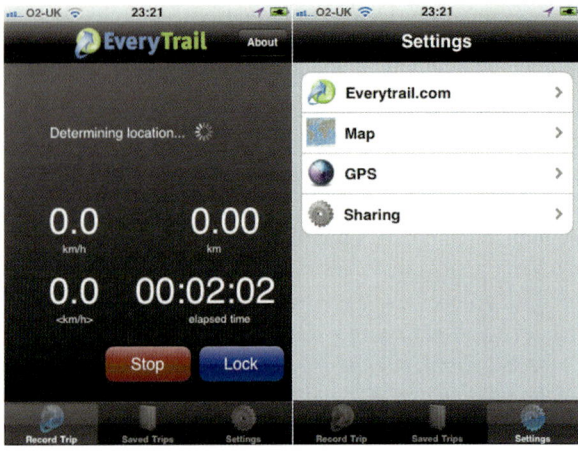

as part of the trip which the track describes. The pictures are uploaded together with the track and can be viewed online. The online track replay function will include the pictures as a slideshow along the track. There is currently no function to import tracks.

You can only record and export. Everytrail also has a bike version for the iPhone. It spots larger numbers that can be read more easily on a high speed trail and works in landscape mode. Trails[123] developed and maintained by Felix Alamouroux is not quite free, it cost £ 2.39 in the iTunes app store[124]. There is a light version for free, but it is limited to some 5 min of tracking. This software has some more functions over the Everytrail. It is possible for example to import data directly. You can access a number of track sites or specify an URL. Standard are Everytrail, Mapmy-run.com and Bikely.com. After choosing the site you can search the public tracks by keyword. The main screen shows the location map, elapsed time, distance and speed. It is possible to save and name waypoints and take pictures. The Trails app uses Open Street Map data to visualise the location. There are two options: one is road, for a simple map and the other one is Terrain and Cycle for a more detailed map. Every time you zoom in or out on the map is reloads the data and depending on the connection this can be a bit slow. In the map view it is also possible to pull out an altitude profile as an overlay on the map. It is possible to edit the track points individually.

Although this is a bit tedious with tracks of more than 400 points it is a neat option to do some rough editing. The exporting functions[125] are either an email, directly to the Everytrail page or to TrailRunner. The email export will be as a GPX and the export to TrailRunner can be sent wirelessly to the computer, both have to be connected to the same network.

---

[123] http://trails.lamouroux.de/.

[124] http://phobos.apple.com/WebObjects/MZStore.woa/wa/viewSoftware?id289190494&mt8.

[125] http://trails.lamouroux.de/exporting-tracks.html.

iTrail[126] is developed by Justin Davis and offers the same functionality as Trails. It also is a paid app and costs £ 1.79 in the iTunes app store. There is no base map function, but it is possible to edit the track points and name them.

Export functions are: Twitter, TrailRunner, trailmapping.com, Google Docs and iTrail Desktop[127]. The Google docs is basically a GPX text file that needs to be copied and pasted to be used. An other option is the iTrail Desktop application. Here again it is possible to send the data between the iPhone and the computer if both are connected to the same private wifi network. There is no real recommendation for one of these apps. For one thing it is because they all do the same and work similar and are compatible with the same software. The differences are the design and the range of functionality. This is reflected in the price tag, but seems reasonable. I am quite happy with the free Everytrail app as I only want to record the track. The Trails app is impressive with its range of function and the beautiful design.

71 *UCL GRAND CHALLENGES—SUSTAINABLE CITIES*[128] UCL Grand Challenges[129] is part of the UCL Research Strategy. UCL has identified new topics of interdisciplinary importance and where new partnerships can deliver novel achievements. The four identified areas are: Sustainable Cities[130], Global Health[131], Intercultural Interaction[132] and Human Wellbeing.

Palette is the new magazine to bring together and document the work at UCL related to Sustainable Cities. The inaugural issue of Palette has just been printed and urbanTick features with a short article in Sect. 5 on page 6. The magazine builds on five sections. Progress reports current activities on the topic that UCL is involved in. Portfolio is a showcase for images produced in the context of research at UCL, Perspective is the section for theories and thoughts of leading UCL academics, Pages is about publications in this area and the section Participation is about forthcoming activities.

CASA[133] features with two more articles in this edition, one is by Mike Batty, "How big can a city get?" and there is also a book review of Andrew Hudson-Smith's[134] "Digital Geography". This first issue of the magazine can be downloaded on the Sustainable Cities homepage or here[135] as a 9 MB PDF file.

---

[126] http://itrailr.googlepages.com/.

[127] http://sites.google.com/site/iphoneitrail/Home/exporting-your-data/itrail-desktop.

[128] *UCL GRAND CHALLENGES—SUSTAINABLE CITIES*, 29 July 2009 12:13, review, sustainability, urbanTick.

[129] http://www.ucl.ac.uk/grand-challenges/.

[130] http://www.ucl.ac.uk/sustainable-cities/.

[131] http://www.ucl.ac.uk/global-health/grandchallenge.

[132] http://www.ucl.ac.uk/intercultural-interaction/.

[133] http://www.casa.ucl.ac.uk/.

[134] http://www.digitalurban.blogspot.com/.

[135] http://www.ucl.ac.uk/sustainable-cities/perspectives/palette-summer09.pdf.

Fig. 22 Image by urbanTick taken from 'You are the City' by Petra Kempf / Detail of one of the sheets

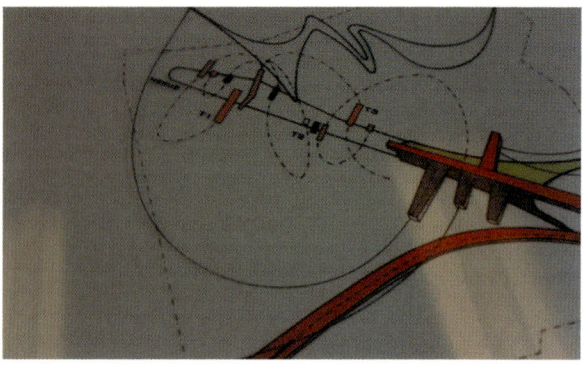

172   *BOOK—YOU ARE THE CITY*[136] You are the City[137] by Petra Kempf[138], Lars Mueller Publisher by Birkhaeuser, 2009. A book that is not really a book might be more of a book than many others. This book here is really not a book, it is a box of sheets and a leaflet. The sheets are colour prints on clear acetate. It is a radical take on city planning with very limited to dos and don'ts. This is rather refreshing and the fact that the transparent sheets allow for creative combination of the presented content goes way beyond telling the "reader" about the new "must" and "don't", but rather directly involves them to participate and shape a number of distinct perspectives on the discussed topic. There is not much more to be said, is there? Well there might be, there are questions about the formality of the visuals, the similarity of the representation, the limitation in the selection of tools and forms. One could argue that is the stuff for discussion and aftermath of the book, as it is still the author's take on the subject and it probably is, but the book does not offer any format for this. So the engagement with the reader ends there, where the sheets can be combined (Fig. 22).

What Birkhaeuser says about the publication: "Cities are hybrid entities based on multilayered and sometimes contradictory organizing principles. As complex networks of geographic, economic, political and cultural segments, they are caught up in a constant process of differentiation. How are we to understand such dynamic processes, especially the complex connections between individuals, whose movements and interactions leave traces in the urban landscape? This publication offers architects, urban planners and general readers interested in city design and growth a novel approach, a mapping tool that creates a framework for understanding the continually changing configuration of the city. With transparent slides, the tool allows one to superimpose various realities like layers and build new urban connections. It invites readers in short to immerse themselves in the complexity of our cities." The book subtitle is "Observation, organization, and transformation of urban settings". With regard to the topic of cycles and rhythms in the city, this publication has a sim-

---

[136] *BOOK—YOU ARE THE CITY*, 31 July 2009 09:31, visualisation, review, cycle, book, urban, graphics.

[137] http://www.springer.com/birkhauser/architecture+&+design/book/978-3-03778-159-3.

[138] http://beta.arch.columbia.edu/users/pk114columbiaedu.

ilar aim to start describing and understand the city in a dynamic sense. Kempf writes in the introduction titled "To the Curios": "Cities are an everyday invention. They are informed and imagined by many people at the time. A city's form is expressed in a vortex of temporal relations, mirrored in the activities of a collective body of individuals interacting with one another." This dynamic approach is also reflected in the naming of the different areas of investigation. The books contains 22 sheets covering four distinct areas, those are: Cosmological Ground; Legislative Agencies; Currents, Flows and Forces; Nodes, Loops and Connections. The naming and the approach can provoke links to Lynch[139]. His five elements plan for the city from his "Image of the City[140]" book were: Nodes, Edge, Path, Landmark, District. Five are much simpler to remember (might be the success of the book) than 22. But obviously there are some more options with a higher number. It does get complicated though. I can list all of them because I have the leaflet in front of me, but the suggestive and at times literal names are easily confused. But maybe this is not the point. Maybe it is more important to create an image though the naming that guides the combination process. The mix of naming strategies is more confusing. Sometimes it is something like Bus Lines or Airport compared to Information Swirls or Under the Ground. The mix of specific and more poetic names probably makes for the distinct aura of the publication. Kempf has worked on a very similar project in 2001. Back then she called it Met(r)onymy 1[141]. Images and style are fairly similar. It seems to be something she started to develop much earlier on. A very interesting comparison between "You are the City" and an earlier book by Zaha Hadid called "Ubiquitous Urbanism" is made on Kosmograd[142]. The formal relationship of the two projects is striking. Interesting because Petra Kempf is Adjunct Assistant Professor at Colombia, the same institution where Zaha Hadid developed her book.

I don't want to leave it here, because this could really create the wrong impression about the book. It is not a copy of something and it is a well thought approach to something new. It really opens the eyes in terms of planning, design approaches but also graphics and communication, 'You are the city—the City is you', has not promised something it will not be able to deliver, It is rather a very real promise and a rather lasting impression.

And if not for all these reasons you want to have one by now, there is one more. Put all the acetates on one pile, look into the sheets from an angle though the reflection (this book is horrible to photograph at a university with this kind of cheap lighting) and enjoy the depth, physical and theoretical this publication is able to create just there in front of you. This is worth buying a book for. Is it a book?

---

[139] http://www.csiss.org/classics/content/62.

[140] http://www.amazon.co.uk/Image-City-Kevin-Lynch/dp/0262620014/ref=sr_1_1?ie=UTF8&qi d1248993802&sr8-1.

[141] http://www.archleague.org/ya/2001/index_kempf.htm.

[142] http://newsfeed.kosmograd.com/kosmograd/2009/05/kempf.html.

173   *GOOGLE LATITUDE ON THE IPHONE—LOCATION BASED SOCIAL NET-WORKING*[143] Google Latitude[144] has featured here earlier[145]; just short after it was launched earlier this year. Since then it has been rather quiet around the service, not only on this blog. There are a few comments after the launch and some first advice on how to use, implement and link it, but then that's it. Regarding the users it is not quite sure on how many people actually use the service. There are probably more that have signed up for it, but do not use it regularly. On the hardware side of it there are also a few problems and hurdles to take. On the iPhone it only runs inside the browser, as Apple has blocked the development of a standalone software in order to "protect" the Maps as the main navigation software. The other hurdle is that no software can run in the background on the iPhone. On other handheld devices such as Android and BlackBerry, Google's list here,[146] it runs as a stand-alone application and can even run in the background. Some services online now include Latitude in their signing up process, in order to provide the customers with accurate location based information. On of them is gps-tours,[147] a website to share walks, hikes and climbing tours. Since the launch of the service a lot of concerns have been raised. In general a large and loud group of people are very concerned about knowing or publishing a persons whereabouts. This not only includes Google Latitude, but location information in general. From GPS to RFID tags everything that could give away a person's location. An example from politics.co.uk[148] shows what the concerns are directed towards: "The dangers are obvious. Stalkers or violent husbands could surreptitiously find out someone's location by throwing a phone in their car boot, for instance. Jealous lovers could install the software while their partner is taking a shower. Employers could force workers to use a Latitude-installed phone." The main problem is, really, that our location is already in the system. It is not so much about this one product, but rather towards a recent development in technology. Google is just a good target because of its size and popularity, but there are a lot of companies that track our movement and habits on a daily basis. In London for example TfL, Transport for London, knows the location roughly of hundred thousands of people, or financial institutions through the use of ATMs: even internet providers know roughly where the computer that you are logging in on is located and there are many more examples and of course speculations. All these information's are not made public to our knowledge. Compared to this with Google Latitude there is the option to share this information with others. Google seems to have given some thought to these concerns prior to launching the service. They have taken a number of measures to help prevent "accidental" use or use through a third person, mainly through integrating it into the Google services and therefore protecting it from third

---

[143] *GOOGLE LATITUDE ON THE IPHONE—LOCATION BASED SOCIAL NETWORKING*, 4 August 2009 11:30, review, location, social network, tracking, iPhone.

[144] http://www.google.co.uk/latitude/intro.html.

[145] http://urbantick.blogspot.com/2009/02/google-longitude-tracking-service.html.

[146] http://www.google.com/support/mobile/bin/answer.py?answer136640.

[147] http://www.gps-tour.info/en/index.html.

[148] http://www.politics.co.uk/feature/legal-and-constitutional/analysis-is-google-latitude-a-problem-$1279630.htm.

person access. But also by implementing a number of steps that lead to the activation of the service.

However for now I have my position on the blog for everyone who is interested. I have given this some thought over the past four years and I am not too concerned about people knowing my location. While working with GPS and tracking every now and then people would ask and laugh whether my wife has access to the data. These sorts of jokes are not only funny but reveal people's concerns, in this case as stereotypes, but still people are thinking about it. I myself have never really seen the location information as a potential risk factor.

Perhaps very naively I usually think of it in terms of my project, but also very personally as a statement of activity, a memory of reality in my daily world of computer, blog and internet. However these concerns are real and have to be addressed. On the other hand people also have to learn to live with the use of this technology and adapt to the new implications of security. I am not saying we just have to accept this as it is, but we have to find ways to improve the situation. On the other hand the actual location information through the Google Latitude service is somewhat crude. I am not sure if this is only on the iPhone, but it is not very accurate. It is very slow too, in terms of response to movement. By only using the browser based service, my location in central London is generally 200–500 m off. I have found that if I first open Maps and define the location, this is usually very quick and gives good accuracy (sometimes a bit off the street inside a building, but all right) and then switch in to the browser the pinpoint is much better. Of course this is partly down to the settings to implement some privacy while public (how complicated is this). A detailed Latitude critique can be read at readwriteweb.com[149]. As an opposition to the concerns raised on personal location information I would like to mention the large communities that are forming around the services to share location information. Google Latitude is by far not the only service available. There are a number of communities. And most of the applications are offering more option, control and supposedly fun than Latitude. In the earlier blog post services were Brightkite[150], Loopt[151] or Pocket Life[152] by Vodafone. They are still around and well used. Some offer now iPhone applications, but surprisingly some are paid apps. An additional service is the one of mapme.at[153]. It does the same and it has a really cool time line feature, similar to the one in timemap[154] developed at the MIT[155]. So to conclude there is a lot more out there than just the Google Latitude and I will have a closer look at these services soon.

---

[149] http://www.readwriteweb.com/archives/google_latitude_on_the_iphone_terrible_compared_to.php.

[150] http://brightkite.com/.

[151] http://www.loopt.com/.

[152] http://www.pocketlife.com/index.html#Login-1898.

[153] http://mapme.at/.

[154] http://urbantick.blogspot.com/2009/01/time-map-some-more-examples.html.

[155] http://code.google.com/p/timemap/.

174   *DIGITAL TOURIST NAVIGATION—TEIGO*[156], Location based information and urban navigation on the iPhone. A project develop at Gobelins l'Ecole de l'Image as a diploma project by five graduate students, Damien Odet, Myriam Penot, David Miège, Léo Chéron and Adrien Felsmann. It is not sure when it is going to come out but it looks really interesting. Already graphically it looks beautiful. It is built as a digital guide that gives you location based information in several different layers. The history layer might be particularly interesting. It is a very formal history layer at the moment with information taken from school books. But looking back at the post about virtual notes, an additional layer with user generated short term history could be very interesting. It would enable you to see what the "tourists" last week have spotted, local outsider knowledge could start building up. This is what the developers say: "Teigo is a new generation urban guide consisting of a mobile phone application, an interactive wall map and an internet site." It offers a cultural and fun way to discover or rediscover a city. The prototype was produced for the city of Paris, but versions for other cities are planned. To relive the historical events of places you visit, Teigo leads you along thematic itineraries during which you will receive interesting tourist information including places to eat and local events. See clip on Vimeo[157]/See all the features and aspects.

Teigo is made for the curious—city dwellers and tourists anxious to discover or rediscover a city. The service is available on several mediums in order to adapt to the largest possible number of users, whether technophiles or not.

175   *BRIGHTKITE GOES AUGMENTED REALITY*[158] Brightkite[159] has something to offer. This was already clear after last weeks post[160] about the service. But there is more coming! Only two days ago they have posted a preview of their next step. As you might guess it is AR based, but it looks brilliant and got me, at least, very excited. To see all the posts on top of the real world through the lens of the camera phone will be a brilliant use of the technology. You could call it state of the art. A lot of services have been announced lately, but this will take social networking on to the next level. At the moment unfortunately it is only Android based, but should soon come to the iPhone too. It looks like the revamp has also brought along some more colours and hopefully an extended length of messages, which was a bit limited so far. Have a look at the clip (Fig. 23).

We just need A LOT more people here in London to use it to make it a lot of fun! So get your iPhones and Androids out and start using Brightkite to generate some content for this AR application! They have teamed up with Layar[161] for the AR stuff. The company has just released an API for their AR browser. This has opened the competition to become the AR browser of choice, as there are other companies in

---

[156] *DIGITAL TOURIST NAVIGATION—TEIGO,* 14 August 2009 09:30, navigation, review, application, iPhone.

[157] http://vimeo.com/5187390.

[158] *BRIGHTKITE GOES AUGMENTED REALITY,* 19 August 2009 09:02, review, location, augmented reality, social network.

[159] http://brightkite.com/.

[160] http://urbantick.blogspot.com/2009/08/virtual-notes-in-real-world-iphone.html.

[161] http://layar.eu/.

Fig. 23 Clip by Brightkite on Vimeo / The first clip showing Brightkite using Layar. (http://vimeo.com/6139889)

the same market. At the moment it is Layar and Wikitude[162], you guessed it, a Wikipedia project, but soon other companies will make their own API available. One of the will be Mobilizy[163], scheduled for next week. Layar has the potential to become a major player, as there is already a lot of content available. Check their blog[164] for examples and pretty clips. Found through GPSObsessed.com[165] and Vimeo[166].

76   *BOOK—ORTSZEIT*[167] A book about time is always something difficult. While time is passing the book stays, could be the metaphor. The book I chose today is different. It talks about the passage of time and this not very quietly. But instead with a very loud bang although the photographs are very quiet and empty they scream—time (Fig. 24).

Fig. 24 Image taken from the book Ortszeit by Stefan Koppelkamm / Book spreads, Zittau, Store-House, 06/1990 and 09/2001

---

[162] http://www.wikitude.org/world_browser.

[163] http://www.mobilizy.com/.

[164] http://layar.com/blog/.

[165] http://gpsobsessed.com/3d-location-based-apps-are-here-brightkite-partners-with-augmented-reality-startup-layar/.

[166] http://vimeo.com/.

[167] *BOOK—ORTSZEIT,* 20 August 2009 11:07, review, photography, time, book.

Fig. 25 Image taken from the book Ortszeit—Local Time by Stefan Koppelkamm / Potsdam, Park Babelsberg, view of the Gliencker Bruecke, 08/1991 and 04/2002

Ortszeit—Localtime[168] is a photo essay by Stefan Koppelkamm[169] with an essay by Ludger Derenthal. The photographer and designer Koppelkamm has after approximately ten years revisited sites he had photographed earlier. Mainly this is around 1990 for the first shot and around 2001 for the following up shot of the same scene or better location. It is all about the vantage point. To access the same location again after such a long time can be quite challenging and some spots must have been inaccessible (Fig. 25).

Portrayed are a number of key buildings from cities and towns of the former GDR shortly after the fall of the Berlin Wall. This was an obvious subject for a few people thinking ahead. And it proves right. It is more than a book about photographs and time. It is a social document about the world we live in and not last about the city as a body. Germany struggled and still struggles with its history of separation and the reunification in 1989. The process is long and multi-layered, it is not only about time. On might expect that change over ten years would be dramatic and towards improvement. But while flipping through the book, it emerges that actually the interesting images are not the ones that show progress from an economic perspective.

Change lives in small details of materials and light. The photographer pays great attention to erasing all trace of change of technology, especially in terms of the final product. This helps to focus on the scene and lets the image speak about what's happened. Features in the images are talking. For example accessories such as cars transport a clear image with atmosphere. But on the other hand you get the funny scene, where everything has changed except from the spatial configuration and the bin on the street corner. Koppelkamm, S., 2006. Ortszeit = Local Time, Stuttgart: Edition Axel Menges. There is a section on the book's website for photographs

---

[168] http://www.amazon.co.uk/Ortszeit-Local-Time-Stefan-Koppelkamm/dp/3936681155/refsr_1_2?ieUTF8&sbooks&qid1250691141&sr8-2.

[169] http://ortszeitlocaltime.de/bilder.php.

that are not in the book[170]. Some brilliant images can be seen there online. There is also a short interview[171], the author was interviewed by Christina Tillmann, Der Tagesspiegel.

77 ANIMAL TRACKING—TRACK YOUR DOG[172] Animals have featured on the blog before, in the area of tracking. It was about Frogs[173]/Frogs[174], Birds[175], Ants[176]/Ants[177], Dogs[178] and Cats[179]. This time it is about dogs again. Purely in a technological sense of tracking of course. About the breed of GPS dog tracking devices. The new model developed by RomaEO[180] has featured on several news sites in the past few days. It comes with a central device and collar as a sender. With the central device the collar is recorded. A maximum of two collars can be tracked at the same time. The spatial limitation is 3 miles. So for hunting a good distance, if you are more sort of a leisure dog type and your dog is not well trained and often runs off, this might not be enough. The device is "tracking" the pet as it is called in the description, but I doubt that it actually records these tracks. This is not mentioned anywhere in the description.

It comes at quite a price[181]. The basic set of handheld and one collar costs about $ 280.00 and an additional collar is again $ 160.00. It is currently only sold within the United States because of radio frequency issues. See clip on Youtube[182]. The company has a range of products for dog (pet) owners. They even showcase a, presumably (judging from the images), iPhone based software[183] for pet tracking. We are looking forward to hearing more about this. A comparable tracking system by Garmin is the Astro 220[184]. It can track up to TEN! dogs (animals) at the same time. The downside here is that the collar transmits only up to every 5 s. If you have a hunting dog, 5 s can be quite a distance. It does track the pack up to seven miles (depending a bit on terrain). It is also priced in a different league, at $ 500.00. So to conclude, the RomaEO is an everyday product for the general public, make some money, leave some responsibility to technology type. You might find it fun for a couple of hours, but it probably wears out.

---

[170] http://www.amazon.co.uk/Ortszeit-Local-Time-Stefan-Koppelkamm/dp/3936681155/refsr_1_2?ieUTF8&sbooks&qid1250691141&sr8-2.

[171] http://ortszeitlocaltime.de/interview.php.

[172] ANIMAL TRACKING—TRACK YOUR DOG, 21 August 2009 09:00, animals, review, tracking, GPS.

[173] http://urbantick.blogspot.com/2009/04/animal-tracking-frogs.html.

[174] http://urbantick.blogspot.com/2009/04/animal-tracking-frogs-second.html.

[175] http://urbantick.blogspot.com/2009/02/mini-tracker-as-tiny-backpacks.html.

[176] http://urbantick.blogspot.com/2009/03/ant-trails.html.

[177] http://urbantick.blogspot.com/2009/07/ants-yearly-effort-to-create-new-colony.html.

[178] http://urbantick.blogspot.com/2009/06/dog-drawing.html.

[179] http://urbantick.blogspot.com/2009/05/whant-to-know-whereabout-of-your-pet.html.

[180] http://www.roameoforpets.com/index.php.

[181] https://www.roameoforpets.com/products_pup.php.

[182] http://www.youtube.com/v/Ypu6UzeoiJs&hlen&fs1&.

[183] http://www.roameoforpets.com/products_petnet.php.

[184] https://buy.garmin.com/shop/shop.do?pID8576.

See clip on Youtube[185]/a rather silly demonstration clip of the pet tracker.

The Garmin Astra on the other hand is a hardcore outdoor gadget for the serious user. It is extendable, durable and costs a lot. There is a whole market out there for the cheap pet tracking products and these companies are pulling all the triggers to convince people they might need this and will be able to use it. Companies like Zoombak[186] offer the whole range of tracking from pet, to kids, to partner. That is a service. If you are more in for the silly side of all this tracking this add might be for you.

178   *TOMTOM FOR THE IPHONE—UPDATE*[187], TomTom[188] announced its navigation software[189] for the iPhone earlier this year at the WWDC. It was a blog post[190] and it also was somehow exciting. It is only two and a half months later and the software is published but it is all not that exciting anymore. It might be a great software and no doubt it works fine, but since the introduction of the 3GS at the same WWDC, so much has changed on the mobile gadget market. Only this month the introduction of the crowd sourced traffic platform WAZE[191] was introduced in the United States and Layar[192] opened up AR layers for a broad range of uses. In fact AR has been the big topic for mobile phone platforms and Android is leading as an AR platform at the moment. TomTom has not yet announced anything for the Android platform. Anyway, onepiece of software cannot do everything; we are well aware of this, but this now pushed the iPhone with its "cannot run anything in the background" policy to its limit. If I ever use the TomTom on my iPhone I want to have the WAZE live traffic update on top of it to give me up to date information and why not have some user generated stuff as AR blobs on the screen as well. See clip on Vimeo[193]/mock up of a navigation software using AR technology.

For me all this fits together and will hopefully eventually merge into something I would more likely call "navigation" software. So navigation in the style of AR would be exciting, but the ever so normal (we now definitely got used to it) "after 200 m turn right" TomTom is not exciting anymore, Nevertheless here is the latest TomTom clip to sweeten the waiting for the actual iPhone car kit.

See clip on Youtube[194] showing the new TomTom clip demonstrating the car kit.

The company has not yet announced the release date for this important element of in car navigation. In fact this is really funny but theoretically the software is

---

[185] http://www.youtube.com/v/0INYjt-2QGs&hlen&fs1&.

[186] http://www.zoombak.com/.

[187] *TOMTOM FOR THE IPHONE—UPDATE,* 24 August 2009 07:07, navigation, gadget, review, software, GPS, iPhone.

[188] http://www.tomtom.com/.

[189] http://iphone.tomtom.com/index.html.

[190] http://urbantick.blogspot.com/search?qtomtom.

[191] http://urbantick.blogspot.com/2009/08/iphone-traffic-update-user-generated-in.html.

[192] http://urbantick.blogspot.com/2009/08/brightkite-goes-augmented-reality.html.

[193] http://vimeo.com/1208591.

[194] http://www.youtube.com/v/Nn0lJFHXMB4&hlen&fs1&.

somehow useless without the car kit. Of course some clever guys came up with a solution. Found through GPSobsessed[195]

THE BLDGBLOG BOOK—HOW TO TALK ABOUT ARCHITECTURE[196] For the last couple of days I am carrying the BLDGBLOG book in my bag. It joined some other books and papers I should read, but instead just keep carrying around believing I might read it. It somehow makes me feel reassured that if there is a chance to read I would read this or that in the bag. The book is not some sort of normal book, it is the book that came out of a blog and not just one blog, but the blog. It is the book summarizing work previously published on the BLDGBLOG.blogspot.com[197] by Geoff Manaugh. The book has been announced on BLDGBLOG for quite a while together with images and content. I only just didn't buy it until very recently. To take a few things up front, it is actually smaller than I expected it to be. Don't know why, maybe because of the "size" (in a number of respects) of the blog I subconsciously expected a massive book. It isn't and that is good. It wouldn't fit in my bag with the other stuff and it wouldn't be a book anymore, but a bible sort of thing. Reading on the back cover of the book though one could think it is some sort of bible. A number of supposedly competent or famous people hype the book together with the author. Not sure what to think about this, it is either a funny joke in the sense of a critical statement or a marketing thing by the publisher. The second would be sad so I will go for the first one.

Turning the blog into a book I suppose is a difficult move. Not from a, people can read it for free on the internet why should they buy the book sort of perspective, but because of the differences in the media format. Digital is not physical and the book definitely is physical. To make the leap between the two media some defining decisions have to be taken in order to allow the new "product" to establish its own character. I have to say I was disappointed when I first held it in my hands at the local store, where it was the only copy. Even though I had deliberately planned to go in and buy it I was thinking about putting it right back on to the shelf and postpone the purchase. But I didn't, paid and put it in my bag. There have been these moments ever since where I have read little bits and pieces in the book purely out of curiosity and I have, over the days flipping and reading, grown to like the book. If you have similar concerns regarding the book I suggest you start reading with the little notes spread in light font as an additional column towards the gutter of the book. These are short and hilariously funny, condensed pieces of information with critical personal thoughts and experiences. At least for me this was the way to get into the flow of the book. As a result I have taken the book out of the bag frequently. To continue on the flow of the book, it is structured in five chapters—presumably the main areas of interest. The articles are published with no information regarding time of publication on the blog, tags or any other blog-unique information. This is confusing at first because it reads familiarly but the orientation is completely different. Once you are used to it, it is free from the constant pressure imposed by the

---

[195] http://gpsobsessed.com/tomtom-iphone-car-kit-teased-on-video/.

[196] *THE BLDGBLOG BOOK—HOW TO TALK ABOUT ARCHITECTURE,* 17 September 2009 10:23, review, book, architecture.

[197] http://bldgblog.blogspot.com/.

blogging environment to link, tie and jump in order not to miss out on the latest development. Finally the read of BLDGBLOG is relaxing. I have to say that I find the chapter titles not immensely catching for my personal interest, but the structure provided helps orientating. I am not convinced that they really summarize the variety of interests and views, connections and summaries presented in the writing. However the content is what you'd expect, it is a great read, funny, challenging and definitely gets you thinking. It gets you thinking about the world, architecture, landscape, maybe the sound or the underground world, but most importantly it get you thinking about your personal world. What are you doing right now, what is happening around you, how do you connect to this and that and what would you do next? For me this is the real achievement and that is why it is worth turning a blog into a book. The blog for me cannot reach the same level of personal involvement. I realize I haven't really said much about the context and the text almost sounds like one of the hypes on the back of the book if not as condensed. Maybe they have a point there. To give away a few pearls of the content that I really enjoyed I will list a few good moments. First I have to go the little notes and posts on the inside of most of the pages, printed in light font. They are a very light red with a very heavy after taste. For example there is the story about the wind and Geoff's experiments with the car windows to adjust the noise the incoming wind makes. He describes how he finds out by trial and error how to adjust the opening in order to be able to listen to the radio while driving. He goes on to dream about orchestrating the same exercise in a house or even a neighbourhood in order to get the wind blowing through the complicated system of doors, windows and fans to make your wind chime in the basement ring. Have a read on page 128—this is great literature. There are also great short texts where Geoff reports fact in a manner of innocence that makes you blush, like "Olympic Climatology" on page 133. For the larger (printed) pieces the interviews are important elements. I think they are really interesting and, together with the images, they are probably the most directly linked pieces to the chapters of the book.

While reading the book you will become familiar with the construction of most of the texts, which are composed in a manner of reporting facts and events in the first few lines but then weaving them further into a comprehensive picture of an imaginative future. This is probably what Geoff means in the introduction when he says: "I've often joked that BLDGBLOG is organized around one thing only: the pleasure principle. ...—because it's fun, and the juxtaposition might take you somewhere. Most importantly, follow your line of interest." (p. 11)

180   *PLY365—GRAPHIC PUBLISHED*[198] A new UCL publication landed on my desk today with a note to thank for my contribution. Although I did not know I was contributing, I was pleased to see the PLY365 track record being published. I remembered that I have submitted a graphic to the annual UCL Grad School image competition last year. I didn't win anything back then and now it is published in the new Grad School Handbook 2009/2010 (Fig. 26).

---

[198] *PLY365—GRAPHIC PUBLISHED,* 22 September 2009 13:49, plymouth365, publication, review, GPS tracks, tracking.

Fig. 26 Image by
urbanTick / The Art of
Research page 12/13

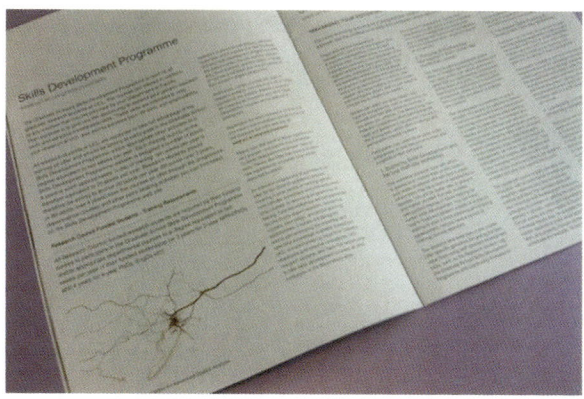

At the same time this data set was the first material to be published on this blog back in October 2008. I had only just completed the recording in Plymouth and moved to London. The original image can be found here[199]. I continued recording my movement with the GPS device and the latest map, London 365, can be found here[200].

NEAREST TUBE—AUGMENTED REALITY APPLICATIONS FOR THE IPHONE[201] With the latest iPhone software update, version 3.1, the long awaited augmented reality applications finally have arrived on the iPhone platform. Already a month back acrossair's[202] Nearest Tube application was hyped on the net and in the news, but now it was introduced rather quietly. It featured on the blog before here. It is now available on the iTunes app store for £ 1.19. I wonder how a software price of £ 1.19 is calculated? Together with it came a bunch of similar public transport applications for example the London Bus application for £ 0.59 by presslite. Of course both developers cover a range of cities with their apps, where you have to buy the app for each city separately, of course. Presslite does cover, London, Paris, Berlin, Lyon, Moscow, Washington, Marseilles, Tokyo, New York, Chicago, Montreal, Toronto, Madrid, Amsterdam, Beijing and Hong Kong. Acrossair[203] on the other hand covers New York and London. I can imagine that it is a battle over this field, as potentially there are a lot of customers. It is for the commuters, but also for tourists and then it is for everyone else who is in the city. I guess that the companies assume that nearly everyone needs their app. I don't think it is that simple, though. For one thing, not everyone has the gadget to actually use the software and two; the idea of getting lost in the city is a myth. The belief that everyone in the city needs this sort of navigation aid is based on the idea that no one knows their way

---

[199] http://urbantick.blogspot.com/2008/10/plymouth365.html.

[200] http://urbantick.blogspot.com/2009/09/London-365-one-year-of-gps-tracks-in.html.

[201] *NEAREST TUBE—AUGMENTED REALITY APPLICATIONS FOR THE IPHONE,* 23 September 2009 09:36, review, orientation, transport, iPhone.

[202] http://urbantick.blogspot.com/2009/09/London-365-one-year-of-gps-tracks-in.html.

[203] http://www.acrossair.com/acrossair_app_augmented_reality_nearesttube_London_for_iPhone_3GS.htm.

Fig. 27 Image by urbanTick / Nearest Tube information in my bathroom

round and constantly gets lost. Well, in a large city such as London it is impossible to know every corner, but I believe that people know their daily route quite well and are perfectly capable of navigating along familiar trails. Only when it comes to out of routine activities on unfamiliar territory are navigation aids used. For example in most cars here in London you can spot an A-Z on the back seat. However, back to the functionality of the applications, the Nearest Tube works beautifully, it is as simple as it gets, both, in terms of graphics and functions. You tab the icon it opens and shows as a camera overlay the direction to the tube stations. The only thing you have to confirm is an iPhone operating system specific question, because the program wants to use the location information to locate the position, so the user has initially to confirm that the software is allowed to do so. Other than this there is no button, no developer logo, no info or 'About', nothing—how nice! You can, however, tab on the displayed Tube sign and it will take you to Google Maps and show the direct route to get there. It is a five star application; it does what it is meant to do and nothing more. The London Bus, on the other hand, does not convince at this stage. It claims to give you bus route information in London, but actually it is limited to central London and to a fraction of the bus lines and only covering major bus stops. Those are basically the tube stations. Although there are a number of bus stops on Tottenham Court Road it directs you either to Tottenham Court Road Station on the south end of the road or to Warren Street Station on the north end of the road (Fig. 27).

Out side the centre, I tried to use it to get in to work this morning around Tufnell Park; the software would not even register the location and therefore would not even give information about distant stations. It also features Augmented Reality but

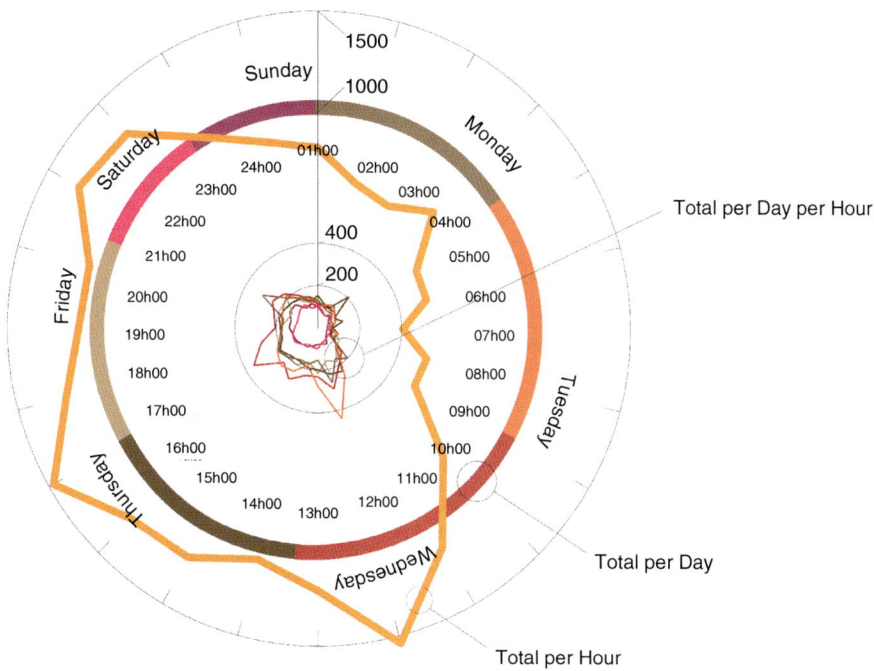

Fig. 28 Image by urbanTick / Graph of blog visits per hour, per day and per day per hour

only as an additional visualisation, whereas Nearest Tube only builds on AR. London Bus is map-based with the option to use AR and it is not as neat as the acrossair[204] version. So Nearest Tube is cool, London Bus is not so cool.

25,000—URBANTICK[205] Some 25,000 visitors on urbanTick today...actually more! The high numbers of visitors on the blog remain stable even over the summer months. It started to increase in May and visitor numbers now are stable around 155 per day over the week (Fig. 28).

Regarding the graph, it represents three sets of data in three rings. From inside to outside, the inner bit is the visits per day per hour. The big peaks are still around midday, mid afternoon and four in the morning representing the shift between Europe and America. The middle ring is representing the number of visits per day, There are differences between weekdays and weekends, where the mid week numbers are still a bit higher than the beginning and the end of the week. Wednesday remains the most popular day, closely followed by Tuesday. The weekends generally have about half the visitors of these popular days, so it is a dramatic difference. The last ring is the total visits per hour. The peaks are mainly the same as last times, the overall line is smoother however with less wiggles. The topic of body and city

---

[204] http://www.acrossair.com/acrossair_app_augmented_reality_nearesttube_London_for_iPhone_3GS.htm.

[205] *25,000—URBANTICK,* 8 October 2009 11:16, graphs, review, history, visits, analysis.

as proposed was the topic for the summer and I am just finishing a working paper on this. Some stuff will of course also go on to the blog. A second working paper focusing on the UrbanDiary project is also under way. Here a lot of bits and pieces have already featured on the blog, but some stuff is still to come. I am currently working on my upgrade and will give a presentation, sort of a mini viva either next month or in December. For this I am trying to finish the two papers. There is also a publication of this blog coming up. Having this platform for a year now, I am planning to publish extracts of it. For this I have joined up with a bunch of researchers working on related topics and they will contribute a short essay to each section. It is all under way and should be ready towards the end of the month. I don't want to give away too much of this but the structure of the publication will be roughly: UrbanDiary urbanMachine urbanNarrative timeSpace bodySpace LocInfo Review

183   *CYCLES AND URBAN MORPHOLOGY—THE HISTORY OF URBAN FORM*[206]
The origin of cities has been the subject of an earlier post[207] with a clear focus on cycles. For an additional post here the starting point is quite a different one. It is the book "History of Urban Form—Before the Industrial Revolutions" by A.E.J. Morris in the third edition. A book of facts and old school history, interpreting the subject rather functionally and with a pretend objectivity. However it is a very popular book and, as the third edition demonstrates, able to maintain its popularity over more than twenty years. The first edition was published in 1972. From the book by Josef H. Reichholf titled "Warum die Menschen sesshaft wurden[208]" the idea of rites and routines where directly involved in the creation of the first settlements and later the creation of the city. In the HUF (History of Urban Form) is acknowledging that the early history of human settlements is still being written, the description blurs early cities/settlements into early cultures such as Aztecs, Maya, Egyptian/Mesopotamia, Greek/Roman or Islamic culture. However, the description in the book starts much earlier in the human history, somewhere in the Neolithic Age when humans are believed to be, in the words of the publication, "... on much the same basis as any of the other animals, by gathering naturally occurring foodstuff ..." (p. 3). From this assumed nomadic life (Might not necessarily imply a nomadic life, some animals do live a territorial life), the humans moved on, around 14,000 BC, to living in caves. Suddenly, settling is possible, but I assume this is what the archaeological evidence is telling us. This is presented as a shift in the concept of living, an improvement over the nomads settling down in a cave. The logical step to follow this shift is the cultivation of plants around 8,000–10,000 years ago, followed by the domestication of animals. Logical, because it is believed that a settled life would make it necessary to source food locally and this food stock would need to be maintained throughout the year. This is then famously described as "The escape from the impasse of savagery was an economic and scientific revolution that made the participants active interacting with nature instead of parasites on nature" (by Childe? in What Happened in History). The book moves then on to describe the "Fertile Crescent" as

---

[206] *CYCLES AND URBAN MORPHOLOGY—THE HISTORY OF URBAN FORM,* 14 October 2009 08:29, review, city, morphology, book.

[207] http://urbantick.blogspot.com/2009/04/on-cycles-beginning-of-urban.html.

[208] http://www.amazon.de/Warum-die-Menschen-sesshaft-wurden/dp/3100629434.

introduced by J Breasted (1935) in Ancient Times. Some 3000 years of slow development later, villages are believed to be established and the first introduction of cities comes at the beginning of the Bronze Age. It follows a statement by Gideon Sjoberg (1965) in The Origin and Evolution of Cities as follows: "a community of substantial size and population density that shelters a variety of non-agricultural specialists, including a literate elite." This description is trying to articulate that again a shift is taking place and no longer everyone is responsible for her/his own food, but some sort of specialisation takes place and exchange of goods between these specialists is invented. For this development, the book lists a number of necessary steps to be taken. Named first is the production of surplus food and the storage of such, as well as other materials that would be needed by the specialists. Then follows the listing of scientific achievements such as writing, mathematics, and astronomy. Only in a third set of additional achievements social organisations is listed. And it is only named in the context of "to ensure continuity of supplies to the urban specialists and to control labour forces for large-scale communal work ..." Mumford is then quoted to state that these requirements were roughly met by around 3000 BC. Surprisingly social organisation is not examined as a structuring of a large group of individuals beyond the family or clan structure—what could be some sort of early politics. However none of these factors are then explored in more detail and none of them feature as defining factors in the chapter on the actual creation of the urban form. To be fair all of them are addressed in a neat row, one after the other, but not as a determining element, rather a feature of the city. Almost in the sense that the city made this possible or it is a "function" of the city. It goes from topography, climate, material, economic, political, religious, pre-urban cadastre, defence, aggrandisement, gridiron, mobility, aesthetics, legislation, infrastructure, social/religious/ethnic groupings and leisure. Anyway there would be a nice example for each of them, but overall it represents clearly a time of thought, the eighties, where everything was neatly divided, separated and isolated to be investigated and then in the exact same state presented—as if the city is made of bricks. To summarise this short introduction to the history of urban form as it were, one could say "it somehow happened". Out of all these objective descriptions of analysis no clear thread emerges along which the evolution cold be examined. The book continues to examine the form of cities. Moving from early settlements examples like Jericho and Catal Huyuk to Jerusalem and Ur quickly to the Greek City State. Here examples of Miletus, Priene and of course Athens are provided. In this section the defence mechanisms of the city are present, but do not dominate. This, however, changes in the following section on Rome and the Empire. The examples here strongly build on the ideal construction of the military base camp, the army castra. The idea of the wall and the strong grid are dominant through out the description of the Roman city. This pre-conception of "the City" as the wall and the grid stands in the way of examining the city form from multiple angles. There are very few references to trade, production or everyday life for example religion. The problem of food production and food storage was earlier noted as the main problem of urban settlements, but have, surprisingly, never featured since as a defining element of city form. If it was, and presumably still is in cities today, this aspect must be considered while defining the urban form. As a consequence of this the city cannot be defined as the grid and the wall, but would need to include the relationship to the surrounding fields for food production as well as, in terms of typology, the locations and types of food storage should be added to the examination of climate impacts. As the book progressed through to the medieval towns there appears to be a big break. The collapse of the Roman Empire also led to the collapse of a lot of Roman-founded cities. Some of them would be rebuilt as medieval towns. However, of course some large and regionally significant settlements manage to maintain their existence, such as London or Verona. The installed by the Roman Empire were neglected throughout and the sophisticated road network, for example, vanished. This meant for medieval times that there was no reliable way to distribute products in bulk. The solution was to establish transport on waterways. Surprisingly Morris states here: "Neither the location of medieval towns nor their form was significantly affected by industry" (p. 96) even though he continues to analyse the typology of medieval town houses as a place combining living and working. The medieval city wall continues to be the defining element of urban form, even though in Britain the wall was, in the fourteenth century, not a significant military need due to the state of peace within the island. However the wall was used to clearly state boundaries to, for example, impose a tax on goods coming through the city gates. There is as an intriguing beauty about the medieval town. It probably derives from a constructed clarity of dominant elements. Apart from the wall, there is a church, a market place and a town hall. Sir Patrick Abercrombie's favourite, it appears was Furnes in Flanders, a pretty business town in 1590. But again the connection to the outside is formally not considered. It appears in some examples in the form of a port that implies some sort of trade. Also new elements in the description are aspects of urban design that are mixed into the description of urban form. A nice example is Telc, which after a devastating fire the town had to be rebuilt.

An unknown designer had for this reconstruction used a musical allegory. This results in a pretty facade bordering the main market space drawing mainly from its uniformity, while integrating individuality to great extent. The Renaissance emphasizes once more the military defence structures, mainly in mainland Europe, especially Italy. Ideal structures are developed mainly with characteristic arrow wall extensions. Whereas in medieval times the wall was designed to be the shortest and most efficient ways to surround the largest possible plot of land the defence strategies became much more sophisticated resulting in a very distinct urban form in the sense of a picture. These ideal towns like Palma Nova or Naarden became icons for the time with a dramatic impact on how towns are perceived -as a one-off object, an artefact in itself. The idea of the city as an object remains throughout the book.

The context of how these cities have developed ever since again shows how interwoven urban form and urban design in this approach are. Cities evolve and even if types of design elements are established the form evolves (Fig. 29).

Examples such as Copenhagen or Karlsruhe can illustrate these thoughts. The connection between travel pattern and morphology of the city is a topic of the research that has not been explored much yet. A starting point could be the perception of space drawn from the UD interviews. from UD txt—"Usually participants have

Fig. 29 Image taken from Wikimedia Commons and Monash University / Copenhagen circa 1700 and Copenhagen today. (http://commons.wikimedia.org/wiki/File:K%C3%B6penhamn_beskjuts_1700.jpg. http://arts.monash.edu.au/saru/symposia/socio-aesthetics/2009/

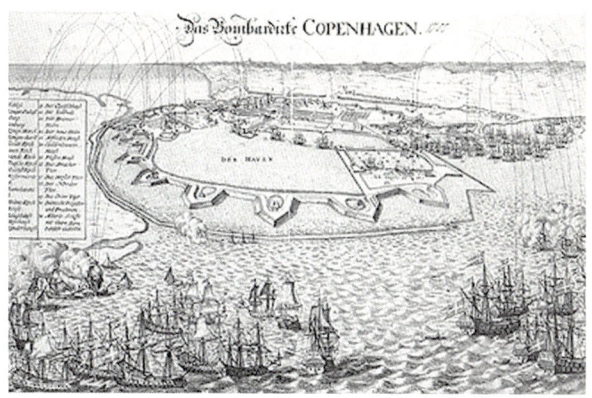

quite a different perception of their spatial habits and will describe them at the beginning of the tracking as diverse and spread over a large area of the city. The first few times they see the data they actually have collected, it is quite a disappointment to them to see that they follow a rather strong routine. Routine seems to be rather negatively perceived and participants often would describe themselves as active, flexible and spontaneous implying a widely spread range of activities with a diverse movement pattern. To describe it they often refer to someone they think is very flexible or very inflexible just to provide for themselves an example of comparison. Routines and rhythm seem to be a not so much discussed subject but rather a topic about which people make a lot of assumptions." If individuality and flexibility, range of patterns and paths are current values of our society, how would this influence and change the current development of the urban morphology? Would it be possible to conclude on current styles and designs or even the next ten years? Also retrospectively could the social values and the urban morphology be connected? Say the Victorian morphology, what would it say about the people of this time's perception of habits and space?

84   *HISTORIC EARTH—OLD MAPS GEOREFERENCED FOR THE IPHONE*[209] Former old map app has transformed and teamed up with a large library and is now Historic Earth. The old map app featured earlier this year on the blog with a review and now we want to look back, previous post HERE[210]. The really big change is the data, the app now has in the background. It draws the data from Historic Map Works[211] a huge database of maps, containing some 1,000,000 maps including United States Property Atlases, Antiquarian Maps, Nautical Charts, Birdseye Views, Special Collections (Celestial Maps, Portraits, and other historical images), Directories and other text documents. Their main business is to provide high quality images of old maps to researchers and map enthusiasts. The main focus is

---

[209] *HISTORIC EARTH—OLD MAPS GEOREFERENCED FOR THE IPHONE,* 16 October 2009 09:30, review, history, identity, mapping.

[210] http://urbantick.blogspot.com/2009/06/iphoneapp-oldmapapp.html.

[211] http://www.historicmapworks.com/.

Fig. 30 Image by urbanTick / Screenshot of Historic Earth iPhone app the Los Angeles Bay area over different times

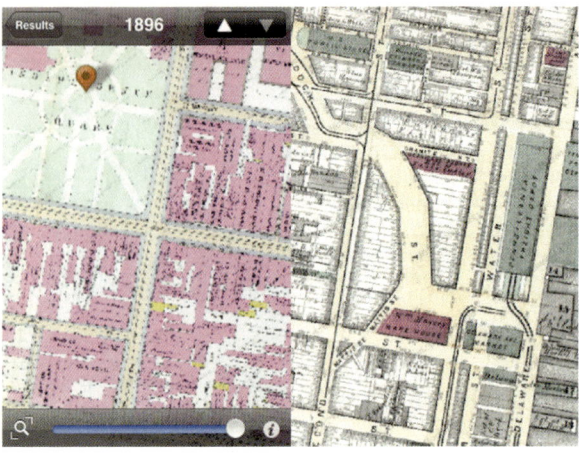

North America, but they stock an increasing number of world maps and others. This means for now that the iPhone app also only covers North America (Fig. 30).

But this is changing, they have a visual counter on their web page to demonstrate how they are making progress, both, increasing the service for the iPhone and geocoding maps in general. The aim is to offer some 130,000 maps in the next month. You can follow them on twitter[212] to check on the status. For facebook lovers here is the fan page[213]. The iPhone app is probably aiming at map enthusiasts mainly really. As for research one probably wants more specific access to the data. However the app is a fascination and is very addictive. It is developed by Emergence Studios[214] as was the old map app. It is introduced as "Historic Earth allows you to map the history of cities, times, buildings and landmarks. View historic maps showing property owners, see buildings constructed and replaced, and watch the landscape change over time." The app is using OSM for the background to reference the layers to the modern map of the location. The overlay, the base can be adjusted in its transparency with a slider, normal gestures as known from Google maps are used to navigate the map. Once in the actual map window it is great: you flip between times with the arrows provided and watch the area change. The trouble really getting into it, as the menu is not intuitive and there is for example no link between the map showing the covered area and the actual historic map (Fig. 31).

However once I figured out that in the settings the "lock frame when switching maps" switch is set to on it is a real pleasure to browse. Not only the area changes, but also the representation techniques and focus of the maps. In this respect it is also a documentation of a changing space perception. It is a bit slow to load here in London, I suppose this is down to all the 32,000 maps having to squeeze into the tube to get across the big blue :) But the frustrating thing is not that it is slow (I

---

[212] http://twitter.com/historicearth.

[213] http://www.facebook.com/historicearth.

[214] http://emergencestudios.com/historicearth/.

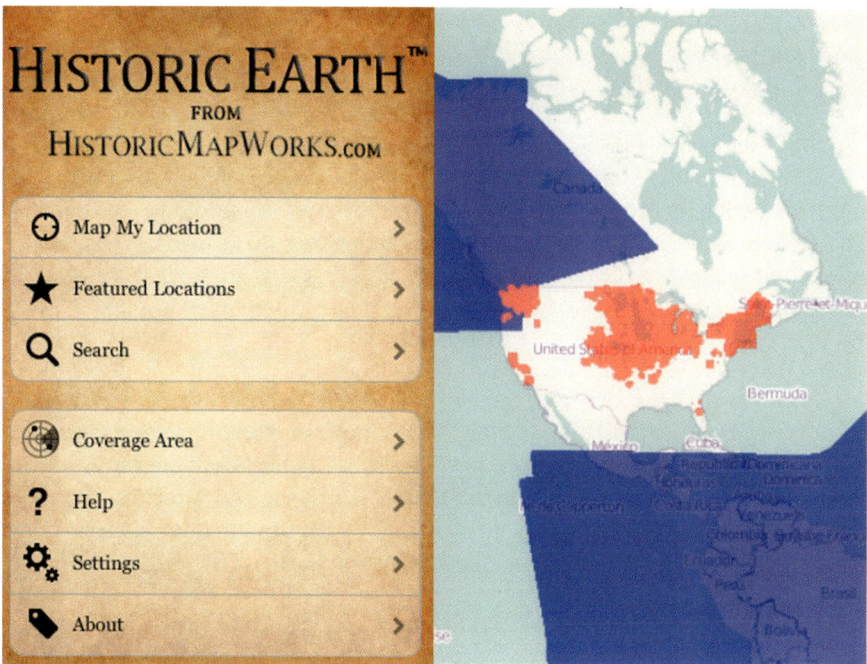

Fig. 31 Image by urbanTick / Screenshot of Historic Earth iPhone app, settings, coverage and menus

don't mind waiting for interesting content), but there is no indicator that something is actually happening. Usually while loading the screen only displays the, sort of, old paper background, but no progress bar or indicator of any sort. It is also one of the very few apps to choose not to display any information of the usual top bar with basic iPhone stats, like quality/type of connection, time and battery life. So there is no way you can tell the device is actually doing something and this has, at least for me, been very irritating I have to admit.

See clip on Youtube[215]/The Historic Earth application on the iPhone.

But sure enough, this is the first release of the app (if you don't count the previous one) and as usual there are some things that just had to be done quickly in the end, but can easily be solved and improved in a following update. The main thing is the quality of the interface and the value of the data available. For both of these points the app scores very high! You can get it for some £ 3.49 from iTunes[216].

IDRN CONFERENCE—REVIEW[217] A review of yesterday's conference on health mapping will give you some insight on the current state of mapping practice in health research and related areas. The day overall was interesting and my poster

---

[215] http://www.youtube.com/v/HQOXASy40nA&hlen&fs1&.

[216] http://itunes.apple.com/WebObjects/MZStore.woa/wa/viewSoftware?id329380870&mt8.

[217] *IDRN CONFERENCE—REVIEW,* 4 November 2009 09:37, iPhone, mobile, review, mapping, mashup.

presentation went well, there were some interesting discussions. The city migration behaviour of individuals seemed interesting for health researchers. However the day was packed with talks and that was the main bit. The first speaker will be Dr. Russell Stothard from the Natural History Museum[218]. He is talking about the use of GPS. His talk has the title 'Using GPS/GIS for Schistosomiasis research—building a better picture of exposure to water contact sites'. First he is pointing out that actually it is possible to geotag an image. Well this is a start. He introduces us to handheld devices available to time and location stamp data such as images. This probably sets the context of the conference. It is a different field from what we are used to. He goes on about the GPS system on how global positioning works. He is working in Africa and this might give a different setting. However somehow I get the feeling that there is still a mystical aura to the continent, you could maybe still get lost down there. He moves on to talk us through the Garmin devices available and there he mentions a nice expression for the back tracking setting, Bread-crumbing. How cool is this. This might lend a new title to the UrbanDiary project as we are bread-crumbing across the city. The fact that there is not a GPS camera at current is presented as very sad, but actually there might be software solutions for this? Interestingly he then starts talking about the location as such and the following slide is titled 'so precisely knowing where things are has never been easier'. Furthermore he points out that actually the location might not be the actual site of where something is, so to say location is not location. He show some of the examples he is working on. It is about a disease in Africa that is using a snail as a host. He is working on the East coast of South Africa. Snail species are quite difficult to tell apart, and the disease is picky, living only in one type of snail. So they have to go out and collect the snails, and take them back to the laboratory to determine what species it is. The location information therefore is important to reconnect the sample with the area of collection. It is a lot about mapping the source (snails) and the impact of the disease. Part of their conclusion then is that the spatial distance from the water source, where the snail hosts live, results in a higher possibility of having the infection. Largely the research is about the life cycle of the disease. He also shows a nice device iGotU[219]. This device was used to track 20 people of a village. They are tracking the people to determine the amount of risk they are exposed to. There are also time aspects as there are only certain times of the day where the snails shed to release the larvae to infect people. He shows a timeLapse of the people's movement over a two day period. This tracking determined quite clearly the contact these people have with the water. It is a very nice example of the use of GPS. However the standard questions remain: what does that actually say. Is this just a scientific stunt? There are the strong cycles these people follow, but somehow these aspects have not yet penetrated the research. If the snail has a cycle and the people have a cycle you can match these up? There might be a chance to change the people's habits to prevent them from getting infected. This might not be as simple as they mostly rely on fishing and this in turn requires a naturally determined schedule in order

---

[218] http://www.nhm.ac.uk/research-curation/staff-directory/zoology/jr-stothard/index.html.

[219] http://www.i-gotu.com/.

to get a good catch. Next speaker is David Aanensen from the Imperial College London[220] talking about 'http://www.spatialepidemiology.net[221]—tools for mapping infectious disease epidemiology'—introducing us to Google Maps use in health research. He also points out there are other services including OSM. So Mash-Ups are the hot key word. He introduces a series of mashups that he has worked on mapping gene sequences, if I have understood him right. He is talking rather casually. The live demo of his websites makes him rather nervous, surprisingly. But it worked well and he was able to demonstrate how it works comparing a set of genes across different countries, by a manual selection done in the mashup. The big question with thee mash-ups probably really is the accessibility for further research. It is mainly a visualisation for the public world wide web, but what now? How can other researchers collaborate or use the provided data? It looks nice but the usefulness is not yet clear. Do they for example offer an API, for other people to access the data and mash it up? He then shows an other example that to some extent partially answers the question: a platform that can be accessed to produce maps. It is based on a copy paste data input field to import data and then map it. He moves on to demonstrate a mobile device application he has developed. Especially for the android. The app does allow you to input data: adding GPS location and sync is done via a web server and directly mapping it on a map. It additionally allows for pulling data from the server to see the new records in context or deciding on where to collect more data. He summarizes the limitations of the technologies. The big problem is the battery life, but also the network coverage and the costs, both for the handset and the contract. He mentions in the end that they have actually just released an iPhone app—let's check EpiCollect[222] on the app store. Haven't been able to find it so far. It follows Dr. Mat Fisher again from Imperial College London[223]. His talk is entitled 'Using Google Earth to identify populations and invasions in emerging fungal infections'. He uses the mapping to predict and link it to analysis, pattern and process. He stresses that the mapping does not tell us anything unless we have a clear design for the research. He shows a clear example of spatial spread of a disease in southern middle America over time, spreading from 1987 from Costa Rica to Panama City in 2008. So he then uses global mapping based on Google Maps to map the other occurrence of the disease on this scale. This makes a lot of sense if you can combine it with other environmental data available globally, such as weather and climate data. Identifying potentially vulnerable locations is very important as the disease is highly spreadable and deadly for amphibians. He provides an example of the extinction of the "Spring frog that happened this year after the introduction of the disease in March 2009". By now the frog is believed to be extinct. The protection of these areas identified as having similar conditions is key. He shows an example of his work hunting frogs across Europe. For the data storage he is in fact using Google docs. He is even using the KML function provided by the

---

[220] http://www1.imperial.ac.uk/medicine/people/d.aanensen/.

[221] http://www.spatialepidemiology.net/.

[222] http://deimos3.apple.com/WebObjects/Core.woa/Browse/pri.org.1632588808.

[223] http://www1.imperial.ac.uk/medicine/people/matthew.fisher/.

Google Docs. Even though it is limited to some four hundred examples. The output is clearly spatial. However this could have been expected as, for one thing he is collecting spatial data and for two animal habitat are spatially determined by conditions. To verify the spatial data he is using the barcode technique. They go ahead and determine the gene of the infection and can show that they are locally connected and individually introduced. So the result shows that the infection is related to UVB, min. temperature and longitude. In an additional example he shows time based location data of samples from the UK and visualises the spread of a virus in amphibians across the UK from 2001 to 2008. After the coffee break speaks Dr. Marianne Sinka and Mr. Will Temperley, University of Oxford[224] about 'Mapping the geographical distribution of the Anopheles vectors[225]'. What are the aspects of mapping malaria data and how can we produce predictable global distribution visuals together with a summary of bionomics, as well as comparable data? She explains how the initial database of vector transitory animals is generated form existing publication sources.

Basically she has subscribed to any malaria related publication source by email and gets news to put directly into the database if related to animal species samples and locations of those. Additionally they add spatial information to the database. Together with a group of experts with detailed knowledge of the locations they have produced area coverage maps. In terms of technology they are using PostgreSQL data base, combining Excel and shape files. Accessing the database is via Python. For the web based stuff they are using Django and Python, but are now developing a Java and Google tool kit based version because of the demand on dynamic content. Together with spatial, physical data I suppose, and climate data they can model potential areas where a certain species can be found. As a result they are aiming at publishing papers this year on the first set of maps with the title 'Web based GIS mapping of molecular/epidemiological database' under the name Protection Agency Centre for Infections. Talk by Dr. Richard Myers, Health They are working on Swine Flu, TB and so on. He runs us through the functional diagram of his functional database. Data Input—Data Storage- User Interface—Data Retrieval and Data Analysis. For his talk he identified a set of three areas that should be looked at to produce a good web based mapping application. The most important aspect, he stresses, is the why and what you want to get out of the mapping exercise, as the web based formation has its limitations. The two other ones are data and sampling, also in terms of the reliability of the data. Interestingly he points out the identification problem with small scale data. They are working with postcode level data. On this level individuals cannot be identified, but the zoom factor is important, as they don't want to have individuals identified in a location. For the website application they are using flash for the visualisation. It looks nice but he points out some downsides to it. It is slow and currently low resolution as well as having limited capacity to show multiple data sets. So he moves on to show examples of Google Maps. His list of pros and cons of using Google Maps for the mapping is rather long. The

---

[224] http://www.map.ox.ac.uk/team/.

[225] http://www.map.ox.ac.uk/.

surprising result is the slowness of it as he points out. What cannot be displayed on a web enabled databases? He concludes with a list, containing confidentiality data, dynamic data, local out breaks, detailed analysis and so on. And the list of what is possible is just as long, mostly technological based here though. Navigation through London comes after lunch, is presented by Tim Fendley[226], Applied Information Group from Legible London[227]—a way finding system for London. He starts with an introduction to navigating London with some hilarious examples of guidance through the city. He continuous with the examples of psychogeography and the urban islands. It is for a change a really refreshing talk with a lot of energy and jokes. It points out how dry and dull the rest of the day was. He then runs us through how they have developed and introduces the new navigation elements. The structure for the new navigation system is all based on the naming of locations. There is also a very detailed process to actually develop the maps and navigation aids. Defining the named areas is tricky and a statement of position. The whole system appears very much connected to the tube stations, as it seems to mainly address the tourists and visitors. It is true that the tube is a simple way to navigate London and building on this is one way of tackling the problem. But I think it still has to prove its use for local people. However as they focus at the moment on central London, most people going around there are in fact visitors. It will be interesting if this gets rolled out over London, to see how people learn to navigate their neighbourhood. Chris Phillips of MapAction[228] is talking about, you guessed it, 'Maps in Action'. Subtitle 'Disaster mapping at the front lines'. They are working with a rapid response mapping team. They get deployed within hours of a disaster to the location. They claim to be local within 24 h. From the equipment box: laptop, GIS, Google Maps/Earth, printer, GPS and camera. There is actually an UN response team, but it takes them about four to five days to get their container shipped into the area. They are working all over the world and the work is obviously very much appreciated by locals suffering from the event. Usually afterwards they are hired to train locals for continuing the job and to prepare for an similar event.

See clip on Youtube[229]/The MapAction in action, documentation video.

He points out the importance of spatial information in affected areas alongside all the equipment. And he mainly draws on the visual aspect of the information, which is used implicitly to understand the information as compared to text information. The title is interesting—'everything happens somewhere'—as a justification of his work, but it might be also his philosophy. He draws on the concept of solving chaos. He also points to some volunteer mapping projects like john the map cartographer[230]—mapping towns on his bicycle. Actually this was a promotion talk for mapping, concluding with everyone can map and everyone should map actu-

---

[226] http://www.appliedinformationgroup.com/people/tim_fendley.shtml.

[227] http://www.tfl.gov.uk/microsites/legible-London/default.aspx.

[228] http://www.mapaction.org/.

[229] http://www.youtube.com/v/k9meFFZxkWY&rel0&color10xb1b1b1&color20xcfcfcf&hl=en&feature=player_embedded&fs1.

[230] http://www.johnthemap.co.uk/pages/index.html.

ally. Peter Yang & Tian-Wei Sheu, National Taichung University, Taiwan with 'An Effective Use of Social Network Analysis for the Study of Taiwanese Employees' Mental Health at Work'. He is focusing on the social network analysis and the aspects of health. The term social capital seems relevant, but hard to define. His use of the analysis is rather focused on networks. He identified five types. Dispersion, Durability, homogeneity, intensity and reciprocity. To get the data he used questionnaires. For the analysis he is using the UCINET 5 for Windows. However the important finding here is probably that location information is not only about maps, but also about networks and connections, crossing points and so on. The last presentation for the conference is given by Dr. Mikaela Keller, Harvard Medical School, USA on 'Mapping the influenza A H1N1 outbreak'. Unfortunately my macBook ran out of battery and I had a chance to follow her talk in more detail. To take it up front she also showed a iPhone application for the project she is working on. It is available on iTunes and simply called healthMap[231]. This is at the same time the project in short, mapping news of diseases. They have invented a internet crawler that works on the basis of text and sentence structure recognition to spot any news in the text, grabbing location and disease, transferring it into the database and producing Google Maps mashup with the data. This information is then accessible to the general public. However this is where the critique of the system comes in. What is the benefit of the information to the general public? And who exactly is this 'general public'? It goes a step further, as the presented iPhone application actually allows the 'general public' to directly submit a 'case', including disease (from a suggestive pull-down menu that tells you up front it must be swine flu) and location of course. You can even include a photograph of the sick person if you'd like to make a point! I find this very dodggy even though the project as a whole has some very interesting aspects. For example the idea of looking at the world as a whole and visualising everyone on the planet as part of the whole. Somehow I have a creeping feeling that some of this research somehow still has a colonial aspect to it. It is interesting to look into problems of distant locations as some sort of export, but not in the sense of working together. Also all this spatial mapping is pointing towards the time-space problem and the issue with location information. It is in fact tied to the idea of the globe (as in the globe on your desk as a rotating ball on a axis that represents an abstraction of the world) and if this view is out date the visualisations are too. So what to do? Is the mapping guild in a crisis because everyone is mapping? All this here seems to be riding on the open source mapping wave. This question is urgent and regarding the take I went to in the evening at the Tate Britain[232] by Doreen Massey[233] a debate around these subjects is ongoing and the question of place and identity are up for challenge, but have to be redefined in the globalized world. I strongly agree with her view on the importance of boundaries for the structuring of places and especially with the argument regarding the human body as the first place it seems obvious to have a definition of the self and the other. And if it is something, it is not

---

[231] http://itunes.apple.com/WebObjects/MZStore.woa/wa/viewSoftware?id328358693&mt8.

[232] http://www.tate.org.uk/britain/eventseducation/talks/19718.htm.

[233] http://www.open.ac.uk/socialsciences/staff/people-profile.php?nameDoreen_Massey.

something else and this makes the distinction between the two. The main aspect is the way boundaries are set up and maintained in terms of the political dimension.

36   *THE FUNCTIONAL CITY—UPDATE*[234] NAi Publishers[235] have kindly supplied me with a brand new print of the 'Functional City'. Some of you might remember the earlier review of the book. The copy I had was printed with a Dutch introduction, whilst the book was in English. The new copy has just arrived and I would like to update this review with a look at the introduction. The introduction sets out the context of the book and especially focuses on the role van Eesteren[236] plays, both within the modernist CIAM group as well as in the book. This is important as the book does both at the same time. It redraws activities of CIAM but also focuses on van Eesteren as, at times, the CIAM's chairman. The introduction makes cleaver use of an event, the exhibition 'The Functional City' that took place in 1935 at the Stedelijk Museum[237] in Amsterdam. Along with this, presented as the climax of the CIAM activities, the events are rolled up from the back to give a broad overview of the details to following in the book. One large, some 5 m long 'historical table' graphically visualised the history of the city. Surprisingly it showed the development of the city as a result of economical, technical and social forces. This is surprising in so far, that in general the term 'social' and 'functional' does not necessarily go well together. But maybe this also points out that the modernist understanding of 'functional' was in fact not as machine like a we construct it. The material and the way it was prepared showed clearly the guiding principle of the CIAM, 'first the analysis and only afterwards the synthetic work, the design' Van Eesteren stated that "the expression 'functional city' best conveys what we expect from a well designed city". He took the human body as a metaphor to explain how the health of the whole is important for individual elements to function properly. Van Eesteren pointed out that the architect's contribution to urban design was necessary for the designing of good extension plans. His main concerns were residential districts and their facilities. He justified the architect's involvement in urban planning with 'he (the architect) is the one who determines the physiognomy of the plan.' He goes on, explaining "the goal is to archive an equilibrium of all of the factors that are of importance for the people to enjoy living their lives. These insights, based on the results of the previous congresses, inexorably drove us to urban planning." Interestingly it appears as if the group is trying to justify its move towards urban planning. They saw themselves as architects in the first place, but took on a different field. This has two aspects to it. One is that the exclusivity of the architect as the maestro and genius, designing a house mostly for rich customer, is not exactly mass-compatible. Few people will be in the position to afford this sort of exclusivity. And secondly the impact (if you want, satisfaction) is not nearly as large for an individual building as it is if you take on the whole city. In conjunction with this goes the instalment of truth with the plan and the resulting power. I think this should not be seen as a nega-

---

[234] *THE FUNCTIONAL CITY—UPDATE,* 12 November 2009 08:43, review, exhibition, city, book, morphology.

[235] http://www.naipublishers.nl/.

[236] http://www.efl-stichting.nl/naamgevers/architect-urbanist/4-11.html.

[237] http://www.stedelijkindestad.nl/.

Fig. 32 Image by Cornelis van Eesteren, taken from cultuurwijzer.nl / Title 'Het Algemeen Uitbreidingsplan van Amsterdam'. (http://www.cultuurwijzer.nl/nwc.gemeentearchiefamsterdam/cultuurwijzer.nl/i000013.html)

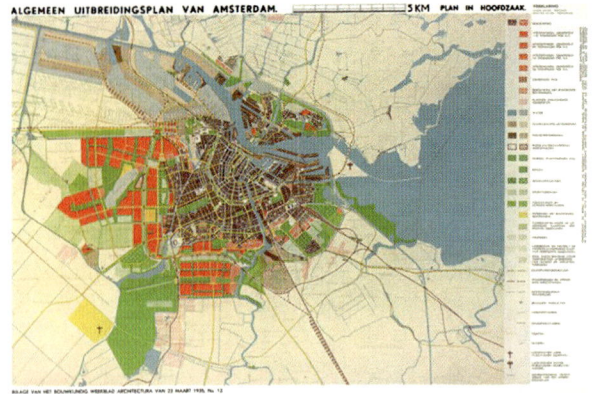

tive aspect to modernist movement, but rather the discovery of the responsibility of planning (Fig. 32).

The exhibition probably showed above all the struggle with a newly discovered possibility, both factual and emotional. In this sense the 'Functional City' can be seen, as the introduction to the book points out, as Berlage's conception architecture as a social art. The idea of the 'Functional City' is, I think, crucial in relation to today's conception of the city. Also the idea of the urbanMachine[238] is based on this construction.

187   *KEVIN LYNCH ONLINE*[239] A lot of the Kevin Lynch material[240] has now been digitalised and put on line by the MIT. The objects in this collection relate to Kevin Lynch's study The Perceptual Form of the City, conducted in Boston, Massachusetts from 1954–1959. The study was done under the direction of Lynch and Professor Gyorgy Kepes at the Massachusetts Institute of Technology Centre for Urban and Regional Studies. Their research findings were the foundation of Lynch's theories on city planning discussed in his seminal work The Image of the City. It says on the page: "The collection includes photographs and records from the Boston phase of the project. The nearly 2,000 black & white photographs, shot by Nishan Bichajian, assistant to Professor Kepes, document the Boston urban environment during the mid-1950s prior to urban renewal. The records document the planning, preparation, and progress of the project (1951–1956), and the research process and findings (1954–1959)". Some stuff can be accessed at the on the dome[241] site. There is also a large collection of black and white photographs that the MIT has put online on flickr. See the slideshow HERE[242].

---

[238] http://urbantick.blogspot.com/search/label/urbanMachine.

[239] *KEVIN LYNCH ONLINE,* 23 November 2009, review, mentalMap, morphology, MIT.

[240] http://libraries.mit.edu/digital/lynch/index.html.

[241] http://dome.mit.edu/handle/1721.3/33656.

[242] http://www.flickr.com/photos/mit-libraries/sets/72157614966285159/.

Bibliography

Adelhof, K., 2008. Urban trends in Berlin and Amsterdam, Berlin: Geographisches Inst. der Humboldt-Univ.

Alder, M., Althaus, P.F. & Giovanoli, D., 1995. Palazzine in Soazza / Palazzine a Soazza: Die Typologie des Korridorhauses / La tipologia della casa a corridoio 1st ed., Basel: Birkhäuser.

Alder, M. & Giovanoli, D., 1997. Soglio: Siedlungen und Bauten / Insediamenti e construzioni 2nd ed., Basel: Birkhäuser.

Alexander, C., 1966. A City Is Not a Tree, London.

Allsopp, B., 1974. Towards a Humane Architecture, London: Muller.

Alsop, W. et al., 2006. Shrinking Cities: Volume 2, Ostfildern: Hatje Cantz.

Andreotti, L. & Costa, X. eds., 1996. Theory of the Dérive and Other Situationist Writings on the City, Barcelona: Museu d'Art Contemporani de Barcelona.

Appleyard, D., Lynch, K. & Myer, J.R., 1964. The View from the Road, Cambridge, MA: MIT Press for the Joint Center for Urban Studies of M.I.T. and Harvard University.

archplus, R., 2007. Situativer Urbanismus - Zu einer beiläufigen Form des Sozialen: archplus 183, ARCH+.

Ball, P., 2005. Critical Mass: How One Thing Leads to Another, London: Arrow Books Ltd.

Barabási, A., 2002. Linked: The New Science of Networks, Cambridge, Mass: Perseus Publishing.

Barman-Krämer, G., Brandl, A. & Unruh, P., 2007. Handbuch zum Stadtrand: Gestaltungsstrategien für den suburbanen Raum 1st ed., Basel: Birkhäuser.

Barthes, R., 1979. The Eiffel Tower, and Other Mythologies, New York: Hill and Wang.

Batty, M., 1980. A Perspective on Urban Systems Analysis, Cardiff: UWIST, Department of Town Planning.

Batty, M., 2005. Cities and Complexity: Understanding Cities with Cellular Automata, Agent-Based Models, and Fractals, Cambridge, MA: MIT Press.

Batty, M., 1980. On Systems Theory and Analysis in Urban Planning: An Assessment, Cardiff: UWIST, Department of Town Planning.

Batty, M., 1970. Spatial Theory and Information Systems, Reading: Urban Systems Research Centre.

Batty, M. & Hudson-Smith, A., 2005. Urban Simulacra: London. Architectural Design, 75(6), 42-47.

Bauhaus, D.S., 2003. Serve City: Interactive Urbanism Mul., Berlin: Jovis.

Bentley, I. et al., 1985. Responsive Environments: A Manual for Designers, Oxford: Architetural Press.

Besten, O.N.N., 2008. Cars, Dogs and Mean People: Environmental Fears and Dislikes of Children in Berlin and Paris. In Urban Trends In Berlin And Amsterdam. Berliner Geographische Arbeiten. Geographisches Inst. der Humboldt-Univ., pp. 116-125. Available at: http://papers.ssrn.com/sol3/papers.cfm?abstract_id=1154559 [Accessed September 16, 2009].

Besten, O.N.N., 2009. Mapping Emotions, Building Belonging: How Children with Different Immigration Backgrounds Experience and Picture Their Parisian and Berliner Neighbourhoods.

SSRN eLibrary. Available at: http://papers.ssrn.com/sol3/papers.cfm?abstract_id=1355288 [Accessed September 16, 2009].

Borden, I. ed., 2001. The Unknown City: Contesting Architecture and Social Space: A Strangely Familiar Project, Cambridge, MA: MIT Press.

Borries, F.V., Walz, S.P. & Bottger, M., 2007. Space Time Play: Computer Games, Architecture and Urbanism - the Next Level, Basel: Birkhäuser.

Boyer, M.C., 1994. The City of Collective Memory: Its Historical Imagery and Architectural Entertainments, Cambridge, MA: MIT Press.

Brent, B. et al., 2007. Spacefighter: The Evolutionary City, Barcelona: Actar.

Bruno, G., 2002. Atlas of Emotion: Journeys in Art, Architecture, and Film, New York: Verso.

Bryson, V., 2007. Gender and the Politics of Time: Feminist Theory and Contemporary Debates, Bristol: Policy Press.

Buckley, W., 1967. Sociology and Modern Systems Theory, London: Prentice Hall.

Burckhardt, L., 2006. Warum ist Landschaft schön?: Die Spaziergangswissenschaft, Berlin: Martin Schmitz Verlag.

Burdett, R. & Sudjic, D., 2008. The Endless City, London: Phaidon Press Inc.

Busch, A., 2003. Geography of Home 1st ed., New York, N.Y., Princeton Architectural Press.

Calvino, I., 1997. Invisible Cities New Ed., London: Vintage.

Capra, F., 1997. Web of Life, London: Flamingo.

Carlstein, T., Parkes, D. & Thrift, N.J. eds., 1978a. Timing Space and Spacing Time, London: Edward Arnold.

Carlstein, T., Parkes, D. & Thrift, N. eds., 1978b. Making Sense of Time, London: Edward Arnold.

Certeau, M.D., 1984. The Practice of Everyday Life, Berkeley, CA: University of California Press.

Chapin, F.S., 1974. Human Activity Patterns in the City: Things People Do in Time and in Space, New York: Wiley-Interscience.

Chapman, K., 1979. People, Pattern and Process: An Introduction to Human Geography, London: E. Arnold.

Collins, G.R., 1959. Linear Planning throughout the World. The Journal of the Society of Architectural Historians, 18(3), 74-93.

Coverley, M., 2006. Psychogeography, Harpenden: Pocket Essentials.

Crang, M., 2001. Rhythms of the City - Temporalised space and motion. In TimeSpace: Geographies of Temporality. Critical geographies. London: Routledge.

Crinson, M. ed., 2005. Urban Memory: History and Amnesia in the Modern City, London: Routledge.

Dekkers, D., 2002. Rheinruhrcity: The Regionmaker Ostfildern: Hatje Cantz.

Du Gay, P., Redman, P. & Evans, J. eds., 2000. Identity: A Reader, London: SAGE.

Elson, M.J., 1974. Activity Spaces and Recreation Trip Behaviour, Oxford: Oxford Polytechnic, Dept. of Town Planning.

Foucault, M., 2001. Order of Things: An Archaeology of the Human Sciences 2nd ed., London: Routledge.

Foucault, M., 2006. Madness and Civilization 2nd ed., London: Routledge.

Franz, B. & Kreb, S. eds., 2005. Landschaftstheorie, Köln: Verlag der Buchhandlung König.

Fuller, R.B., 1982. Critical Path 2nd ed., St. Martin's Griffin.

Gausa, M. et al., 2003. Metapolis Dictionary of Advanced Architecture: English Edition, Barcelona: Actar.

Giddens, A., 1986. The Constitution of Society: Outline of the Theory of Structuration, Cambridge: Polity Press.

Glennie, P. & Thrift, N., 2009. Shaping the Day: A History of Timekeeping in England and Wales, 1300-1800, Oxford: Oxford University Press.

Gould, P. & White, R., 1974. Mental Maps, Harmondsworth: Penguin.

GQ, 2009. Die Woche in Bildern. *GQ Germany*, (April).

Grosz, E.A., 1995. Space, Time, and Perversion: Essays on the Politics of Bodies, New York: Routledge.

Grosz, E., 1998. Bodies-Cities. In H. J. Nast, ed. Places Through the Body. London: Routledge.

Hagerstrand, T., 1978. Survival and Arena. In Timing Space and Spacing Time - Human Activity and Time Geography. London: Edward Arnold.

Halberger, F., 1994. Introduction to Chronobiology - Variability: from foe to friend, of mice and men, Medtronic. Available at: http://www.msi.umn.edu/~halberg/introd/index.html.

Hall, P.G., 1988. Cities of Tomorrow: An Intellectual History of Urban Planning and Design in the Twentieth Century, Oxford: Basil Blackwell.

Hall, T., 2000. Urban Geography 2nd ED 2nd ed., Abingon: Routledge.

Haslam, D., 2004. Schrumpfende Städte, Ostfildern: Hatje Cantz Verlag.

Hillier, B., 1996. Space Is the Machine: A Configurational Theory of Architecture, New York: Cambridge University Press.

Hillier, B. & Hanson, J., 1984. The Social Logic of Space, Cambridge: Cambridge University Press.

Hobbes, T., 1651. Leviathan, Available at: http://www.gutenberg.org/etext/3207 [Accessed October 1, 2009].

Hough, M., 1984. City Form and Natural Process: Towards a New Urban Vernacular, London: Croom Helm.

Hölldobler, B. & Wilson, E., 2008. The Superorganism: The Beauty, Elegance, and Strangeness of Insect Societies 1st ed., London: W.W. Norton & Co.

Howard, S.E., Osborn, S.F.J. & Osborn, F.J., 1965. Garden cities of to-morrow, Cambridge, MA: MIT Press.

Hudson-Smith, A., 2003. Digitally Distributed Urban Environments: The Prospects for Online Planning. PhD Thesis. University College London, the Bartlett School of Architecture.

Jackson, J.B., 2000. The Stranger's Path. In Landscape in Sight. London: Yale University Press.

Kaika, M., 2005. City of Flows: Modernity, Nature, and the City, New York: Routledge.

Kapler, T. & Wright, W., 2004. GeoTime Information Visualisation. In Austin, Texas: IEEE Info-Vis.

Kelly, K., 1995. Out of Control: The New Biology of Machines, Social Systems, & the Economic World, Cambridge, MA: Perseus Books.

Kempf, P., 2009. You are the City Pap/Trspy., Baden: Lars Müller Publishers.

Koolhaas, R., 2006. Delirious New York: Ein retroaktives Manifest für Manhattan 3rd ed., Achen: Arch+.

Koppelkamm, S., 2006. Ortszeit = Local Time, Stuttgart: Edition Axel Menges.

Kostof, S., 1991. The City Shaped: Urban Patterns and Meanings Through History, London: Thames and Hudson.

Kwan, M., 2004. GIS Methods In Time-Geographic Research: Geocomputation And Geovisualisation Of Human Activity Patterns. Geografiska Annaler Series A-Physical Geography, 86 B(4), 267-280.

Kwan, M.-P. & Lee, J., 2003. Geovisualization of Human Activity Patterns Using 3D GIS: A Time-Geographic Approach. In Spatially Integrated Social Science: Examples in Best Practice. Oxford: Oxford University Press.

Latham, A. ed., 2009. Key Concepts in Urban Geography, Los Angeles: Sage.

Leapman, M., 2004. London, Vis a Vis, Cheltenham: European Schoolbooks.

Lefebvre, H., 2004. Rhythmanalysis: Space, Time and Everyday Life, London: Continuum.

Lefebvre, H., 1991. The Production of Space, Oxford: Basil Blackwell.

Ley, D., 1972. The Black Inner City as Frontier Outpost: Images and Behavior of a Philadelphia Neighborhood. Available at: http://worldcat.org/oclc/6643324 [Accessed September 16, 2009].

Loew, M., 2001. Raumsoziologie 1st ed., Frankfurt am Main: Suhrkamp.

Lynch, K., 1984. Good City Form, Cambridge, Mass: MIT Press.

Lynch, K., 1960. The Image of the City, Cambridge, MA: MIT Press.

Lynch, K., 1972. What Time Is This Place?, Cambridge, MA: MIT Press.

Maas, W., Rijs, J.V. & ESARQ, 2000. Costa Iberica: Upbeat to the Leisure City, Barcelona: Actar.

Manaugh, G., 2009. The BLDGBLOG Book, San Francisco, CA: Chronicle Books.

Marshall, S., 2009. Cities, Design & Evolution, Abingdon: Routledge.

Marshall, S., 2005. Streets & patterns, London: Spon.

Martin, G. ed., 2001. Time-Geography Matters. In TimeSpace: Geographies of Temporality. Critical geographies. London: Routledge.

Massey, D.B., 2005. For Space, London: SAGE.

Matei, S., 2003. Mental Maps: Social and spatial research on emotional and affective implications of maps and space. Available at: http://www.mentalmaps.info/ [Accessed September 16, 2009].

McDonough, T. ed., 2002. Guy Debord and the Situationist International: Texts and Documents, Cambridge, MA: MIT Press.

Mitchell, W.J., 1999. E-Topia: "urban Life, Jim - but Not as We Know It", Cambridge, MA: MIT Press.

Moertenboeck, P. & Mooshammer, H., 2008. Networked Cultures, Rotterdam: NAi Publisher.

Morris, A.E.J., 1994. History of Urban Form: Before the Industrial Revolutions 3rd ed., Harlow: Longman Scientific & Technical.

Muybridge, E., 1979. Muybridge's Complete Human and Animal Locomotion, New York: Dover Publications.

Nast, H.J. & Pile, S. eds., 1998. Places Through the Body, London: Routledge.

Nesbitt, K., 1996. Theorizing a new agenda for architecture, New York: Princeton Architectural Press.

Neuhaus, F., 2010. Cycles in Urban Environments: Investigating Temporal Rhythms, Saarbrücken: LAP Lambert Academic Publishing.

Office, F.M.A., 1998. Small, Medium, Large, Extra-Large: Office for Metropolitan Architecture, Rem Koolhaas, and Bruce Mau 2nd ed., New York, N.Y: Monacelli Press.

Pile, S. & Thrift, N.J. eds., 2000. City A-Z, London: Routledge.

Pocock, D.C.D., 1978. Images of the Urban Environment, London: Macmillan.

Prasad, R., 2005. Applied Satellite Navigation Using GPS, GALILEO, and Augmentation Systems, Boston, MA: Artech House.

Psarra, S., 2009. Architecture and Narrative: The Formation of Space and Cultural Meaning, Abingdon: Routledge.

Refinetti, R., 2006. Circadian Physiology 2nd ed., Boca Raton: Taylor & Francis.

Reichholf, J., 2008. Warum die Menschen sesshaft wurden: Das größte Rätsel unserer Geschichte 2nd ed., Frankfurt: Fischer.

Richards, E.G., 1998. Mapping Time: The Calendar and Its History, New York: Oxford University Press.

Rost, J.M., 2002. Komplexe Systeme, Frankfurt: Fischer (Tb.).

Rowe, C. & Koetter, F., 1997. Collage City 5th ed., Basel: Birkhäuser.

Sadler, S., 1999. The Situationist City, Cambridge, MA: MIT Press.

Sassen, S., 1996. Metropolen des Weltmarkts. Die neue Rolle der Global Cities, Frankfurt: Campus Fachbuch.

Shane, D.G., 2005. Recombinant Urbanism: Conceptual Modeling in Architecture, Urban Design and City Theory, Chichester: John Wiley & Sons.

Slinkachu, 2009. Little People in the City: The Street Art of Slinkachu, Macmillan UK.

Somer, K., Van, E.&.V.L.S. & Amsterdam, (., 2007. The Functional City: The CIAM and Cornelis Van Eesteren, 1928-1960, Rotterdam: NAi Publishers.

Spencer, J., 2003. Global Positioning System: A Field Guide for the Social Sciences, Malden, MA: Blackwell Pub.

Spuybroek, L., 2004. Nox: machining architecture; Bauten und Projekte, London: Thames and Hudson.

Strogatz, S.H., 2004. Sync: The Emerging Science of Spontaneous Order, London: Penguin Books Ltd.

Sumrell, R. & Varnelis, K., 2007. Blue Monday: Stories of Absurd Realities and Natural Philosophies, Barcelona: Actar.

Susteren, A.V., 2004. Metropolitan World Atlas, 010 Uitgeverij.

Thrift, N.J. & May, J. eds., 2001. TimeSpace: Geographies of Temporality, London: Routledge.

Tschumi, B., 1996. Architecture and Disjunction, Cambridge, MA: MIT Press.

Tsui, J.B., 2005. Fundamentals of Global Positioning System Receivers: A Software Approach 2nd ed., Hoboken, NJ: John Wiley & Sons Inc.

Tuan, Y., 1977. Space and Place: The Perspective of Experience, Minneapolis, MN: University of Minnesota Press.

Tuan, Y., 1990. Topophilia: A Study of Environmental Perception, Attitudes, and Values, New York: Columbia University Press.

Unwin, D., 1981. Introductory Spatial Analysis, London: Methuen.

Volk, T., 1995. Metapatterns: Across Space, Time and Mind, New edition., New York: Columbia University Press.

Vyzoviti, S., 2004. Folding Architecture: Spatial, Structural and Organizational Diagrams illustrated edition., Book Industry Services (BIS).

Warf, B., 2008. Time-Space Compression: Historical Geographies, London: Routledge.

Weyl, H., 1983. Symmetry, Princeton, N.J.: Princeton University Press.

Whorf, B.L., 1956. The Hopi language, Chicago: Univ. of Chicago Libr.

Whyte, W.H., 1960. The Organization Man, Harmondsworth: Penguin.

Whyte, W.H., 1980. The Social Life of Small Urban Spaces, Washington, D.C: Conservation Foundation.

Zerubavel, E., 1985. Hidden Rhythms: Schedules and Calendars in Social Life, Berkeley, CA: University of California Press.

Zerubavel, E., 1989. The Seven Day Circle, Chigago, IL: University of Chicago Press.

Index

F. Neuhaus (ed.), *Studies in Temporal Urbanism,*
DOI 10.1007/978-94-007-0937-9, © Springer Science+Business Media B.V. 2011